Delilah Montoya

DELILAH

MONTOYA

Activating
Chicana
Resistance

Josie Lopez

University of New Mexico Press | Albuquerque Museum | Albuquerque

Contents

Acknowledgments

Delilah Montoya: Activating Chicana Resistance is a profound celebration of the Chicano and Latino communities with which Delilah Montoya has collaborated for decades. Her sustained examination of history and culture reverberates in the activism found across her series of works. Presenting women boxers possessing dignity and strength, the resilience of immigrants crossing the border, and the proud expressions of faith, language, art, creativity, and survival, Montoya expresses the power of community. The Albuquerque Museum extends our gratitude to Delilah for generously collaborating with us on this important exhibition and catalog.

While this project celebrates a regional artist representing stories of various communities, we also look forward to its role as a major contribution to the study of twentieth-century American photography in general. Too often, artists working within their community are considered only as representatives of that community, and not as creators of images of contemporary significance. Dr. Tomás Ybarra-Frausto coined the term "glocal" to reference the global relevance of the profound local experience. In her images, Delilah tells those universal stories.

The Albuquerque Museum is grateful to those who have helped make this exhibition and catalog possible. We thank the City of Albuquerque's Department of Arts and Culture, Albuquerque Museum Board of Trustees, Albuquerque Museum Foundation Board of Directors, the Art Advisory Committee, and the volunteer museum guides for their strong support of the museum's exhibitions and programs. To the many individuals and organizations who have contributed objects to the museum's permanent collection, thank you for your generosity. All donors to the collection are credited in the object captions.

This exhibition was a collective effort and could not have been realized without the contributions of our curatorial, collections, and design staff, including Ellen Castrone, Meara Christopher, Keith Lee, Stephen Hutchins, and Jen Montaño. Special thanks to Curatorial Assistant Magaly Jiménez Baca for her efforts in organizing the project and forging an expansive and generous connection with the curator and artist. Special thanks to Josie Lopez for continuing to forge an engaged curatorial practice.

The catalog text was a collaborative writing endeavor that involved an in-depth visual and cultural analysis of Montoya's series of works by Lopez. The catalog also includes conversations between Delilah Montoya and Demetria Martinez. Special thanks to Demetria and other collaborators, including Mónica Sánchez, Orlando Lara, Maria Elena Alvarez, and Tina Hernandez for participating in the conversations included in the catalog.

We also thank Stephen Hull at the University of New Mexico Press and his editorial and design teams for their thoughtful contributions to the catalog.

We extend special thanks and gratitude to the Terra Foundation for generously supporting this catalog and the associated exhibition organized by the Albuquerque Museum.

ANDREW CONNORS
Director, Albuquerque Museum

Foreword
A Living Dialogue
Art, Identity, and Community

There are countless reasons why this catalog is important. Above all, it celebrates the work of Delilah Montoya—a body of artwork created over decades by an accomplished and multifaceted artist that speaks powerfully to identity, community, and culture.

This catalog also marks a significant moment for the Albuquerque Museum: the acquisition of an important collection of Montoya's works in 2024. This acquisition emerged from the museum's commitment to critically examining its collection, asking not only *who is represented*? But, just as crucially, *who is not*? This effort, led by Dr. Josie Lopez, beginning in 2019, revealed significant underrepresentation of women in general as well as contemporary Native American, contemporary Hispanic/Latino, Asian American, and Black artists. This imbalance was deeply consequential. The Albuquerque Museum exists within a minority-majority state, where more than 45 percent of our population identifies as Hispanic, Latino, or Chicano. To authentically serve our community, our collection must reflect its diversity—not only demographically, but through the depth and richness of cultural expression.

Delilah Montoya's work speaks directly to this need. An award-winning and revered Chicana artist, she does not look *at* her community from the outside but speaks *with* it from within. Her images are not distant observations or neutral documentations; they are grounded in collaboration, dialogue, and shared experience. Individuals in her photographs are not passive subjects—they are active participants. Montoya's process honors their voices and stories, resulting in work that resonates with authenticity and layered meaning.

I vividly remember the first time I encountered Delilah's work in the Art Museum at the National Hispanic Cultural Center, in Albuquerque's South Valley. On display was a striking large-format photograph of Doña Sebastiana—not a typical carved representation, but a living embodiment performed by theater artist Mónica Sánchez, in collaboration with Montoya.

Many of Montoya's photographic portraits re-humanize iconic figures—such as Doña Sebastiana, La Malinche, or La Llorona. At other times, she uses portraits to celebrate mothers, families, prisoners, boxers, writers, and immigrants—those often overlooked in dominant cultural narratives—portraying them as empowered figures in their own right.

Montoya's photography, printmaking, and iconic installations remind us that behind every cultural symbol is a real place or an actual person—and within every individual across history lies a layered story and a voice that still speaks. Through intentional collaboration and the lens of her camera, Montoya transforms individuals and places into powerful conduits for understanding history, community, and self.

These pages are filled with images that illuminate and intrigue—images grounded in both cultural memory and individual identity. Delilah Montoya's artwork offers more than documentation; it offers conversation. It invites us to look deeper, to listen more closely, and to engage more fully with the richness of the cultural landscape—past, present, and future.

Finally, in an era when images can be accessed anywhere, anytime, and on any screen, it is worth reflecting on why art books matter. The physical book itself matters, and investment in an art book celebrating the work of Delilah Montoya matters. To hold a book—turning its pages, lingering over each image, engaging in a focused and tactile way—is an experience of particular value. A well-crafted art book is more than an archive; it is an invitation to slow looking, deep reflection, and an intimacy that digital platforms rarely achieve. This art book is also about collaboration and conversation with Josie Lopez, the artist, and her co-conspirators. For visual art as resonant as Montoya's, the printed page becomes a space where the work lives and breathes—a bridge between artist and audience, between individual and community.

As you turn these pages, I invite you to reflect on the vital role of artists like Delilah Montoya who bring forth powerful images *and* stories that inspire—harnessing the enduring power of art to reflect, connect, and transform our understanding of ourselves and one another.

SHELLE VANETTEN DE SANCHEZ
Director, Department of Arts and Culture, City of Albuquerque
2025

Delilah Montoya's decades-long engagement with printmaking, photography, and large-scale installations is embedded in a practice of activism and disruption. She asks a key question across all of her works. "What is the colonial body?" The contested spaces of identity, land, feminine power, and the struggle for justice are inextricably tied to this question, which marks both a historical rupture and the emergence of Mestizaje. Chicanx bodies, according to Montoya, are colonial bodies born out of struggle and violence but also shaped by the intersections of culture and belief systems that are bound up with a sense of dignity and community.

Born in Texas, raised in the Midwest, and now returning to New Mexico, where she has spent much of her career in Albuquerque, Montoya's work is deeply rooted in her interactions with the communities she lived in and worked with. Synthesizing a diversity of syncretic forms and practices, her projects confront spirituality, gender norms, and cultural identity, challenging viewer perceptions through a unique lens intently trained on the roots of Chicanx identity. From the beginning, Montoya's work has not only situated and defined her Chicana identity, but it has also served as a tool rooted in activism—demanding that Chicanx voices, stories, bodies, and histories be seen. Montoya's work involves learning about herself and the world around her while simultaneously reflecting images of survival and resistance back to the communities and individuals she has collaborated with. According to Montoya,

> By exploring the aesthetic history that speaks to my community, I learned to make art about my world as seen through the eyes of a mestiza. One must engage their community to best represent it. So much of what I do is the same. The same commitment to the *Plan de Aztlán* where the artists were called to action. For me, that is to originate an aesthetic that speaks about our community and develops a sense of self. Community has always been at the core of my work. Developing work around this idea shifts over time as the community expands and faces new challenges. Yet so many of those challenges remain the same: poverty, little representation in education or civic institutions, and mass incarceration. The new challenges are with the ever-increasing Latinx communities that are very young and energetic and whose needs are numerous. This Latinx art community is at a critical mass and must be nurtured to be heard.

In many conversations about her trajectory as an artist, Montoya references the Chicano movement as an integral aspect of her work and worldview. The *Plan de Aztlán*, drafted in 1969 at the Chicano Youth Liberation Conference in Denver, Colorado, is a key document that helped define the Chicano movement. It outlines a vision for cultural pride, self-determination, and social justice, advocating for the empowerment of Mexican Americans through unity, education reform, and political activism. The plan invokes "Aztlán," the mythical homeland of the Aztecs, as a unifying symbol of cultural pride and resilience. It emphasizes acknowledging the Indigenous roots of Chicano history and rejecting assimilation into mainstream American culture.[1] The plan stresses the need for Chicanos to control their communities, including local governance, education, and economic resources. It also proposes the formation of a unified political party to represent Chicano interests and address systemic injustices.[2] Collective action is central to the plan, urging Chicanos to unite to confront shared struggles. This solidarity is framed as essential for achieving liberation.[3] The plan advocates for Chicano-owned businesses and cooperative ventures to reduce dependence on exploitative systems and to broaden the economic goals of the Chicano movement.[4] It critiques the American education system for erasing Chicano history and culture and demands bilingual education and the inclusion of Chicano heritage in school curricula.[5] The plan frames the Chicano struggle as part of a global movement for justice and liberation, emphasizing resistance against racism, exploitation, and oppression.[6]

As Montoya describes above, the Chicano movement was an integral aspect of advocating for and connecting with the communities she was part of in Denver, Albuquerque, Houston, and California. While she considers Albuquerque her home, her understanding of Chicano identity is informed by her broad-ranging interactions with various Chicanx and Latinx communities, collaborators, and artists involved in activist projects. The connections she found across many collaborations was the desire to hone a complex and layered understanding of what it means to be a Chicana. For Montoya, that connection was defined by the kind of activism that emanated from the Chicano movement. In many conversations, Montoya has also reflected on how ideas and identity can shift and change over time, but the core of collaborating and engaging with her community is central for the movements that may have started in the 1970s but are just as relevant today.

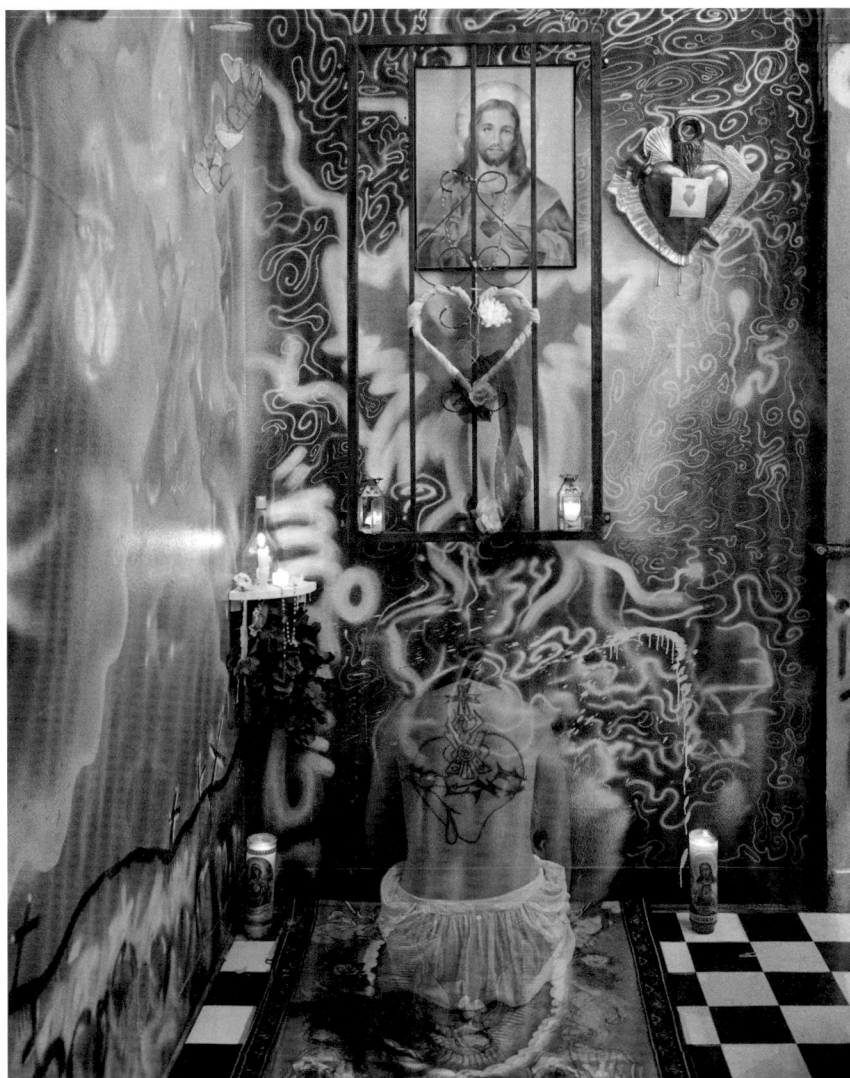

Montoya has long been included in the broader story of Chicanx art and photography. She participated in exhibitions like *Chicano Art: Resistance and Affirmation, 1965–1985*, and *Our America: Latino Presence in American Art*. She was a co-curator and artist in *Chicana Badgirls: Las Hociconas*. Montoya has been included in several groundbreaking exhibitions examining Latina and Chicana history and identity, including the recent exhibition *La Malinche: Traitor, Survivor, Icon*. These are just a few important examples of the hundreds of exhibitions Montoya has participated in the United States and globally.

Montoya works in series, building up bodies of work to fully interrogate different aspects of history and identity as well as push the limits of a variety of genres, techniques, and approaches to making art. This publication and accompanying exhibition are organized based on the series that Montoya has created over the past four decades. Each chapter includes an analysis of the series and conversations between Montoya and journalist Demetria Martinez and other collaborators. This text also includes descriptions of Montoya's artistic practice, highlighting her intentional and often technically experimental approaches to melding photography, printmaking, and the production of large-scale installations.

Each chapter explores specific themes demonstrating how Montoya's work is embedded in a form of activism that seeks to disrupt how Chicanx and Latinx communities are seen and understood. Historical specificity is the foundation of many of Montoya's series. All of her projects are based on a deep level of research. For example, she studied the Dresden Codex as source material for her *Codex Delilah*. She sought the origins of Aztec and European traditions for the *Sagrado Corazón* series. She has interrogated the historical development of issues that impact broader Latinx communities and identities, including colonialism, the border, and incarceration. Her vantage point is one of a Mestiza, and she fully interrogates the strength and resilience of women through historical figures like La Malinche, La Virgen de Guadalupe, and La Llorona. She captures and utilizes images of women boxers, activists, and *malcriadas* (bad girls) to show how Chicanas see themselves within the worlds they inhabit.

Concepts of double colonization are prevalent in each of Montoya's series. Laura Gomez states, "The American Southwest was subject to two different colonial regimes. The first was the Spanish colonization of all of Mexico in the sixteenth and seventeenth centuries. The second layer of colonization of the region occurred with the U.S. military invasion of Mexico and subsequent incorporation of Mexico's vast territory."[7] Understanding Chicanx identity is inextricably linked with this concept of layers of colonialism, and Montoya is keenly aware of this connection between history and identity formation.

In addition to double colonization and the Chicano movement, the history of New Mexico and its lands are important in several of Montoya's series. The trajectory of Chicanx identity in New Mexico is unique and often framed within the tri-cultural myth, which espouses the notion that Indigenous, Anglo, and Hispanic peoples have lived peacefully together for centuries. This narrative denies the conflicts and wars that determined land ownership, sovereignty, and deep-rooted connections to Mexican and Indigenous cultures and identities. Caught in the social expectations of assimilation, first from the Spanish Empire and Catholic Church and later from US Imperialist forces, Chicanx identity is layered and complex, requiring a deeper look at how cultural memory continues to shape our communities' quest for self-determination. Montoya pushes against the boundaries of what it means to be Mestizo in New Mexico, arguing that all of these histories, cultures, and identities shape who we are. Rather than asking if we are American enough or Mexican enough, Montoya asserts that Nuevo Mexicano Chicanos embrace their own lived experiences and expressions of community, spirituality, and culture.

Montoya speaks to the importance of revealing truth in her images. She works with her subjects as collaborators to capture their truth. This process, however, is not one of simply documenting a specific time, place, or person. Rather, Montoya uses the photograph as a tool. Her processes embedded in printmaking, collaging, large-scale installations, and bookmaking move her art beyond the photograph itself. Each series is a constellation of many works connected through multivalent narratives while traversing the past, present, and future.

Chicana activism is central in Montoya's work, but it is a form of activism that underscores a universal message rooted in the quest for equality and for a deeper understanding that colonialism persists. She is interested in confronting the viewer's assumptions about Chicanx and Latinx identity.[8] While some of the works presented here were made in the 1980s and 1990s, their interaction with the Borderlands, immigration, incarceration, and detention are even more relevant in 2025 as communities face mass deportation and heightened xenophobic rhetoric.

D elilah Montoya has most often been described as a narrative or documentary photographer. Her artistic practice, however, is also profoundly rooted in printmaking. She uses photography as a tool to create artworks that are often experimental, pushing the boundaries of both mediums. Montoya studied serigraphy with Jim Kraft, lithography with John Sommers, and collotype processes with Ann O'Keefe, to name a few. In conversation with Demetria Martinez, she talked about printmaking as a collaborative process where printers work with artists to achieve the result the artist envisions. Montoya decided, early on, that she wanted to hone both a creative vision and the technical expertise to achieve that vision.

Printmaking, as both a medium and a process, has long functioned as a site of cultural resistance, political activism, and historical reclamation. Artists and collectives such as Malaquías Montoya, Esther Hernandez, Rupert García, the Royal Chicano Air Force (RCAF), Cuban posters, and in Mexico, the Taller de Gráfica Popular are a vital part of the Latinx graphic art historical narrative. Self Help Graphics (SHG) in Los Angeles has been a site for collaborative printmaking for over fifty years. Montoya connected with SHG earlier in her career and maintained connections there. In 1999, she participated in the first iteration of the Maestras Atelier, which included over ten Chicana artists at varying stages in their careers. The project involved each artist creating a unique print, participating in group critiques, and being part of a collaborative workshop. At the time, Montoya was working on her series, which incorporated images of Guadalupe.[1]

Montoya has stated that her practice seeks to move beyond the "straight photograph"—a form often associated with documentary or narrative images—to instead treat the photographic print as a physical object imbued with the historical, cultural, and spiritual themes that are the foundation of Chicanx identity. In addition to thematic concerns and the process of capturing photographic images, Montoya's series are also driven by the technical decisions she makes—choice of substrate, ink density, and overlay of imagery. These choices ultimately determine her creative process. According to Montoya, "The intent is to be moved by my instinct to select a technique, integrate its expressive potential, and extend it through the final presentation."[2]

While other artists have worked across the mediums of printmaking

ONE Printmaking and Photography

and photography, Montoya is one of very few Chicana contemporary artists who have embraced these mediums. In March 1968, the Museum of Modern Art in New York presented a survey of photographic prints that spanned over a century. According to Peter C. Bunnell, director of the exhibition,

> A distinction between two traditional aesthetic approaches: the first is where the straightforward image is interpreted illusionistically, that is, *through* the picture plane; and the second is that in which the emphasis is on the print itself, as a distinct object and an extension of the image. The latter approach seeks to make the medium visible, while the former wishes to make it invisible. . . . The show is an effort to point out the distinct expressive potentials of these differing means, not just to catalog the processes used in printing. To the extent that the individuals represented by their work have been able to integrate their technical methods with the initial vision, avoiding a sense of arty contrivance, the prints are read as clear and vital works in their own right.[3]

This exhibition is just one example of examining photographic printmaking; it provides an early example of artists utilizing technical and aesthetic approaches to printmaking to create their own visual languages. Other key examples include *Photography and Printmaking* at the V&A Museum in 1978. In 2023, the National Gallery organized an exhibition titled *Etched by Light: Photogravures from the Collection, 1840–1940*. RISD Museum organized an exhibition titled *Process Work: Intersections of Photography and Print ca. 1825 to Today*. The exhibition description reads, "Across a presentation of over 40 historic and contemporary photogravures, collotypes, photolithography and relief prints, this exhibition poses the question: What are the social, aesthetic, and technological possibilities that emerge from the marriage between photography and print, both then and now?"[4]

Montoya's utilization of printmaking techniques is central to understanding her process. Printmakers are problem solvers who constantly use their technical skills to determine how to achieve the end result. Consequently, they are continually experimenting with new methods and approaches. The process of printmaking itself furthers the thematic and aesthetic power of Montoya's works. In *Contact: Art and the Pull of the Print*, Jennifer L. Roberts states, "A print is an object that has been made by transferring an image between two surfaces in contact. Every print is the result of a process of contact and release which links it immediately to themes of touch, presence, and intimacy, but also to themes of loss, separation, and memory."[5] This definition beautifully reveals that technical process is not separate from Montoya's complex interactions with history and identity but rather an integral part of her visual language.

The basic printmaking process includes creating an image on a matrix (usually a plate, stone, block, or screen). Ink is applied to the matrix, and the image is transferred to a support, usually paper. The transfer happens by applying pressure, typically with a press. Roberts goes on to say that prints are created through pressure, while photographic images are made through the transfer of light.[6] A closer look at different printmaking methods across Montoya's series demonstrates the multilayered and interconnected components capturing images, transferring images, and ultimately transforming images into art objects.

In *Cristo Crucificado*, Montoya depicts the Cristo de las Esquipulas, which is housed at the Santuario de Chimayo. There is more than one story regarding the origin of the cross, but it is said that the church was built to host the crucifix, which is still a religious and cultural symbol important in northern New Mexico. His lowered head and suffering body are rendered with high-contrast mezzotint screens for CMY color and two kodalith ortho films to create the key image with brown and black ink. Multicolor serigraphs involve creating a separate screen for each color, a precise registration system to make sure that each color aligns when transferred, and each color layer has to be transferred onto the substrate one at a time. Christ's lowered head, closed eyes, and injured body conjures a religious response, but the image is not merely a universal representation of Christianity; rather, it links Christ's suffering to the concept of the colonial body. Christian conversion was a brutal element in the history of colonialism. Montoya references centuries-old visual languages practiced by *santeros* (woodcarvers) in New Mexico. She is also using the visual language of *retablos*, Mexican devotional paintings.

Cristo Crucificado was one of Montoya's early forays into printmaking following her exploration of Phillip Zimmerman's book, *Options for Color Separations*. She used a technique of colorizing black-and-white photographs using four screens: cyan, magenta, yellow, and a black key. Montoya utilized a lith mask to produce color formed through mezzotint patterns. A mask is essentially a sheet of material with cut out areas that block ink from reaching certain parts of the printing matrix, allowing for the creation of specific design elements on the final print.[7] She used a similar process in *Untitled* and *Who Says Girls Can't Swing*.

Tijerina Tantrum, created at Self Help Graphics, foregrounds Reies López Tijerina, a key figure in New Mexico's land grant movement, who fought for the restitution of lands taken after the 1848 Treaty of Guadalupe

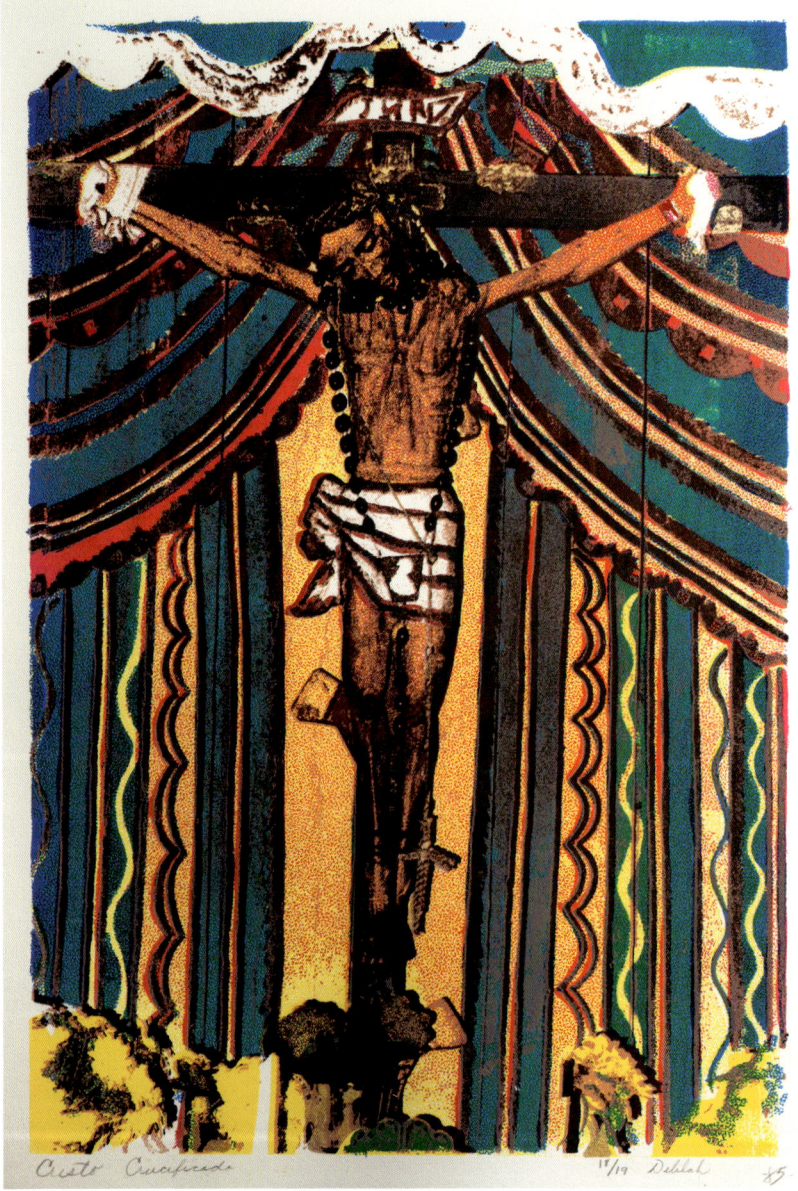

Delilah Montoya
Cristo Crucificado
1985
Serigraph, ed. 18/19
28½ × 22¼
Collection of the artist

(*opposite page, top*)
Delilah Montoya
Untitled
1984
Serigraph, ed. 8/9
13⅜ × 19⁵⁄₁₆ in.
Collection of the artist

(*bottom*) Delilah
Montoya
*Who Says Girls Can't
Swing*
1984
Serigraph, ed. 3/9
14⅜ × 19¾ in.
Collection of the artist

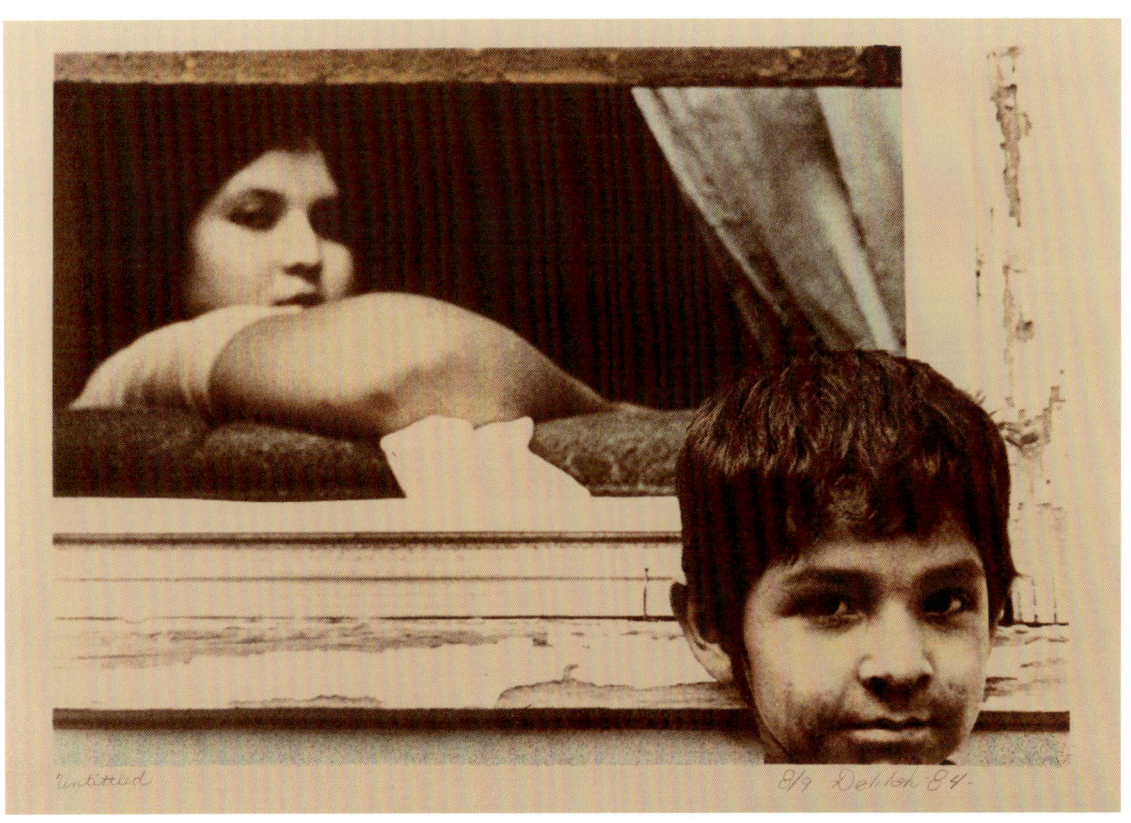

"Untitled"   8/9 Delilah 84

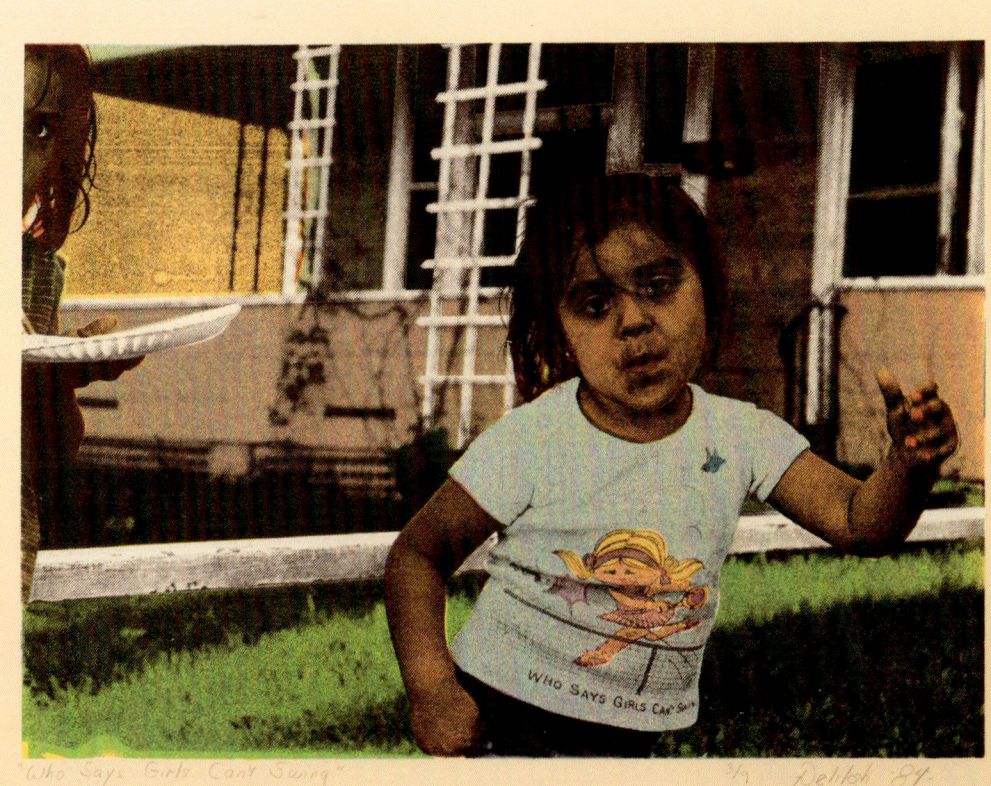

"Who Says Girls Can't Swing"   3/9   Delilah 84

Hidalgo. The United States took one-third of Mexico's territory. The print is a compilation of photographic images arranged in a grid. The central part of the grid is a montage of color images of a female figure dancing. The depictions of the dancing figure are framed by black-and-white images showing protests, the land, and historical portraits of the Chicanx communities whose culture and whose narratives were deliberately erased or rewritten. The serigraph is based on photographs and film stills, but Montoya reworks the photographic image through the printmaking process. Both *Cristo Crucificado* and *Tijerina Tantrum* include visible halftones and dots of varying sizes, which are used to create the illusion of different shades of a single color. To the human eye, these tiny dots blend and appear as a single gradient. Montoya, however, deliberately draws attention to the dots, making it visibly clear that she is using a printmaking approach as an act of acknowledging complex layers of identity—both religious and historical.

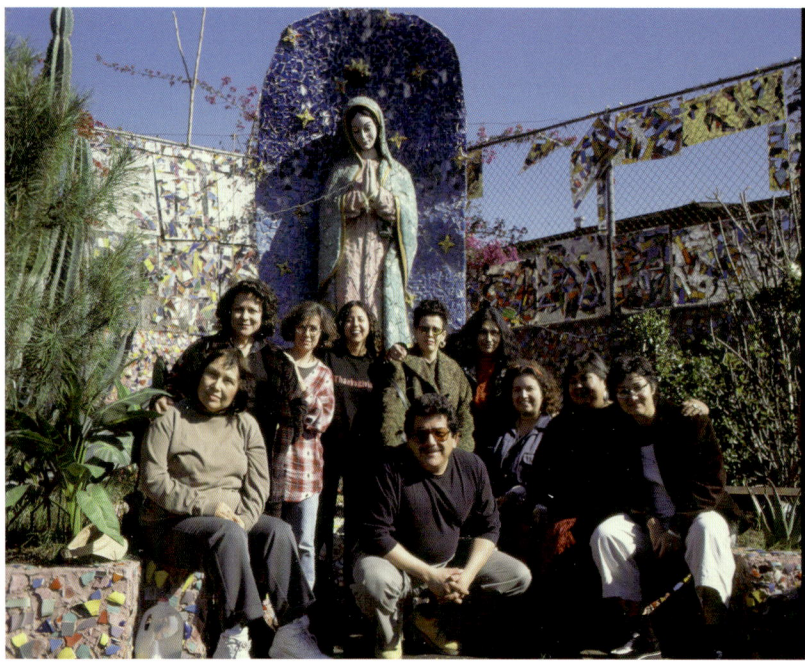

Self Help Graphics Maestra Atelier 1999
left to right: Artists: Yolanda Lopez, Barbara Carrasco, Delilah Montoya, Flavianna Rodríguez, Diane Gamboa, Margaret Guzmán, Pat Gomez, and Yreina D. Cervántez; Scholar: Laura E. Pérez; Interim Director of Self Help Graphic: Tomás Benítez.

(*opposite page*)
Delilah Montoya
Tijerina Tantrum
1989
Serigraph, ed. 61/63
30 × 23½ in.
Albuquerque Museum, museum purchase and gift of the artist
PC2022.32.19

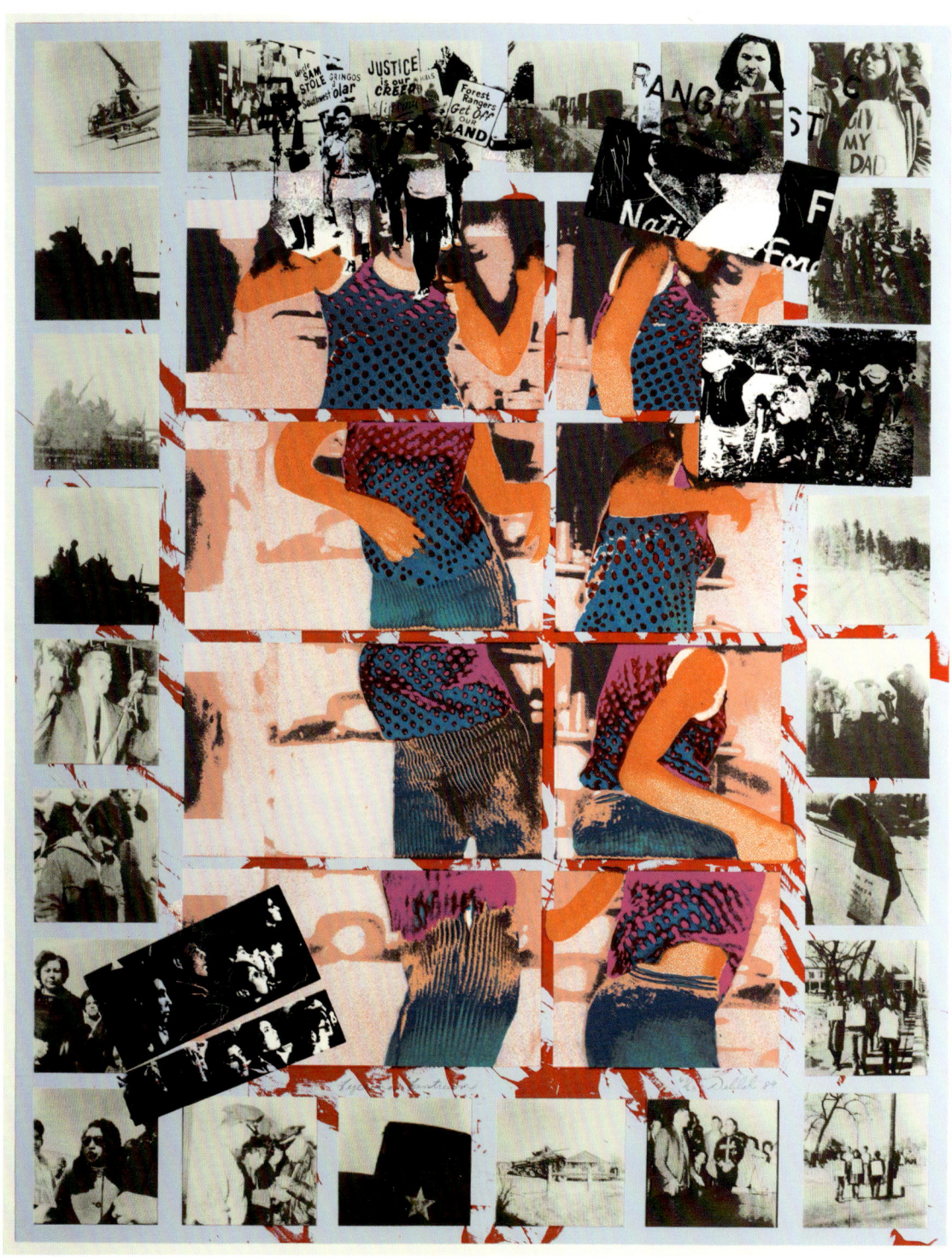

Instead of using CYMK screens for *Tijerina Tantrum*, Montoya created layers of colors by masking sections of the photograph and then printing those sections. According to Montoya, "Layered on top of those colors is a photographic image exposed as a halftone plate and then printed as a black key. A flat newspaper gray was printed before the final key for the news images."[8] In the interior grid, the dance called the Tijerina Tantrum is a series of photographic stills from a family super 8 film clip of Montoya's Auntie Gina. High-contrast kodalith layers of flat planes and large uniformed dots are blended to add the color, producing a posterized aesthetic. In these earlier prints, Montoya is clearly testing the boundaries of how to incorporate photography and printmaking techniques to achieve a specific visual language that is also embedded in history, spirituality, and identity, which can be seen in the untitled print from the *Guadalupano* series shown in chapter 6.

Delilah Montoya's 2008 print, *Smile Now, Cry Later*, is also a serigraph that subverts the genre of portraiture. The title, *Smile Now, Cry Later*, as seen on the female boxer's tattoo, represents duality, fate, and the inevitable consequences of one's actions. The female figure who proudly defies the typically posed female portrait confronts the viewer. Her direct gaze,

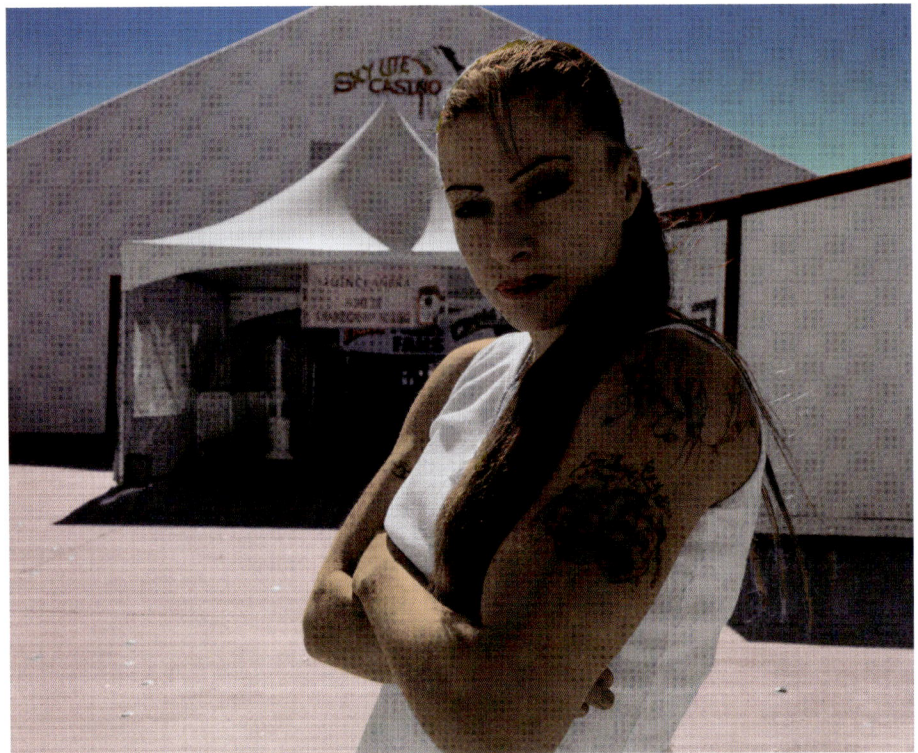

Delilah Montoya
Smile Now ~ Cry Later
2008
Serigraph, ed. 15/46
22⅛ × 29 in.
Collection of the artist

folded arms featuring her tattoo, and flexed muscles represent an intersection of a powerful form of femininity occupying what are traditionally masculine spaces. Montoya's experimentation with color separations and overlays is more difficult to discern because her technique of utilizing mezzotint and halftone work to produce an image that appears to both reflect light and activate the surface of the paper as a print.

The work emerges from Montoya's extensive series documenting female boxers, *Women Boxers: The New Warriors*, which is further discussed in chapter 8. The series challenges societal notions of femininity and power and presents these athletes with dignity as they navigate the professional realm of sport. Montoya's print aligns with her broader themes of inhabiting and remaking visual genres. *Smile Now, Cry Later* is a striking synthesis of feminist intervention, Chicana resilience, and technical printmaking expertise. Through this work, Montoya not only documents but actively reshapes visual narratives around Latina agency. The serigraph becomes both a tribute to and a challenge against traditional narratives of femininity and struggle, ultimately reinforcing Montoya's broader artistic project of revealing underlying truths through layered, multi-referential compositions.

Much later, in 2019, Montoya was invited to participate in *New Monuments for New Cities [A]Part* for the High Line initiative in New York City, Houston, Austin, Chicago, and Toronto. She collaborated with Sin Huellas member Jimmy Castillo to produce a poster that honored the families separated at the border. The Sin Huellas Artist Collective is a multiracial, multimedia artist and activist collective that works with former immigrant detainees and organizers to create alter-narratives of immigrant incarceration, deportation, and resistance. The following passage is the statement that accompanied *[A]Part*:

> Our nation, our city, is home to the multitudes. Where families define us as a country by carving out their lives with love, work, play, and cooperation. The sum of this constitutes our humanity . . . our liberties. Every family ripped apart experiences the unthinkable. Policies that systematically separate families re-calibrate our moral compass. "[A]part" is a monument to the families holding steady as they are pulled apart. These families are a part of our sovereign body, our nation, our community, and our home. As a

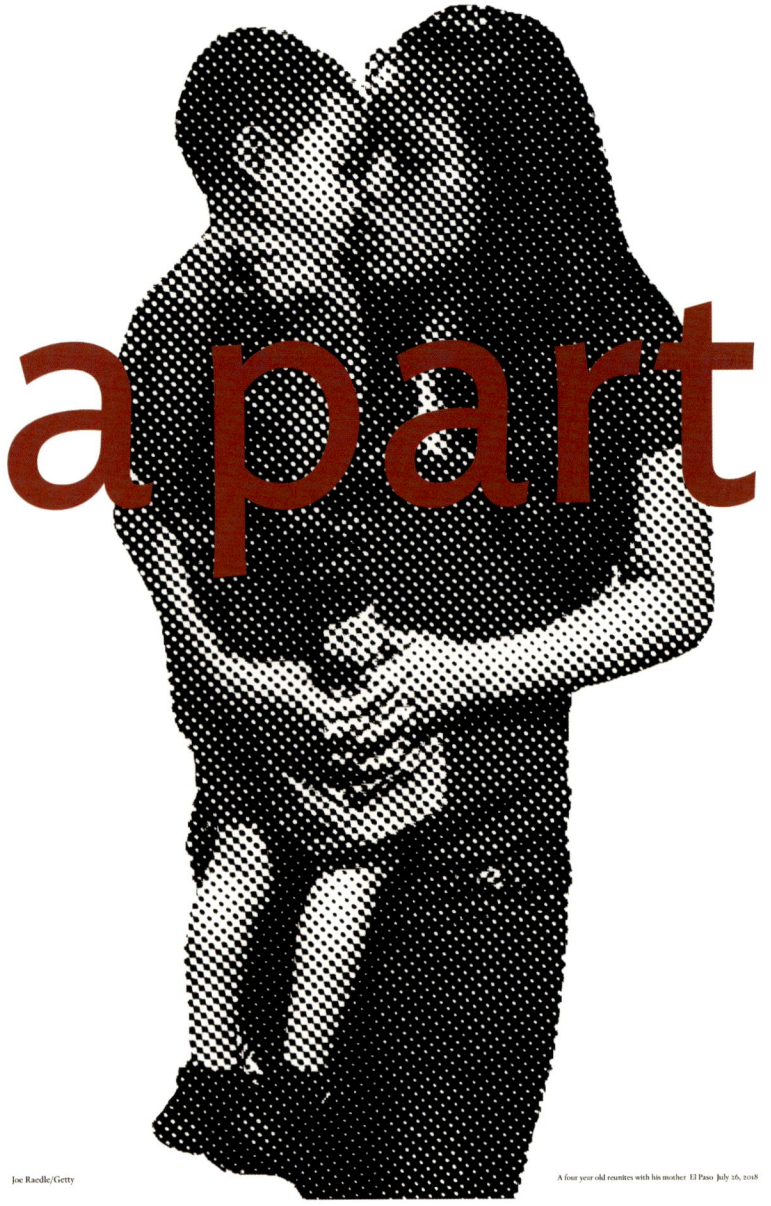

Joe Raedle/Getty

A four year old reunites with his mother El Paso July 26, 2018

Delilah Montoya
A[PART]
2018
Dye sublimation on
aluminum
20 × 30 in.
Collection of the artist
Photograph: Joe Raedle/
Getty Images News via
Getty Images

memorial to the strength of love that bonds them, this monument realigns our moral compass in the direction of humanity. This monument is an art/activist action by the Sin Huellas collective members, Jimmy Castillo and Delilah Montoya.[9]

While the poster was produced as an inkjet reproduction, Montoya's continued engagement with the dot matrix as a visual form reappears many years after her earlier prints. In this case, the intimate portrait of a mother holding her child is disrupted by the dot matrix, forcing the viewer to grapple with the devastating reality of family separation. Montoya is intentionally disrupting the genre of portraiture by layering the image with patterns that are a nod to printmaking.

In her print *Los Dos Corazones*, Montoya pays homage to her close friend, renowned sculptor Luis Jiménez, who passed away in 2006. A photograph of Jiménez, taken by Montoya in 2005, near his ranch in New Mexico, is lovingly placed in the locket she holds. Mementos that they shared, including rose petals and the locket charms that were gifts from

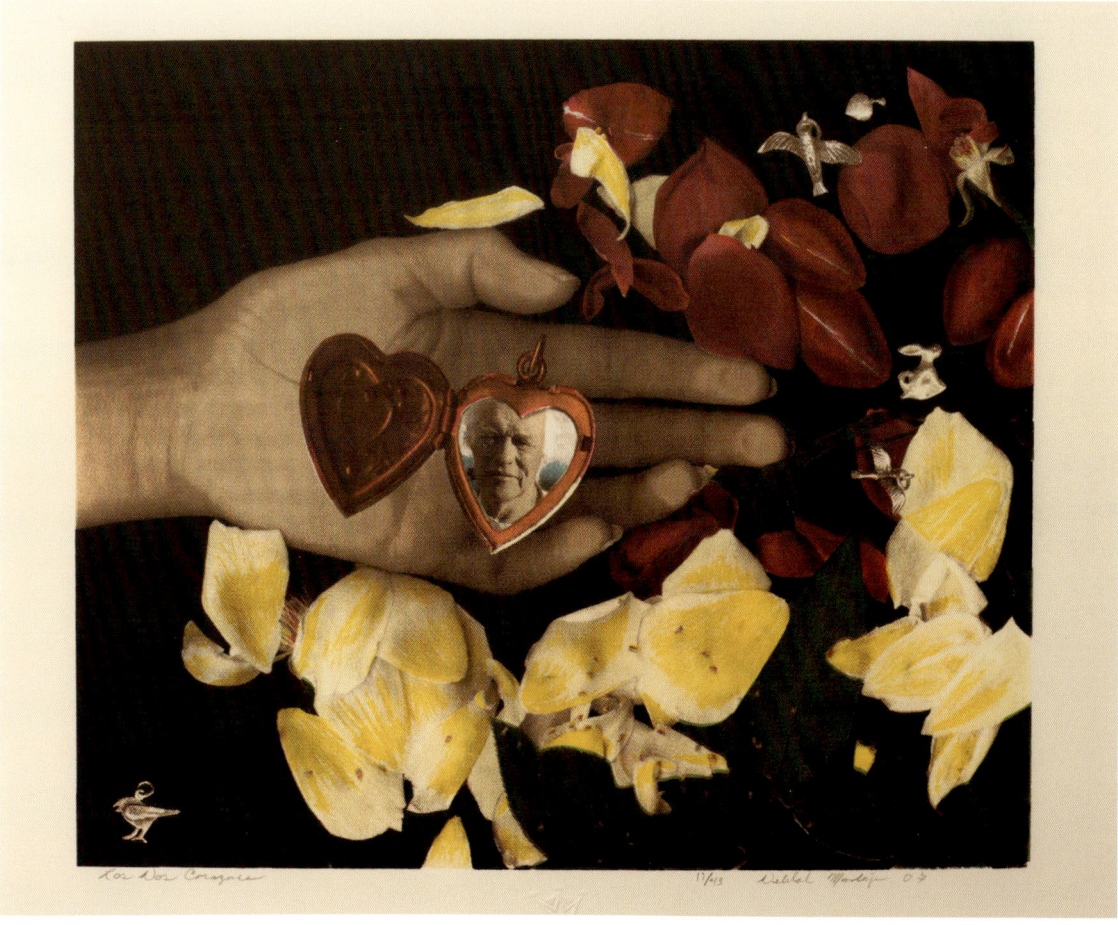

Delilah Montoya
Los Dos Corazones
2007
Serigraph, ed. 11/43
22⅛ × 29 in.
Collection of the artist

Jiménez, are part of a composition that is also an altar of remembrance. "Luis was a very warm, caring individual, and I hope people can get this sense of him when looking at this print," she says. The image of Montoya's hand appears as if it is pressed up against glass, giving the impression that memories are being shared as if preserved in a glass box. *Doz Corazones* and *Smile Now, Cry Later* were created in Austin at Coronado Studios. At this point, Montoya worked out how to create the mezzotint and halftone layers using a computer.

Modern Democracy, After Goya's "Disasters of War" is a reflection on the consequences of war inspired by Francisco Goya's statement, "Grande hazaña! Con muertos!" which means "Great deeds, with dead men!" The print was created at the Texas Collaborative Art Studio in 2011–2012 using a photogravure polymer printmaking technique. The print is based on one of Luis Jiménez's final prints, which was published at Flatbed Press in Austin, Texas. Jiménez's sources of inspiration for his print were the tragic war in Iraq and Goya's *Disasters of War*. In studying Jiménez's print, Montoya states, "I became aware that, as citizens, our affiliation to 'freedom' is bound to a 'democratic' process that motivates us, not necessarily by reason, but rather by a consuming patriotic commitment. To extend this thought beyond the boundaries of the United States, we as citizens of the world are bound to a submissive duty known as nationalism that serves the interests of those who control governments, and thus, as the print suggests, modern democracy is born/borne." Montoya forcefully engages with the searing social critique of power structures found in Goya's prints, but the reference also celebrates Goya's masterful practice of intaglio printmaking.

Montoya used polymer photogravure, which is a contemporary printmaking technique that merges the traditional process of intaglio printmaking with photographic processes. It involves the transfer of a photographic image onto a light-sensitive polymer plate. Light exposure hardens the polymer, capturing the tonal values of the image on the plate, creating an etched or relief surface. The result is an image with fine detail and an excellent tonal range. After exposure, the plate is washed, dried, cured, and inked. Using an etching press, the image is transferred onto paper. As in many of her other prints and installations, the materiality of the work is just as important as the image itself. The polymer photogravure process resulted in soft, velvety blacks and a delicate interplay between ink and the

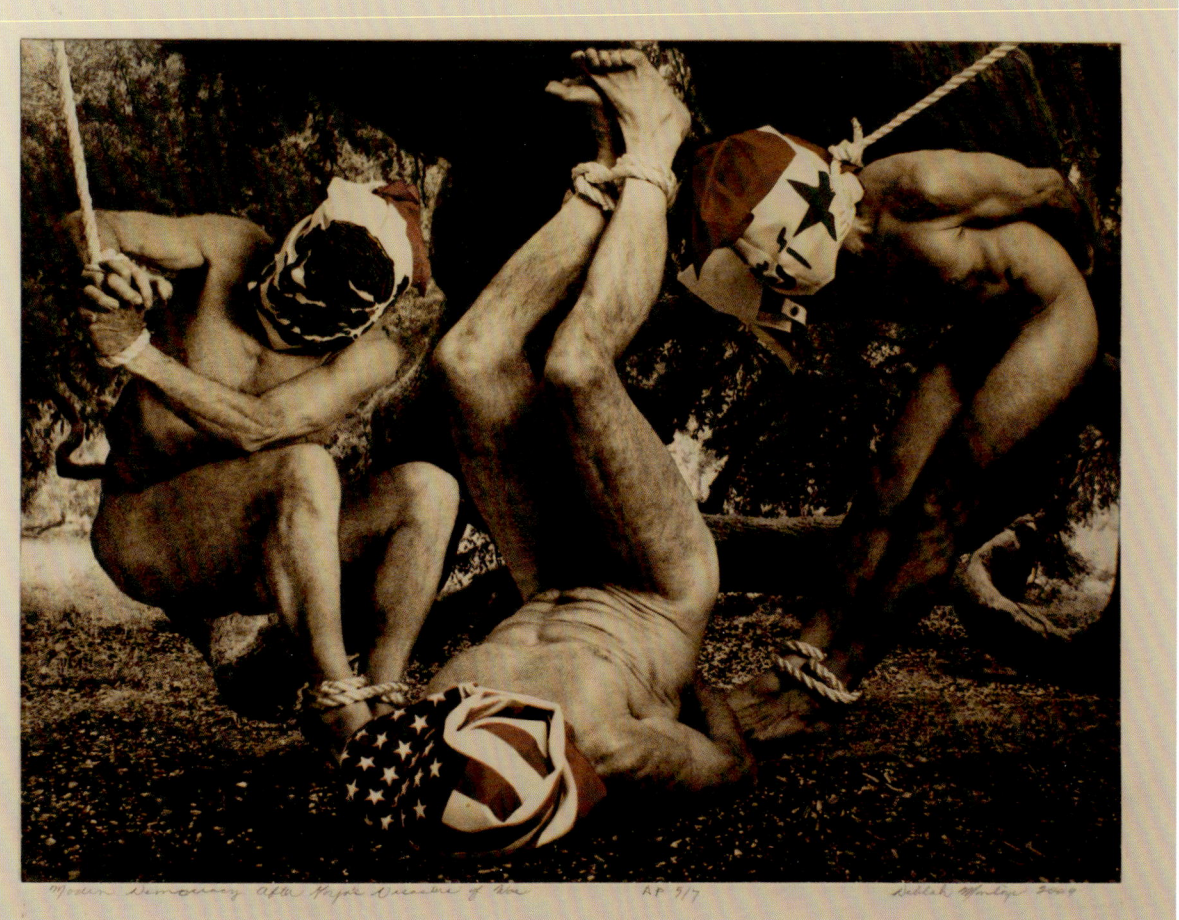

Delilah Montoya
Modern Democracy After
Goya's Disasters of War
2009
Polymer etching, AP 5/7
24⅕ × 19¾ in.
Collection of the artist

texture of the paper, offering a presence that is very different from digital prints.

While the fusion of printmaking and photography is prevalent in many of Montoya's series, she also disrupts the idea of "straight photography" by creating larger installation works and photomurals that transform various objects into a multilayered experience. *Saints and Sinners* engages with the spiritual and penitential practices of the Hermanos Penitentes, a religious order of Northern New Mexico. The installation consists of multiple elements—a photographic mural, an altar, and fourteen glass jars representing the Stations of the Cross, each containing symbolic artifacts. Together, these elements transform the space into an interactive ritual of remembrance.

The photo mural—a large-scale black-and-white image of Montoya's grandfather's *morada*—is the central visual element of *Saints and Sinners*. The grid pattern used to construct the mural disrupts the notion of a singular perspective, fracturing the image into multiple viewpoints. The crumbling adobe structure, the streaks of light penetrating the wooden slats, and the dust-laden surfaces all evoke a space of abandonment. Yet, the specific story and presence of Montoya's grandfather and her experience in the space remains. More universally, there is an enduring sacredness, situating the morada as both a site of loss and continued spiritual resonance.

Below the mural, the altar installation engages the audience in active participation. The earthen red floor, the flickering candles, and the trapezoidal *banco* (bench) inscribed with the word "sin" create a space where viewers must physically kneel to examine the glass jars, reenacting gestures of devotion found in Catholic spiritual practices. The fourteen jars, each containing objects symbolizing the Passion of Christ, serve as microcosmic encapsulations of Montoya's broader themes—spiritual suffering, cultural displacement, and the persistence of faith. These symbolic interventions transform the Stations of the Cross into a contemporary Chicano experience, reworking Christian iconography through a lens of spiritual resilience. Below is Montoya's first-hand description of her process.

Delilah Montoya: The Process of Making Saints and Sinners

Saints and Sinners is a nod to Amalia Mesa-Bains and Patrick Nagatani. While at the CARA exhibition opening, I saw Amalia's impressive *An Ofrenda for Dolores del Rio* and Patrick's work at the University of New Mexico. I liked the scale of their works and how the photographs presented along with intentional objects transformed space. Installation art is a mode of production where the experience is the aim of the compilation. *Saints and Sinners* presents a subjective experience rooted in Chicanx political concerns, history, and identity.

Saints and Sinners was my master's thesis in 1990. It was an opportunity to learn more about my grandfather's *morada* and the Penitente Brotherhood, which shaped my family's history. *Saints and Sinners* investigates spiritualism found within the Chicano homeland in Northern New Mexico. The Hermandad (a penitential Christian brotherhood) expresses the act of penance through the passion of Christ and was a binding force that unified the Spanish colonial communities of Northern New Mexico. The Hermandad helped mend the fragmentation caused by the Mexican War when New Mexico was ceded to the United States. By keeping the ancient theology alive, they kept spiritual, social, and cultural identity intact, helping to activate our cultural orientation.

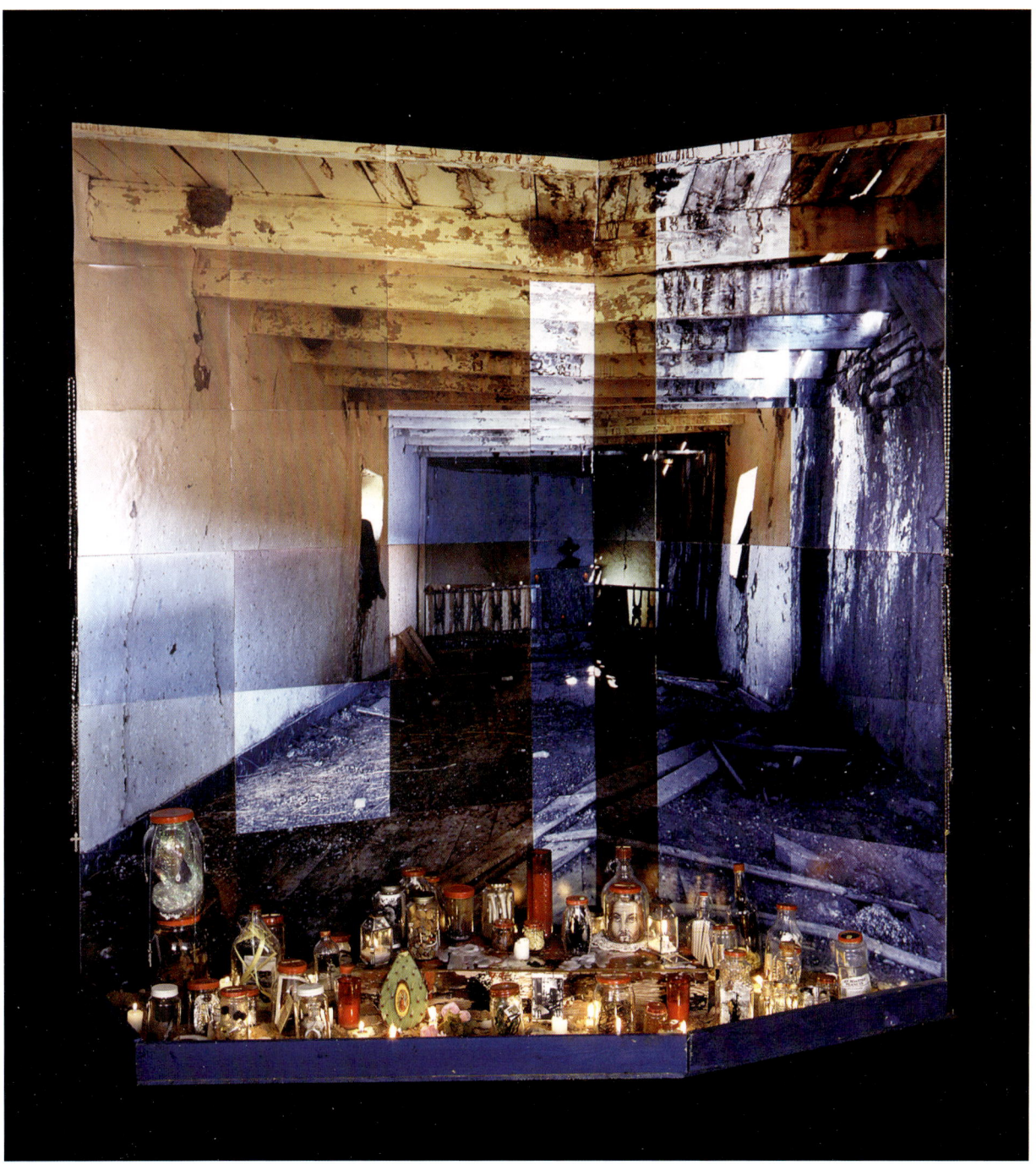

Delilah Montoya

Saints and Sinners

1990

Collaged chromogenic prints mounted on wooden frame

96 × 120 in.

Albuquerque Museum, gift of the artist

PC2022.32.14

Mysticism, alchemy, and sacrifice are evocative of both Christian and Mesoamerican thought.

To help develop a definition of Aztlán, I focused on the New Mexican Santos and spaces of recognized spiritual power, such as the Santuario de Chimayo. I read *Santos and Saints*, a 1974 book by Thomas Steele that cataloged nineteenth-century New Mexican Santeros. Steele described the making of a saint as a holy action, and the purity of the Santero's heart gave value to the work and not necessarily the craftsmanship. My grandfather came to mind, the image of him devoutly praying in his room for so many years, blind, contained within narrow physical boundaries, yet those very boundaries were expansive in the spiritual realm. Could he create a traditional *santo*? Was this the religious fervor that a true Santero accessed? What kind of art is this? It is not directed by craftsmanship but a conceptual attitude that captures the core of representation.

Saints and Sinners is a juxtaposition of two opposing forces. Thinking about its political implications, I coined the term saintly sinners: the Judases of our society. Yet this opened another door: Was Judas born to betray Christ, was he destined for evil, did he have a free will? Again, my attention turned to my grandfather sitting in his cloister of prayer and memory, to my mother's criticism of his heavy drinking, to his carefully feeling his way with a cane to the coal shed, his favorite hiding spot of his pint. I remember watching him pray over his wife's coffin, begging that she take him with her. Was my grandfather also a saintly sinner? What is the measuring stick that moved him from one extreme to the other? This is the theology I contemplated while constructing the installation.

The mural-sized photograph that functions as a backdrop for an altar was the interior of "San Isidro," my grandfather's morada, located outside of Las Vegas, New Mexico between Rosiada and San Manuelitas. This area was my grandfather's childhood and spiritual home; he was born on a *ranchito* adjacent to the morada. Here, my ancestors opened their souls to God. Even in my childhood, the morada was abandoned. I vividly remember the red crepe paper hanging from the *vigas*. Each time I visited, it was in further deterioration.

At the time of the photo shoot, the rock under the adobe plaster was beginning to show. The red tin roof had holes allowing streaks of light to shine on the altar. At the front of the morada, behind the main altar, the wall is curved into a semi-arch. Swallows nested on the vigas and eaves, leaving a tremendous amount of droppings everywhere. The walls were splattered with a white coloration, lending a surreal sentiment.

To produce the greatest resolution so that the photograph could be blown up to mural size, I decided to photograph the morada with a 4 × 5 camera. I needed help with the equipment, so I invited Cecilio García-Camarillo to join me on the shoot. Also, I was apprehensive about going into the abandoned morada alone. On the night before the shoot, I had a dream about an elegantly designed, gold-inlaid red cross. The cross disturbed me. Upon discussing this dream with Cecilio, he revealed a similar incident involving a daydream he experienced while jogging: In his daydream, I entered the morada, then went back to the truck to get a guitar, and returned as a child. I played the guitar to the spirits asking the sacred space permission to make art of the morada.

San Isidro contains a heightened energy level; it was a spiritual center where souls were revealed to God. I know that my grandfather visited the morada through his prayers; in his mind, it exists as he saw it before his blindness set in. The bright, blood-red tin roof was held by four sturdy rock walls that were cleanly plastered. Planked with a rough wood floor, the interior was humble but clean. The walls were once freshly painted pink with a dark royal blue baseboard, and the windows were covered with white lace curtains. When the front door was opened the morning sunbathed the saints and candles on the altar. It was here, by performing the penitential rites, my grandfather received his passage to manhood. It was important to ask permission to use this space for artmaking.

Cecilio felt innocence was needed to obtain permission, so he asked his daughter Oraibi to help with the ritual by playing the guitar in the morada before the shoot. To help send the message, I lit candles on the altar as Oraibi strummed the guitar. In Spanish, Cecilio asked permission as a prayer for the transformation. Immediately afterwards, a swallow cooed. We interpreted that as a positive omen to proceed. For the next hour and a half, I photographed every angle, wall, and corner of the morada, and I distinctly remember that throughout this period, the swallows remained silent. Just as I took the last shot, the last candle went out.

The mural, which is 9 feet by 7 1/2 feet, is a composite print constructed from two shots that are identical except for a color cast. One has a cold blue cast caused by using tungsten film under daylight conditions, and the other has a warm cast that recorded the morning light. A grid pattern is used to insert warm and blue photo sections that create a crucifix, fitting together like a puzzle. The right side of the mural is predominantly warm, and the left side is cool, creating a tension of opposites. The blue cast suggests the moonlight, referencing night or perhaps the darkening during the *tenieblas* Hermandad ceremony. The left side is warm like the morning sun, perhaps a resurrection. These divisions, likewise, represent the transmutation of the soul as it changes from one state to the other. The mural's theme is dualism: one side is night, sin, death, and darkness juxtaposed against day, grace, resurrection, and light.

Cecilio pointed out a church in the South Valley with interesting sculptures, which he believed was a morada. He commented that the icons might be significant to my research. The site was indeed a morada, and the outside sculptures represented the Stations of the Cross, sculpted with cement. I immediately knew I had to photograph them. I was aware of the fact that during holy week the morada would be active. On Good Friday, I went there hoping to receive permission to photograph the sculptures. To my surprise, I bumped into Charley Gallegos, a carpenter and coworker at the University of New Mexico. He was an herman at that morada. I requested permission to document the sculptures, but he explained that it was not allowed, for the stations were sacred, but if I was really serious about photographing them, he would make an appeal to the artist, Hermano Juan. It was this incident that started a mentorship with Hermano Juan Sandoval.

As the mayor and founder of San José Morada in Albuquerque, Hermano Juan was a spiritual leader and artist. A strong-minded, compassionate, sincere Hermano de Nuestro Senor de Nasareno, Hermano Juan, as an artist, receives inspiration from the heart. Drawing upon his faith to formulate an aesthetic and religious understanding of his subject, he meditated before executing the work, believing that creating is an internalized process. He was careful about where the work was placed and who owned it. He believes that once his work is taken out of its environment, it can lose potency.

When I made an appeal to Hermano Juan to photograph his Stations of the Cross outside of the San José Morada, he asked about my intentions. I explained that I wanted to photograph the station for an art project. I discussed my interest in religious iconography used and created by Chicanos. He permitted me to photograph, but only under specific conditions. Since he never exhibits his work in galleries or museums, the same must apply to the photographs. Also, the photos must not be sold. He implied that I

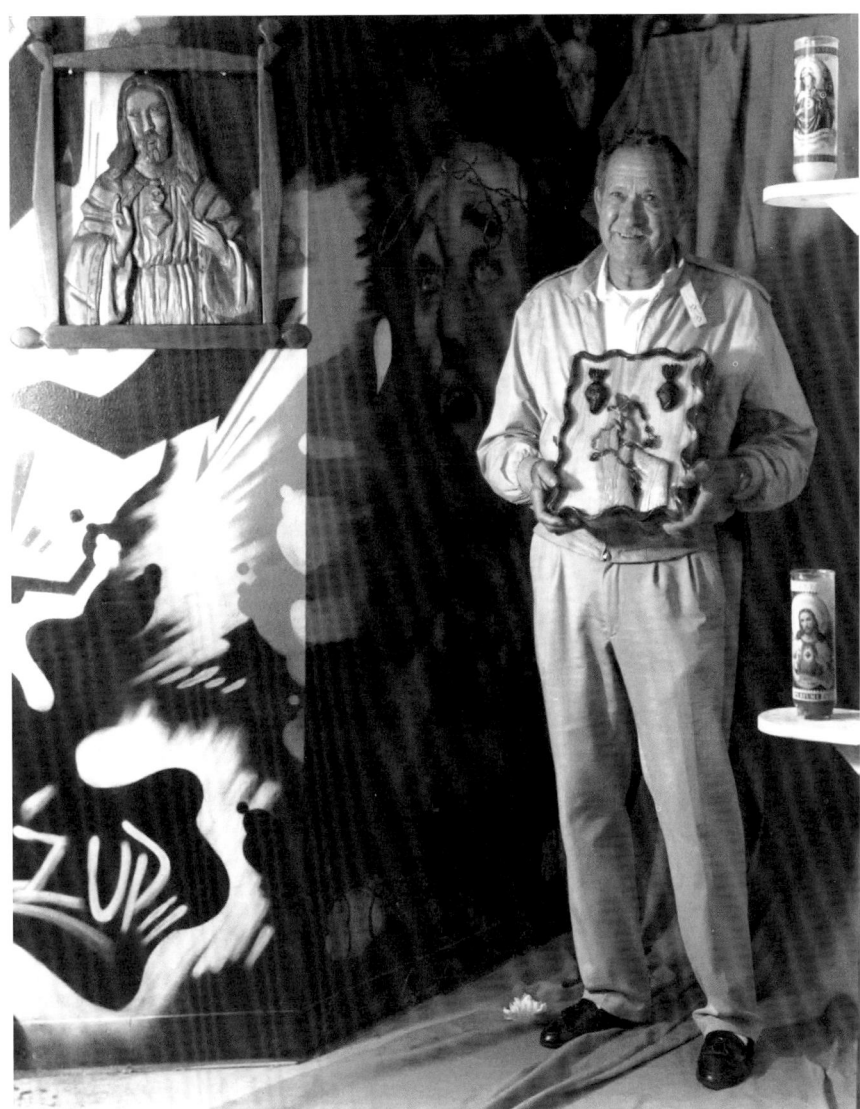

Delilah Montoya
Hermano Mayor Juan Sandoval
1990
Silver gelatin print
8 × 10 in. contact
Collection of the artist

study the stations and learn about their symbolism. He suggested that the end result of photographing the images should be for spiritual reasons. I decided to accept his approach to art since it gave me the most comprehensive method for approaching my project *Saints and Sinners.*

The fourteen jars with gold crosses on red lids represent this collaboration between Hermano Juan's expression of the Passion of Christ and my learning from that experience. They were executed through a process of meditation in much the same manner a Hermano would use the Via Dolorosa to reflect on the parable of each station to understand its message. The Station of the Cross represents a contemporary message I symbolically reconstructed inside a glass jar. They reference the alchemist's method of transmutation, which places an inferior material with a catalyst so that it would change to a superior material. The glass jars can be thought of as the body, and the contents as a soul. Like a spirit, each jar is unique and possesses the ability to change.

The fourteen glass jars represent the Passion of Christ and contain the following items:

1. Jesus is condemned—rose thorns;
2. Christ receives the cross—fishing hooks, weights, and a photograph of a Hermano carrying a cross;
3. Jesus falls the first time—crow feathers, tattered rose;
4. Jesus meets his mother (*el encuentro*)—open jar with Christ child and photo of Ms. Gallegos with her grandson, small jar contains a suspended jar with a transparency of a fetus; a small vial with a rose stem and three red thrones (the fourth sorrow of Mary);
5. Simon helps Jesus—old door hook holding up a crystal;
6. Veronica wipes the face of Christ—*pano* (handkerchief) with a ballpoint pen drawing of Christ, the artist is a state penitentiary prisoner;
7. Jesus falls the second time—jug with warning labels filled with water from the Rio Grande;
8. Jesus speaks to the women of Jerusalem—photograph with a teenager sitting and an explosion in the background; electrical wires are in the foreground;
9. Jesus falls the third time—syringe, ceramic arms, and ashes;
10. Jesus is stripped of his garments—photograph of telephone lines;
11. Jesus is nailed to the cross—jar of old rusty nails; vial with five red thorns (fifth sorrow of Mary);
12. Jesus dies—arbitrary notices with a crucifix wrapped in black cloth; vial with six thorns (sixth sorrow of Mary);
13. Jesus is taken down—palm leaves with a photograph of a resurrection;
14. Jesus is placed in the tomb—eight vials containing seeds, one vial with seven thorns (seventh sorrow of Mary)

The placement of the altar on the ground echoes Christianized Mesoamerican Native altar spaces in Latin American churches, which consists of burning candles on the floor with food offerings. The floor is a metaphor for sacred earth. To further support the notion of sacred earth, I employed adobe, the building material for the morada, as the substrate upon which to assemble the altar. The altar is a trapezoid shallow box framed with 2 × 4-inch boards painted blue, which is related to the blue baseboard of the Mural. The adobe dirt is spread evenly inside the box. Lit candles, a red and black banco, and jars are placed on the earthen altar. The banco is a low shelf constructed from red and black planks now weathered and with the paint blistering off. The word "sin" is spray-painted on the top. It provides a surface for the offerings of candles and jars.

The installation, *Saints and Sinners*, inspires audience interaction. I received items donated by the community, including the rosaries by my mother, Amalia Garcia. When lit, on opening night, the flickering candles created movement, a visual effect that attracted an audience. The jars drew people into a closer investigation of the installation. Some held the jars while examining their contents; others knelt on the floor to view the candles and objects placed on the altar. Several even repositioned the jars and lit candles while weaving their own stories of the scene. Visually, the viewer is bowing in front of the cross. This interaction of the public not only contributed to and enhanced the success of the installation but, in my estimation, also positively completed the entire process of *Saints and Sinners*.

Delilah Montoya
*Glass Jar with Crucifix—
Station of the Cross #10:
Jesus Stripped*
1992
Cibachrome print
15½ × 19½ in.
New Mexico Museum
of Art, gift of Jonathan
Abrams and Fay Pfaelzer
Abrams, 2009
2009.04.4ab

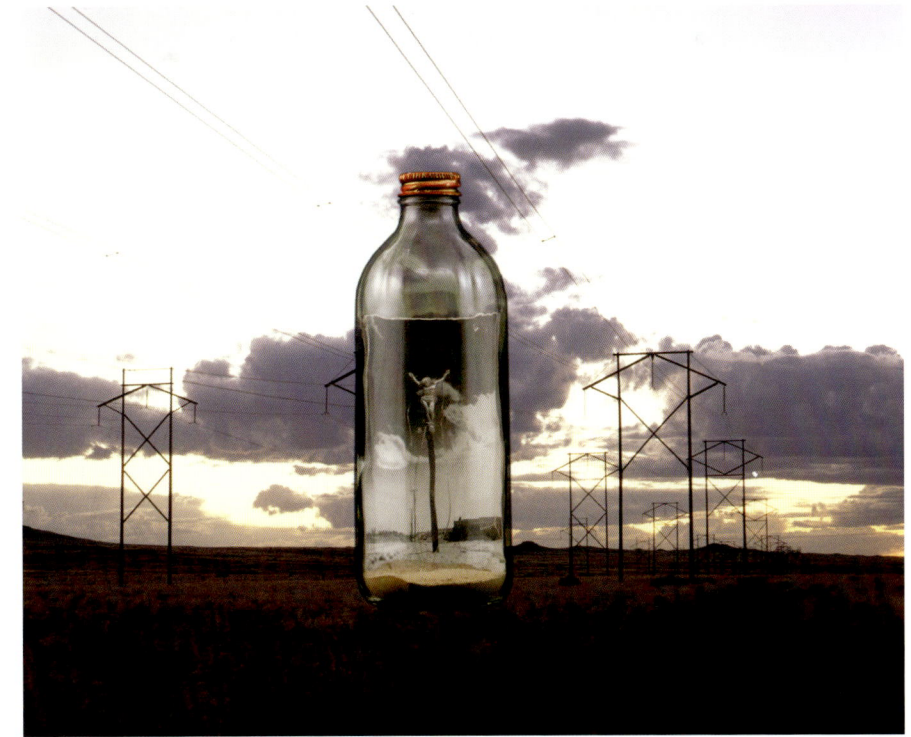

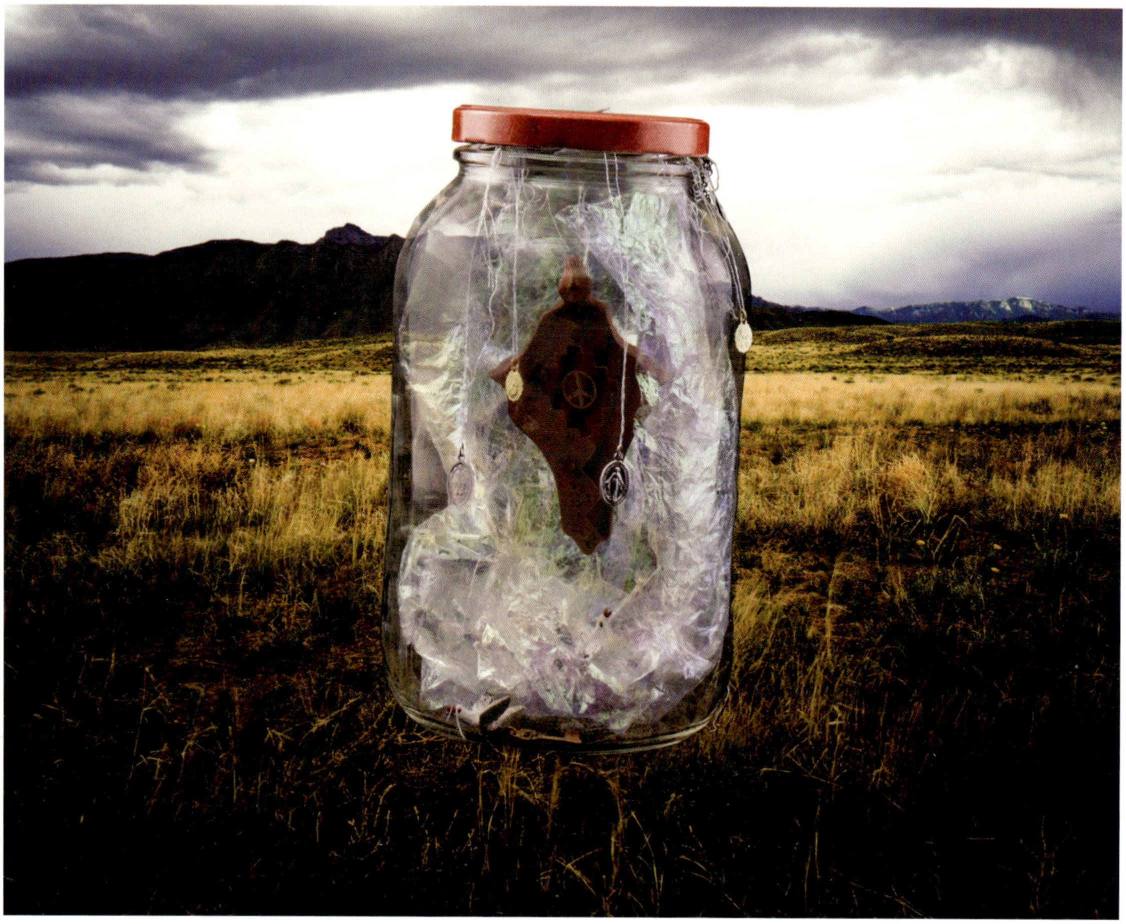

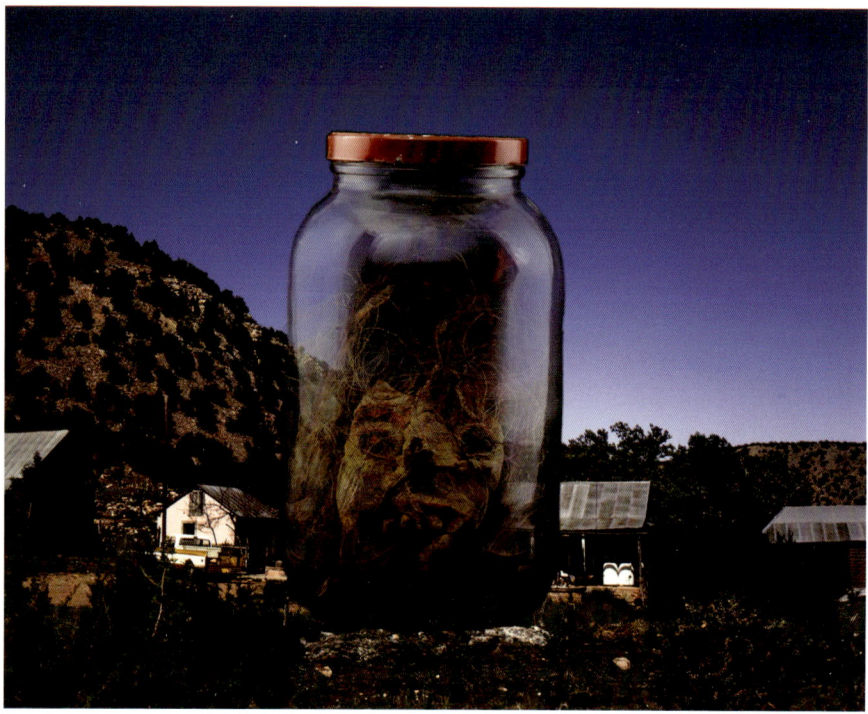

(*top*) Delilah Montoya
El Cielo
1992
Cibachrome print
15½ × 19½ in.
Collection of the artist

(*left*) Delilah Montoya
El Inferno
1992
Cibachrome print
15½ × 19½ in.
Collection of the artist

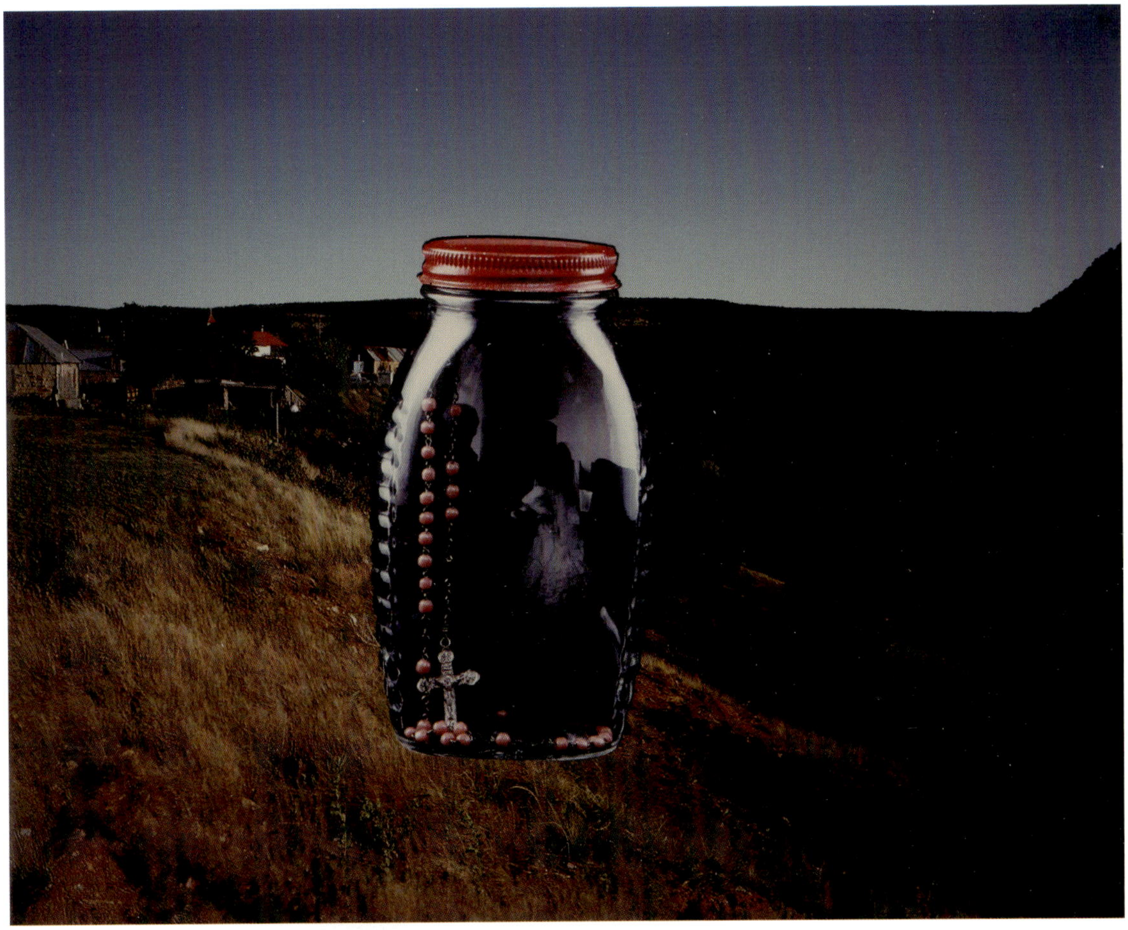

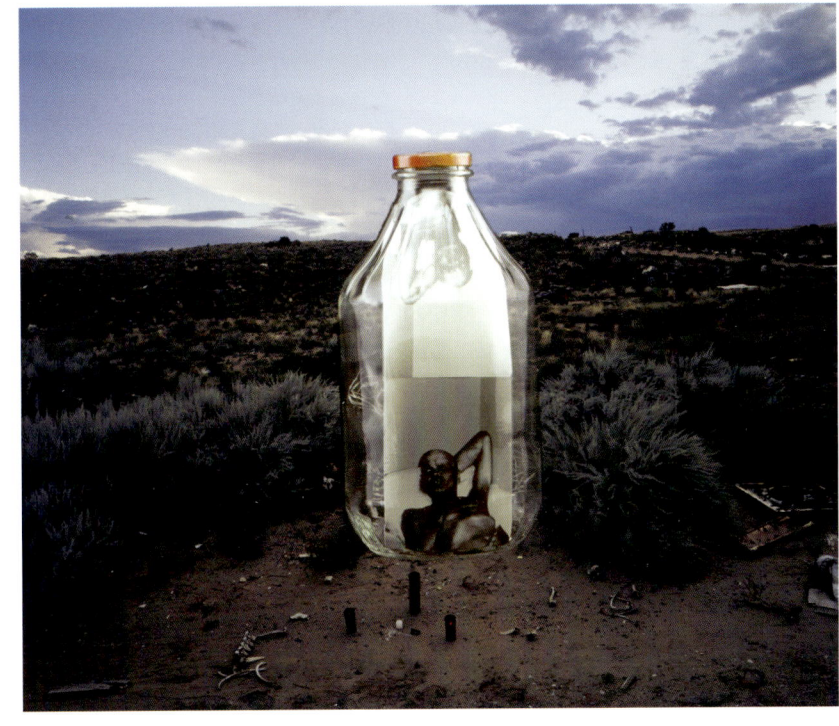

(*top*) Delilah Montoya
The Blessing
ca. 1992
Cibachrome print
15½ × 19⅕ in.
Collection of the artist

(*right*) Delilah Montoya
Women of Jerusalem
ca. 1992
Cibachrome print
15½ × 19⅕ in.

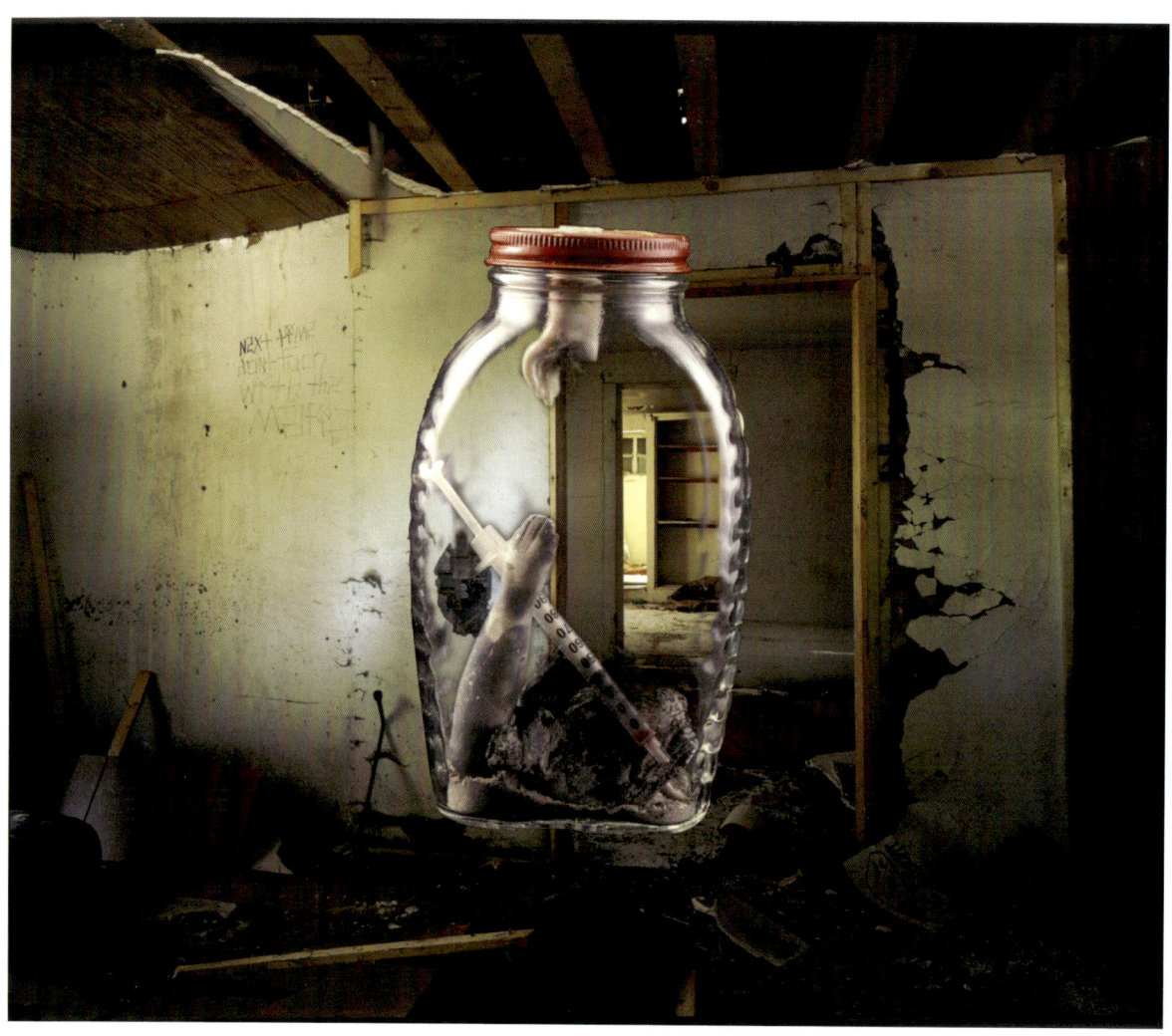

Delilah Montoya
Station #7
ca. 1992
Cibachrome print
15½ × 19½ in.
Collection of the artist

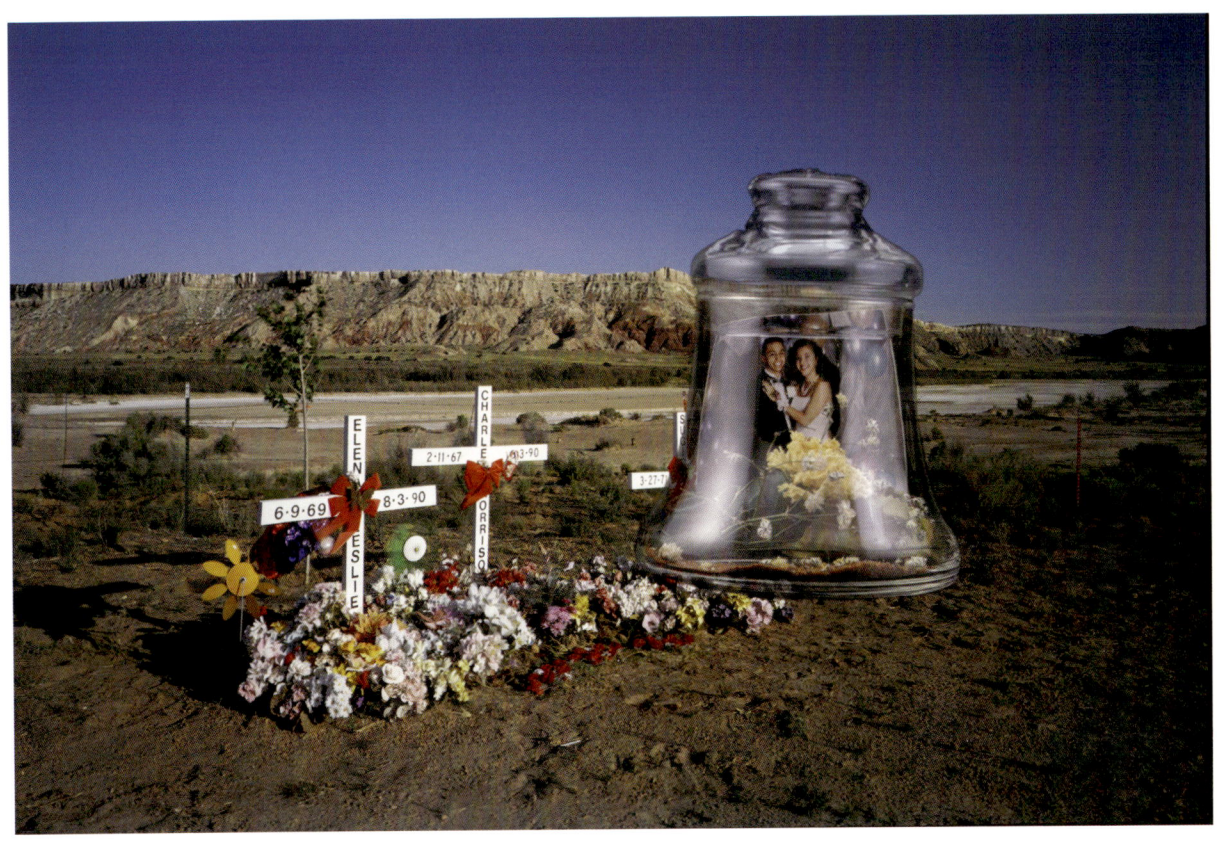

Delilah Montoya

Til Death Do We Part

1992

ca. 1992

Cibachrome print

15½ × 19½ in.

Collection of the artist

odex Delilah: A Journey from Mexicatl to Chicana consists of seven panels with painted figures, text, and photographic images affixed to *amate* paper (Mexican bark), which is similar to the paper used in the original codices of Mexico. In these codices, Indigenous scribes communicated events, rituals, calendar systems, tribute, and more. The *Dresden Codex* is one of only four Mayan codices that exist in the world today. Housed in the collection of Saxon State and University Library, Dresden. Montoya looked to this pre-Columbian example as source material for *Codex Delilah: 6 Deer Journey from Mexicatl to Chicana*, which was included in the exhibition, *The Chicano Codices: Encountering Art of the Americas*, curated by Marcos Tranquilino Sánchez for the Mexican Museum in San Francisco. The exhibition was a response to the celebrations marking the passage of 500 years since Columbus arrived in the Americas. Artists and activists spoke out against the histories and impacts of colonialism that were ignored.[1]

Codex Delilah: A Journey from Mexicatl to Chicana* includes three registers that function to reveal the interconnected relationships of each realm. The upper register is the cosmic realm inhabited by Mesoamerican deities. 6 Deer's journey unfolds as a visual narrative in the center or earthly realm, and the text by Cecilio Garcia-Camarillo inhabits the underworld.[2] Mayan date glyphs separate each of the seven panels, signaling the passage of time from preconquest to 2012, which marked the beginning of a new age according to the Mayan calendar. In her proposal for the project, Montoya discusses both the formal elements of the codex and the pre-Columbian visual language that she drew from, which included the flattening of space, ambiguous perspective between background and foreground, sky and ground, linear depictions that further reinforce the flattening of the figures, and selective use of color.[3]

Montoya's codex is constructed of amate paper. Montoya says, "This paper is not considered a true paper since it is not made with a pulp mash. To make amate, the outer tree bark is peeled, and the inner bark is boiled and soaked in water overnight, then beaten with a smooth, flat stone until it becomes pulp. A glutinous substance, taken from orchid bulbs, is added, and then this paste is formed. The paste is pounded with flat rocks into sheets and dried in the sun. This is a specialized process that the Otomi Culture has developed over thousands of years." Montoya purchased the amate paper at a *mercado* in Ciudad Juarez in the mid-eighties. She says,

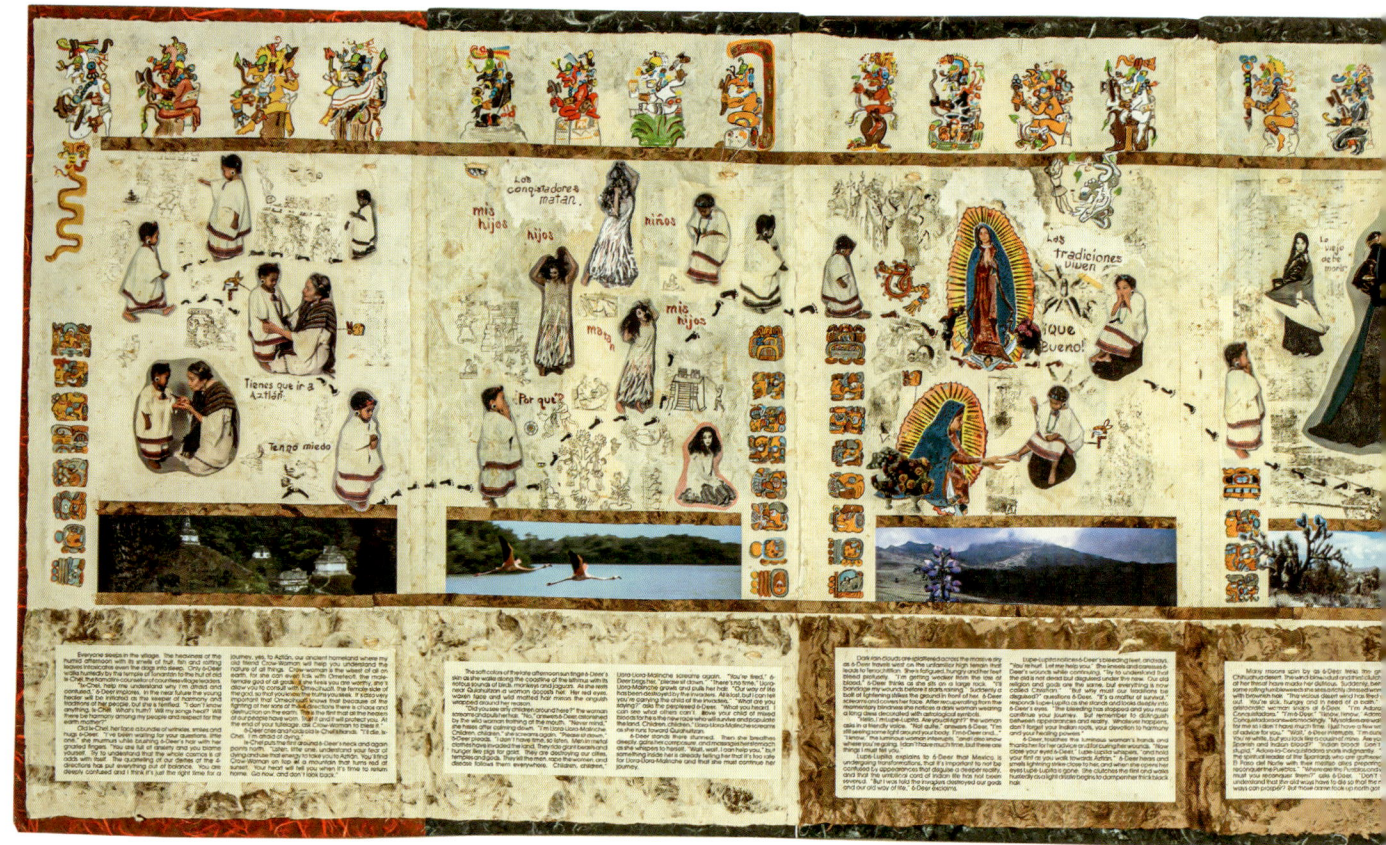

Delilah Montoya
Codex Delilah: A Journey from Mexicatl to Chicana
1992
Painted amate paper on board,
photographs, and string
30¼ × 102¼ in.
University of New Mexico
University Libraries, Center for
Southwest Research and Special
Collections

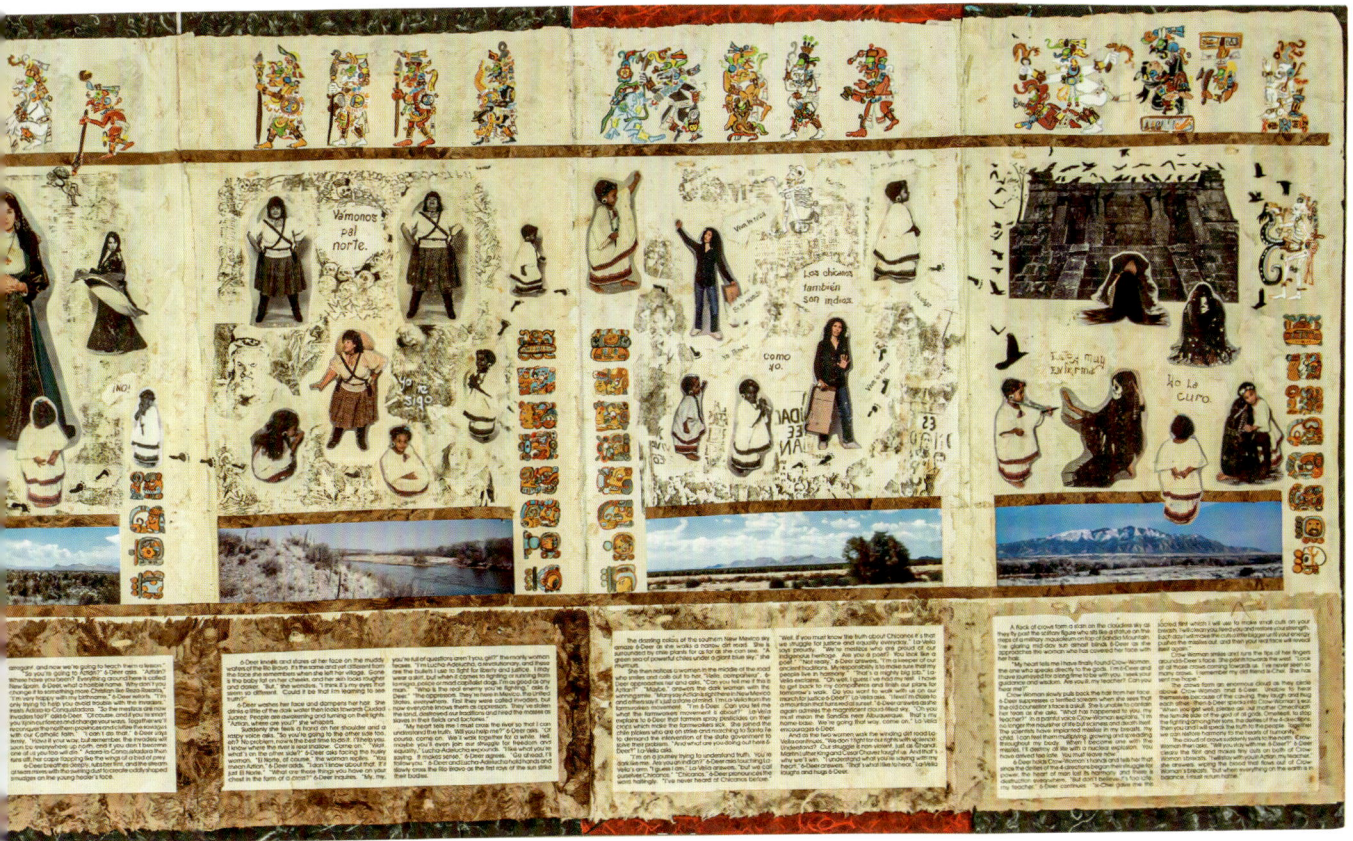

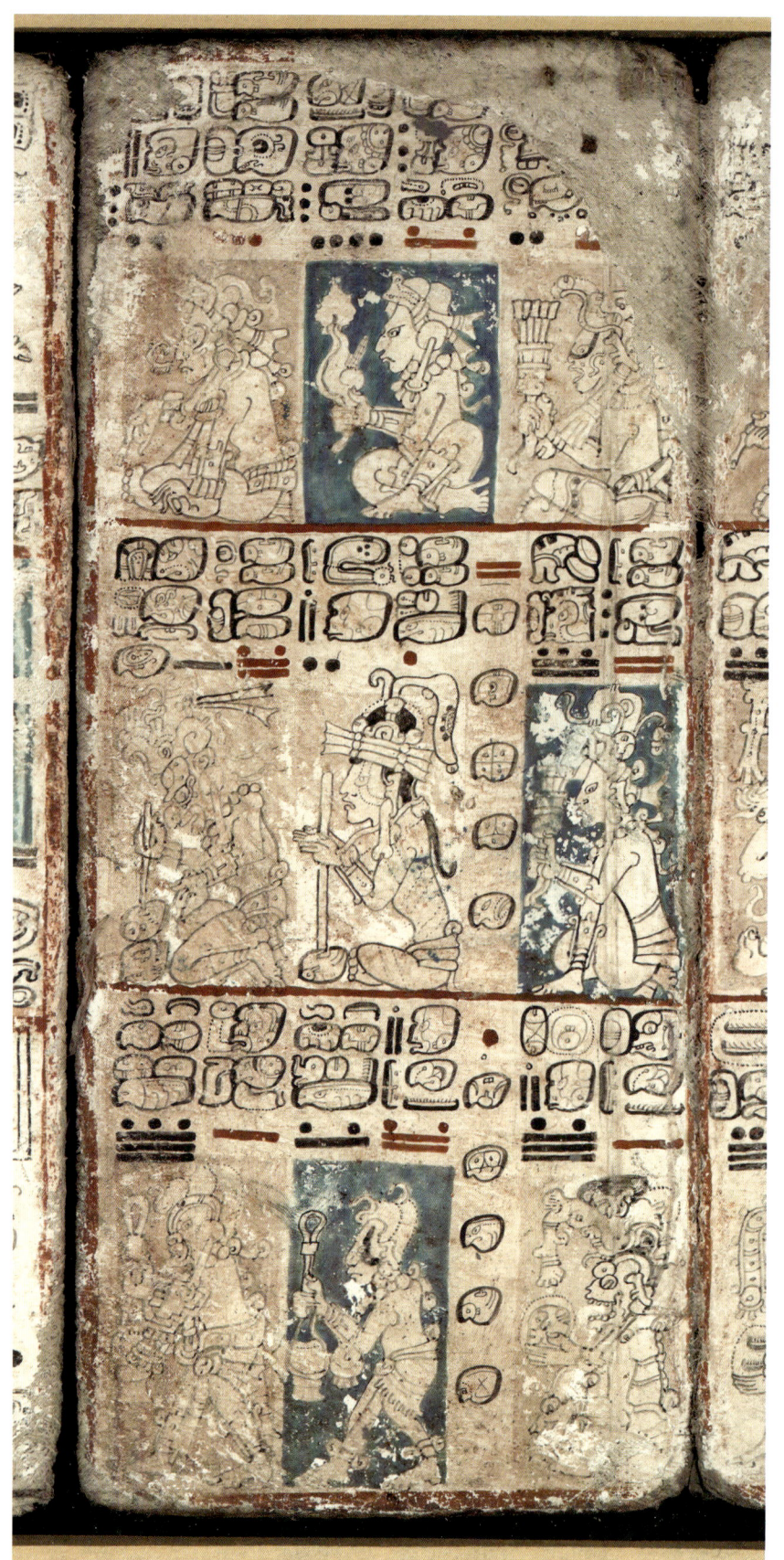

Unidentified Artist
Dresden Codex
ca. 1300–1521
Chalk, soot ink, and pigment on amate paper
8.07 × 140.16 in.
Saxon State and University Library Dresden

"In 1992, when I was invited to participate in the Chicano Codices, I pulled out my stash of Amate. I knew this paper was just waiting for Codex Delilah to be made." [4] The compilation of collaged photographs, drawings, heat transfer stickers, and other printed material were held together by the very type of substrate that was used in the original codices.

In each panel, the upper realm depicts a cosmic battle between four Chaacs representing four aspects of the Mayan rain god as Bacabs. Each resides in a different cardinal direction and is associated with a specific color: red is east, white is north, black is west, and yellow is south. Montoya also references a fifth god who could hold the key to cosmic balance. In the earlier panels, the gods appear relatively calm, but as time goes on, they become more animated and engage in battle, signaling a cosmic imbalance.

Meanwhile, in the earthly realm, 6 Deer also moves through time. In the first panel, she is frightened and does not want to leave her home. She encounters Ix-Chel, who tells her that she must find Crow Woman to understand the nature of all things. Panel two is 1530, where 6 Deer meets Llora-Llora-Malinche, who is mourning the death and destruction of conquest but also ushering in the birth of Mestizaje. In panel three, she meets Nuestra Senora de Guadalupe in 1540, marking the intersection of Christian and Indigenous beliefs. In 1688, 6 Deer encountered La Conquistadora, who was the saint Spanish colonists evoked to reconquer Native American territory after the Pueblo Revolt of 1680. In panel five, 6 Deer encounters Lucha-Adelucha, a *soldadera* fighting in the Mexican Revolution in 1910. In panel six, she meets a Chicana activist in the chile fields of the north. In the final panel, she moves into the future and finds Crow Woman, ill and struggling, but 6 Deer agrees to stay until the world is in balance. Each of the women 6 Deer encounters is a complex historical figure connected to various deities, legends, and folkloric protagonists. According to Montoya, "Together they represent a mestiza feminist vision of a woman whose roles as weaver, child bearer, healer, warrior, and soothsayer gives life and death to her people.[5]

Each panel represents a specific moment in time and reflects the deeply researched format of the *Dresden Codex* and many icons of Chicana history and identity. What is not readily apparent, however, is the process Montoya used in creating the images in the central register. The glyphs representing the deities and dates are hand-drawn and painted, but the female figures, including 6 Deer, are friends, family, and activists from Albuquerque who were photographed as they embodied their own histories. In this sense, Montoya is not only constructing an understanding of Chicana identity and history, but she is also mapping those stories onto what, at the time, was her present community.

As mentioned earlier, the idea of Aztlán as a mythical homeland is embedded in the Chicano movement. It is part of embracing an Indigenous antiquity while contesting colonial perspectives. Mapping was one of the tools utilized to conquer and claim lands in both instances of colonization. At the bottom of the central register, just below 6 Deer's graphically depicted journey, Montoya includes images of the landscapes that 6 Deer traversed. Actual depictions of the land disrupt the concept of mapping as a way of possessing land and instead demonstrate how the land, the human journey, and the cosmic narrative are all interconnected.

The Albuquerque Museum included the *Codex Delilah* in the Center for Southwest Research collection in the exhibition, *Malinche: Traitor, Survivor, Icon* in 2022.[6] At that time, viewers were experiencing a work made ten years earlier, in 1992. In 1992, however, Montoya looked ten years to the future, as 2012 marked the beginning of a new age. Interestingly, as in many of Montoya's works, the messages the codex relayed from the future were just as relevant in the past. In the end, 6 Deer is grappling with a world in which the earth is suffering. Still, the stories, strength, and resilience of the lessons learned from her journey from Mexicatl to Chicana root her in her identity and become her source of healing, strength, and survival that will carry into the future.

Codex Delilah: A Journey from Mexicatl to Chicana

Created in 2001
Illustrated by Delilah Montoya
Written by Cecilio García-Camarillo (1944–2002)

Panel 1: Everyone sleeps in the village (pg. 38). The heaviness of the humid afternoon with its smells of fruit, fish, and rotting leaves intoxicates even the dogs into sleep. Only 6 Deer walks hurriedly by the temple of Tonantzín to the hut of old Ix-Chel, the *tlamatini*-counsellor of countless village leaders.

"Ix-Chel, help me understand why I'm afraid and confused," 6 Deer

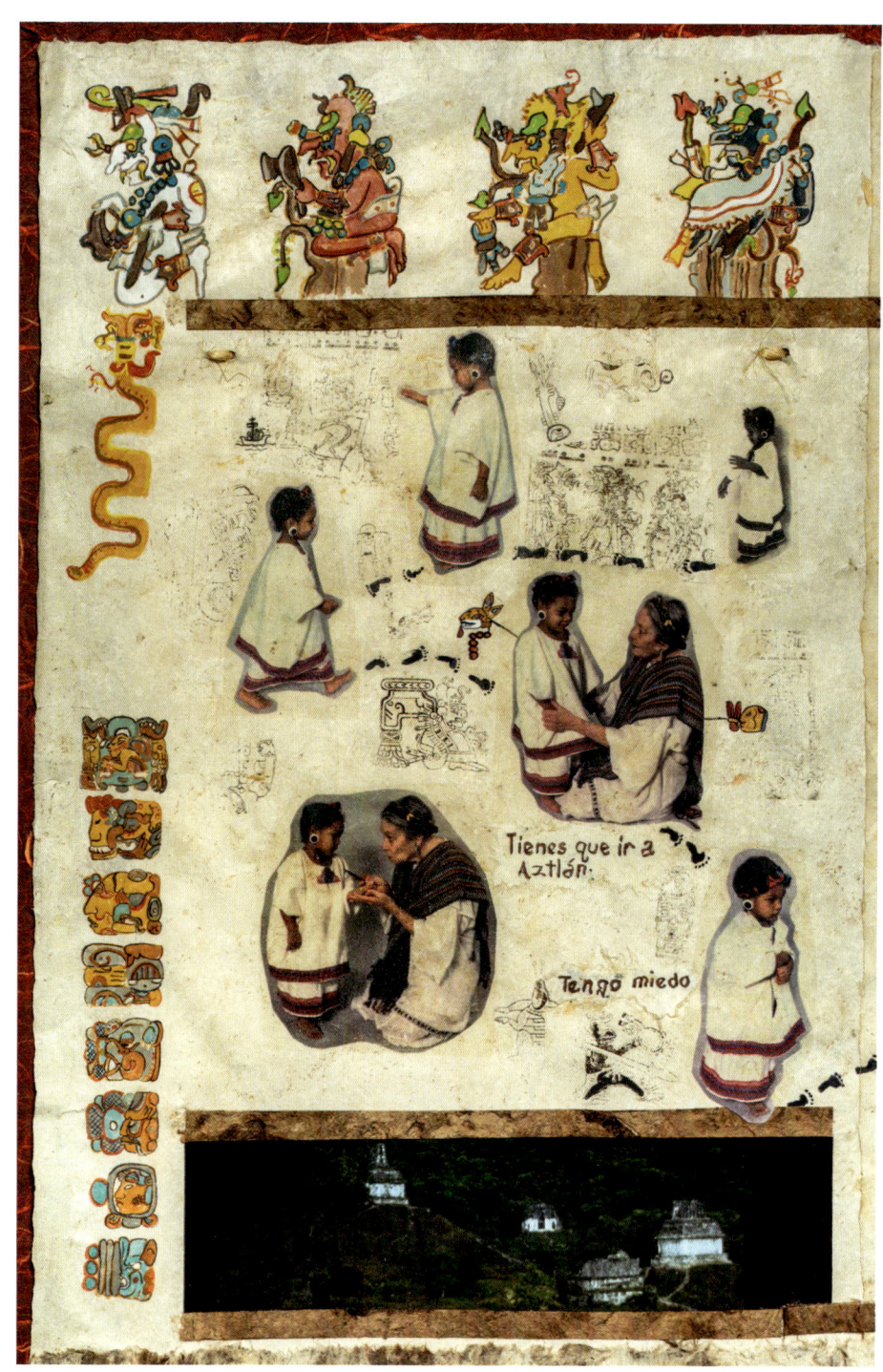

Delilah Montoya
*Codex Delilah: A Journey
from Mexicatl to Chicana*
Detail: Panel 1, Ix-Chel
sends 6 Deer on a
journey

implores. In the near future, the young healer will be initiated as the keeper of harmony and traditions of her people, but she is terrified. "I don't know anything, Ix-Chel. What is truth? Will my songs heal? Will there be harmony among my people and respect for the earth mother?"

Old Ix-Chel, her face a bundle of wrinkles, smiles and hugs 6 Deer. "I've been waiting for your questions, little one," she murmurs while brushing 6 Deer's hair with her gnarled fingers. "You are full of anxiety, and you blame yourself. Try to understand that the whole cosmos is at odds with itself. The quarreling of our deities of the four directions has put everything out of balance. You are deeply confused, and I think it's just the right time for a journey, yes, to Aztlán, our ancient homeland where my old friend Crow Woman will help you understand the nature of all things. Crow Woman is the wisest of all on earth, for she can even talk with Ometeotl, the male-female god of all gods. If she feels you are worthy, she'll allow you to consult with Omecihuatl, the female side of the god, so that you know the truths you seek. It's also very important that Omecihuatl knows that because of the fighting of her sons of the four directions there is chaos and destruction on the earth. This is the flint that all the healers of our people have worn. Trust it and it will protect you. At the end of your tutelage, ask Crow Woman to bless it." 6 Deer cries and holds old Ix-Chel's hands. "I'll die, Ix-Chel. I'm afraid of dying."

Ix-Chel puts the flint around 6 Deer's neck and again points north. "Listen, little one, understand your fear of dying and use that energy to take you to Aztlán. You'll find Crow Woman on top of a mountain that turns red at sunset. Your heart will tell you when it's time to return home. Go now, and don't look back."

Panel 2: The soft colors of the late afternoon sun tinge 6 Deer's skin as she walks along the coastline of the isthmus with its riotous sounds of birds and monkeys and jaguars (pg. 40). As she rests near Quiahuitzan a woman accosts her. Her red eyes, waxen face, and wild matted hair mirrors the anguish wrapped around her reason.

"Did you see any children around here?" the woman screams and pulls her hair.

"No," answers 6 Deer, astonished by the wild woman frothing at the mouth.

"Never mind," she hisses after calming down. "I'm Llora-Llora-Malinche.

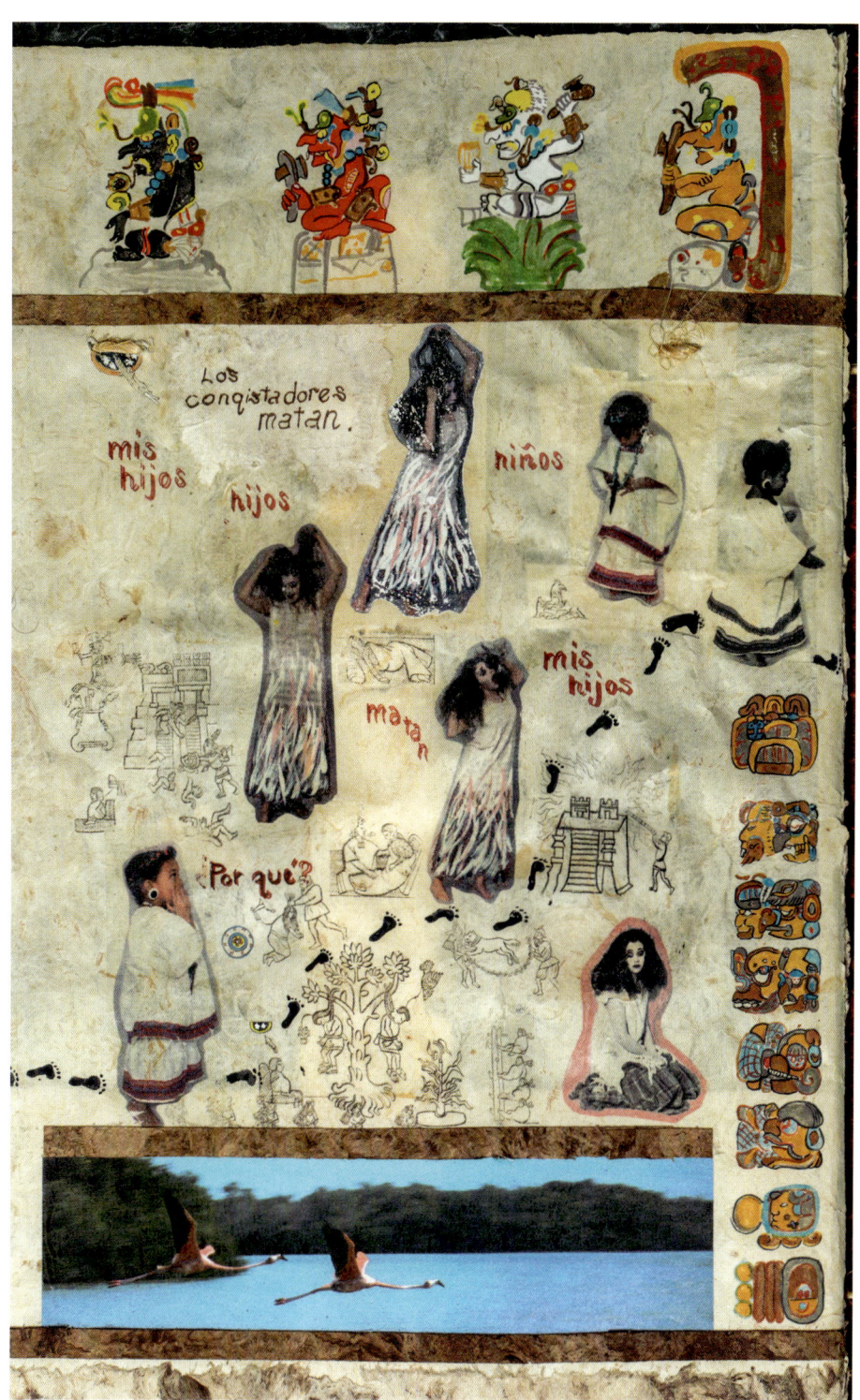

Delilah Montoya
*Codex Delilah: A Journey
from Mexicatl to Chicana*
Detail: Panel 2, 6 Deer
meets Llora-Llora-
Malinche

Children, children," she screams again.

"Please sit down," 6 Deer pleads. "I don't have time, so listen. Men in metal clothes have invaded the land. They ride giant beasts and hunger like pigs for gold. They are destroying our cities, temples and gods. They kill the men, rape the women, and disease follows them everywhere.

"Children, children," Llora-Llora-Malinche screams again.

"You're tired," 6 Deer begs her, "please sit down."

"There's no time," Llora-Llora-Malinche growls and pulls her hair. "Our way of life has been destroyed by the invaders. All is lost, but I can tell you're carrying the child of the invaders."

"What are you saying?" asks the perplexed 6 Deer.

"What you heard. I can see what others can't. Love your child of mixed bloods for he is the new race who will survive and populate the land. Children, children," Llora-Llora-Malinche screams as she runs toward Quiahuitzan.

6 Deer stands there stunned. Then she breaths deeply, gains her composure, and massages her stomach as she whispers to herself, "Wait, wait, I can help you," but something inside her is already telling her that it's too late for Llora-Llora-Malinche and that she must continue her journey.

Panel 3: Dark rain clouds are splattered across the massive sky as 6 Deer travels west on the unfamiliar high terrain that leads to Tenochtitlan (pg. 42). She is fatigued, hungry, and her feet bleed profusely. *I'm getting weaker from the loss of blood*, 6 Deer thinks as she sits on a large rock. *I'll bandage my wounds before it starts raining*. Suddenly a bolt of lightning strikes the ground in front of her. 6 Deer screams and covers her face. After recuperating from the momentary blindness she notices a dark woman wearing a long dress decorated with astrological symbols.

"Hello, I'm Lupe-Lupita. Are you all right?" the woman asks in a friendly voice.

"Not quite," answers 6 Deer, "I'm still seeing some light around your body. I'm 6 Deer and . . ."

"I know," the luminous woman interrupts, "and I also know where you're going. I don't have much time, but there are things I must tell you."

Lupe-Lupita explains to 6 Deer that Mexico is undergoing transformations, that it's important to not be confused by appearances that disguise

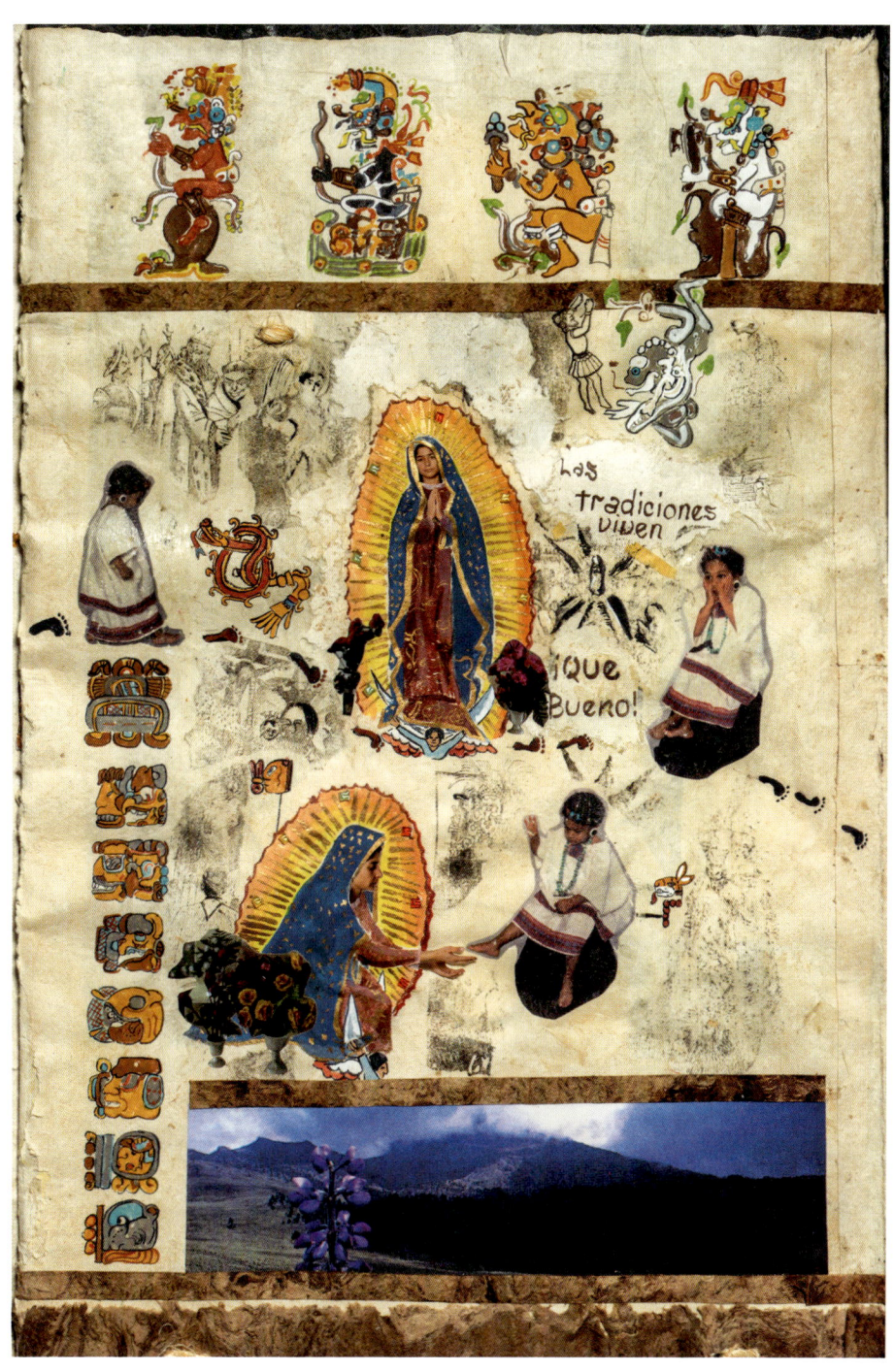

Delilah Montoya
*Codex Delilah: A Journey
from Mexicatl to Chicana*
Detail: Panel 3, 6 Deer
meets Lupe-Lupita

a deeper reality, and that the umbilical cord of Indian life has not been severed. "But I was told the invaders destroyed our gods and our old way of life," 6 Deer exclaims.

Lupe-Lupita notices 6 Deer's bleeding feet, and says, "You're hurt. Let me help you." She kneels and caresses 6 Deer's wounds while continuing, "Try to understand that the old is not dead but disguised under the new. Our old religion and gods are the same, but everything is now called Christian."

"But why must our traditions be disguised?" questions 6 Deer.

"It's a matter of survival," responds Lupe-Lupita as she stands and looks deeply into 6 Deer's eyes. "The bleeding has stopped, and you must continue your journey. But remember to distinguish between appearances and reality. Whatever happens, don't forget your Indian roots, your devotion to harmony, and your healing powers."

6 Deer touches the luminous woman's hands and thanks her for her advice and for curing her wounds. "Now close your eyes, 6 Deer," Lupe-Lupita whispers, "and hold your flint as you walk towards Aztlán." 6 Deer hears and smells lightning strike close to her, and when she opens her eyes Lupe-Lupita is gone. She clutches the flint and walks hurriedly as a light drizzle begins to dampen her thick black hair.

Panel 4: Many moons spin by as 6 Deer treks the great Chihuahua desert (pg. 44). The wind-blown dust and thirst clutching at her throat have made her delirious. Suddenly, behind some rolling tumbleweeds she sees a richly dressed woman with brownish hair.

"The vicious desert wind has tired you out. You're sick, hungry and in need of a bath," the aristocratic woman snaps at 6 Deer. "I'm Adora-la-Conquistadora."

"I'm 6 Deer."

"I know, I know," Adora-la-Conquistadora answers mockingly. "My soldiers are waiting for me, so I don't have much time. I just have a few words of advice for you."

"Wait," 6 Deer interrupts, "I'm curious. You're white, but you look like a cousin of mine. Are you of Spanish and Indian blood?"

"Indian blood! Don't be stupid," Adora-la-Conquistadora snarls indignantly. "I'm the spiritual leader of the Spaniards who are gathered at El Paso del Norte with their mestizo allies preparing to reconquer the Pueblos."

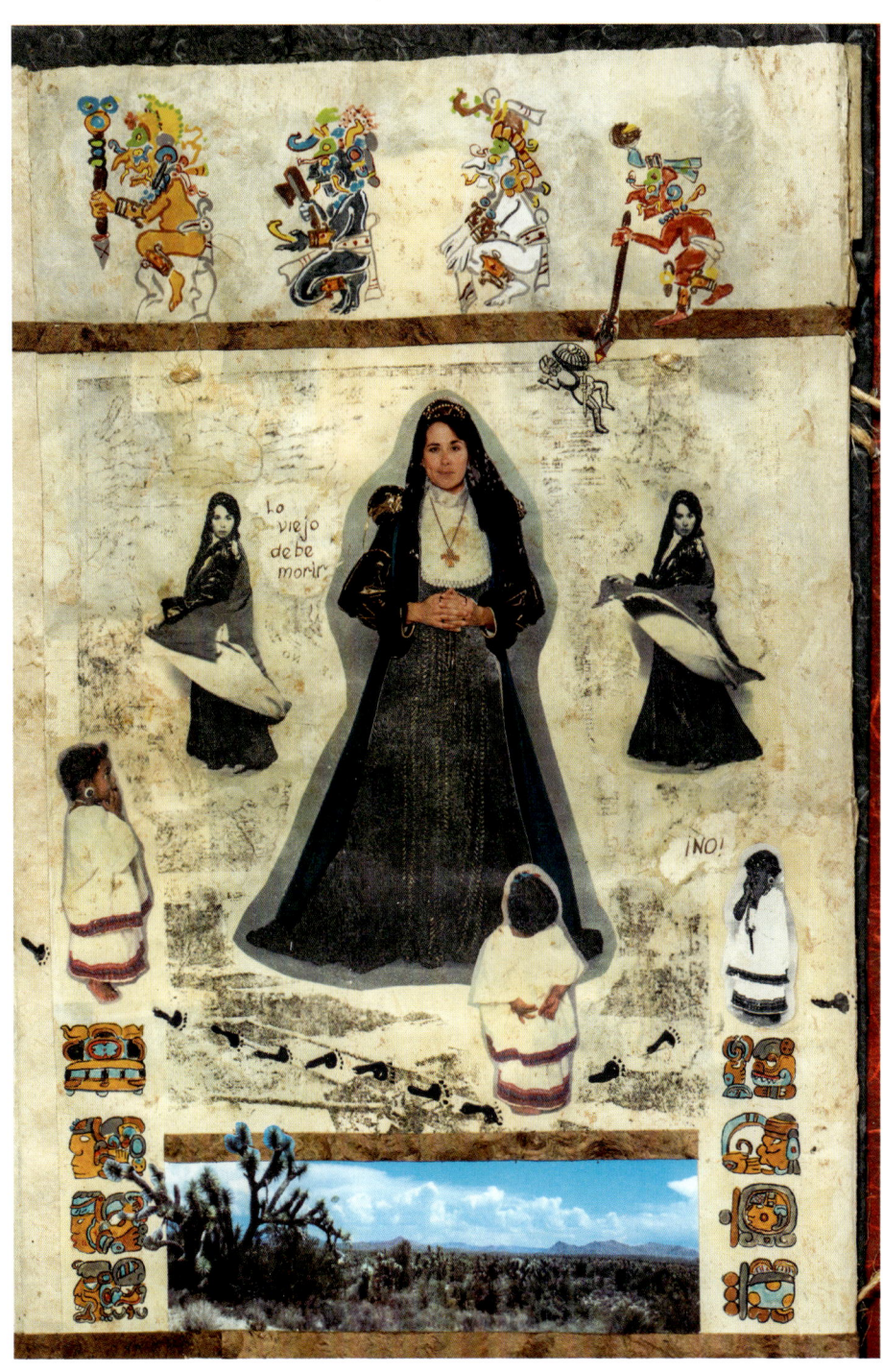

Delilah Montoya
*Codex Delilah: A Journey
from Mexicatl to Chicana*
Detail: Panel 4, 6 Deer
meets Adora-la-Con-
quistadora

"Where are the Pueblos and why must you reconquer them?" asks 6 Deer.

"Don't you understand that the old ways have to die so that the new ways can prosper? But those damn fools up north got too arrogant, and now we're going to teach them a lesson."

"So you're going to Aztlán?" 6 Deer asks.

"Aztlán? Where have you been? Everything around here is called New Spain. 6 Deer, what a horrible name. Why don't you change it to something more Christian like Reza-Rosario."

"I'm very happy with my birthname," 6 Deer retorts.

"I'm only trying to help you avoid trouble with the invaders," insists Adora-la-Conquistadora.

"So the mestizos are now invaders too?" asks 6 Deer.

"Of course, and if you're smart you'll join our forces and change your ways. Together we'll reconquer the northern provinces and civilize the savages with our Catholic faith."

"I can't do that," 6 Deer says firmly.

"Have it your way, but remember, the invaders will soon be everywhere up north, and if you don't become one of us you too will die." Adora-la-Conquistadora then runs off, her cape flapping like the wings of a bird of prey.

6 Deer breathes deeply, rubs her flint, and the stream of tears mixes with the swirling dust to create oddly shaped smudges on the young healer's face.

Panel 5: 6 Deer kneels and stares at her face on the muddy waters of the Río Bravo (pg. 46). It is the same and yet different from the face she remembers when she left her village. Gone is the baby fat on her cheeks, and her skin looks rougher and darker. *But*, she wonders, *I think it's my eyes that seem so different. Could it be that I am learning to see truth?*

6 Deer washes her face and dampens her hair. She drinks a little of the dark water then looks towards Ciudad Juárez. People are awakening and turning on their lights.

"Aztlán, where are you?" she whispers.

Suddenly she feels a hand on her shoulder and a raspy voice asks, "So you're going to the other side too, eh? No problem, now is the best time to do it. I'll help you. I know where the river is real shallow. Come on."

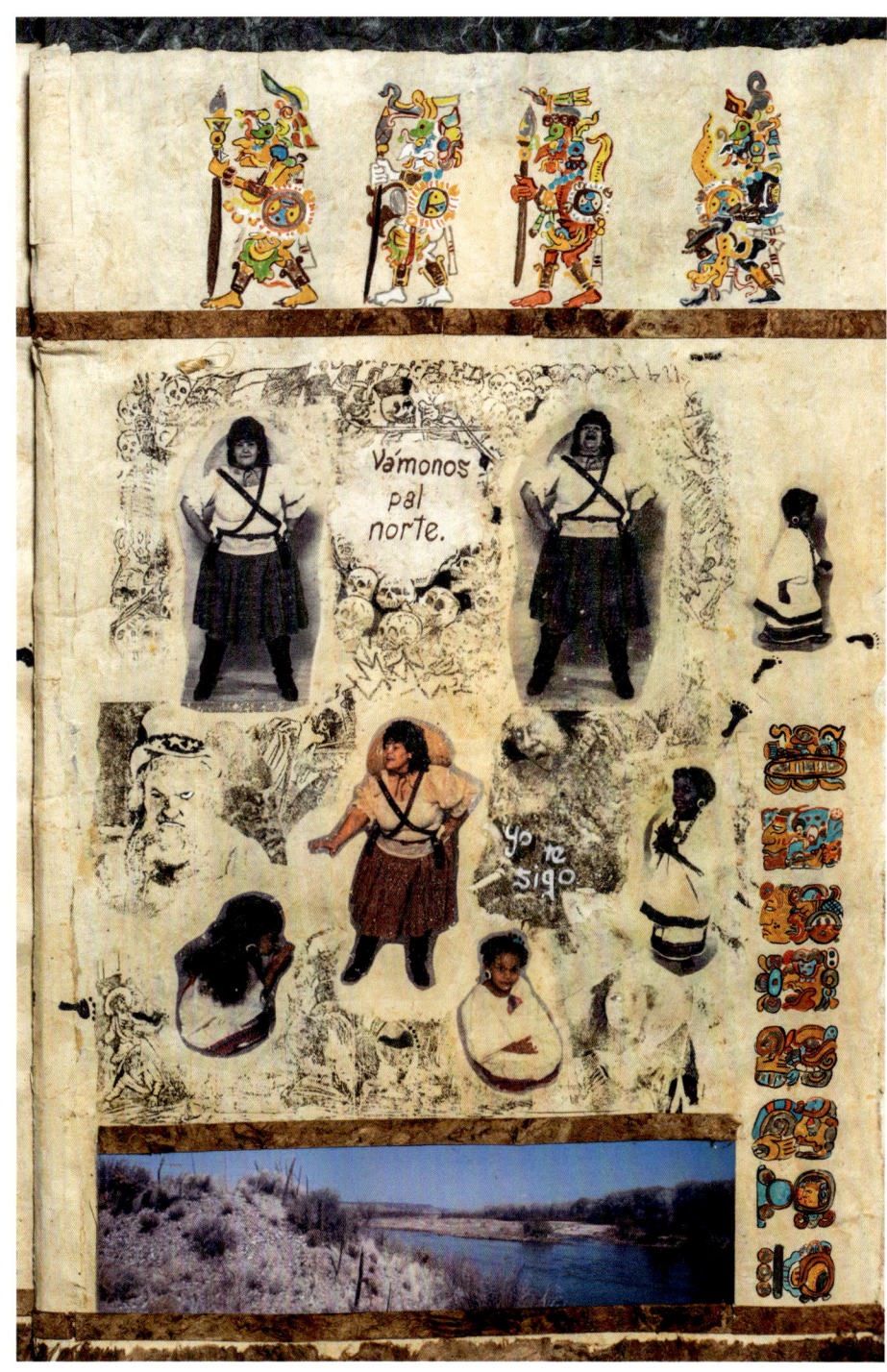

Delilah Montoya
*Codex Delilah: A Journey
from Mexicatl to Chicana*
Detail: Panel 5, 6 Deer
meets Lucha-Adelucha

"Wait, what's on the other side?" 6 Deer asks facing the husky woman.

"El Norte, of course." the woman replies.

"You mean Aztlán," 6 Deer adds.

"I don't know about that. It's just El Norte."

"What are those things you have on your chest in the form of a cross?" 6 Deer inquires.

"My, my, you're full of questions aren't you, girl?" the manly woman teases. "I'm Lucha-Adelucha, a revolutionary, and these are the bullets I use to fight for liberty and justice. I may wear a skirt, but when it comes to fighting or running from la migra, police or mad capitalist dogs, I'm as good as any man."

"Who is the real enemy you're fighting?" asks 6 Deer."

"The oppressors. They're here in Mexico, the United States, everywhere. First they were called invaders, but now everyone knows them as oppressors. They've stolen the land, destroyed our traditions, and hired the masses as slaves in their fields and factories."

"My heart tells me I must cross the river so that I can understand the truth. Will you help me?" 6 Deer asks.

"Of course, come on. We'll walk together for a while. Hell, maybe you'll even join our struggle for freedom and equality," Lucha-Adelucha expounds.

"I like what you're saying. It makes sense," 6 Deer agrees.

"Go ahead, I'll follow you." 6 Deer and Lucha-Adelucha hold hands and slowly cross the Río Bravo as the first rays of the sun strike their bodies.

Panel 6: The dazzling colors of the southern New Mexico sunset amaze 6 Deer as she walks a narrow dirt road (pg. 48). She is surrounded by chile plants for as far as she can see. "A green sea of powerful chiles under a sky on fire," she murmurs.

She then notices a woman in the middle of the road who smiles and calls out to her, "Hello, compañera."

6 Deer approaches her and asks, "Can you tell me if this is Aztlán?"

"Maybe," answers the dark woman with the winning smile. "Many say Aztlán is right here in New Mexico and others say it's just a state of mind. I'm La-Velia from the farmworker's movement."

"I'm 6 Deer. Can you tell me what the farmworkers movement is about?"

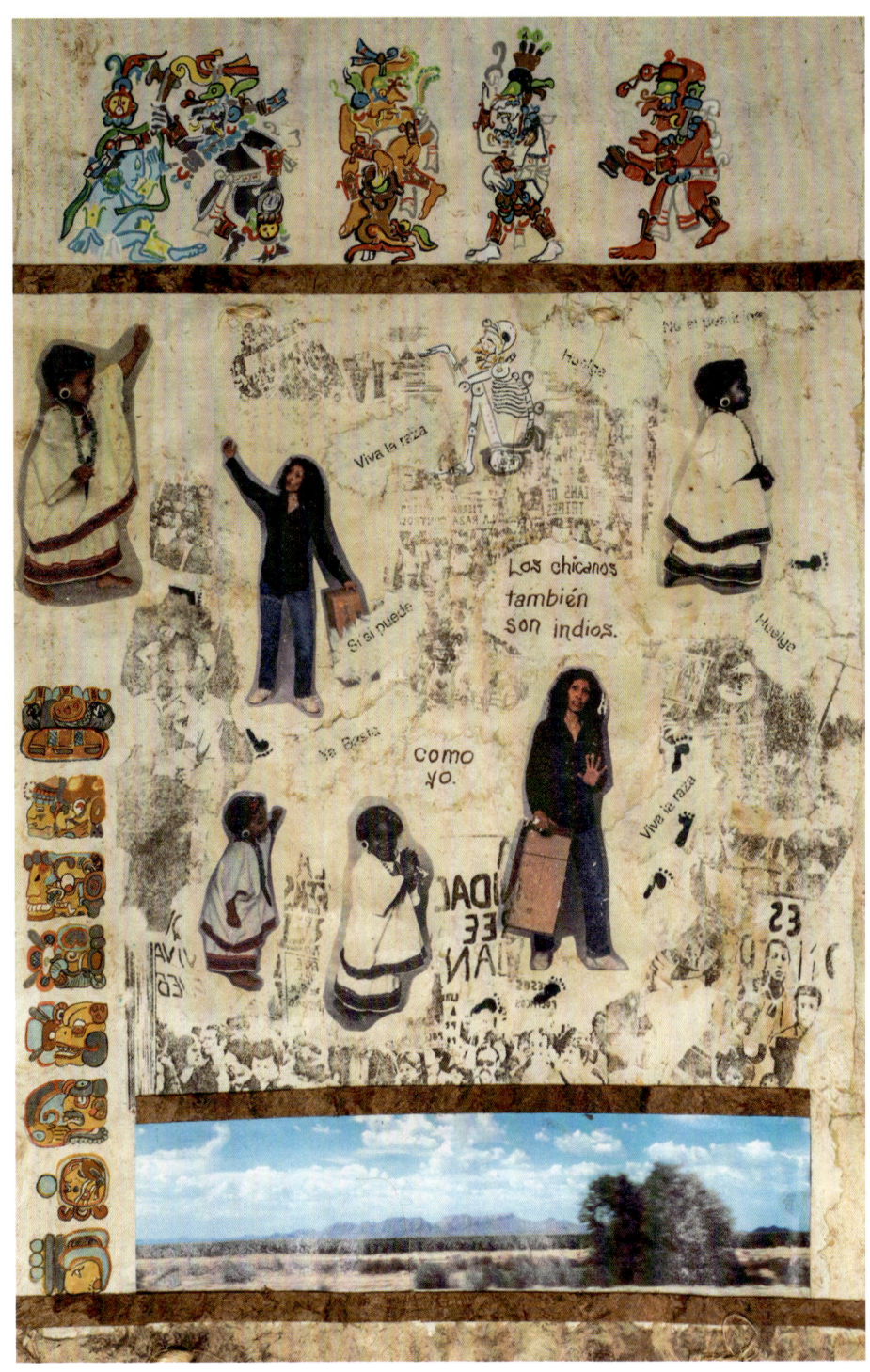

Delilah Montoya
*Codex Delilah: A Journey
from Mexicatl to Chicana*
Detail: Panel 6, 6 Deer
meets La-Velia

La-Velia explains to 6 Deer that farmers spray pesticides on their crops which make the farmworkers sick. She joined the chile pickers who are on strike and marching to Santa Fe to demand the intervention of the state government to solve their problem.

"And what are you doing out here 6 Deer?" La-Velia asks.

"I'm on a journey trying to understand truth. You're dark like me. Are you an Indian?" 6 Deer asks touching La-Velia's arm.

"I guess I am," La-Velia answers, "but we call ourselves Chicanos."

"Chicanos," 6 Deer pronounces the word haltingly. "I've never heard of Chicanos before."

"Well, if you must know the truth about Chicanos it's that we struggle for justice and equality every day," La-Velia says proudly. "We're mestizos who are proud of our indigenous heritage. Are you a poet? You look like a poet."

"Not really," 6 Deer answers, "I'm a keeper of our ancient traditions. My responsibility is to make sure that my people live in harmony."

"That's a mighty big job," La-Velia exclaims. "Oh well, I guess I've had my rest. I have to get back to my compañeros and finish our plans for tomorrow's walk. Do you want to walk with us on our march for justice 6 Deer?" La-Velia asks.

"I feel I'm close to a mountain that turns red at sunset," 6 Deer answers as she again admires the iridescent sky.

"Oh you must mean the Sandías near Albuquerque. That's my home-base. We're going that way, come on," La-Velia encourages 6 Deer.

And as the two women walk the winding dirt road La-Velia continues, "We don't fight for our rights with violence. Understand? Our struggle is non-violent, just as Ghandi, Martin Luther King and César Chávez taught us. And that's why we'll win."

"I understand what you're saying with my heart," 6 Deer answers.

"That's what I like to hear," La-Velia laughs and hugs 6 Deer.

Panel 7: A flock of crows form a stain on the cloudless sky as they fly past the solitary figure who sits like a statue on top of Sandía Mountain (pg. 50). The glaring mid-day sun almost blinds 6 Deer as she approaches the woman who has covered her face with her hair.

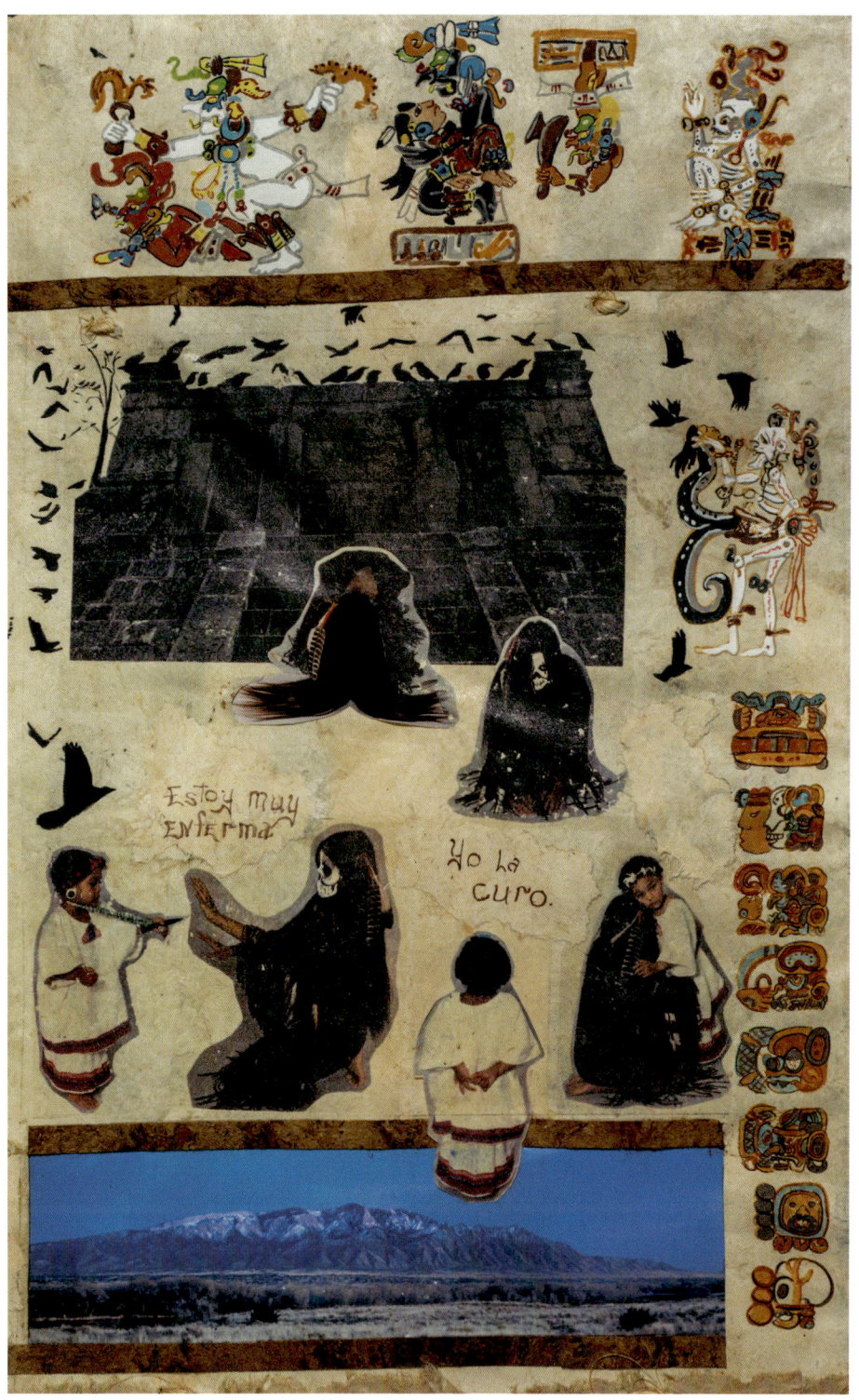

Delilah Montoya
*Codex Delilah: A Journey
from Mexicatl to Chicana*
Detail: Panel 7, 6 Deer
finds Crow Woman

"My heart tells me I have finally found Crow Woman, the one who speaks directly to the gods. I'm 6 Deer and I have journeyed for a long time to be with you. I seek your guidance and wisdom. Are you ill, my teacher? Can you hear me?"

Crow Woman slowly pulls back the hair from her face. 6 Deer suppresses a terrified scream when she sees that the old counsellor's face is a skull. She is unable to contain her tears as she asks, "What has happened to you, my teacher?"

In a painful voice Crow Woman explains, "I'm no longer the nourisher of life but sickness and death itself. The scientists have implanted missiles in my breasts, my child. I can feel them multiplying, growing, and spreading throughout my body. When I become one with the missiles, I'll destroy all life with a nuclear explosion. You have arrived too late. You must leave now."

6 Deer holds Crow Woman's hands and tells her that since the deities of the four directions began their struggle for power, the heart of man lost its harmony and there is destruction everywhere. "But don't believe it's too late, my teacher," 6 Deer continues. "Ix-Chel gave me this sacred flint which I will use to make small cuts on your breasts. I will clean you, feed you and restore your strength. Each day I will make the cuts a little bigger until your energy pushes the missiles out, and then your real face will reveal itself again."

Crow Woman smiles and runs the tips of her fingers around 6 Deer's face. She points towards the west. "Look at all those crows coming towards us. I've never seen so many crows. I remember my old friend Ix-Chel. She has sent me hope."

The crows form an enormous cloud as they circle above Crow Woman and 6 Deer. Unable to hear themselves because of the cawing, they laugh and hug each other. Then 6 Deer speaks into Crow Woman's ear, "When you get well, please ask our mother Omecihuatl, the female side of the god of all gods, Ometeotl, to stop the fighting among her sons, the deities of the four directions. Then you and I will speak the truth to the people. Together we can restore harmony to the hearts of humanity."

The cloud of crows suddenly swirls to the north. Crow Woman then

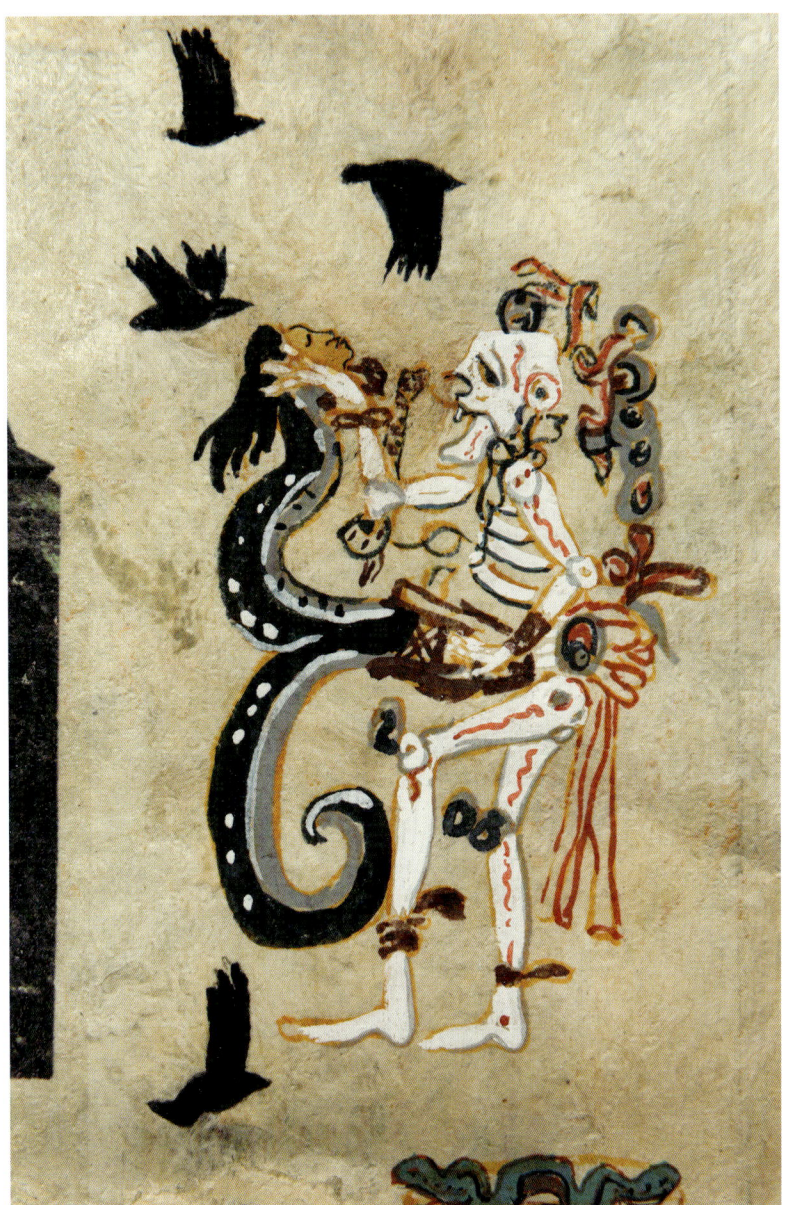

Delilah Montoya
Codex Delilah: A Journey from Mexicatl to Chicana
Detail: Panel 7, 6 Deer finds Crow Woman

asks, "Will you stay with me, 6 Deer?" 6 Deer cleans the flint and makes tiny cuts on both of Crow-Woman's breasts.

"I will stay with you in Aztlán, my teacher," she answers, wiping the blood that flows out of Crow Woman's breasts. "But when everything on the earth is in balance, I must return home."

As part of her MFA project at the University of New Mexico, Delilah Montoya created a series of collotype prints portraying her Chicano community in Albuquerque through the lens of the Sacred Heart icon. Montoya wrote a thesis on her findings of the history, ritual meaning, and syncretic foundations of the symbol both from the perspective of European belief systems and pre-Columbian Aztec rituals practiced by the Nahua people. In her text, she reveals the layered colonial histories and enduring spiritual transformations that shaped the religious and cultural landscape of New Spain, particularly concerning Nahua traditions and the introduction of the baroque Sacred Heart. The text discusses how Christian colonial authorities aimed to establish the omnipresence of their god by integrating local Indigenous spiritual concepts into Catholic iconography. Despite the colonial suppression of Nahua religious practices, Indigenous beliefs remained a persistent undercurrent in colonial society, influencing family structures, economic systems, and artistic traditions. The convergence of the Nahua *yollotl* (heart) with the European Sacred Heart reflects this process of syncretism, demonstrating the complex survival of Indigenous worldviews within the imposed Christian framework. Through the series of prints informed by this research, Montoya demonstrates how Chicanx cultural and spiritual practices are not just history or memory but a persistent, constantly shifting negotiation of identity.

Montoya references Octavio Paz, who articulated the profound trauma experienced by the Nahua people following the Spanish conquest. Beyond military defeat and forced servitude, the most devastating loss was the obliteration of their social and religious order, signified by the destruction of temples and cultural monuments. Paz describes this rupture as both an annihilation of the Nahua ruling elite—priests and aristocracy—and an erasure of their symbolic world. Yet, within the cyclical view of time inherent in Nahua cosmology, destruction also implied renewal, suggesting that while their gods disappeared from official narratives, they persisted in concealed, reconfigured forms within the fabric of colonial life.

Montoya collaborated with artists, community members, family, and friends to explore a variety of themes and concepts related to art, history, Chicanx Identity, feminine icons, and more. She wanted to collapse the space between the photographer and the subject and transform the interaction into a collaborative space. While individual narratives are present

55

within each print, the broader series is a visual representation of a collective Chicanx consciousness. In the end, the project was a collaboration depicting how the subjects saw themselves and what was most precious to them.

Montoya is also disrupting the genres of ethnographic photography and the colonial practices of categorizing and depicting types of people. In conversations and in her own writings, she talks about Edward S. Curtis's interest in photographing the other, including Native Americans and Mestizos in the Southwest. These images became the mode through which Europe saw the so-called New World and, in some cases, how those communities being depicted began to see themselves. Montoya is pushing back against the history of photography and the contemporary pressure for Latinx communities to fit into the mainstream. By capturing individual stories that are specific to people she knows, Montoya is presenting a portrait of the community back to the community itself. Simultaneously, she is creating a more universal mosaic of what it means to engage in a collective expression of community.

El Sagrado Corazón began as a series of twenty-six collotypes, all of which Montoya painstakingly printed herself using the process she shares below. Each layered composition includes objects, backdrops, and clothing specific to each story. Montoya invited Michael Esfera to organize graffiti artists from the community to spray paint the walls of her studio, which were then used as backdrops. She worked with each sitter to determine how they wanted to incorporate their own objects into the photograph, asking, "What is in your heart?" While the project involved deep collaboration, the final prints were situated within the broader creative vision that evolved through Montoya's visual language and printmaking process.

El Sagrado Corazón is a profound reworking of Catholic sacred imagery. Montoya remakes the iconography of the Sacred Heart, a symbol traditionally imbued with divine compassion. She confronts the colonial weight of evangelization to interrogate its role in both suppressing and co-opting religious power and beliefs. *God's Gift*, *El Misterio*, and *Pasion* include collaborators whose backs are facing the camera. Each of these prints includes sacred imagery in different forms—tattoos, candles, backdrops, and imagery of Christ. The collotypes evoke the hallowed surfaces of devotional painting, yet the obscured faces and ritual performance remind the viewer that religious images are themselves historical constructs, subject to reinterpretation. By integrating elements as diverse as soft halos, the luminescence of votive candles, and graffiti art, Montoya relays that the sacred is not confined to a pristine altar but is continually remade in everyday spaces. Her reimagining of the sacred thus functions as a visual representation of both the past and the present.[1]

Montoya's disruption of the genre of portraiture enacts a broader understanding of community and family. In works like *Los Jovenes* and *La Familia*, Montoya reveals the strength of connection between friends and family, demonstrating that community is a central component of survival and pride. In these prints, many of the sitters look directly at the camera with assertive gazes and assertive poses and gestures affirming a collective

Delilah Montoya
God's Gift (from the portfolio *El Sagrado Corazón*)
Suranjith Gunasekara
1993
Collotype on d'Arches Hot Press, ed. 1/1
9⅞ × 7¾ in.
Albuquerque Museum, museum purchase and gift of the artist
PC2022.32.12

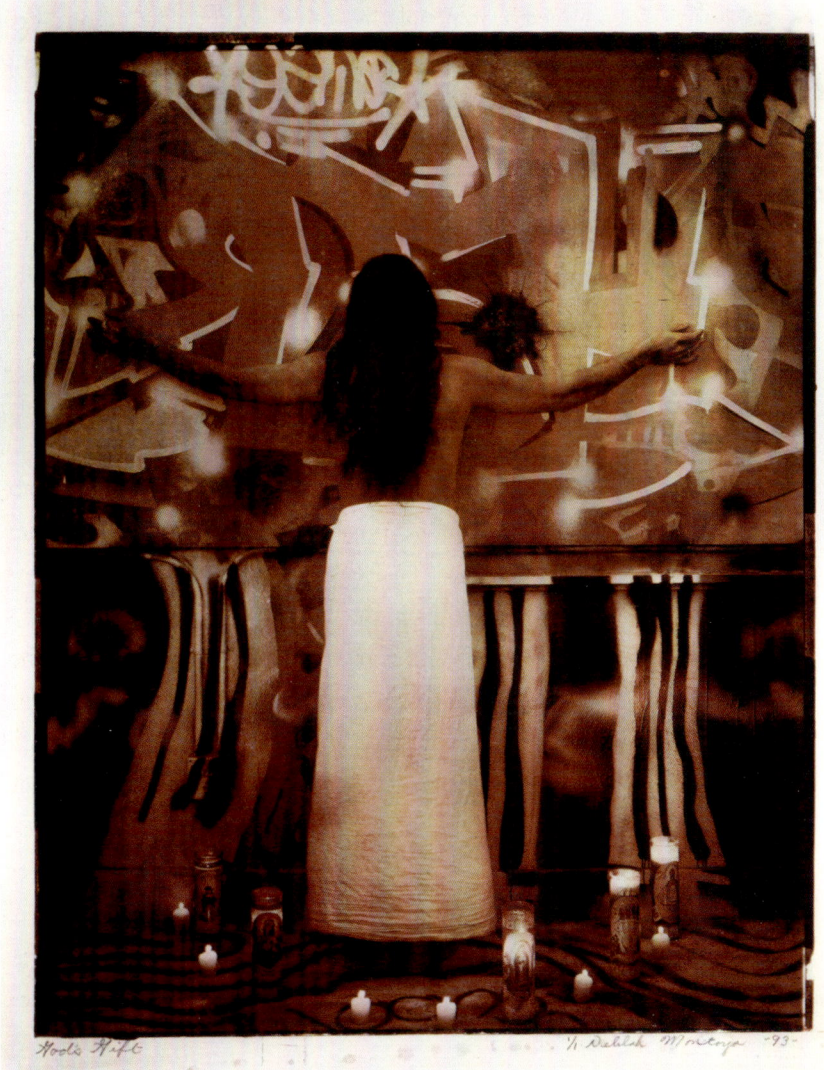

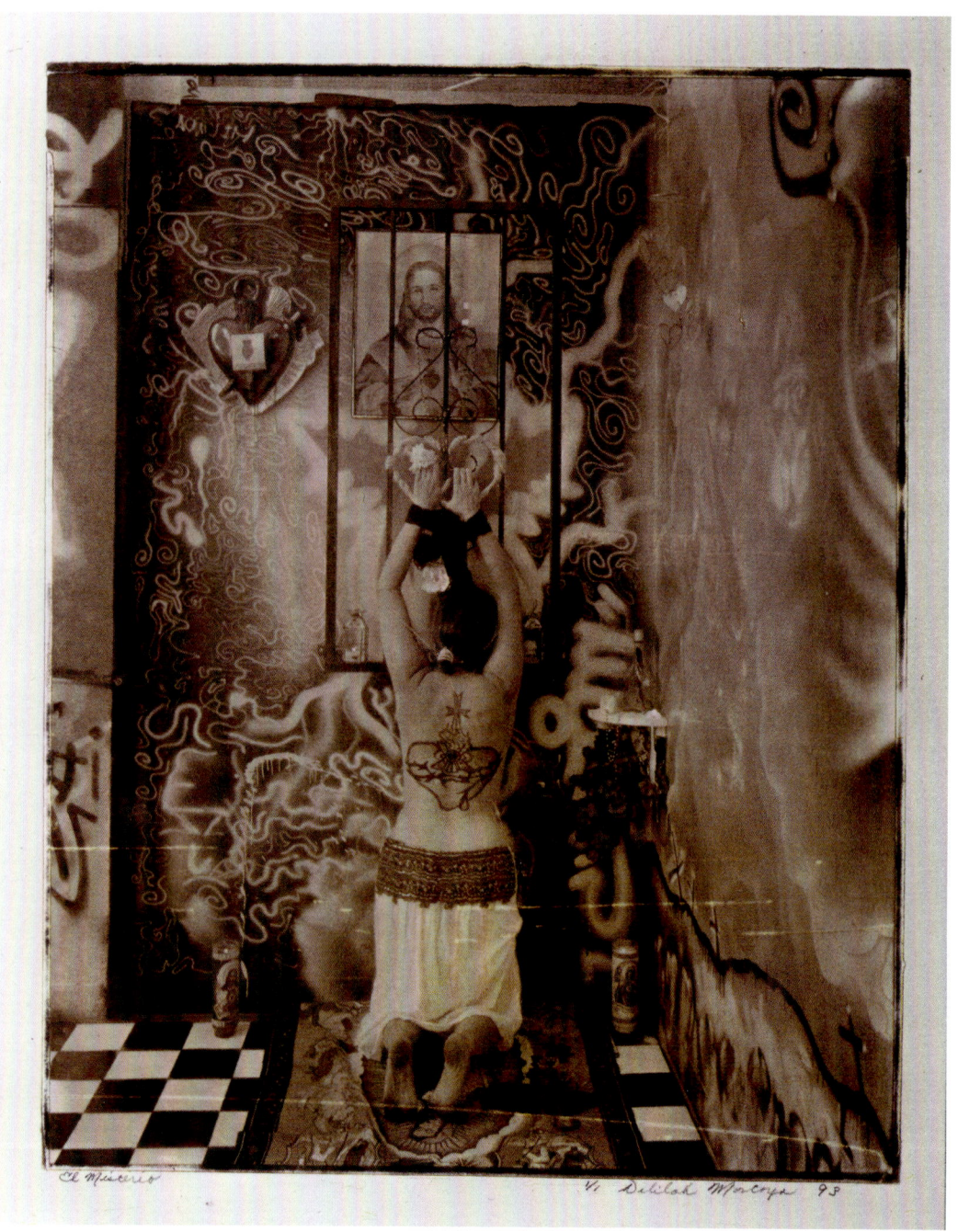

Delilah Montoya

El Misterio (from the portfolio *El Sagrado Corazón*)

Self-portrait

Collotype on d'Arches Hot Press, ed. 1/1

9⅞ × 7¾ in.

Albuquerque Museum, museum purchase and gift of the artist

PC2022.32.11

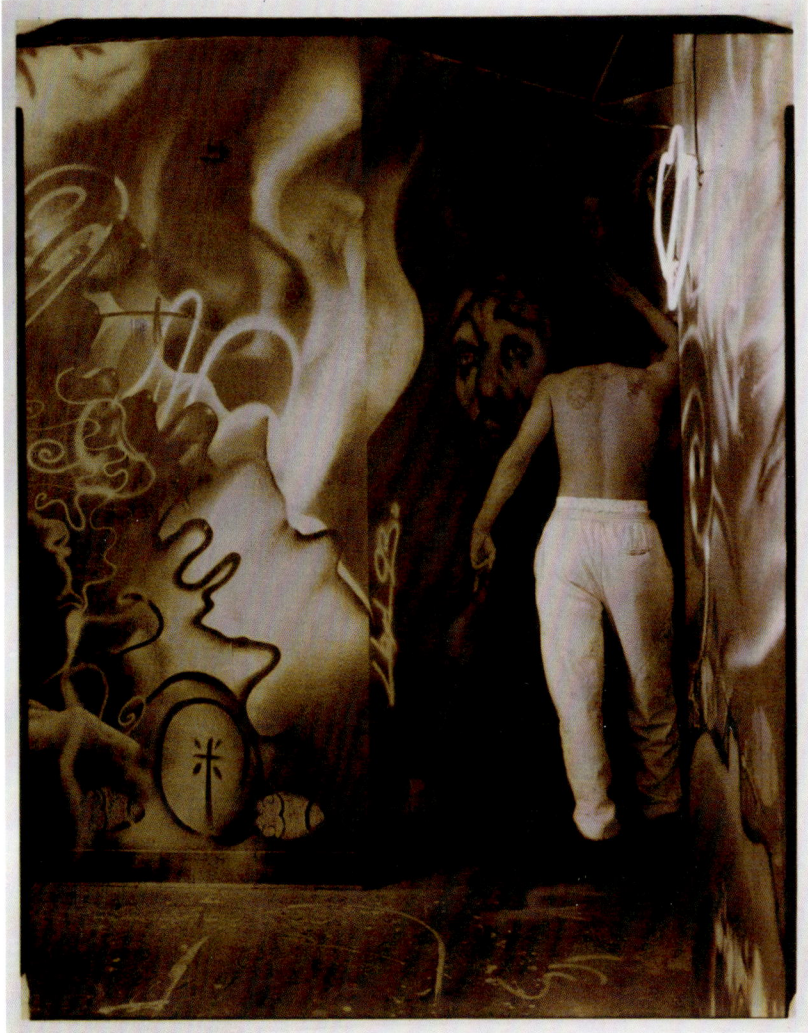

Delilah Montoya
Pasión (from the portfo-
lio *El Sagrado Corazón*)
Gary Jaramillo
1993
Collotype on d'Arches
Hot Press, ed. 1/1
9⅞ × 7¾ in.
Smithsonian American
Art Museum, museum
purchase through the
Horace W. Goldsmith
Foundation
1998.88.1

identity that is both shared and personal. In *Los Jovenes*, the social aspect of gathering with friends is central, while in *Jesus's Carburetor Repair*, taking pride in work is important to him. Mothers with their young children demonstrate that raising families is precious in their lives. These images reveal that relationships in Chicanx communities are what the collaborators defined as most important to them. Connections forged through shared histories and an understanding that the passing down of history and culture are also part of the spiritual fabric that defines Chicanismo for this community. The interstices between formal portraiture and installation art in these prints also underscore a collaborative process—one in which Montoya enlists community members both as subjects and as

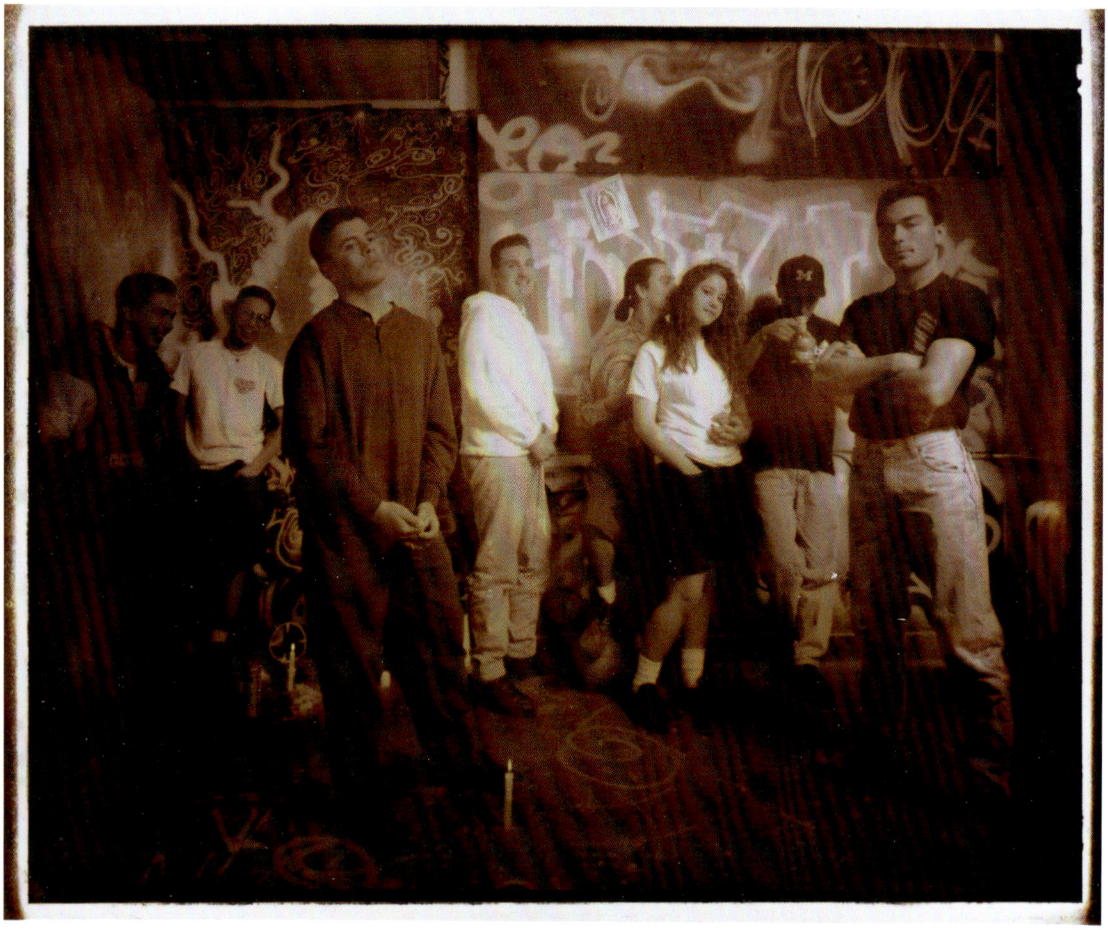

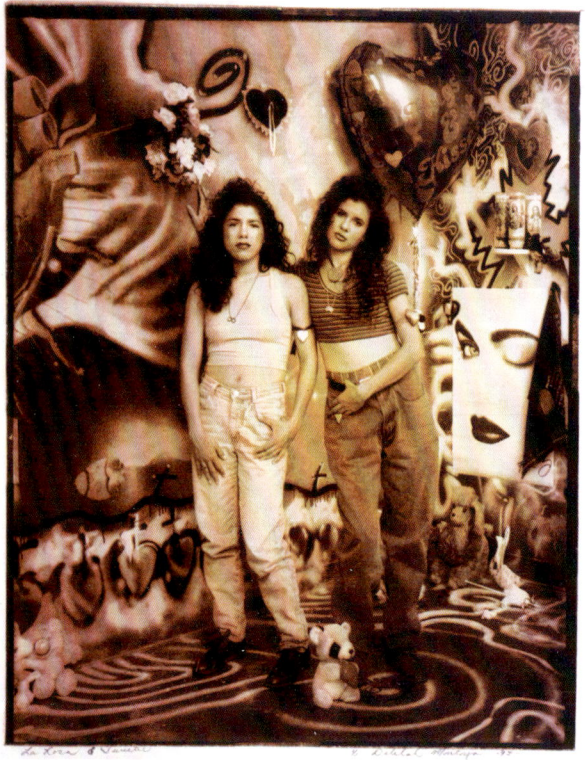

(*top*) Delilah Montoya
Los Jovenes (from the portfolio *El Sagrado Corazón*)
Andrew Marcom, Auggie, J. T., Miguel Baca,
Michael Esfera, Vidalia Chavez, Jaime Silva, and
Ray Saavedra
1993
Collotype on d'Arches Hot Press, ed. 1/1
7¾ × 9⅞ in.
Los Angeles County Museum of Art, purchased
with funds provided by the Ralph M. Parsons Fund
AC1994.173.2

(*left*) Delilah Montoya
La Loca y Sweetie (from the portfolio *El Sagrado
Corazón*)
Anita Garcia, Susan Marquez
1993
Collotype on d'Arches Hot Press, ed. 1/1
9⅞ × 7¾ in.
Collection of the artist

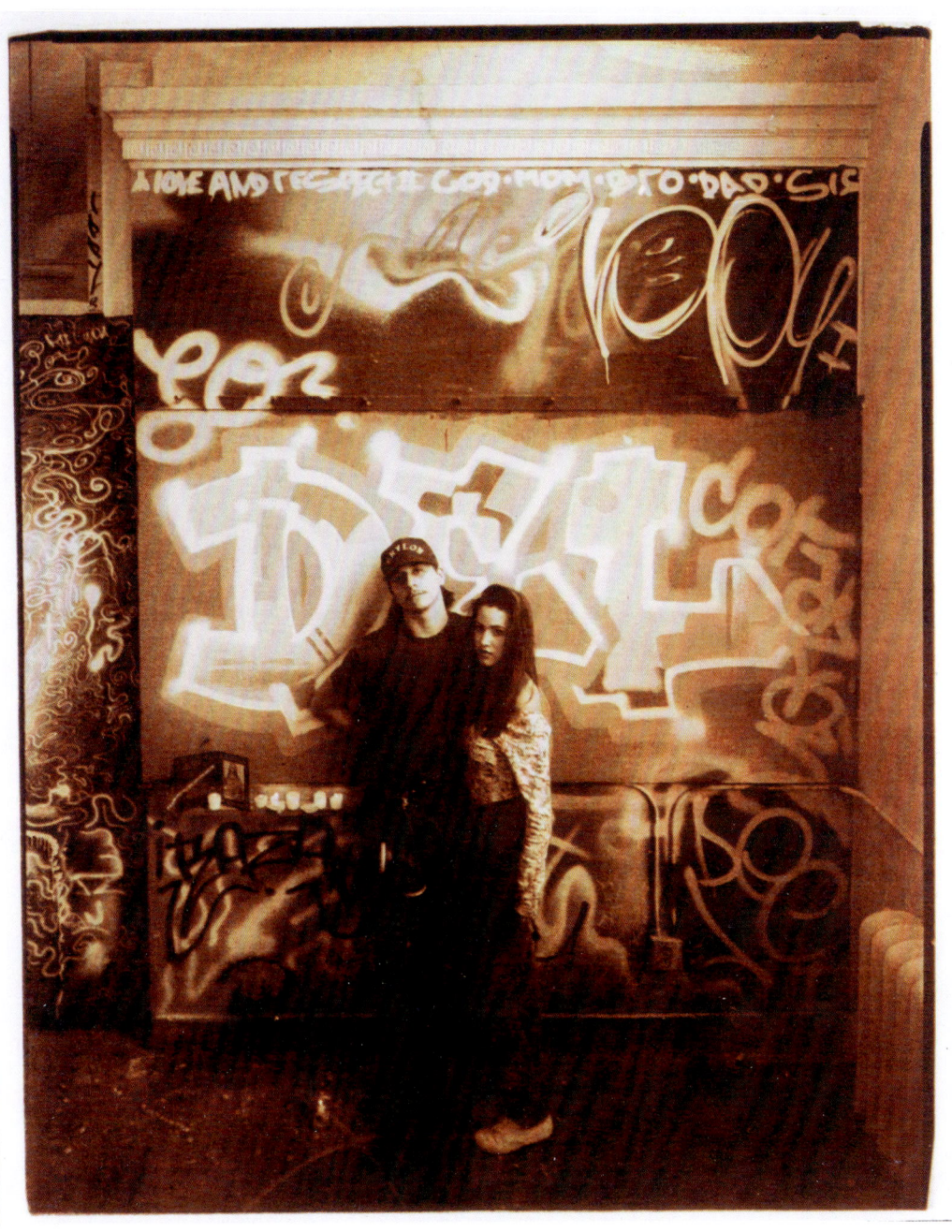

Delilah Montoya
Los Del Corazón (from the portfolio *El Sagrado Corazón*)
Michael Esfera, Cielo Garcia
1993
Collotype on d'Arches Hot Press, ed. 1/1
9⅞ × 7¾ in.
Collection of the artist

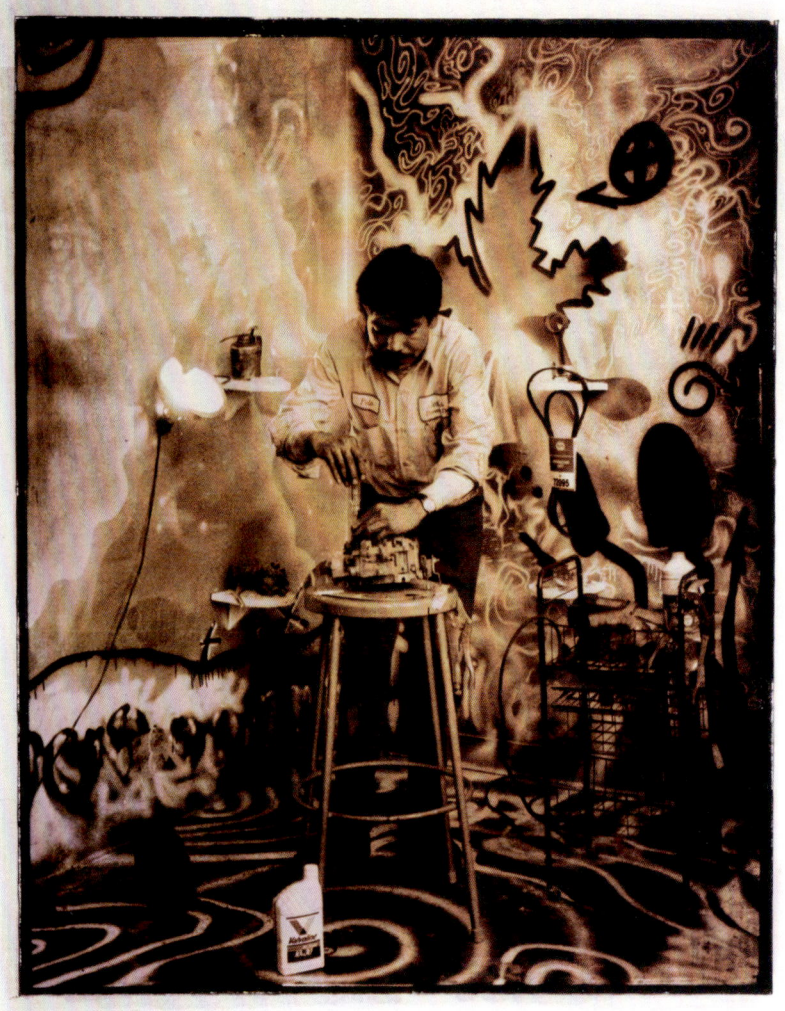

Delilah Montoya
Jesus' Carburetor Repair
(from the portfolio *El Sagrado Corazón*)
Apolonio Garcia
1993
Collotype on d'Arches
Hot Press, ed. 1/1
9⅞ × 7¾ in.
Collection of the artist

co-creators of a renewed visual language that makes the Chicanx body visible. While the objects that resulted in these interactions are what the viewer currently sees, the project would not have been possible without the relationships Montoya forged in her own community.

In addition to collaborating with young artists and community members, Montoya also wanted to celebrate and honor several important Chicanx Albuquerque artists, including the poet Cecilio García-Camarillo, who was a dear friend she collaborated with on many projects. Renowned writer Rudolfo Anaya poses for a portrait surrounded by fabrics and objects that reflect his connections to the culture and history of New Mexico which he wrote about in many of his books. Eva Encinias, who developed one of the

Delilah Montoya
El Corazón de Maria
(from the portfolio *El
Sagrado Corazón*)
Maria Delgado
1993
Collotype on d'Arches
Hot Press, ed. 1/1
9⅞ × 7¾ in.
Collection of the artist

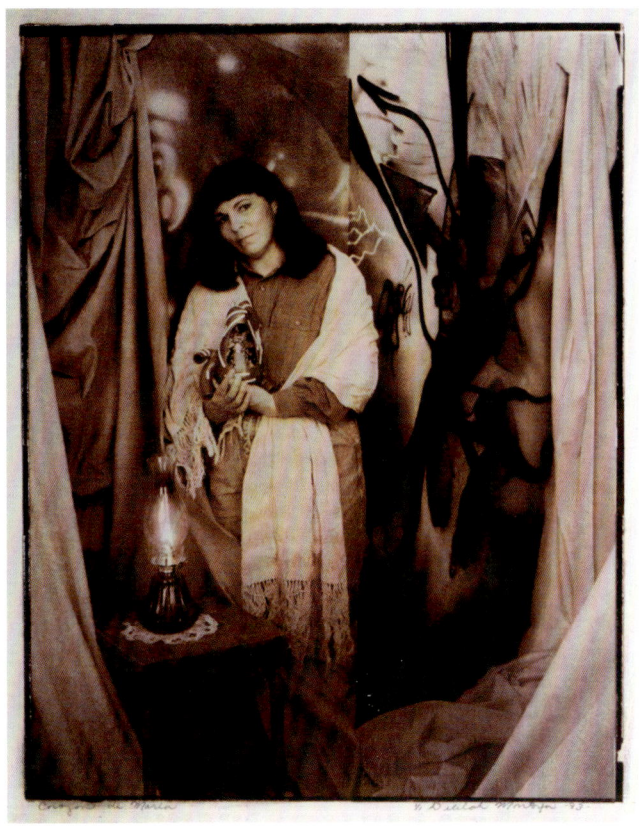

Delilah Montoya
Mom's Angels (from the portfolio
El Sagrado Corazón)
Maggie Sharpe, Carmen Sharpe,
Maria Elena Alvarez
1993
Collotype on d'Arches Hot
Press, ed. 1/1
9⅞ × 7¾ in.
Museum of Fine Art Houston,
the Sonia and Kaye Marvins
Portrait Collection, gift of Mike
and Mickey Marvins
95.19

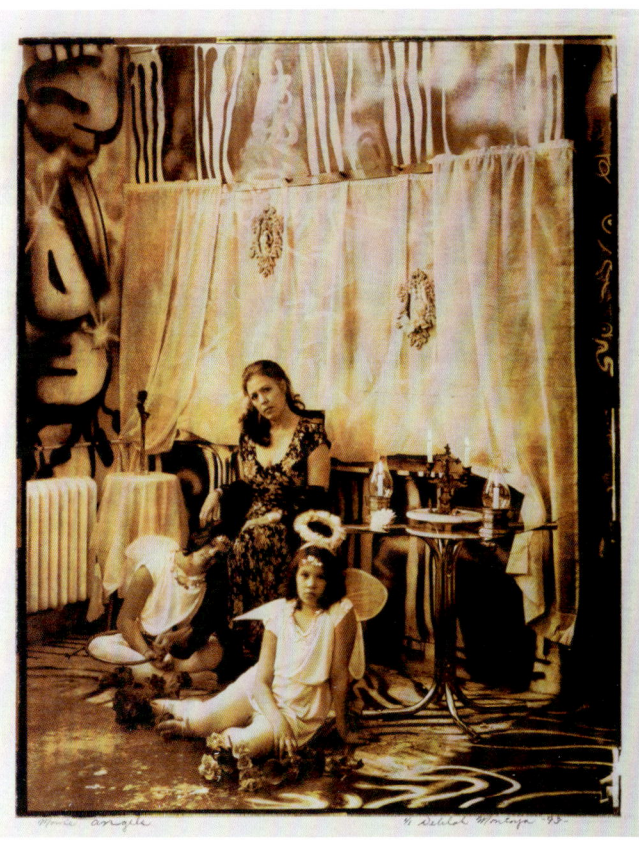

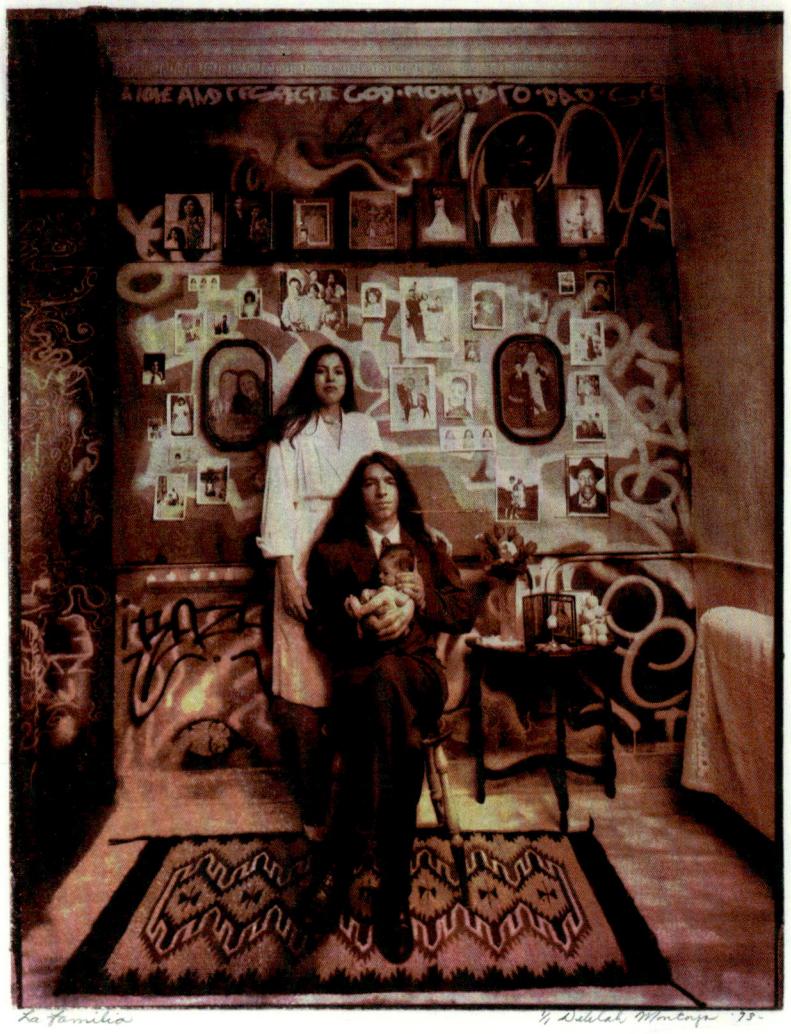

La Familia

Delilah Montoya
La Familia (from the
portfolio *El Sagrado
Corazón*)
Joseph, Roberta, and
Andres Gallegos
1993
Collotype on d'Arches
Hot Press, ed. 1/1
9⅞ × 7¾ in.
Collection of the artist

premier flamenco communities in the world, demonstrates the power and
beauty of her art. Montoya captures a full range of creativity that emerges
from a connection to Albuquerque as a historical home of many Latinos
and a place of vibrant creativity. From young people and the working class
to the creative powerhouses that have shaped Albuquerque's Chicanx narratives, each sitter affirms their role and importance in advancing cultural
awareness.

Several collaborators selected important historical figures and icons
reaching back to the concept and idea of Aztlán while also demonstrating how Mexican and Indigenous rituals and practices are connected yet
manifest differently in New Mexico. La Malinche, for example, is often

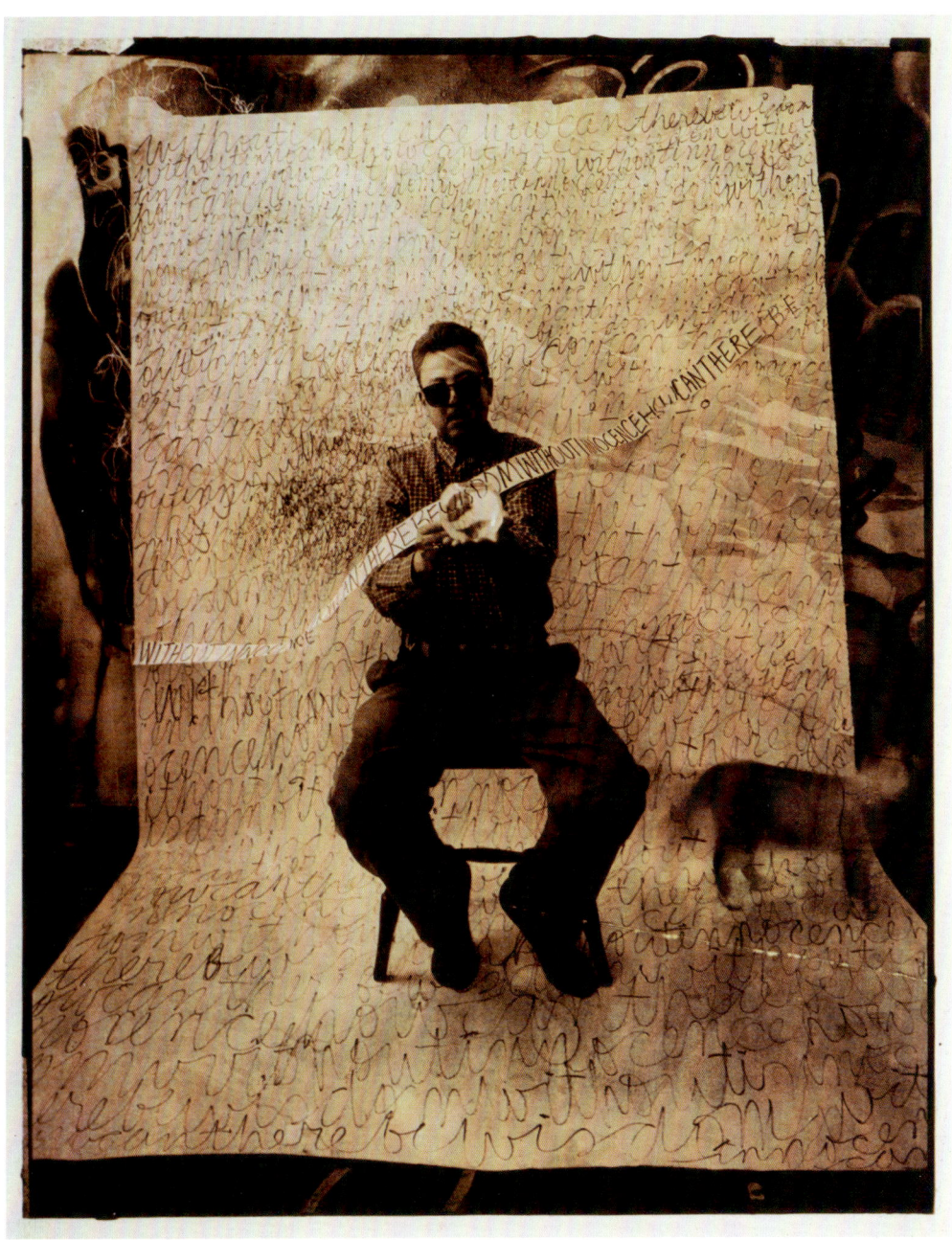

Delilah Montoya
*Without Innocence How Can There Be
Wisdom* (from the portfolio *El Sagrado
Corazón*)
Cecilio Garcia-Camarillo
1993
Collotype on d'Arches Hot Press, ed. 1/1
9⅞ × 7¾ in.
Collection of the artist

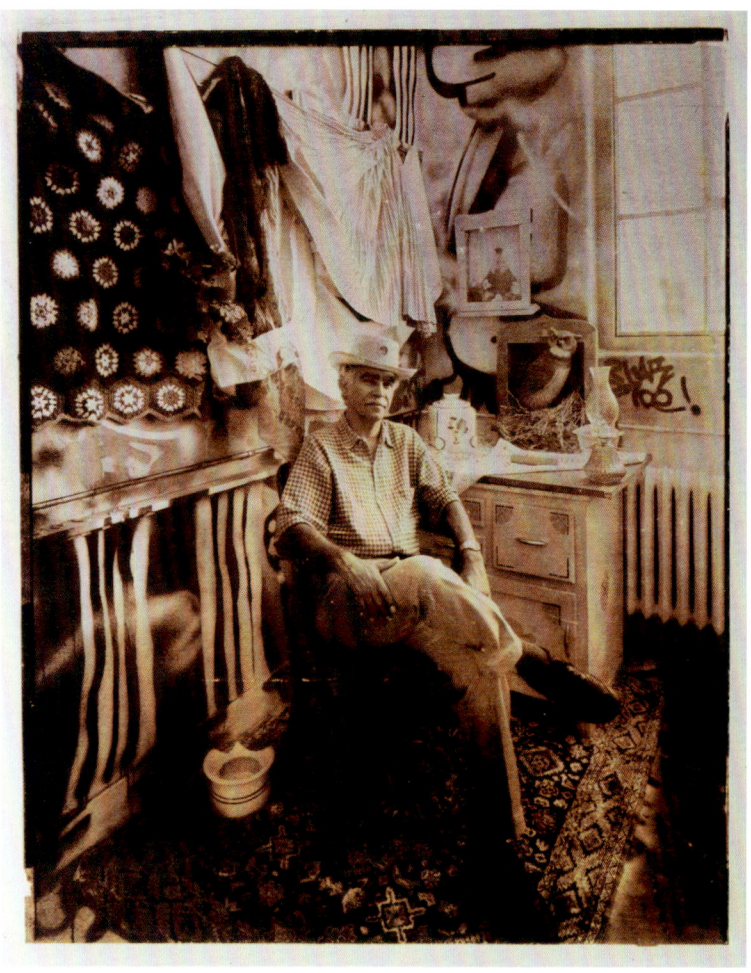

Delilah Montoya
Rudolfo (from the portfolio
El Sagrado Corazón)
Rudy Anaya
1993
Collotype on d'Arches Hot
Press, ed. 1/1
9⅞ × 7¾ in.
Collection of the artist

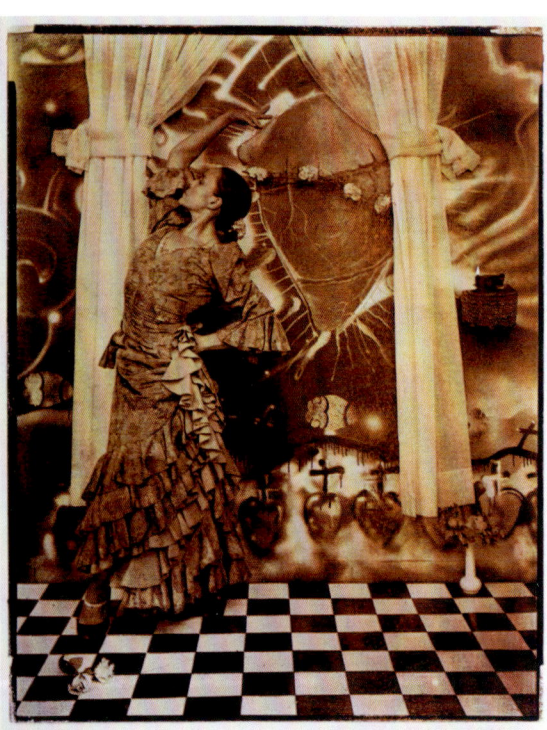

Delilah Montoya
El Grito de la Gitana (from
the portfolio *El Sagrado
Corazón*)
Eva Enciñias
1993
Collotype on d'Arches Hot
Press, ed. 1/1
9⅞ × 7¾ in.
Smithsonian American Art
Museum, museum purchase
through the Horace W. Gold-
smith Foundation
1998.88.3

described as a traitor who became Cortez's translator. She is also known as the mother of Mestizaje. In New Mexico, however, she appears as a young innocent girl often wearing a First Holy Communion dress in traditional Matachin rituals and dances performed in both Pueblo and Chicanx communities. *La Genizara* represents the many young women who were enslaved in the eighteenth century.[2] *El Aborto* references Frida Kahlo. Madonna and Child and a Curandera (healer) explore the many roles that women play. *El Sagrado Corazón*, overall, depicts a full range of powerful women finding their strength through cultural memory but also within their own lived experience.

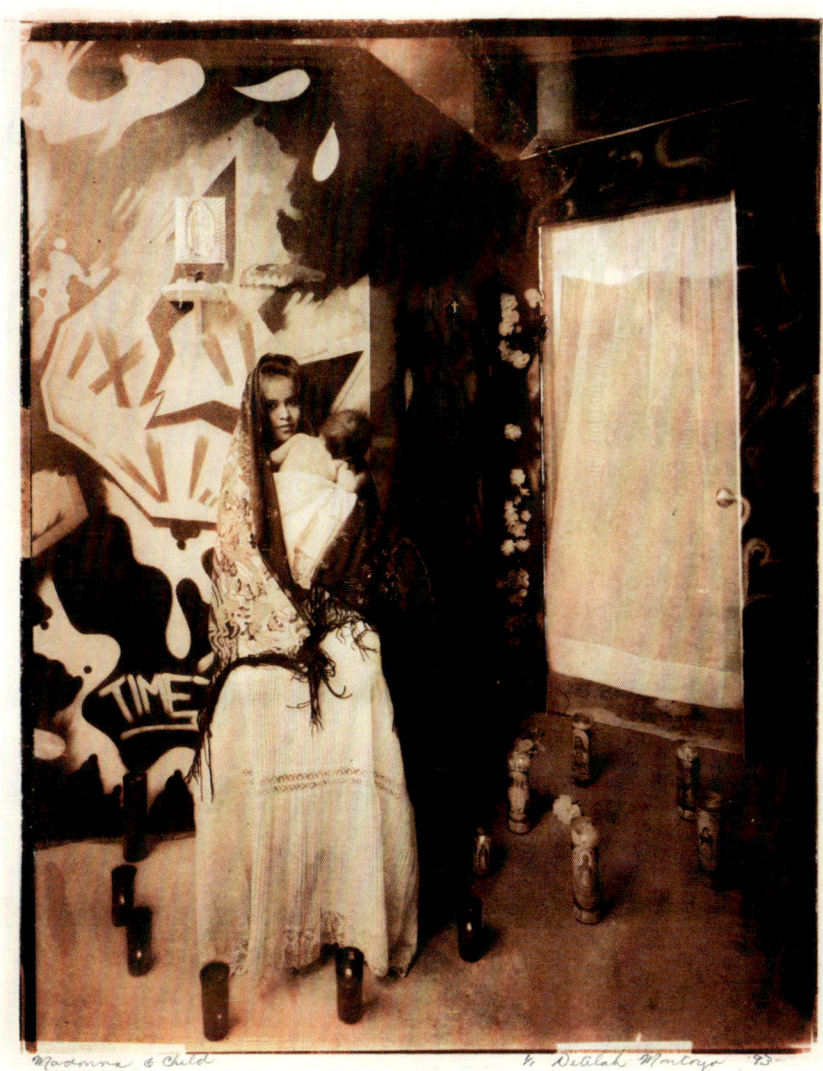

Delilah Montoya
Madonna and Child
(from the portfolio *El Sagrado Corazón*)
Arlene, David Madrid
1993
Collotype on d'Arches
Hot Press, ed. 1/1
9⅞ × 7¾ in.
Collection of the artist

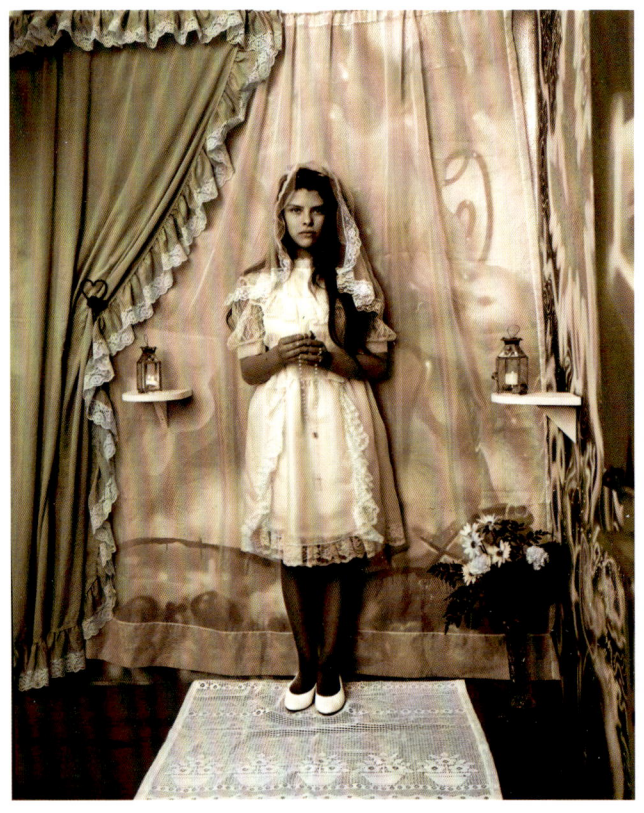

Delilah Montoya
La Malinche (from the port-
folio *El Sagrado Corazón*)
Marisa González
1993
Collotype on d'Arches Hot
Press, ed. 1/1
9⅞ × 7¾ in.
Albuquerque Museum,
museum purchase and gift of
the artist
PC2022.32.21

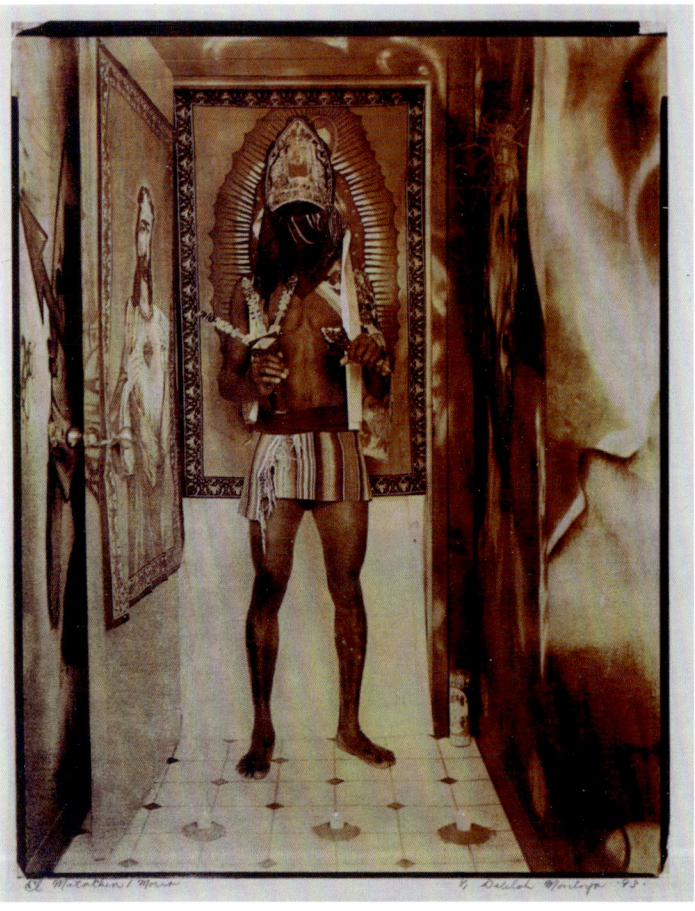

Delilah Montoya
El Matachin/Moro (from
the portfolio *El Sagrado
Corazón*)
Wasi
1993
Collotype on d'Arches Hot
Press, ed. 1/1
9⅞ × 7¾ in.
Collection of the artist

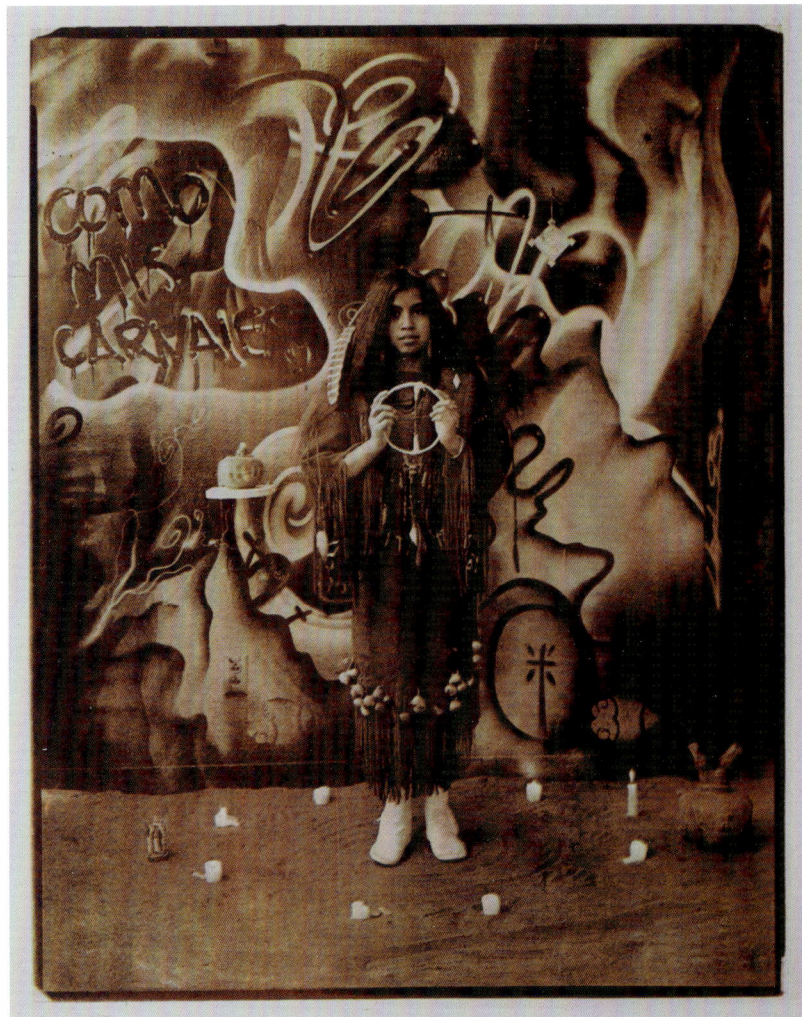

Delilah Montoya
La Genizara (from the portfolio *El Sagrado Corazón*)
Darlene Madrid
1993
Collotype on d'Arches Hot Press, ed. 1/1
9⅞ × 7¾ in.
Collection of the artist

Some of the prints were more elaborate spaces of ritual performance, referencing both death and the Aztec ritual of sacrifice. Masks, *calaveras* (skeletons), candles, and feathers are used as props to create scenes that are simultaneously pre-Columbian and surreal, interrogating how death is also part of the syncretic practices Montoya explores. Throughout her series, Montoya is cognizant of the interconnected relationships that exist not only across time but also across realms. The series of twenty-six collotypes was the original scope of *El Sagrado Corazón*. Montoya also created silver gelatin prints, which added a different aesthetic to the way photographs are viewed. While the deep richness of oil-based inks on textured paper provide images with a soft glow, the rich contrasts of light in the

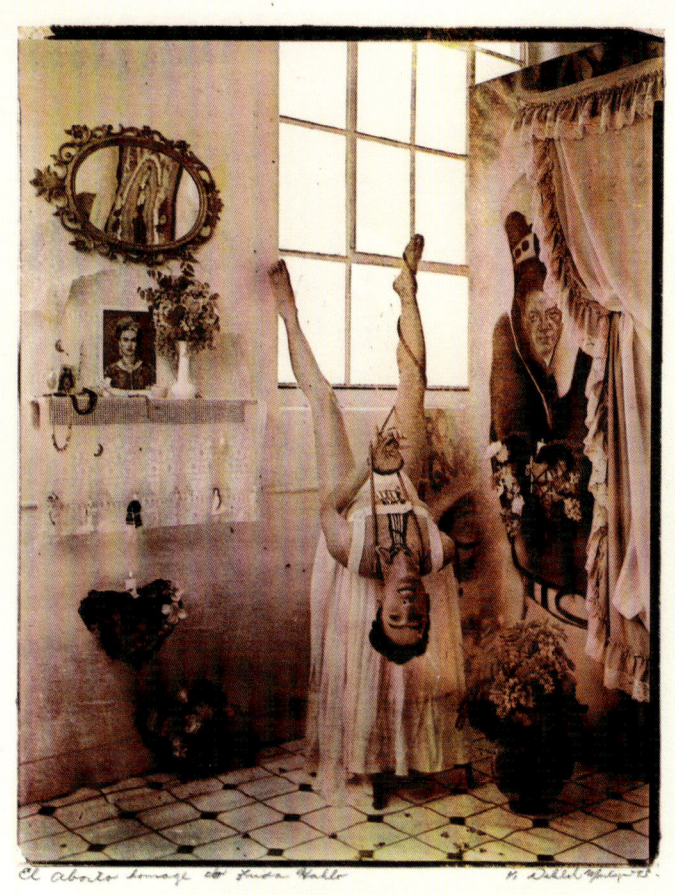

Delilah Montoya
El Aborto in Homage to Frida Kahlo (from the portfolio *El Sagrado Corazón*)
Alicia Perea
1993
Collotype on d'Arches Hot Press, ed. 1/1
9⅞ × 7¾ in.
Collection of the artist

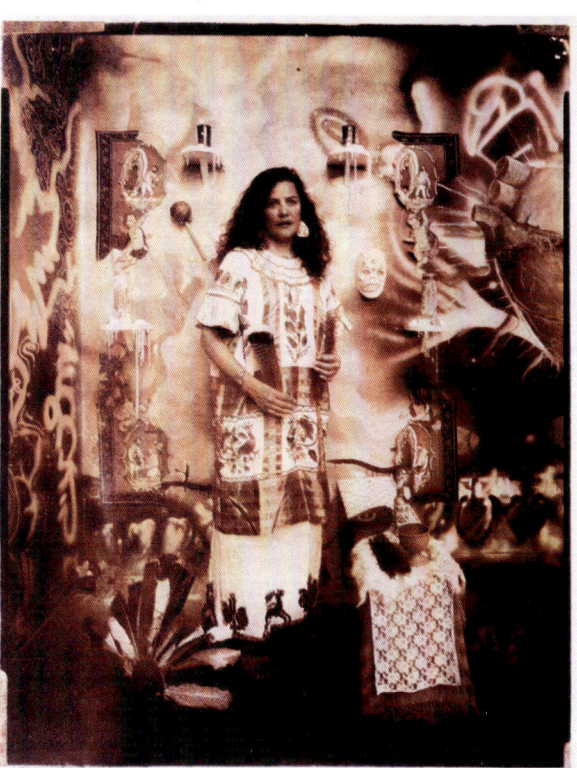

Delilah Montoya
Curanderisma (from the portfolio *El Sagrado Corazón*)
Elena Avila
1993
Collotype on d'Arches Hot Press, ed. 1/1
9⅞ × 7¾ in.
Collection of the artist

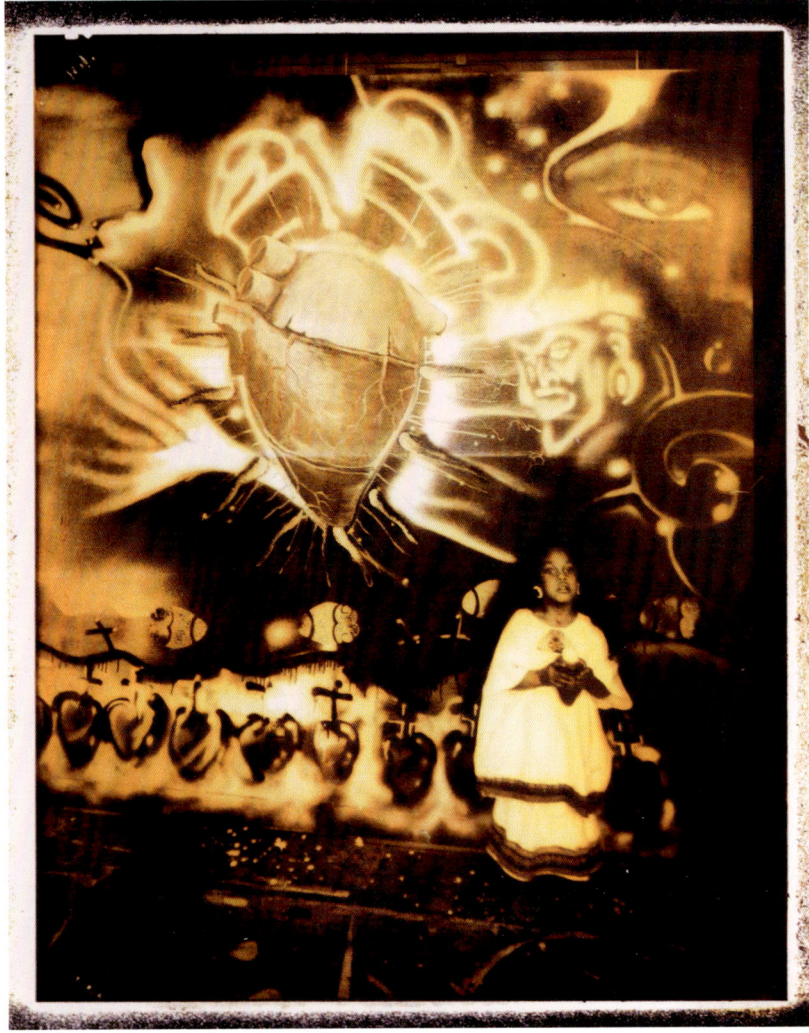

Delilah Montoya
Teyolia (from the portfolio *El Sagrado Corazón*)
Samera Merriman
1993
Collotype on d'Arches Hot Press, ed. 1/1
9⅞ × 7¾ in.
Smithsonian American Art Museum, museum purchase through the Horace W. Goldsmith Foundation
1998.88.4

black and white silver gelatin prints create a different kind of nostalgia and history. These approaches to different materials allowed Montoya to determine how the art object would ultimately take shape.

In Conversation with Delilah Montoya, Maria Elena Alvarez, and Demetria Martinez: *Sagrado Corazón*

Demetria: In reflecting on your *Sagrado Corazón* series, I couldn't help but think of Aztec sacrifices, the cutting out of the heart to keep the sun moving across the sky. So many of our altars, our candles, and our holy cards include images of a usually pale European Jesus pointing to his heart. Your work, of course, is rooted in a very different narrative of the heart. Your images uplift Chicanx culture and communities in Albuquerque. Could you say more about that?

Delilah: When making *Sagrado Corazón*, I was taking a course on pre-Columbian art with Flora Clancy. I was interested in Nahua philosophy and what they thought about the heart. The Sacred Heart does not appear in Catholicism until after the conquest. Catholicism and the baroque aesthetic were global during the period of conquest. Europeans brought ideas to the places they were conquering. A whole civilization was trying to consume and conquer another civilization. In turn, Aztec culture and beliefs were unfolding for the Franciscans. They were exposed to new people and realized that the Aztecs practiced a deep-rooted theology of their own, which in turn influenced Catholicism. In my research, I discovered that Nahua religious and cultural practices survived even after the conquest. Within our cultura, somehow, it still survives in how we approach and understand things. The Sacred Heart is just one example of cultural memory.

It is a portrait of Jesus and Mary revealing their hearts. I wanted to create a portrait of the Chicano community in Albuquerque, revealing their hearts. The collaborative process was a key element in the project. I took a lot of art history, so I was familiar with the genre of portraiture. I was also thinking about the Native American portraits by Edward Curtis. Those images were a preconception of what Curtis wanted to think about and how he wanted to depict the Native American community. I wanted to do something where we can be remembered for who we were and are.

Demetria: Delilah, looking at those images, which are quite beautiful, it occurs to me that it has as much to do with the fact that you're not an outsider looking in. But you're a member of the community that you're depicting. Your work is collaborative, and you've used that word frequently to talk about your work in relationship to the Chicano community.

Delilah: It also goes back to printmaking. When I started taking serigraphy with Jim Kraft, I learned that you could transfer a photographic image into prints. I knew how to print photographs as silver gelatins and even use kodalith layers for special effects. But what I didn't know how to do was to transfer the image into inks and to make multiple passes. I continued to explore printmaking at UNM and the Tamarind and found a real emphasis on collaboration and working collaboratively with the artist. It is important to be intuitive, and you have to listen to what the artist wants to achieve in making the image. Even though I decided to make my work on my own art rather than becoming a printer, I liked the idea of collaboration.

Portraiture allowed me to collaborate on another level with the person I was photographing. The image itself is a product of my ideas and the ideas of the subject. And then, of course, as the printmaker, I would further develop the work, which enabled me to nourish the photograph. The portrait then went beyond what Curtis was doing because the shared process and our shared identity infused the portraits with a truth about who Chicanxs are and where their heart is individually and collectively.

Demetria: Maria Elena, your collaboration with Delilah was quite extensive. For the *Casta* series, you opened up your home, much like you opened your heart for the *Corazón* series. Looking back, what did you take away from your involvement with her and her work? Was there something you learned about yourself through the process?

Maria Elena: I experienced what it truly means to be part of an artistic process and to contribute to someone else's creative vision. Being close to Delilah allowed me to understand the direction she was taking with her images.

Delilah: I always thought of you as a writer, as writing itself is a creative process. You have always been a natural collaborator.

Demetria: So, to be part of someone else's visual creative process—what was it about the *Sagrado Corazón* that interested you, Delilah?

Delilah: At that time, graffiti artists and Chicanx art were not respected. Over the years, Chicano art gained acceptance and validation. I wanted to help recognize these art forms as a vital expression of our culture. This project was deeply connected to our heritage—a reflection of the Corazón was cast alongside the graffiti artists. It also served as a way to unite the community.

Delilah: How old were your children at the time of the shoot, Maria Elena?

Maria Elena: Maggie was nine, and Carmen was eight.

Delilah: They were young, and I vividly remember how you balanced your career while being a single mom. You were a powerhouse, breaking barriers and creating opportunities for many of the often-overlooked Chicano artists in Albuquerque.

Marie Elena: I am proud of what I accomplished as the art editor for the *Albuquerque Journal*. Before my tenure, the publication's art coverage had a predominantly white Eurocentric focus, often overlooking the contributions of Hispano/Chicano artists. Their creative work was dismissed as simplistic and unrefined.

Delilah: In the *Corazón* series, the image of you and the girls is truly beautiful. One thing I'm curious about—when I reflect on my upbringing, I associate the Sacred Heart as a religious symbol. For you, was the Sacred Heart a religious symbol, or did it hold a more profound cultural significance?

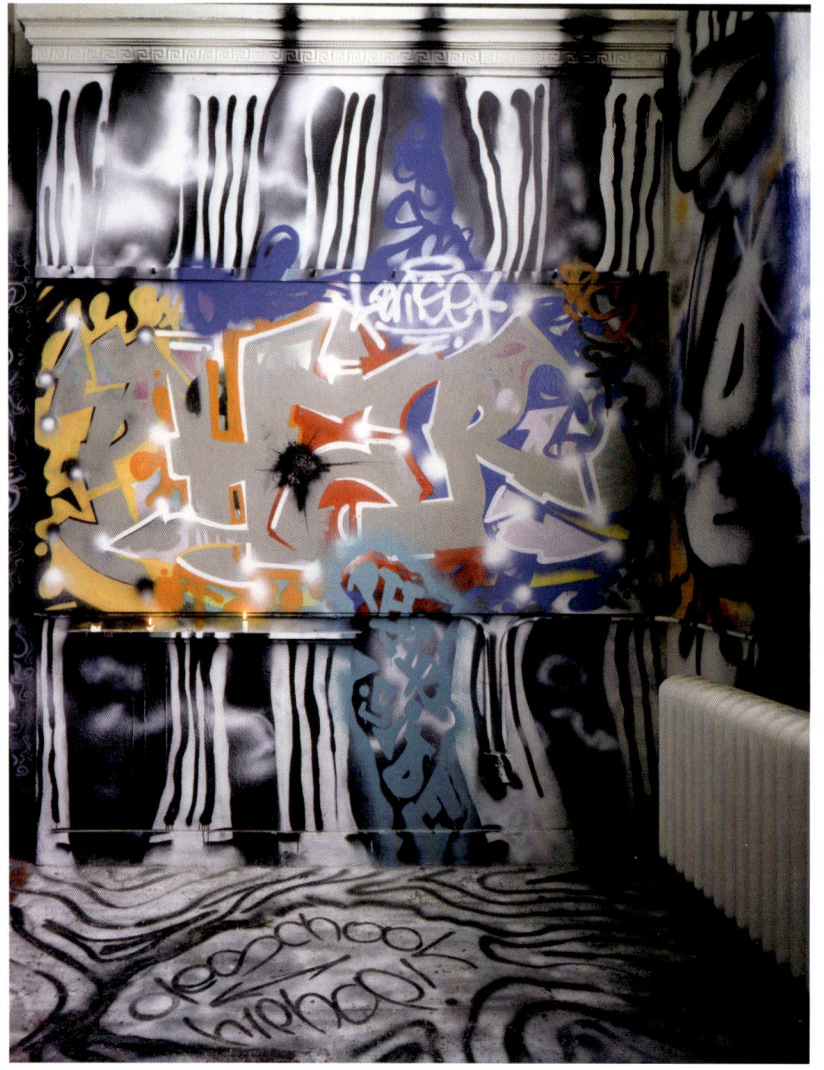

Right west-facing wall, University of New Mexico Graduate Studio, 1992 New Mexico Museum of Art Installation 2014 Syncretism Artist: Delilah Montoya Tlakwilo (Glyph Maker): Michael Esfera

Maria Elena: For my mother, the Sacred Heart didn't hold much significance, but for my deeply religious grandmother, it held a spiritual significance to her religious beliefs. I didn't fully grasp its meaning until I read your master's thesis on the history of the *Sagrado Corazón*. I found your research tracing its origins back to Aztec culture groundbreaking. What fascinated me most was the revelation that the Sacred Heart doesn't appear in Catholicism or Christianity until after the conquest and is rarely depicted in European religious art.

Delilah: As I looked at images of Jesus and Mary revealing their hearts, I felt inspired to depict the Chicano community rebuilding their own hearts. I remember how, despite everything you had on your plate—working full time and balancing so many responsibilities in a very Anglo newsroom—you maintained a commitment to connect with Chicanx artists and the local Hispano art community to ensure their stories were told.

Maria Elena: Actually, the community reached out to me because they hadn't seen a Hispanic woman on the arts desk before. I was from northern New Mexico and had been editor of *Hispanic Magazine*, a national monthly magazine. This is where I first discovered the diversity and talent of Chicano/Hispano artists from around the country. When I got to Albuquerque, it was easy for me to recognize the local artistry and talent. I was drawn into a circle of talent, now celebrated writers and artists like Demetria, Francisco Lefebre, Luis Tapia, and Rudy Fernandez. There was this huge, vibrant community, and I fit right in.

Demetria: Elena, how did you feel when you saw the image of you and your daughters—the sheer beauty of it? What emotions did it bring up for you?

Maria Elena: I was very proud to be part of the project, and today, so are my girls. Delilah's work was groundbreaking.

Delilah: Several works from the series went to the Smithsonian. There were exhibitions in California and across the United States. A lot of the work got sold. They are collotypes, and I think I'm the only Chicana making those kinds of prints. I like thinking about the process and materials.

Maria Elena: Did you see yourself documenting a time in history?

Delilah: Documentary projects typically have a clear message or goal—they aim to capture something specific from the photographer's perspective. My work, however, isn't strictly documentary. There's an element of subjectivity to it. It's my way of understanding and engaging with the world around me, and in doing so, I learn more about myself. In my process, I manipulate the photograph itself. I don't view it as purely objective or subjective. Maria Elena, when we worked together on the *Sagrado Corazón* series, we had a conversation, and I asked, "What is your heart?" If you were to reveal your heart, what would it be? What does your heart look like? It didn't take long for you to answer—my children.

Maria Elena: Oh yeah, we identified them as angels.

Delilah: They were your angels and in them lived your heart. So, we decided, let's do this. Let's make them your angels. We collaborated to create that image. A documentary photographer typically captures an image as it is, but what we did was different—we created the image together. That collaborative process is something I've always been drawn to.

Collotype Process by Delilah Montoya

The *Sagrado Corazón* series was created using the collotypes process. Ann O'Keefe introduced me to the process during her post-MFA study at UNM. The collotype is the first photographic printmaking process invented by Alphonse-Louis Poitevin in 1855. This type of print is the only screenless photomechanical process that produces a high-quality print from a continuous-tone photographic negative. Nineteenth-century photographs were published using this method. Great works such as Muybridge's *Animal Locomotion* survive as collotypes. Unlike silver gelatin prints, collotypes are incredibly stable because they are printed on rag paper with oil-based inks. The stability of the materials interested me. I liked the idea of making a *Sagrado Corazón* print that could last for centuries like the Sacred Heart itself has.

The process starts with a treated dichromate-sensitized gelatin matrix, as O'Keefe showed me an unexposed panchromatic sheet of film soaked in a dichromate solution does the trick. Once dried it is then exposed in contact with a photographic negative under ultraviolet light. At this point, you can see the negative's imprint on the surface of the gelatin matrix. The matrix is then washed in cool water, which removes the dichromate and stops the light-sensitive chemical reaction. The cool water causes the gelatin matrix to microscopically reticulate as a random surface that acts as a halftone screen so the tones of a photograph can be printed. The matrix is hung up to dry. Meanwhile, nine to ten sheets of Arches watercolor hot press paper are torn and punched with pin registration holes.

Once the matrix dries, a plate is made by adhering the matrix to a plexiglass sheet with spray mount. The plate is pin registered so multiple passes of ink can be printed onto a single sheet of paper. To prepare the plate to accept ink, the gelatin matrix is swollen with a water-based compound of glycerin poured evenly across the surface and soaked for an hour. Meanwhile, the ink and press are made ready. After an hour, an ammonia compound is poured over the matrix and wiped off with a soft paper towel. The matrix surface is soft like butter, so the wipe must be gentle so as not to lay scratches on the image. Once the plate is clean and damp, it is ready to accept ink.

I used a hard roller to lay a thin coat of ink onto the matrix surface. The viscosity of the ink varied to produce a full tone, warm-colored print. I started with a loose yellow ink layer, then stiffened the ink until I printed a final black key. This required seven layers of ink, each pass required preparing the matrix to accept ink. The matrix was rolled up with ink for each sheet passed through the lithograph press. The same ten sheets of paper were printed for each run of color; this meant that the matrix stayed in perfect registration each time a new layer of color was added and a sheet of paper was dropped onto the matrix. Because the process is tricky, not all the inked sheets were successful. If I was lucky, five to seven prints were good. The rest of the prints were destroyed. I learned that when printing collotypes, lightning strikes during the New Mexico monsoons help to make the best printing experience. The air had ions, and the collotype process seemed to like that.

Casta paintings emerged in New Spain during the eighteenth century as a visual and cultural tool to articulate the complex system of racial hierarchies instituted by Spanish colonial authorities. These paintings depicted families arranged in panels that illustrated the myriad possibilities of racial mixing—involving Spanish, Indigenous, and African ancestries—and codified these mixtures into a rigid, socially constructed hierarchy.

Scholars like Magaly Carrera have argued that these images served not only as art but as a means to "image" identity in a colonial context. In her work, *Imaging Identity in New Spain*, Carrera examines how casta paintings reveal the colonial desire to document and control the racialized identities emerging in the New World. They offered a visual rhetoric that both mirrored and reinforced the structured social order, emphasizing a naturalized order of races that underpinned colonial policy and everyday life. The paintings were made in New Spain with the intention of sending them to Spain, demonstrating an effort to keep the races separate and maintain the purity of Spanish blood in the Americas.

Ilona Katzew's analysis in *Casta Paintings: Images of Race in 18th Century Mexico* complements this view by detailing how these artworks meticulously cataloged not only the visible physical traits but also the implied social and moral standings of the subjects. Katzew argues that the paintings were part of a broader cultural project: they made the "invisible" rules of racial classification visible to the colonial elite. They served as an enduring record of the racial dynamics that defined New Spain.

Together, these perspectives underscore how casta paintings were both products and producers of a colonial ideology. This visual language rendered the complexities of racial mixing into a neatly ordered system. Their legacy continues to influence contemporary discussions about race and identity as artists and scholars continue to revisit these images to explore the lingering impact of colonial categorizations in the Americas. In reality, of course, racial mixing was prevalent, and the systemized attempts to maintain racial purity became constructs through which individuals claimed European descent and attempted to suppress Indigenous and Black heritage.

Using casta paintings as source material, Montoya seeks to disrupt not only the process of categorizing people racially but also to hone a deeper meaning of Mestizaje to forge an understanding that the colonial body is also a global body. According to Montoya, "The *Nuestra Calidad* photographs adhere to a common structure: A family is asked to sit for a portrait in the setting of their choice; I edit the photographs and then accompany them with racial identifying information. However, unlike the descriptive titles and labels used in colonial casta paintings, I introduce racial heritage by juxtaposing the photos with DNA genetic analysis." In addition to the portraits and DNA data, Montoya recorded stories from the participating families. She also created maps to visually demonstrate how DNA is literally a marker of human history and movement across the globe. The act of mapping is also related to colonialism and the conquest of land. In this project, Montoya uses each component of the installation to create a different kind of claim, namely an understanding that multiracial and multiethnic identity building is a strength not something used to categorize people in order to define class, status, and generational wealth through both blood and land.

In Conversation with Delilah Montoya and Demetria Martinez:
Contemporary Casta Portraiture: Nuestra Calidad

Demetria: Your contemporary casta portraits were a highly complex undertaking spanning your interest in seventeenth-century casta paintings and the contemporary science of DNA. The paintings, of course, were creations of New Spain. They visually categorized people based on their racial heritage. They showed the mixing of Spanish, Indigenous, and African ancestry. The paintings had an insidious purpose. Of course, they were used to maintain the power structure of the Spanish colonial system by reinforcing the idea of so-called blood purity. And the superiority of Spanish heritage. How did you become interested in the paintings, and how did you go on to approach families for the project, which included the stories of their DNA?

Delilah: *Contemporary Casta Portraiture: Nuestra Calidad* took a long time to complete. I had been thinking about it for most of my career. Curiosity often guides my creative process. When you go into art history and academia, people rarely think about things like the Sacred Heart. It was just assumed that this is the way it was. The cross-pollination of culture is not always self-evident to the dominant culture. As a Chicana, it is evident to me. I saw some casta paintings in the early seventies in Omaha, Nebraska, at the Chicano Awareness Center. We had a youth

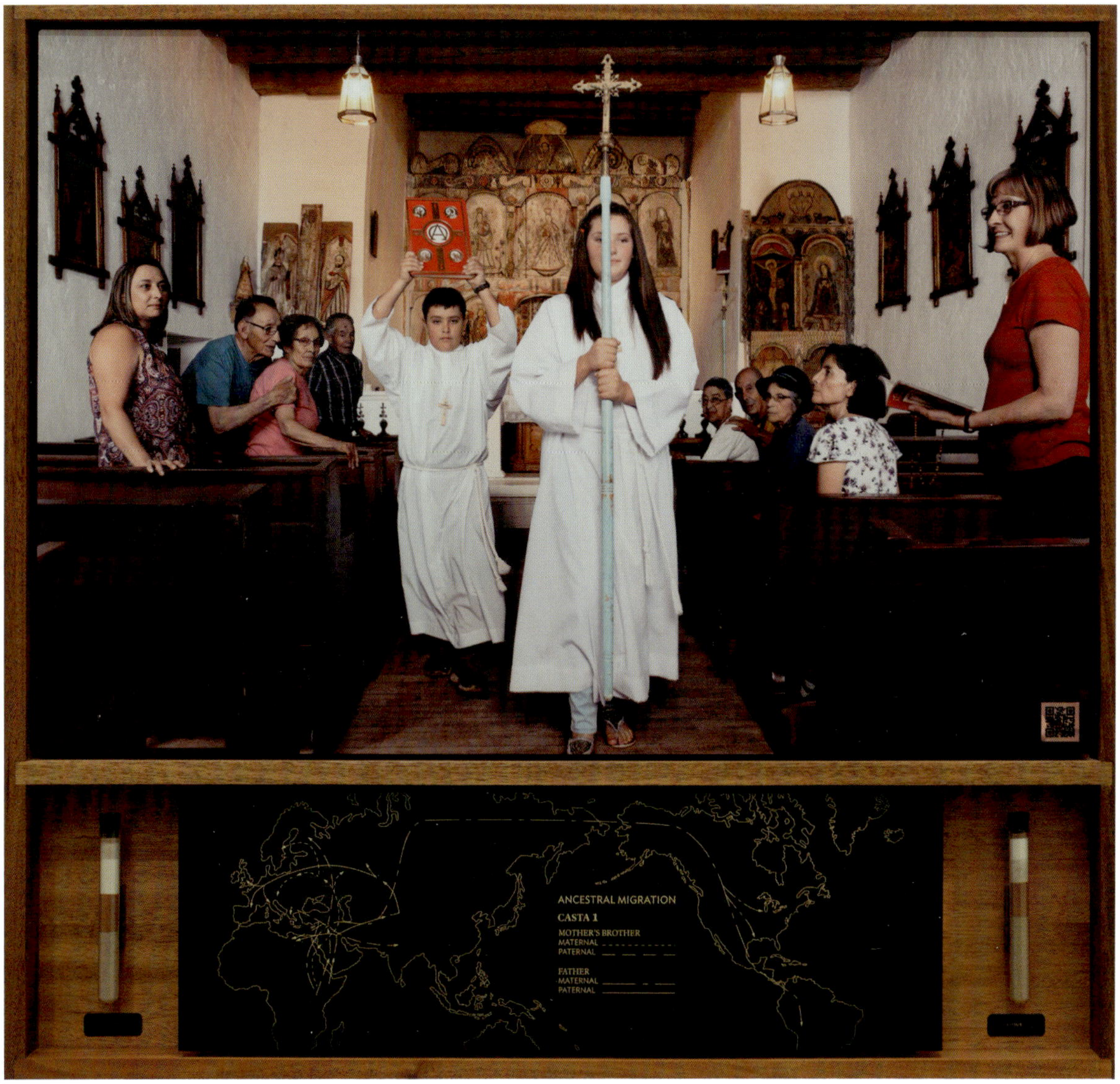

Delilah Montoya
Casta 1 (from the series *Contemporary Casta Portraiture: "Nuestra Calidad"*)
2018
Dye sublimation prints on aluminum set in wood frames, metal etching, and test tubes filled with various sands
36 × 38 in.
Collection of the artist

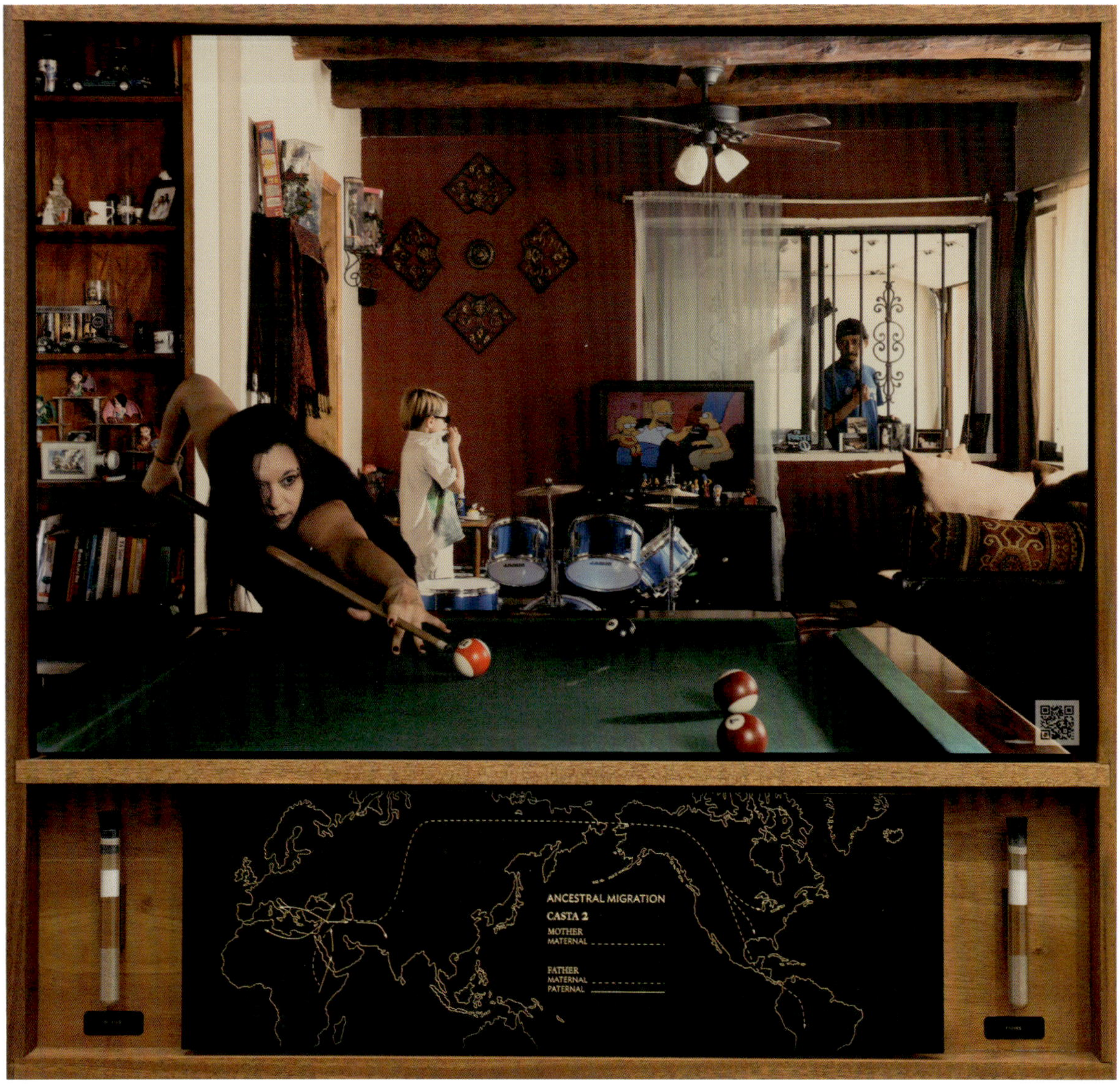

Delilah Montoya
Casta 2 (from the series *Contemporary Casta Portraiture: "Nuestra Calidad"*)
2018
Dye sublimation prints on aluminum set in wood frames, metal etching, and test tubes filled with various sands
36 × 38 in.
Collection of the artist

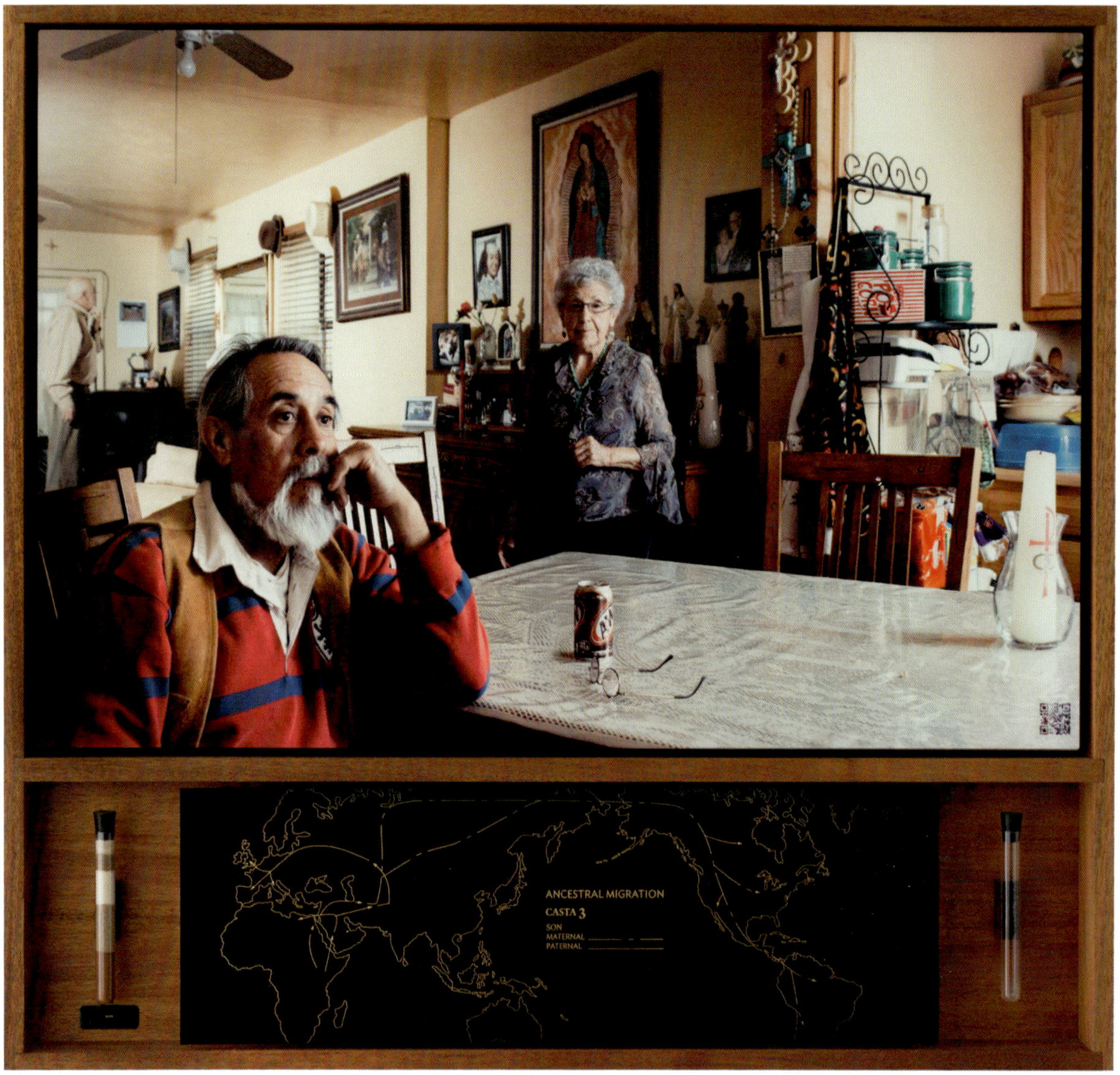

Delilah Montoya
Casta 3 (from the series *Contemporary*
Casta Portraiture: "Nuestra Calidad")
2018
Dye sublimation prints on aluminum set
in wood frames, metal etching, and test
tubes filled with various sands
36 × 38 in.
Collection of the artist

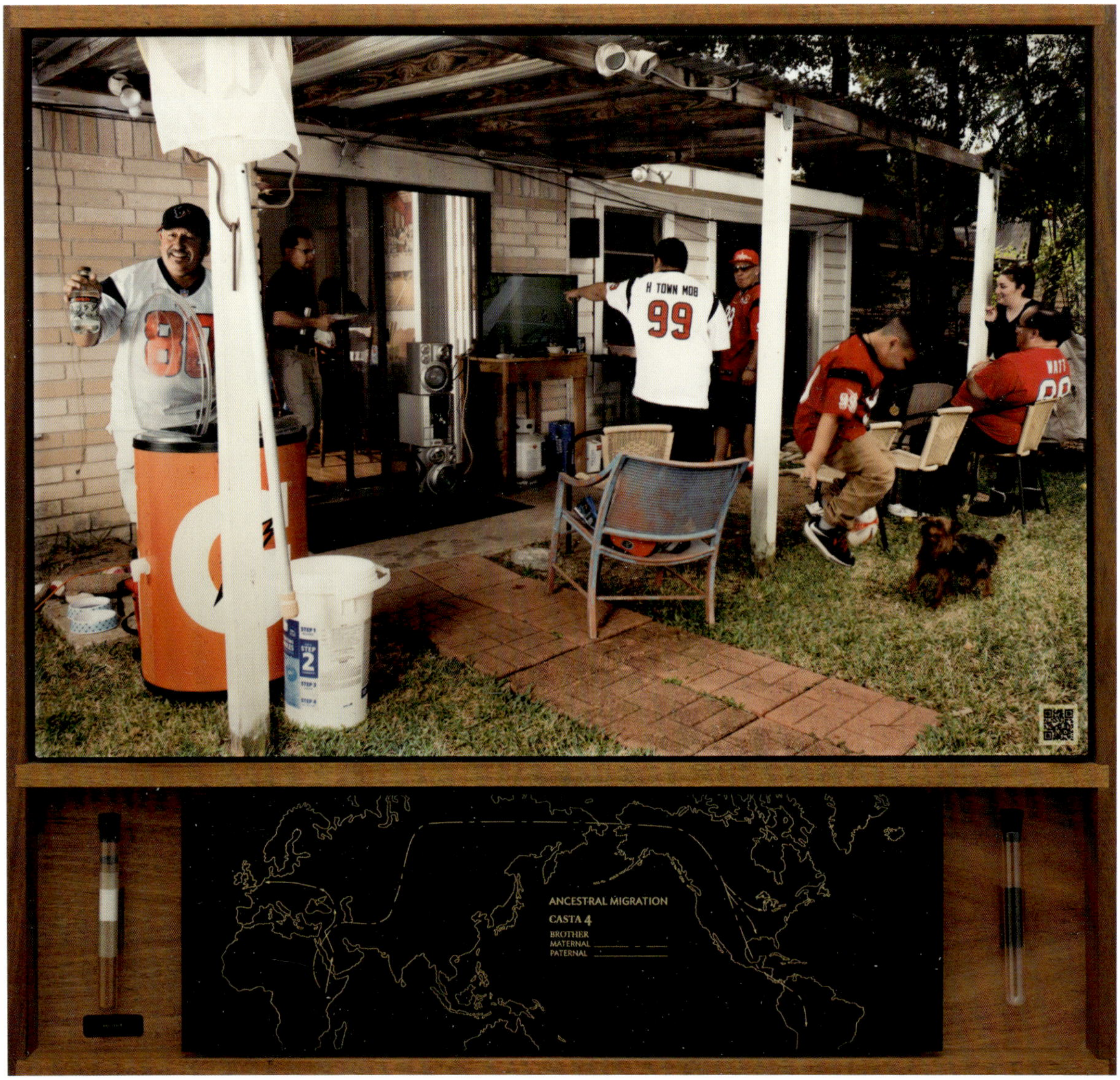

Delilah Montoya
Casta 4 (from the series *Contemporary Casta Portraiture: "Nuestra Calidad"*)
2018
Dye sublimation prints on aluminum set in wood frames, metal etching, and test tubes filled with various sands
36 × 38 in.
Collection of the artist

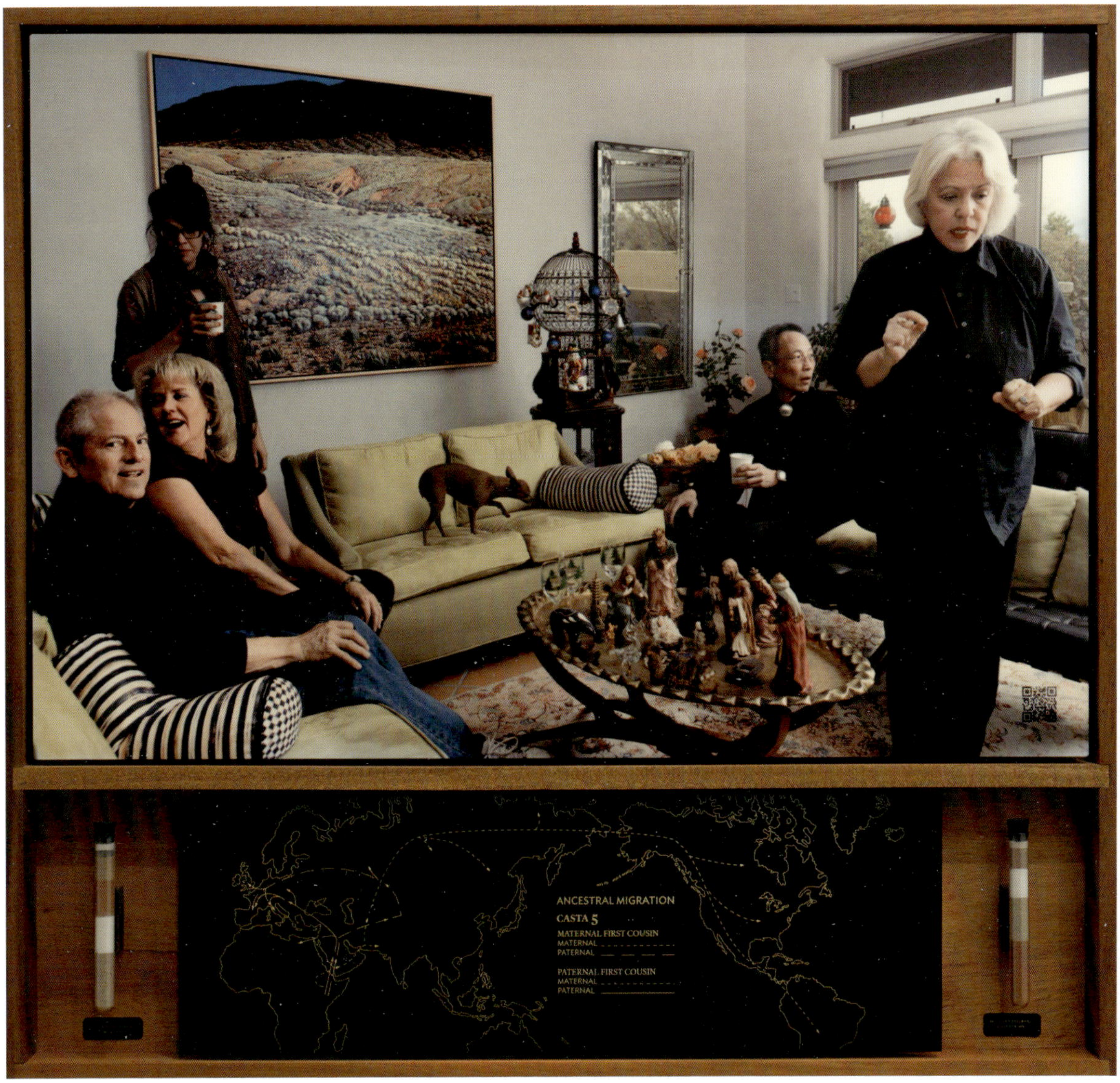

Delilah Montoya
Casta 5 (from the series *Contemporary Casta Portraiture: "Nuestra Calidad"*)
2018
Dye sublimation prints on aluminum set in wood frames, metal etching, and test tubes filled with various sands
36 × 38 in.
Collection of the artist

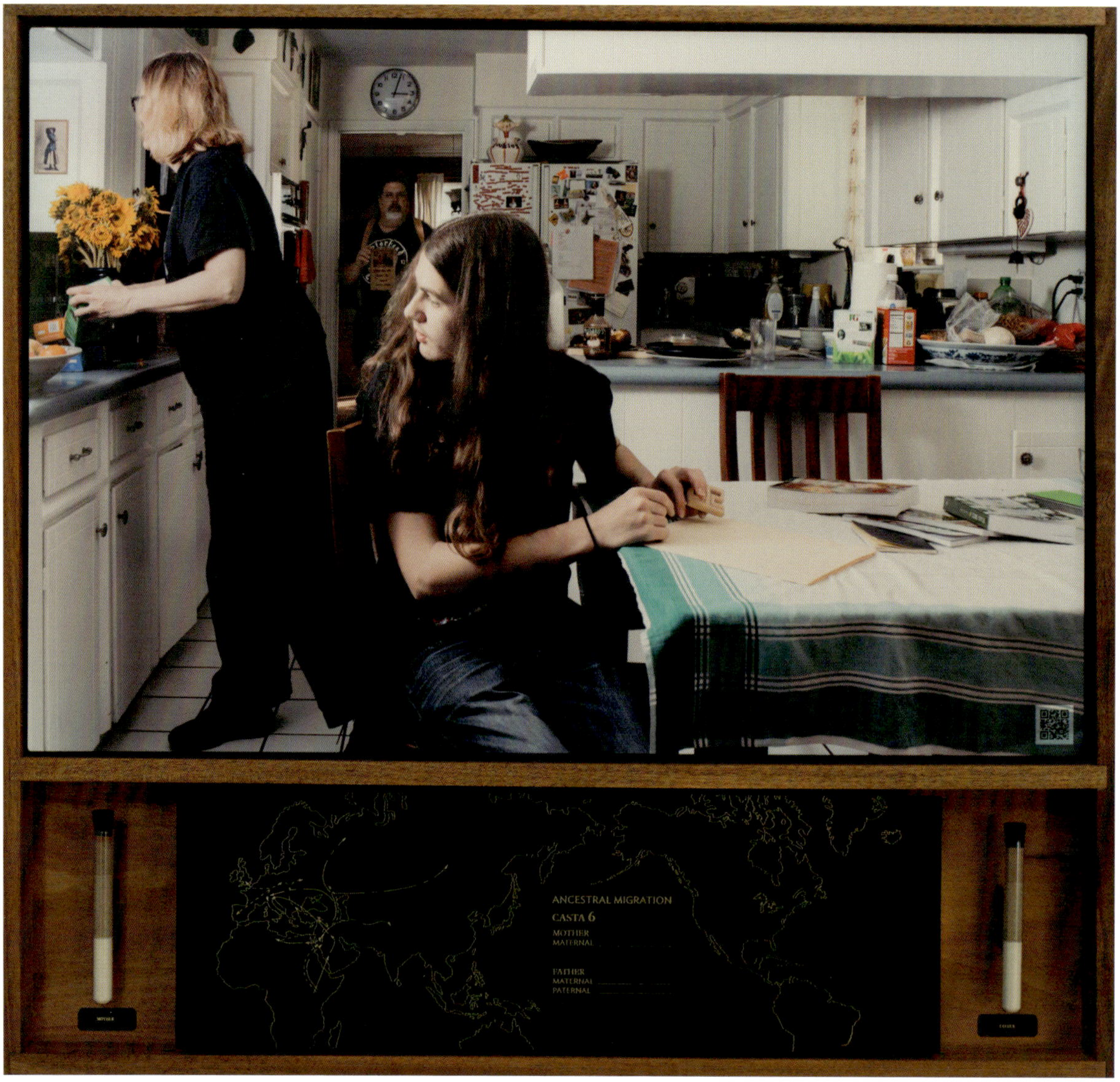

Delilah Montoya
Casta 6 (from the series *Contemporary
Casta Portraiture: "Nuestra Calidad"*)
2018
Dye sublimation prints on aluminum set
in wood frames, metal etching, and test
tubes filled with various sands
36 × 38 in.
Collection of the artist

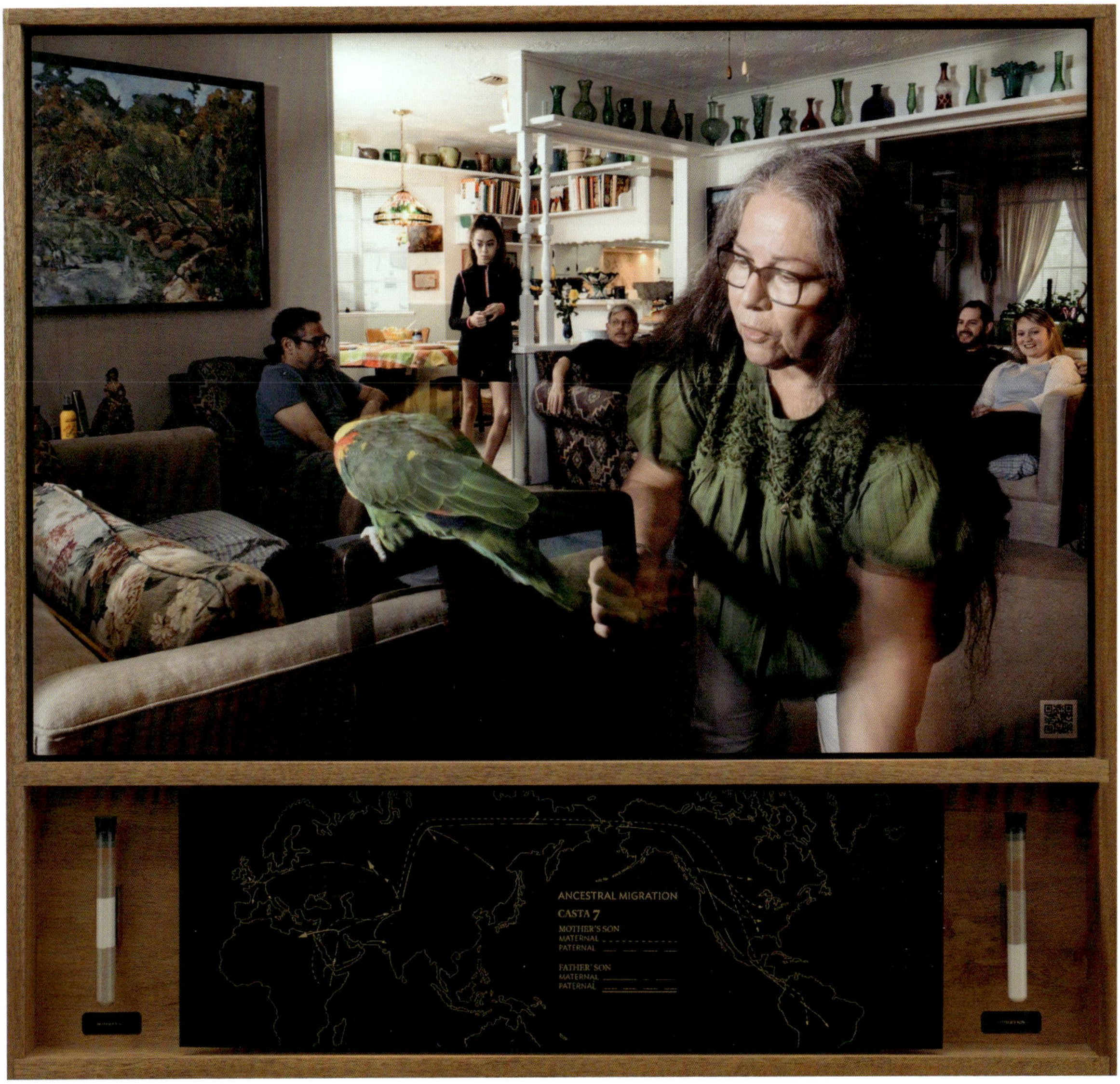

Delilah Montoya
Casta 7 (from the series *Contemporary
Casta Portraiture: "Nuestra Calidad"*)
2018
Dye sublimation prints on aluminum set
in wood frames, metal etching, and test
tubes filled with various sands
36 × 38 in.
Collection of the artist

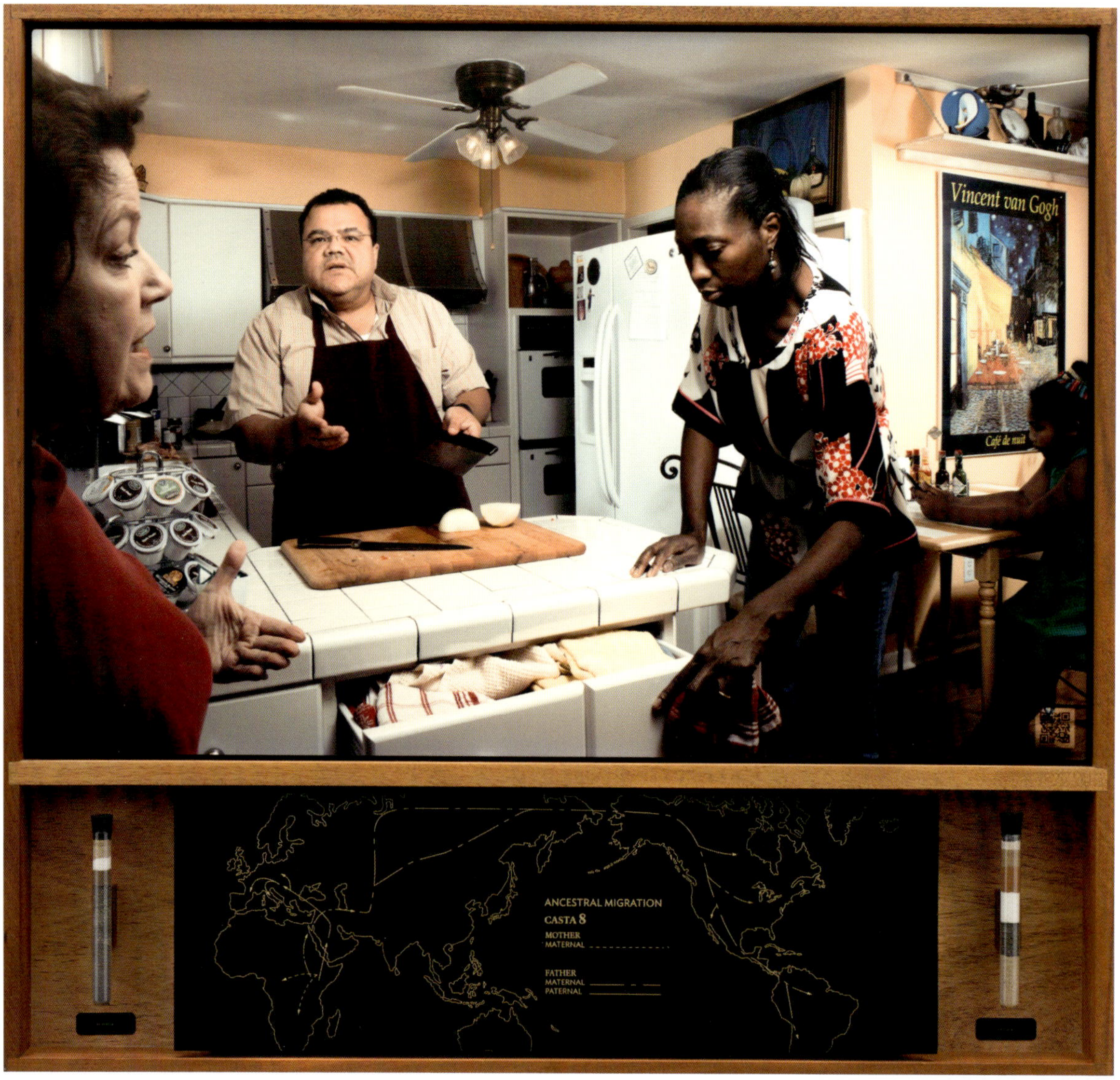

Delilah Montoya
Casta 8 (from the series *Contemporary
Casta Portraiture: "Nuestra Calidad"*)
2018
Dye sublimation prints on aluminum set
in wood frames, metal etching, and test
tubes filled with various sands
36 × 38 in.
Collection of the artist

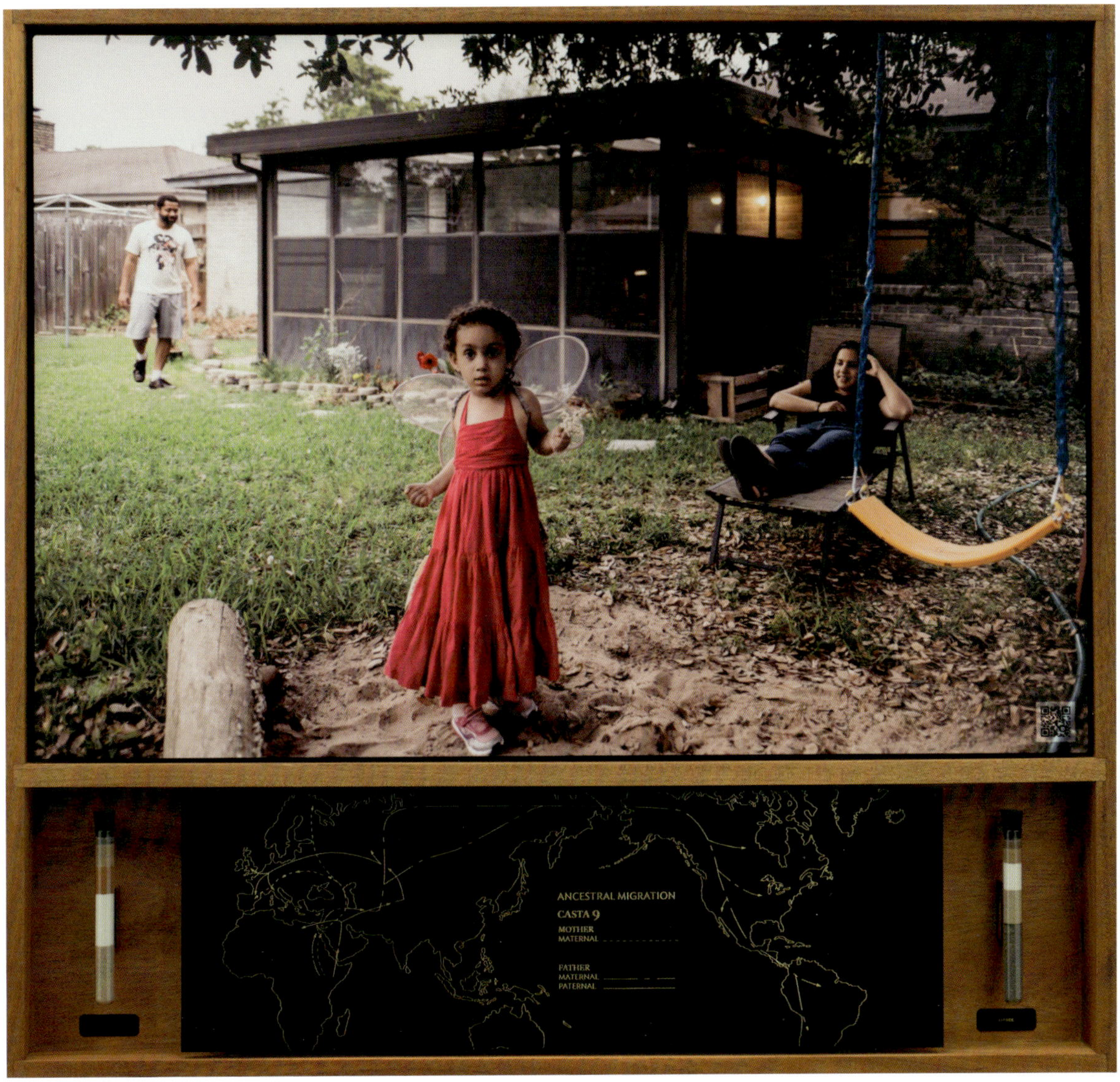

Delilah Montoya
Casta 9 (from the series *Contemporary
Casta Portraiture: "Nuestra Calidad"*)
2018
Dye sublimation prints on aluminum set
in wood frames, metal etching, and test
tubes filled with various sands
36 × 38 in.
Collection of the artist

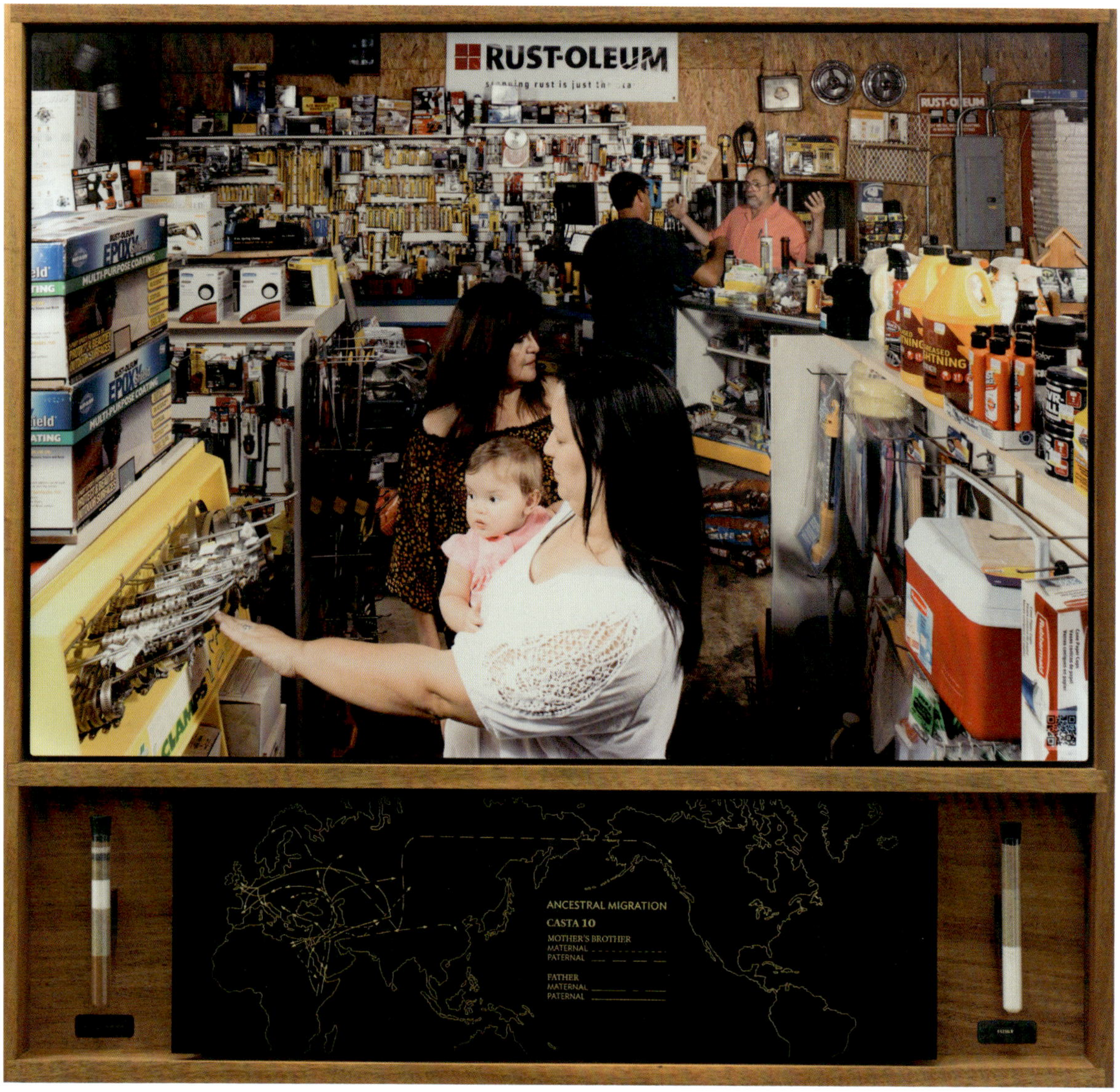

Delilah Montoya
Casta 10 (from the series *Contemporary Casta Portraiture: "Nuestra Calidad"*)
2018
Dye sublimation prints on aluminum set in wood frames, metal etching, and test tubes filled with various sands
36 × 38 in.
Collection of the artist

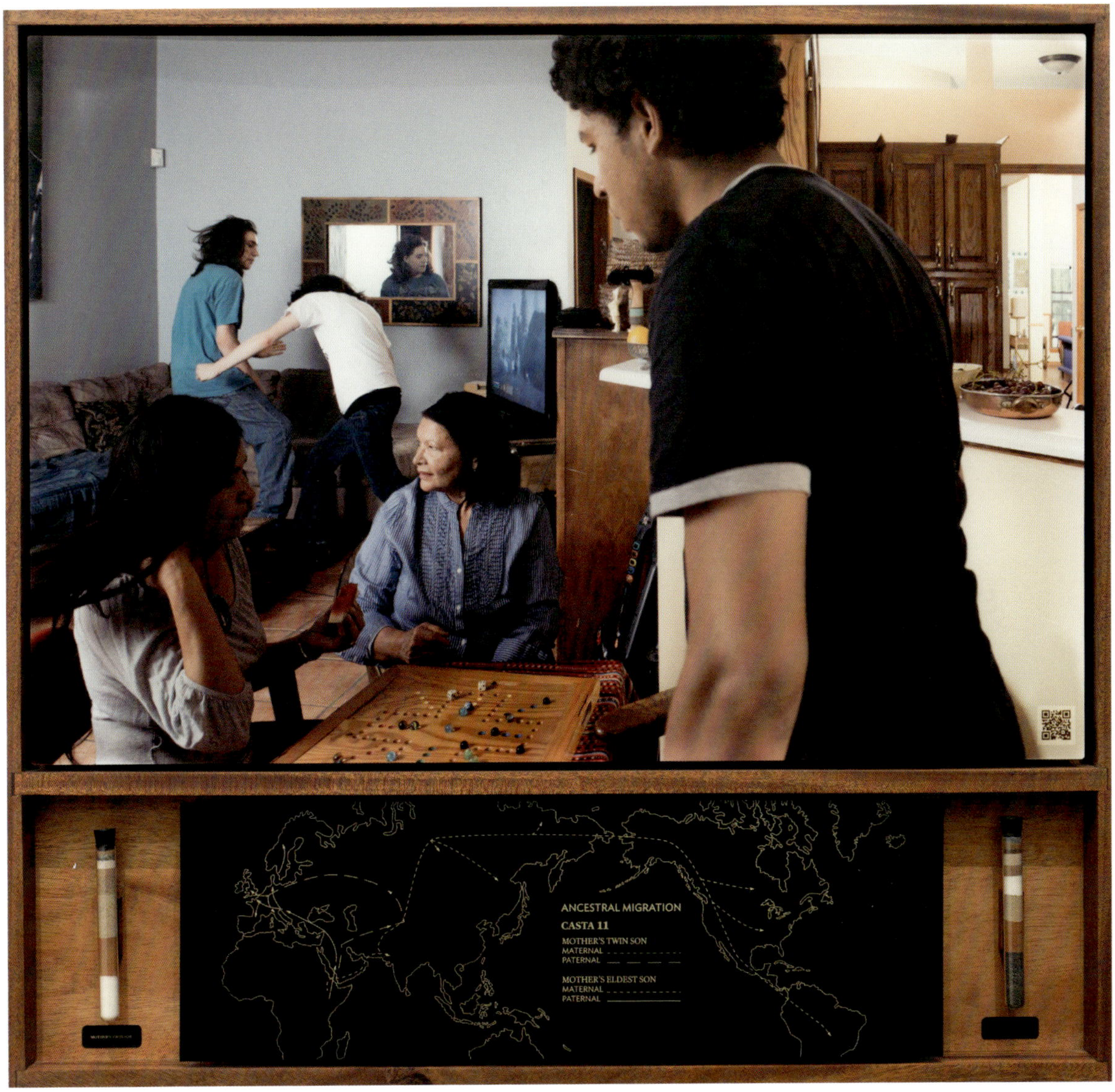

Delilah Montoya
Casta 11 (from the series *Contemporary Casta Portraiture: "Nuestra Calidad"*)
2018
Dye sublimation prints on aluminum set in wood frames, metal etching, and test tubes filled with various sands
36 × 38 in.
Collection of the artist

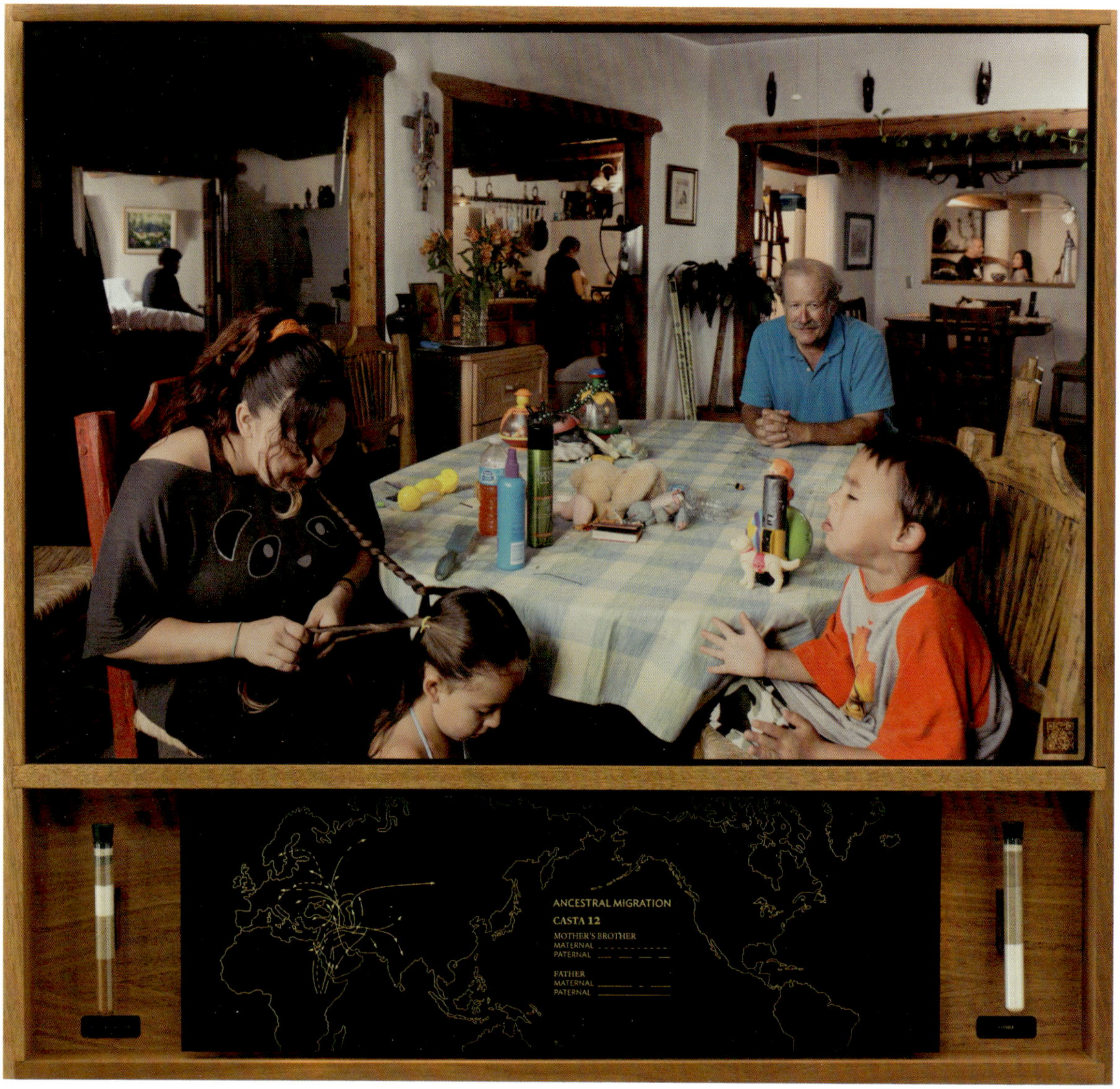

Delilah Montoya
Casta 12 (from the series *Contemporary Casta Portraiture: "Nuestra Calidad"*)
2018
Dye sublimation prints on aluminum set in wood frames, metal etching, and test tubes filled with various sands
36 × 38 in.
Collection of the artist

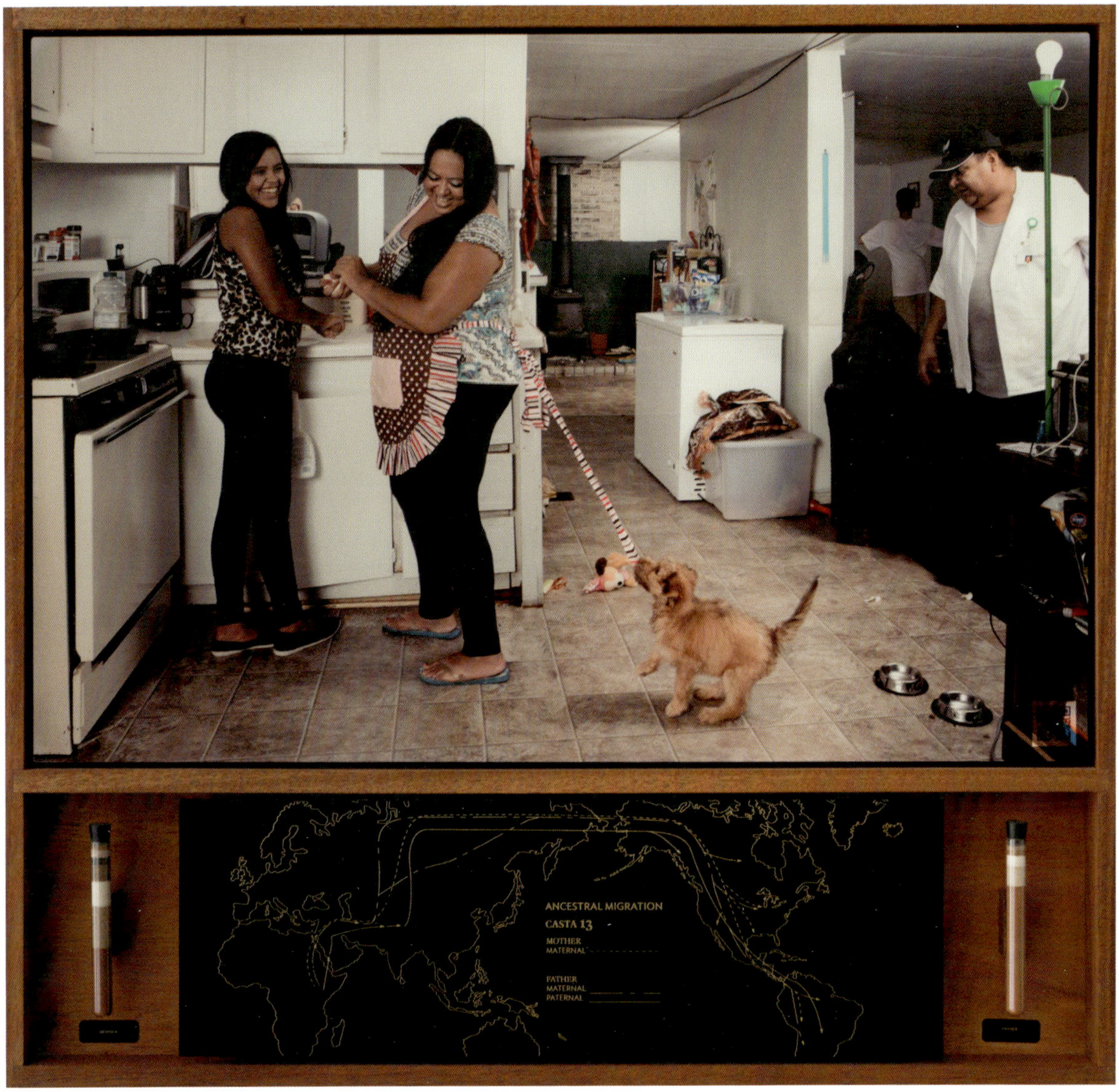

Delilah Montoya
Casta 13 (from the series *Contemporary
Casta Portraiture: "Nuestra Calidad"*)
2018
Dye sublimation prints on aluminum set
in wood frames, metal etching, and test
tubes filled with various sands
36 × 38 in.
Collection of the artist

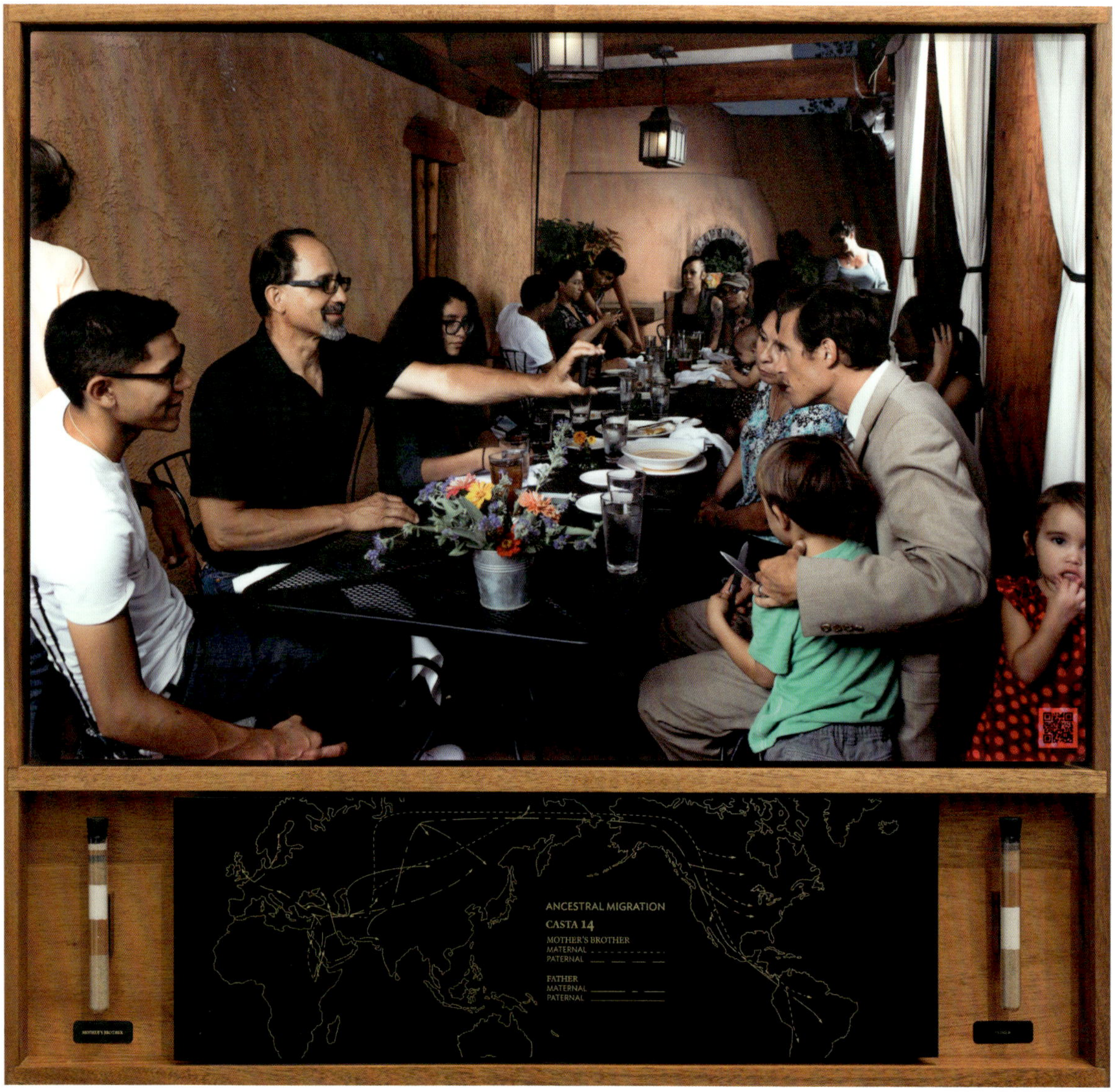

Delilah Montoya
Casta 14 (from the series *Contemporary Casta Portraiture: "Nuestra Calidad"*)
2018
Dye sublimation prints on aluminum set in wood frames, metal etching, and test tubes filled with various sands
36 × 38 in.
Collection of the artist

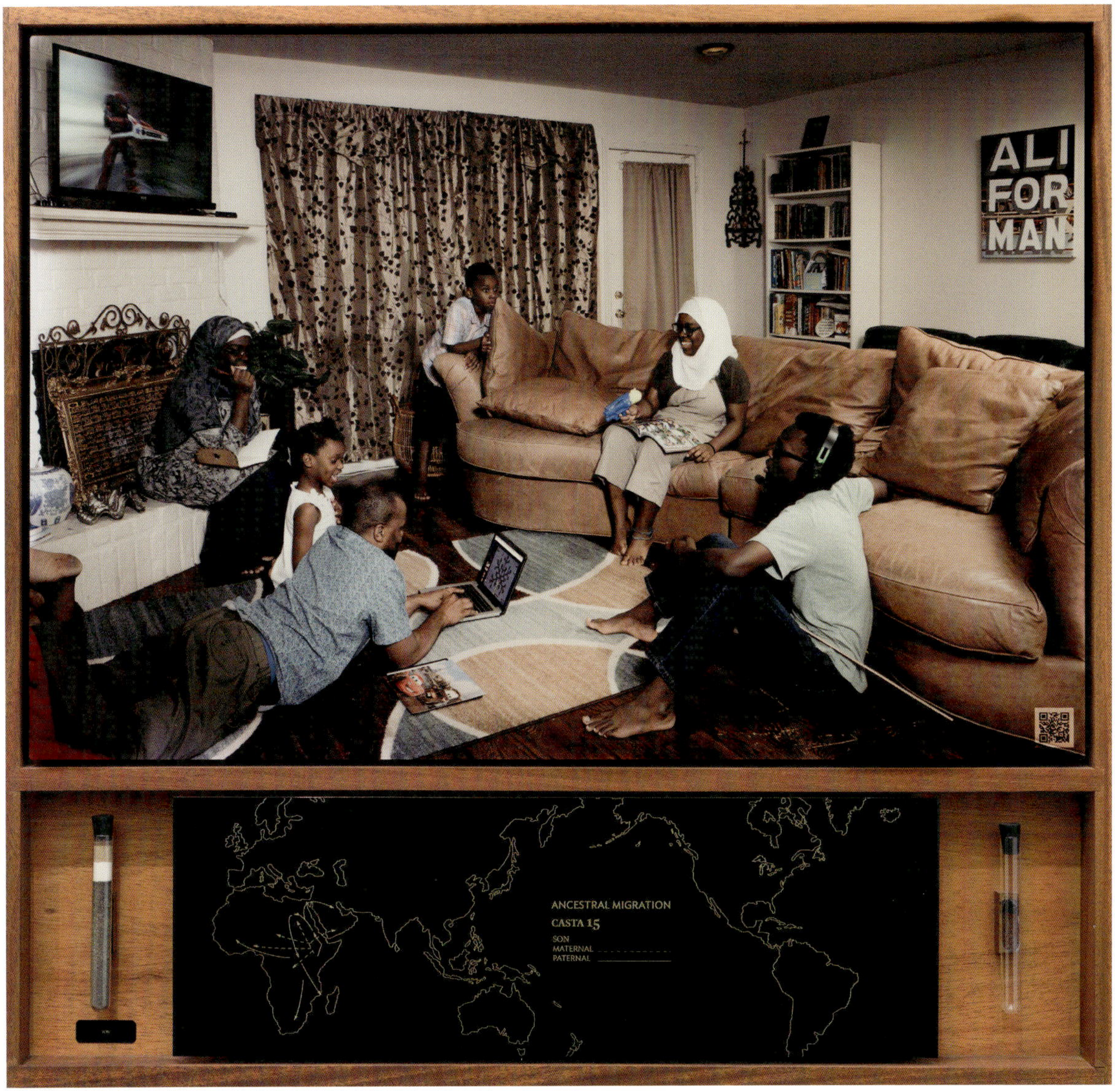

Delilah Montoya
Casta 15 (from the series *Contemporary
Casta Portraiture: "Nuestra Calidad"*)
2018
Dye sublimation prints on aluminum set
in wood frames, metal etching, and test
tubes filled with various sands
36 × 38 in.
Collection of the artist

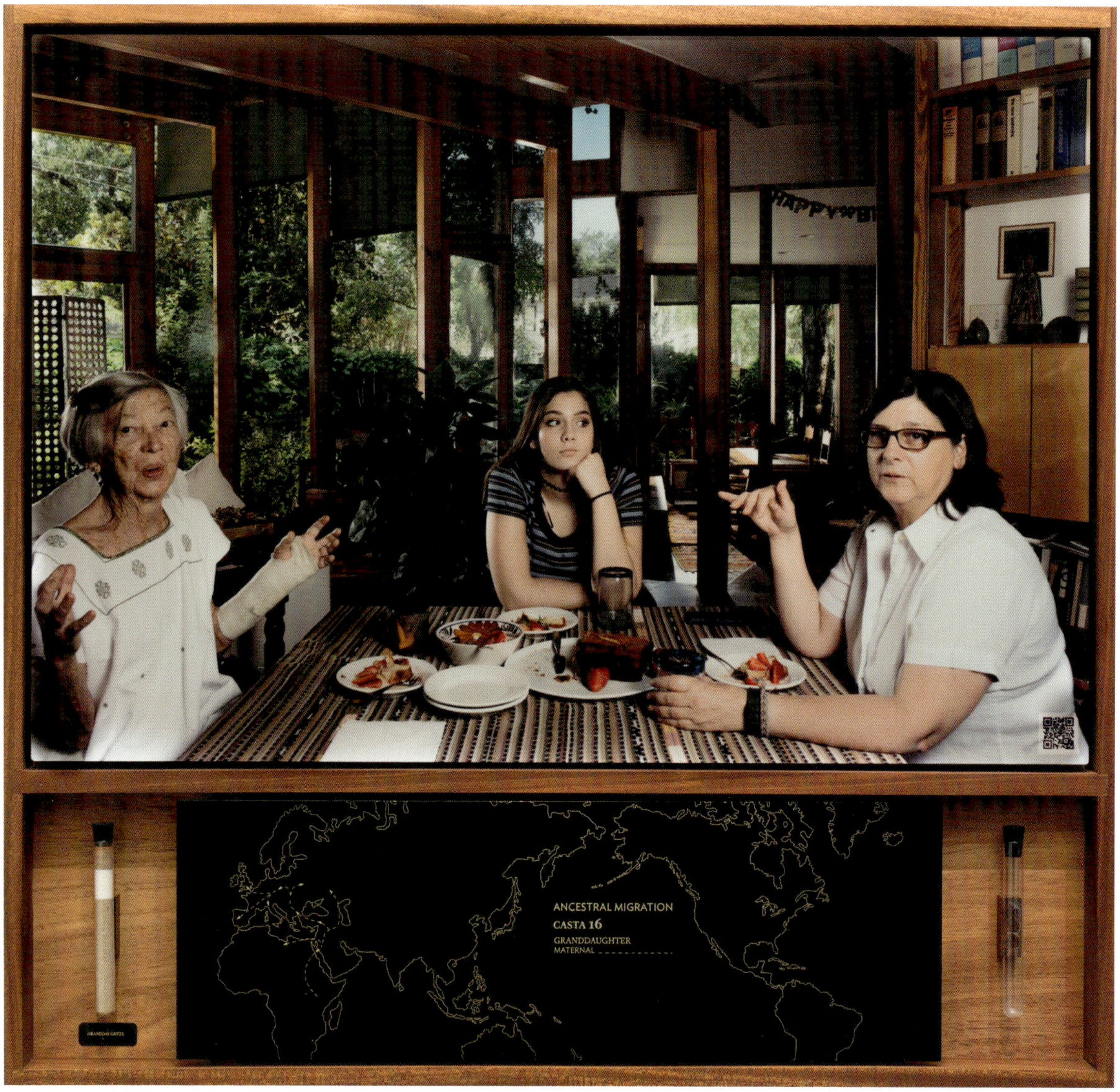

Delilah Montoya
Casta 16 (from the series *Contemporary
Casta Portraiture: "Nuestra Calidad"*)
2018
Dye sublimation prints on aluminum set
in wood frames, metal etching, and test
tubes filled with various sands
36 × 38 in.
Collection of the artist

group that would gather in that space where pictures and other materials were posted. There was this whole portfolio of casta paintings, and it was presented in terms of nationalism that defined Mexican identity. I realized that the castas were about race and represented an explanation of Mestizaje. Somehow, I accepted that thinking that this is Mestizaje, this is nationalism. Somewhere down the line, I realized, this is race, and this is colonialism. These portraits explain why things happen the way they do now. They demonstrate that the colonial fabric is still very much around us, and we're ensnared in it. I decided to mimic the Spanish Colonial castas to document that the same racialized ideologies are still present. I started by doing a lot of research to understand how people read these images historically.

Demetria: How did you bring these ideas home to the Chicanx communities and the individuals that you interviewed? And how did you incorporate DNA into the project?

Delilah: I wanted to engage with the idea of sovereignty. What does it look like in the United States? One of the things that I read on colonizing was a description of the colonial body. The king and queen or colonial rulers would be the head and the subjects their body. Who is the colonial body? Who are the people that sovereignty was built from in the United States? I realized it was Native Americans, African Americans, and Latinxs. These are the people on which sovereignty built itself. I wanted to bring this idea together with the castas because that is what it does; the castas demonstrated the colonized body and who that colonized body was. That colonized body is racially mixed and has been racially mixed for hundreds of years, literally hundreds of years. We are not immigrants. And so what we see, especially with the immigration policies and birthright citizenship that are going on now, is an attempt to control the colonized body.

The casta paintings also intersected with enlightenment ideas that included observation and labeling everybody. That was science. Because they were into this whole idea of categorization, and through this categorization, they believed things would become more apparent, and truth would be revealed. I realized that's what we're doing with the DNA testing now. What I found interesting about DNA testing is that it is seen as science and as truth, just as during the Casta paintings, the labeling was considered to be scientific truth. It was during that period when the idea of cleaning of the blood was prevalent. We still have the cleaning of the blood. It's still happening.

Demetria: Tell us more about the interviews that you did with the families. What kind of things were you hearing from them in telling their stories?

Delilah: I also wanted to address different sectors of society, moving from prison culture all the way up to corporate culture through the various families that I found to collaborate with. Ultimately, my collaborators were those who knew of my work. I needed them to trust me and be on board with what I was doing and thinking. Those I collaborated with were really generous with their time and appreciated my ideas relating to sovereignty and racial mixing. The project was organized in such a way that the collaborator had control of the narrative and of what I was going to photograph and who was going to be DNA tested.

I first visited with them, explaining that I wouldn't use names because names were not used in the castas. I wanted it to be anonymous, and I also wanted to protect them. This meant that the subjects essentially became types. The viewer would have to identify their casta type. As a result, the viewers confront their own biases. I wanted the viewer to become uncomfortable and unpack their preconceived notions because this process is so intuitive. We've been raised around it. We've been taught to think this way.

As part of photographing, we determined where I would set up the camera and lights. I asked them to be actors in their own lives together as a family. Each session took about two hours. This was followed up with DNA testing. I was talking to Surpik Angelini, the founder of Transart in Houston, Texas. As a mentor and curator, she helped me think through this, so it was a great collaboration. She was interested in some of the same ideas and suggested that it would be interesting to hear what the families had to say about their respective photographs. And that is when I came up with the idea of the QR code, which was pretty new at the time. I asked a family member to look at the photograph and talk about what they saw or wanted other people to know about their family portrait. It is essential to look at the portraits while listening to their monologues. It is a real-time experience. The stories offer insight into who that family is, so these monologues are important to the work. These monologues are very expressive.

Monologue from *Casta 9*

> Three of us in the backyard. We look like a pretty unified group with my Haitian Cuban background and Julie's midwestern US and Northern Argentina thing going on. Our daughter makes perfect sense, right? Coming from the two of us, the phenotype is right. In Haiti, I go into certain neighborhoods, and a stranger would see me and call me blanc. But of course, if I go into like a rich neighborhood in Haiti, then I'm Black again. Even within the island, racially fluid, but here, just Black. The first nations here in the US are strong, beautiful, and rich. In Haiti, there's nothing but the blood. You find it in the DNA. There's no memory, so you have whole ethnic groups that disappear. The African blood that survives in Julie, the African communities were decimated. There was an outbreak of fever, and all Argentine blacks were quarantined together, and so they quickly got sick. I wouldn't be surprised if there was also migration. Yeah, Brazil is right there, you know. You cross the border, and all of a sudden Africa is alive again. Families tell themselves these stories, and I'm a big fan of productive lies, and I have no problem with those coexisting with the truth.

Demetria: It is fascinating because you are interviewing individuals from Albuquerque and Houston. And yet, looking at these maps, you see a global community, a global people.

Delilah: The colonized body is global. That's why the name for our identity keeps changing. We're not just one thing because we're all of it. What you tend to see happen over and over again, of course, is that the maternal side is generally indigenous to the Americas and the paternal side comes right out of Europe. Whenever I take on any of these projects, I learn about the world around me. In my mind's eye, I begin to understand it and unpack it. That's why I take on these projects. I'm curious. I'm curious about why things are the way they are and why we are experiencing the world this way.

In Conversation with Delilah Montoya, Maria Elena Alvarez, and Demetria Martinez: *Contemporary Casta Portraiture: Nuestra Calidad*

Delilah: The collaborative process was essential in the *Casta* series. I was asking a lot from the families I collaborated with. I was asking to be in their homes, to record their stories, and to photograph their children. And by the way, can I have your DNA too? That takes a lot of chutzpah.

Maria Elena: As an anthropologist and a sociologist, I was fascinated when Delilah described the casta project. I was already deeply interested in the history of the caste system in the Americas. I had done some reading on how the Spaniards identified mixed races. In the project, you not only invited my immediate family but also extended family members. But all the elders had died. So it's just me and my cousin. We wanted to understand as much as we could in the DNA itself. My DNA was 35 percent Mediterranean on mom's side and 35 percent Native American on dad's side. So when you put them together, my DNA is 50 percent Native American. The next largest percentage is Mediterranean.

Delilah: The family monologue was one of the components I wanted to layer into the *Casta* series. I asked one family member to talk about their casta image and recorded it. It felt like the stories in spoken word would give context and texture to the project. It would make the families vital and real. I embedded a QR code into the picture so viewers could access the monologues and listen to each family's story. So, the viewer at that point comes in direct contact with the participant. At first, it was difficult to get people to use the code. But then, when it went up in Chicago all of a sudden it got so many hits that I had to buy the subscription for the QR codes to keep them active.

Another important medium Montoya turned to repeatedly was bookmaking. *Codex Delilah: A Journey from Mexicatl to Chicana*, *Crickets in My Mind*, and *Shooting the Tourist* are three examples of series of works that Montoya compiled into a book form. In 1978, Montoya left Omaha and moved to west Denver, an inner-city barrio. The move marked a transition from a small Latinx community to a bustling, vibrant, and expansive primarily Chicanx urban center. Montoya describes her arrival, "What a marvelous feeling to step on a bus and see la raza. I experienced many firsts: pollution, segregation, traffic jams, and graffiti. I witnessed the red glow of the city night sky, and life seemed very different." The barrio that Montoya describes is Inca Street. Before leaving and returning to Albuquerque, Montoya photographed her neighborhood with the hopes of capturing not only the visual experience of the neighborhood but also the sounds, the commotion, and the soul of the community. At the time, Montoya was unsure how the project would take shape or how the photographs would live.[1]

Decades later, Montoya returned to the photographs when she and Cecilio García- Camarillo worked on an artist book together. *Crickets in My Mind* is a literary meditation developed by García-Camarillo. In 1992, he and Montoya worked together to pair some Inca Street photographs with five literary works he wrote exploring the concept of *sensualismo*. While Montoya and García-Camarillo are both Chicano artists, they wanted to express how Chicanismo could be seen through multivalent perspectives, including male and female, visual and literary, and the real versus the invisible. The idea was to create multiple levels of perception to reveal underlying truths. Sensualismo is a political ideology that reveals the dark side of our world. Six copies of the collaborative artist book were produced and promoted by Mano Isquierda in Albuquerque. According to the gallery description, *Crickets in My Mind* gives witness to "sensualismo"—the appetite of the flesh for the flesh. Sensualismo represents a primitivism embodied within the mores, institutions, and lifestyles of our time and found within the dark side of our being. The point of disclosure is to reveal sensualismo within our world, that is, the impact of outside forces that cause the world to seem disjointed."[2]

The design of the book is also central to the project. Specific materials like human hair, handmade paper, bronze shavings, flint, lithograph and serigraph prints of the photographs, acetate overlays, and hand-printed text all contribute to how the work is experienced. Montoya compiled the images and constructed the book by hand. The first section of the nineteen-page book reads,

1. Ramon, the Philosopher

> These last few days, I've seen posters around town announcing my being here tonight at St Mary's University to talk with you about "sensualismo," and I've been wondering what has gone through the minds of those of you that read the posters and came face to face with that word. Well, let me tell you, it's a very heavy thing. I've been at it for forty years, and it has been beautiful looking for what was missing not only in my life, but in the bloodstream of the government, churches, and institutions. When I first started on the journey, I was trying to solve the enigma behind the hollow mythology that governed the two worlds that I saw, one dying.[3]

The text and images work together to produce an experience that is both universal and specific. The photographs were initially scenes captured on the streets in which Montoya's approach references Weegee and Diane Arbus. Through various layers of printmaking and assemblage, however, Montoya transforms them into meditations. The prints reflect the people of the community specifically but also embed those images within constellations of shape, color, and line to produce visual reflections intermingled with García-Camarillo's political message of sensualismo, which describes the need to consume otherness.[4]

(*opposite page, top*)
Delilah Montoya and
Cecilio García-Camarillo
Crickets In My Mind, page 5
1992
Lithography and serigraphy
on rice paper
20 × 14¾ in.
University of New Mexico
University Libraries, Center
for Southwest Research and
Special Collections

(*opposite page, bottom*)
Delilah Montoya and Cecilio
García-Camarillo
Crickets In My Mind, front
cover
Human and horse hair, brass
shaving, paper pulp, and
organic material
20. × 16. in.
University of New Mexico
University Libraries, Center
for Southwest Research and
Special Collections

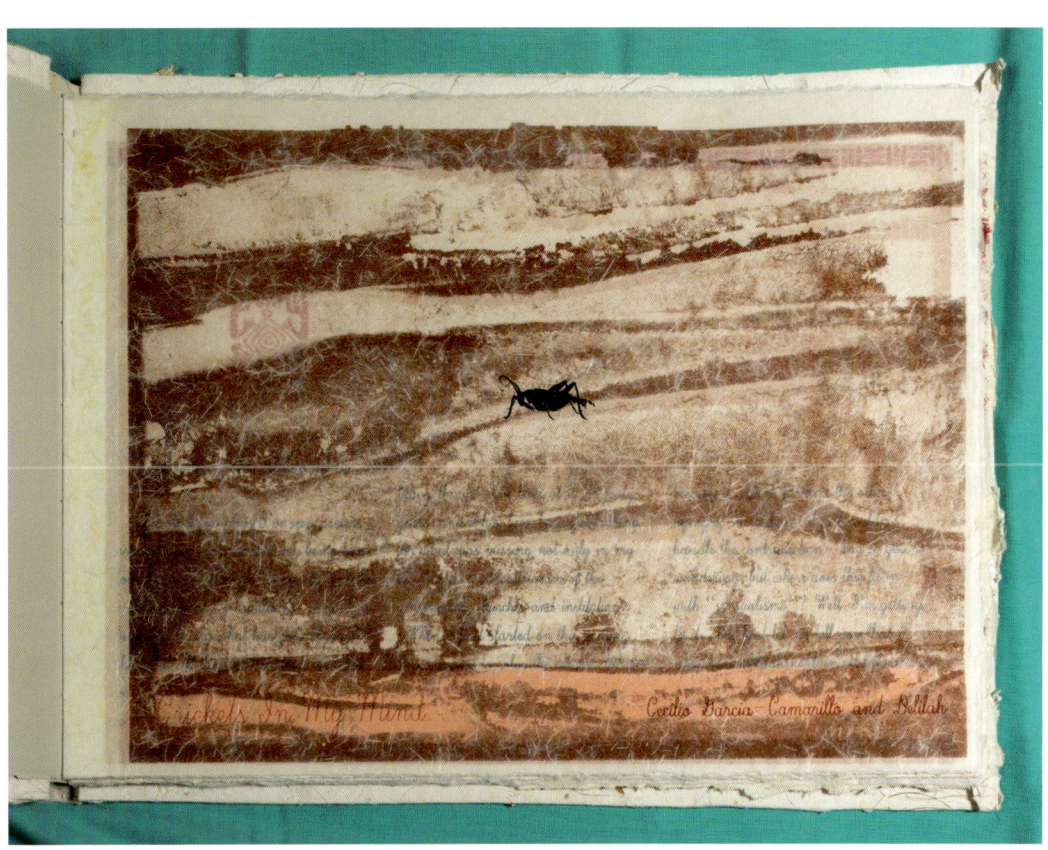

Crickets In My Mind   Cecilio Garcia-Camarillo and Delilah

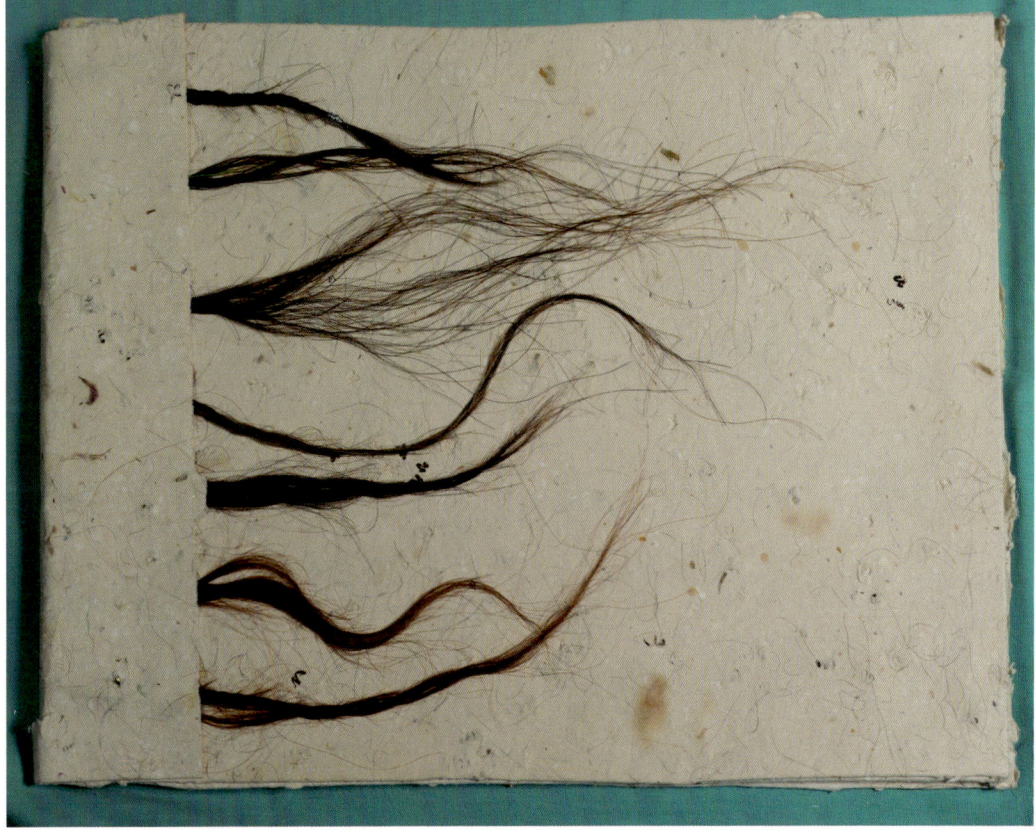

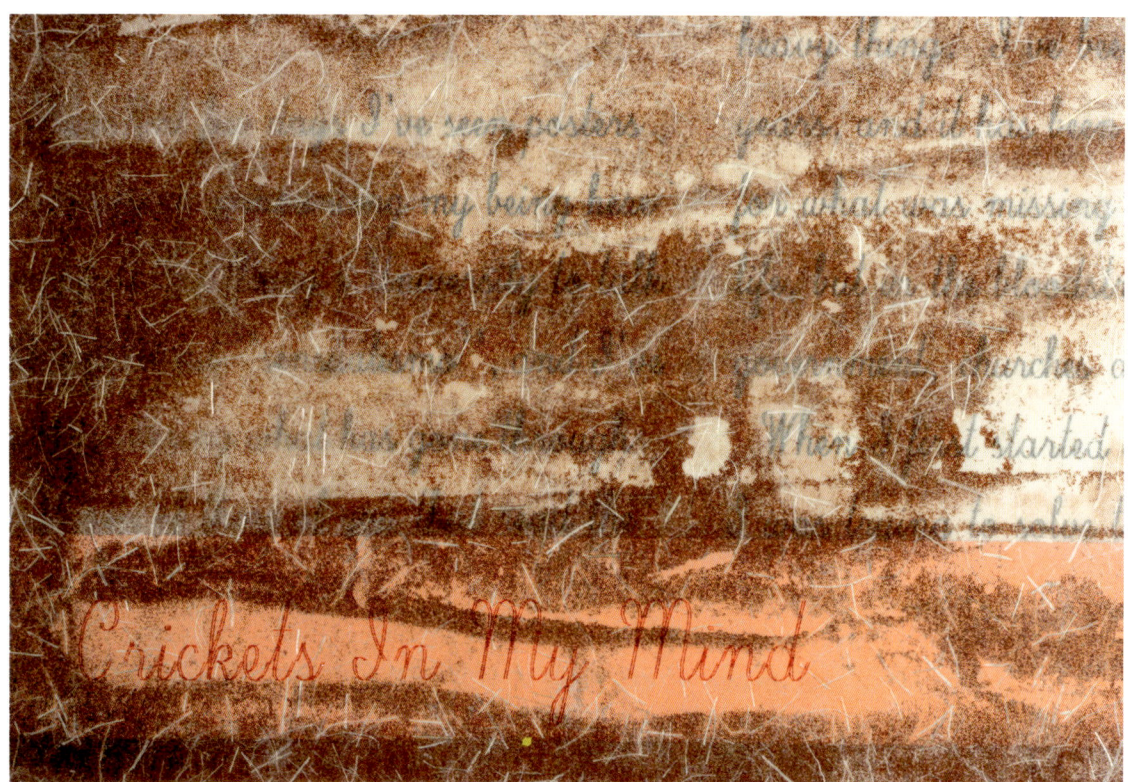

Crickets In My Mind

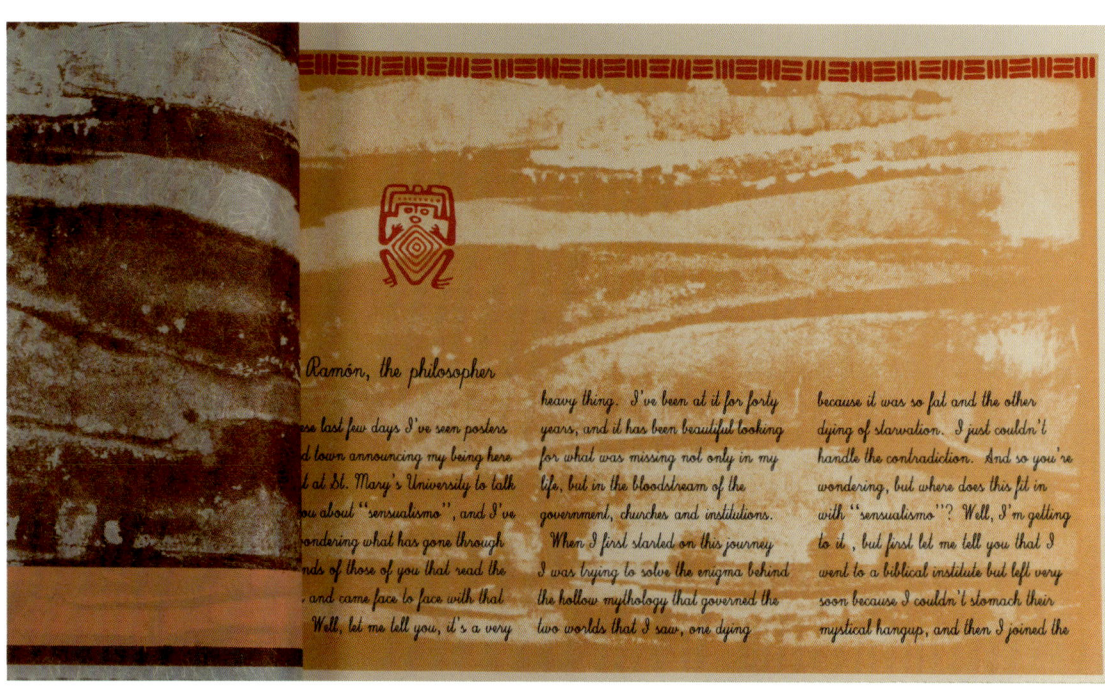

Ramón, the philosopher

...ese last few days I've seen posters ...d town announcing my being here ...t at St. Mary's University to talk ...ou about "sensualismo", and I've ...ondering what has gone through ...nds of those of you that read the ...and came face to face with that ...Well, let me tell you, it's a very heavy thing. I've been at it for forty years, and it has been beautiful looking for what was missing not only in my life, but in the bloodstream of the government, churches and institutions.

When I first started on this journey I was trying to solve the enigma behind the hollow mythology that governed the two worlds that I saw, one dying because it was so fat and the other dying of starvation. I just couldn't handle the contradiction. And so you're wondering, but where does this fit in with "sensualismo"? Well, I'm getting to it, but first let me tell you that I went to a biblical institute but left very soon because I couldn't stomach their mystical hangup, and then I joined the

(*opposite page, top*) Delilah Montoya and Cecilio García-Camarillo
Crickets In My Mind, page 6 detail
1992
Lithography and serigraphy on rice paper
20 × 14¾ in.
University of New Mexico University Libraries, Center for Southwest Research and Special Collections

(*opposite page, bottom*) Delilah Montoya and Cecilio García-Camarillo
Crickets in My Mind, page 6–7 detail
1992
Lithography and serigraphy on Fabriano and rice paper
20 × 14¾ in.
University of New Mexico University Libraries, Center for Southwest Research and Special Collections

(*above*) Delilah Montoya and Cecilio García-Camarillo
Crickets in My Mind, page 8 detail
1992
Lithography and serigraphy on Fabriano paper
20 × 14¾ in.
University of New Mexico University Libraries, Center for Southwest Research and Special Collections

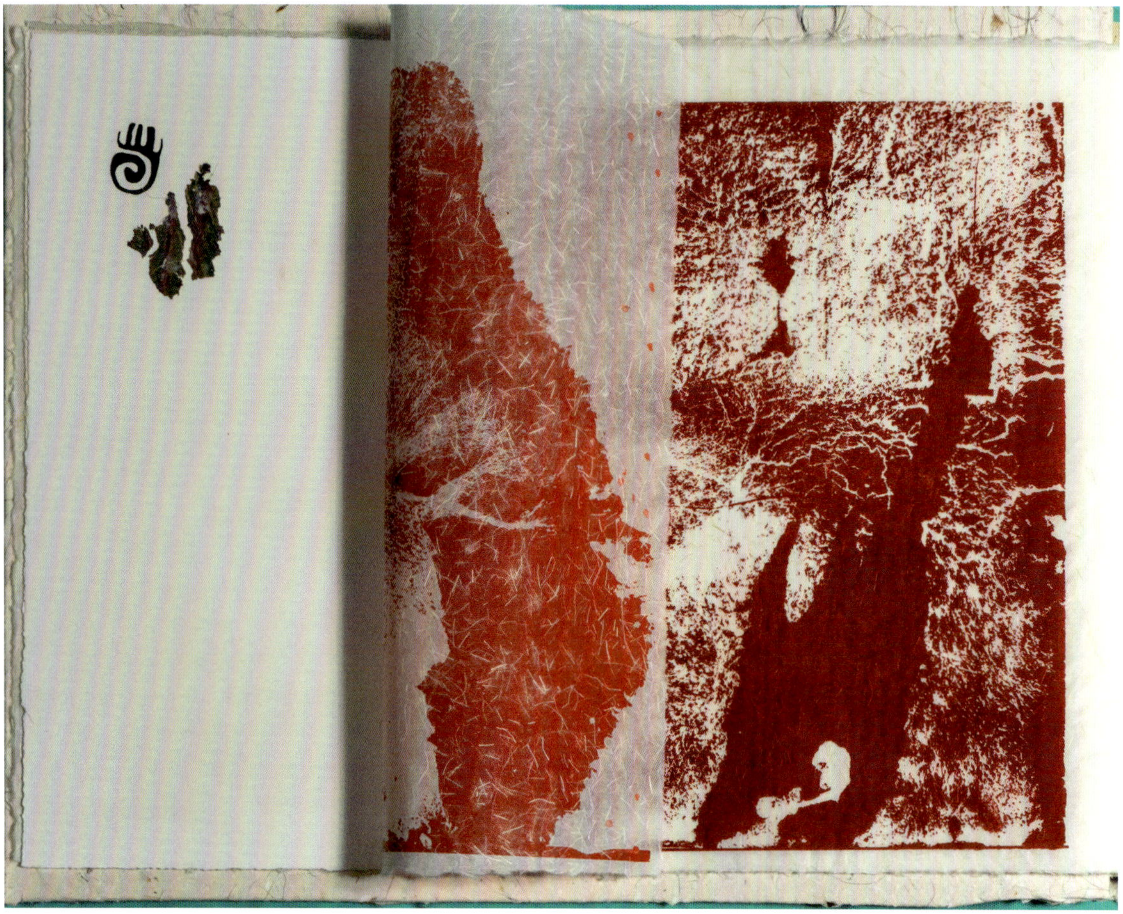

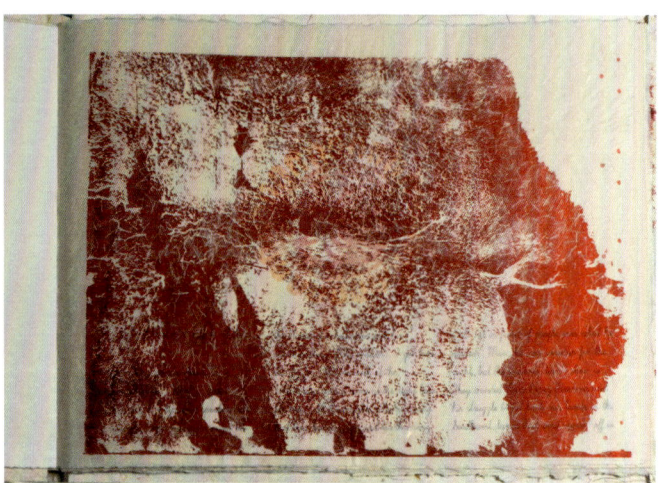

(*top*) Delilah Montoya and Cecilio García-Camarillo
Crickets in My Mind, page 10–12 detail
1992
Lithography on rice paper
20 × 14¾ in.
University of New Mexico University Libraries, Center for Southwest Research and Special Collections

(*bottom*) Delilah Montoya and Cecilio García-Camarillo
Crickets in My Mind, page 11
1992
Lithography and serigraphy on rice paper
20 × 14¾ in.
University of New Mexico University Libraries, Center for Southwest Research and Special Collections

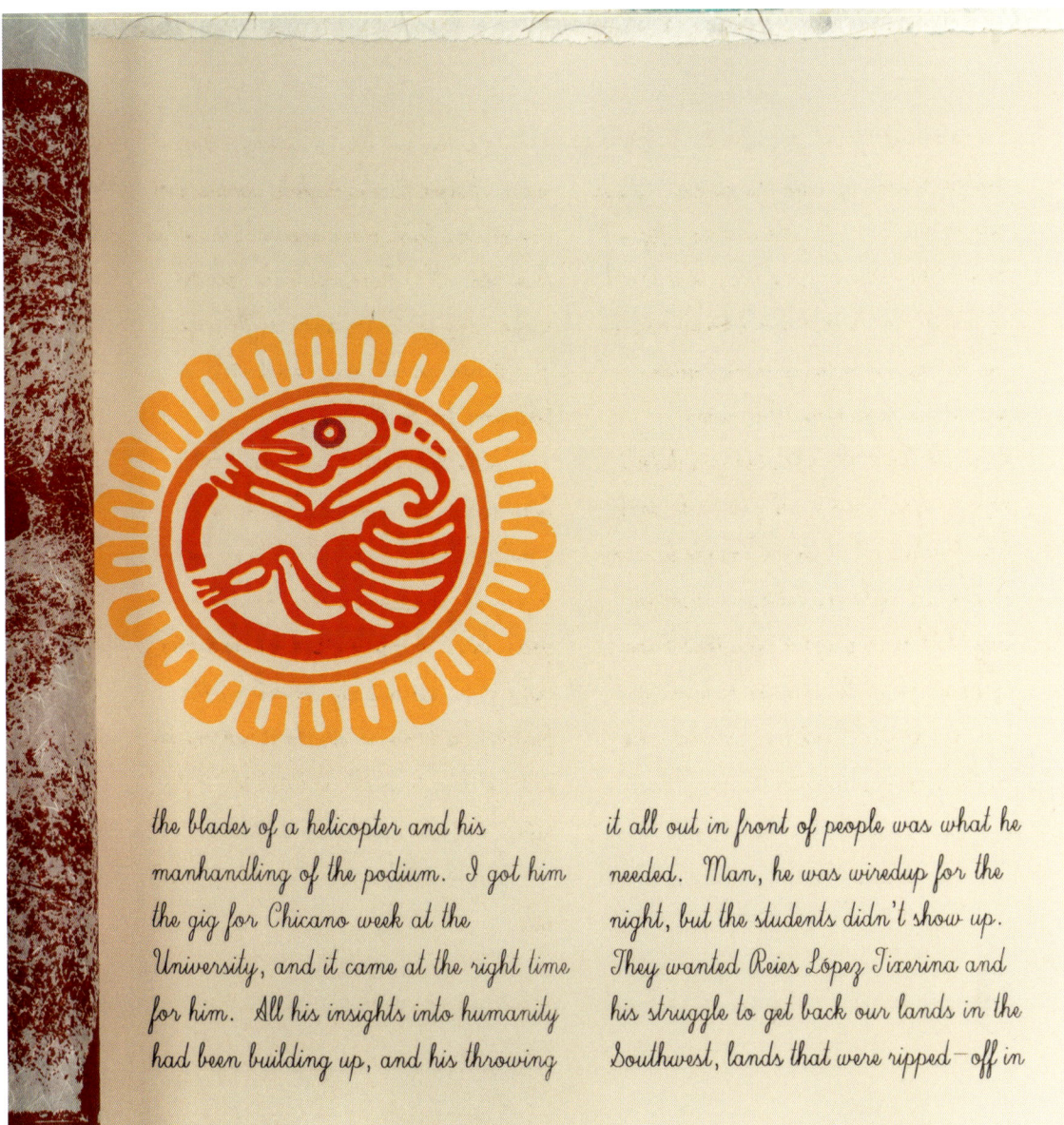

the blades of a helicopter and his manhandling of the podium. I got him the gig for Chicano week at the University, and it came at the right time for him. All his insights into humanity had been building up, and his throwing it all out in front of people was what he needed. Man, he was wiredup for the night, but the students didn't show up. They wanted Reies López Tixerina and his struggle to get back our lands in the Southwest, lands that were ripped-off in

Delilah Montoya and Cecilio García-Camarillo
Crickets in My Mind, page 12–13 detail
1992
Lithography and serigraphy on Fabriano paper
20 × 14¾ in.
University of New Mexico University Libraries, Center for Southwest Research and Special Collections

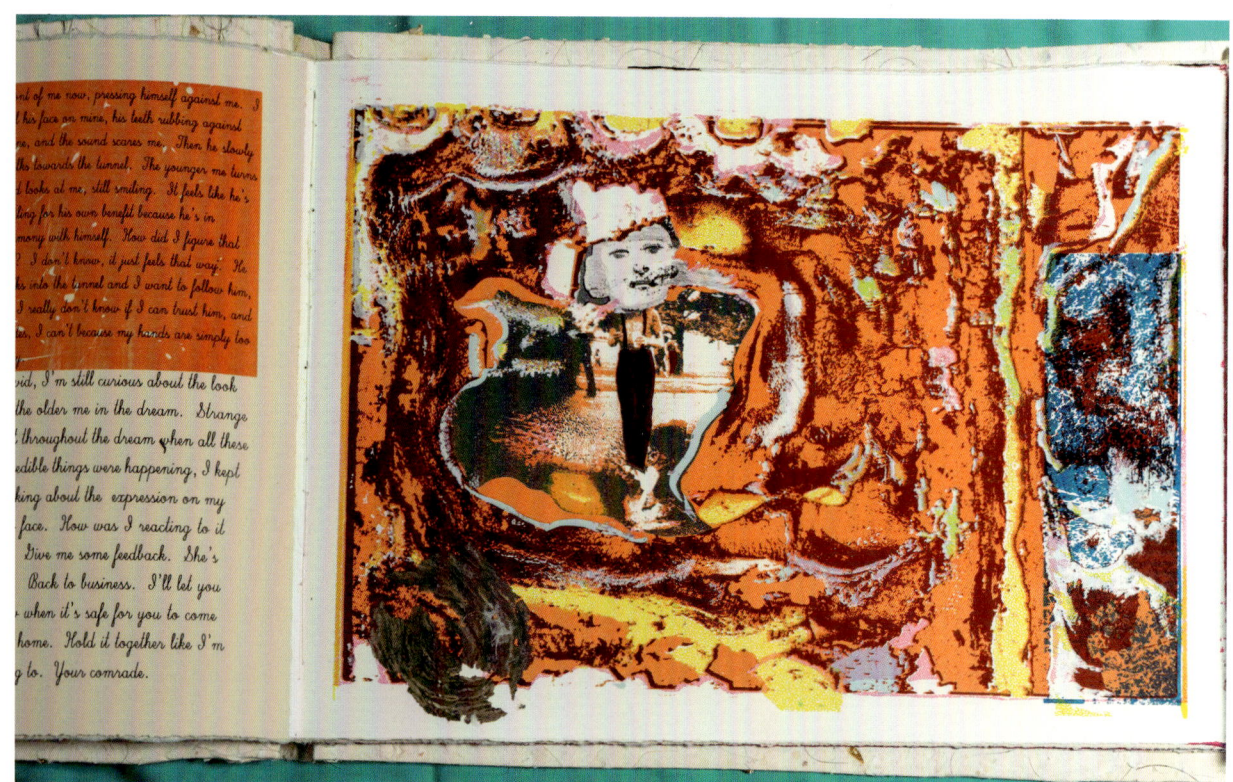

...nt of me now, pressing himself against me. I
...t his face on mine, his teeth rubbing against
...me, and the sound scares me. Then he slowly
...s towards the tunnel. The younger me turns
...d looks at me, still smiling. It feels like he's
...ting for his own benefit because he's in
...mony with himself. How did I figure that
...? I don't know, it just feels that way". He
...s into the tunnel and I want to follow him,
...I really don't know if I can trust him, and
...es, I can't because my hands are simply too

...vid, I'm still curious about the look
...the older me in the dream. Strange
...t throughout the dream when all these
...edible things were happening, I kept
...king about the expression on my
...face. How was I reacting to it.
...Give me some feedback. She's
...Back to business. I'll let you
...when it's safe for you to come
...home. Hold it together like I'm
...g to. Your comrade.

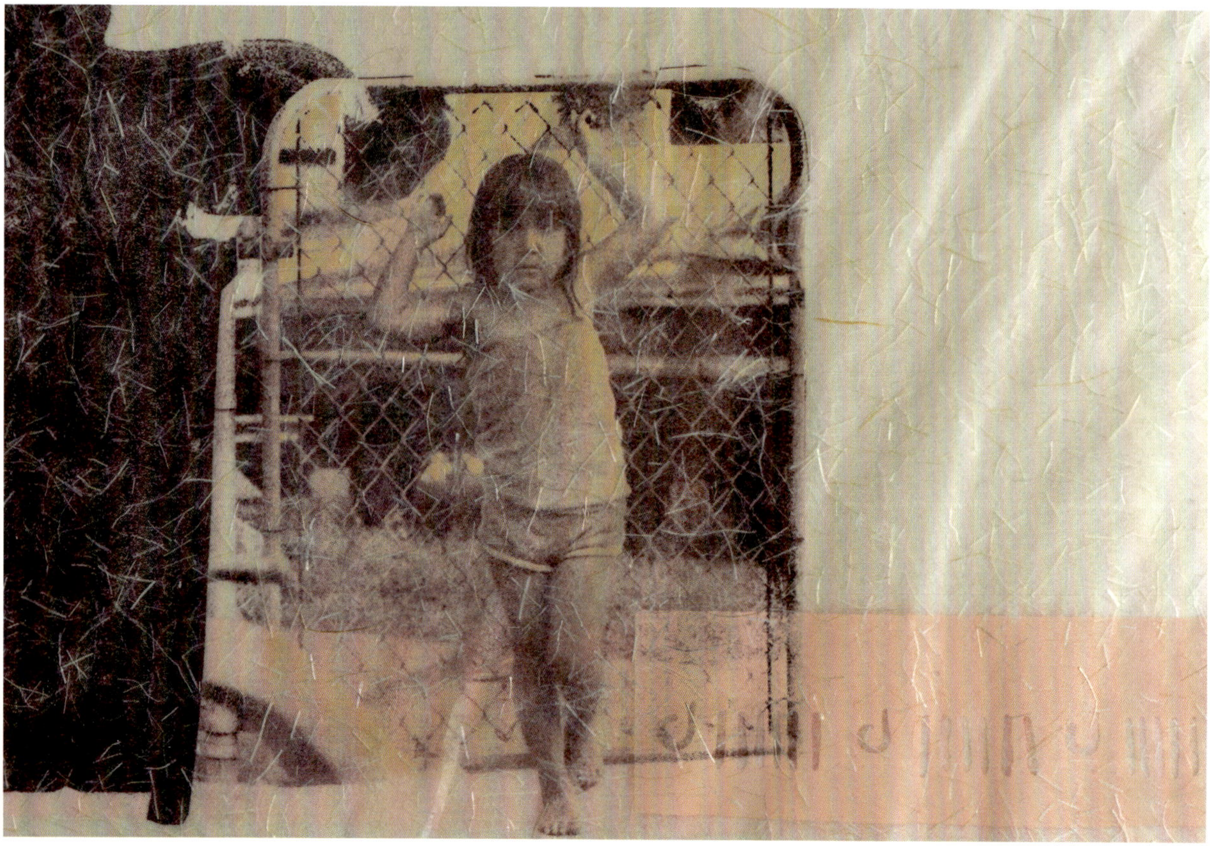

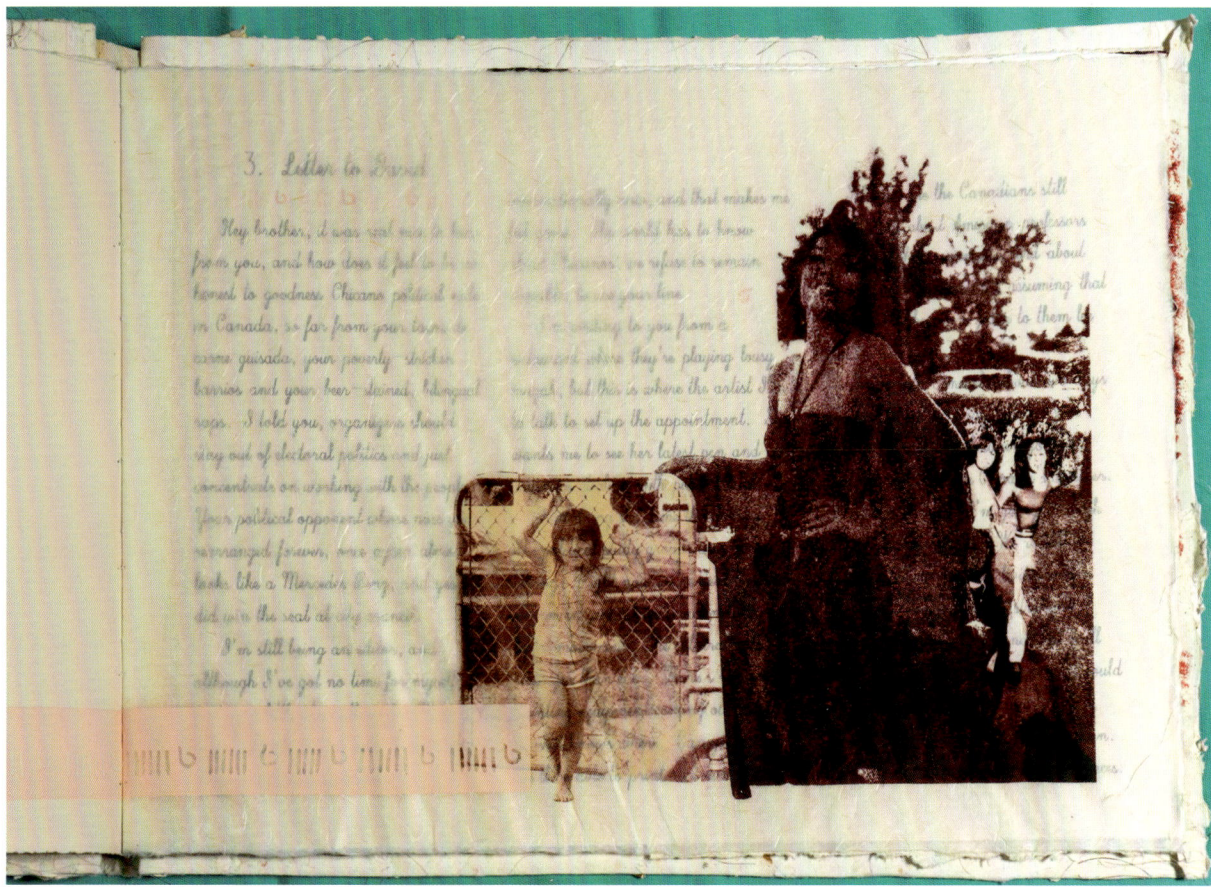

(*opposite page, top*) Delilah Montoya and Cecilio García-Camarillo
Crickets In My Mind, page 21 (from the series *Inca Street*)
1992
Lithography and serigraphy on Arches Hot Press
20 × 14¾ in.
University of New Mexico University Libraries, Center for Southwest Research and Special Collections

(*opposite page, bottom*) Delilah Montoya and Cecilio García-Camarillo
Crickets In My Mind, page 18, detail (from the series *Inca Street*)
1992
Lithography and serigraphy on rice paper
20 × 14¾ in.
University of New Mexico University Libraries, Center for Southwest Research and Special Collections

(*above*) Delilah Montoya and Cecilio García-Camarillo
Crickets In My Mind, page 17 (from the series *Inca Street*)
1992
Lithography and serigraphy on rice paper
20 × 14¾ in.
University of New Mexico University Libraries, Center for Southwest Research and Special Collections

This is the same cruddy situation I grew up in. Igualita. Chingao, and I always dreamed of something different. Harmony, me entiendes? Yeah, I know "The past repeats itself".

I want to share a dream I had last night. Ramón Tijerina, the old barrio philosopher, gave a talk a few nights ago. He blew up the few people that showed up with his "sensualismo" bombs. You've heard it all, I'm sure. Well, he was in the dream, and so was an old hitch-hiker I picked up yesterday. And how could I forget my old, alcoholic Papá, the main man in my life that I hardly know cause he was never around. Let's see if it's Freudian enough for you.

I'm walking up a staircase, feeling a little nervous, and my hands are very tired. At the top is a door. Everything's so silent. The door opens and a boy smiles at me. After a while I realize that it's me, with the same haircut and my favorite checkered shirt of middle school years. I try to figure out the smile on the younger me. It's not diabolical or frightened, but more like a smile apart. But what starts worrying me is that I can't figure out how I'm reacting to the presence of the younger me. Damn it, what's the expression on my face. The younger me keeps smiling. I want to touch him, but my hands weigh so much. The younger me moves aside and I walk into a large room with dim lights. On one side there's a tunnel and on the other a huge wall that seems to be made of gelatin. The younger me is now behind the gelatin. His smiling head has detached from its body and floats through the gelatin and comes at me. Now it's Ramón Tijerina smiling his smile of knowledge. Then it's the old hitch-hiker with his smile of pain. Then it becomes Papá drunk out of his mind. His eyes are bloodshot and half-closed. Saliva rolls down the absurd smile. Now the body of the younger me walks through the gelatin wall and connects with the head. The younger me smiles at me once again. He's in front of me now, pressing himself against me. I feel his face on mine, his teeth rubbing against mine, and the sound scares me. Then he slowly walks towards the tunnel. The younger me turns and looks at me, still smiling. It feels like he's smiling for his own benefit because he's in harmony with himself. How did I figure that out? I don't know, it just feels that way. He walks into the tunnel and I want to follow him, but I really don't know if I can trust him, and besides, I can't because my hands are simply too heavy.

David, I'm still curious about the look on the older me in the dream. Strange that throughout the dream when all these incredible things were happening, I kept thinking about the expression on my own face. How was I reacting to it all? Give me some feedback. She's here. Back to business. I'll let you know when it's safe for you to come back home. Hold it together like I'm trying to. Your comrade.

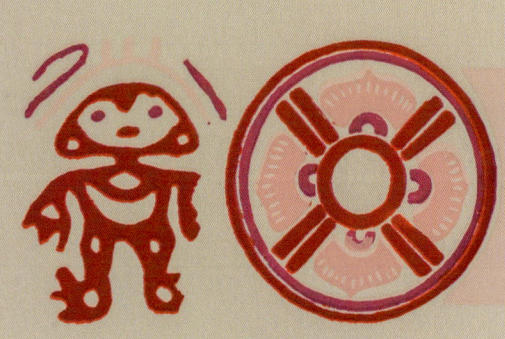

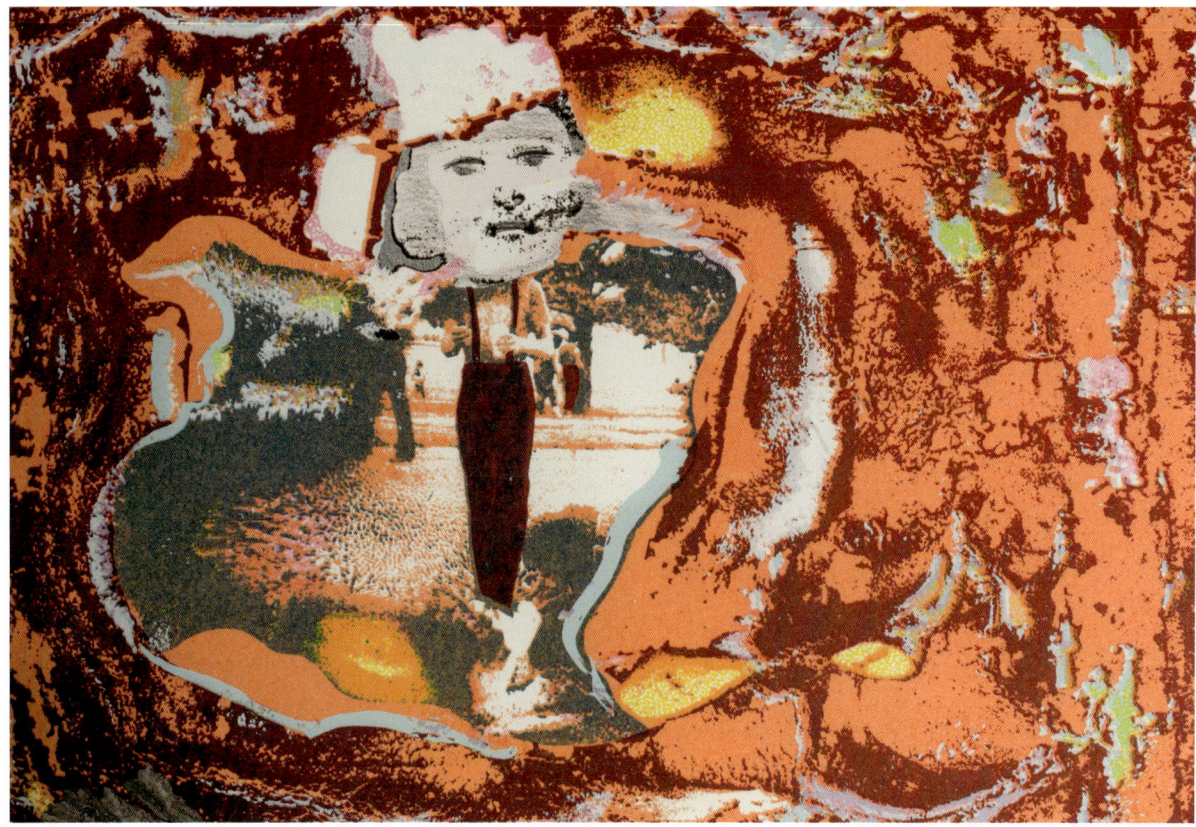

(*opposite page, top*) Delilah Montoya and Cecilio García-Camarillo
Crickets in My Mind, page 20
1992
Lithography and serigraphy on Fabriano paper
20 × 14¾ in.
University of New Mexico University Libraries, Center for Southwest Research and Special Collections

(*opposite page, bottom*) Delilah Montoya and Cecilio García-Camarillo
Crickets in My Mind, page 16 detail
1992
Lithography and serigraphy on Fabriano paper
20 × 14¾ in.
University of New Mexico University Libraries, Center for Southwest Research and Special Collections

(*above*) Delilah Montoya and Cecilio García-Camarillo
Crickets in My Mind, page 21
1992
Lithography and serigraphy on Arches Hot Press
20 × 14¾ in.
University of New Mexico University Libraries, Center for Southwest Research and Special Collections

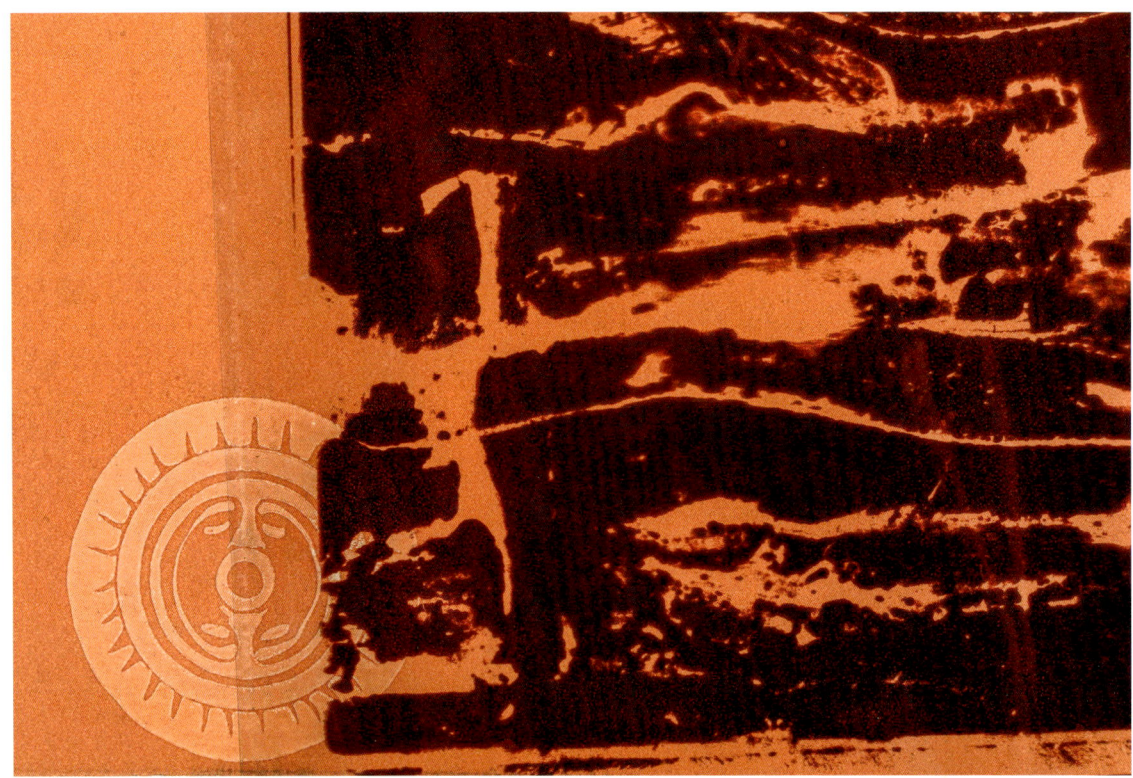

(*top*) Delilah Montoya and Cecilio García-Camarillo
Crickets in My Mind, page 28, 30 detail
1992
Lithography and serigraphy on Arches Hot Press and
mylar
20 × 14¾ in.
University of New Mexico University Libraries, Center
for Southwest Research and Special Collections

(*bottom*) Delilah Montoya and Cecilio García-Camarillo
Crickets in My Mind, page 28 detail
1992
Lithography and serigraphy on Arches Hot Press
20 × 14¾ in.
University of New Mexico University Libraries, Center
for Southwest Research and Special Collections

(*opposite page*) Delilah Montoya and
Cecilio García-Camarillo
Crickets in My Mind, page 29 detail
1992
Lithography on mylar
20 × 14¾ in.
University of New Mexico University
Libraries, Center for Southwest Research
and Special Collections

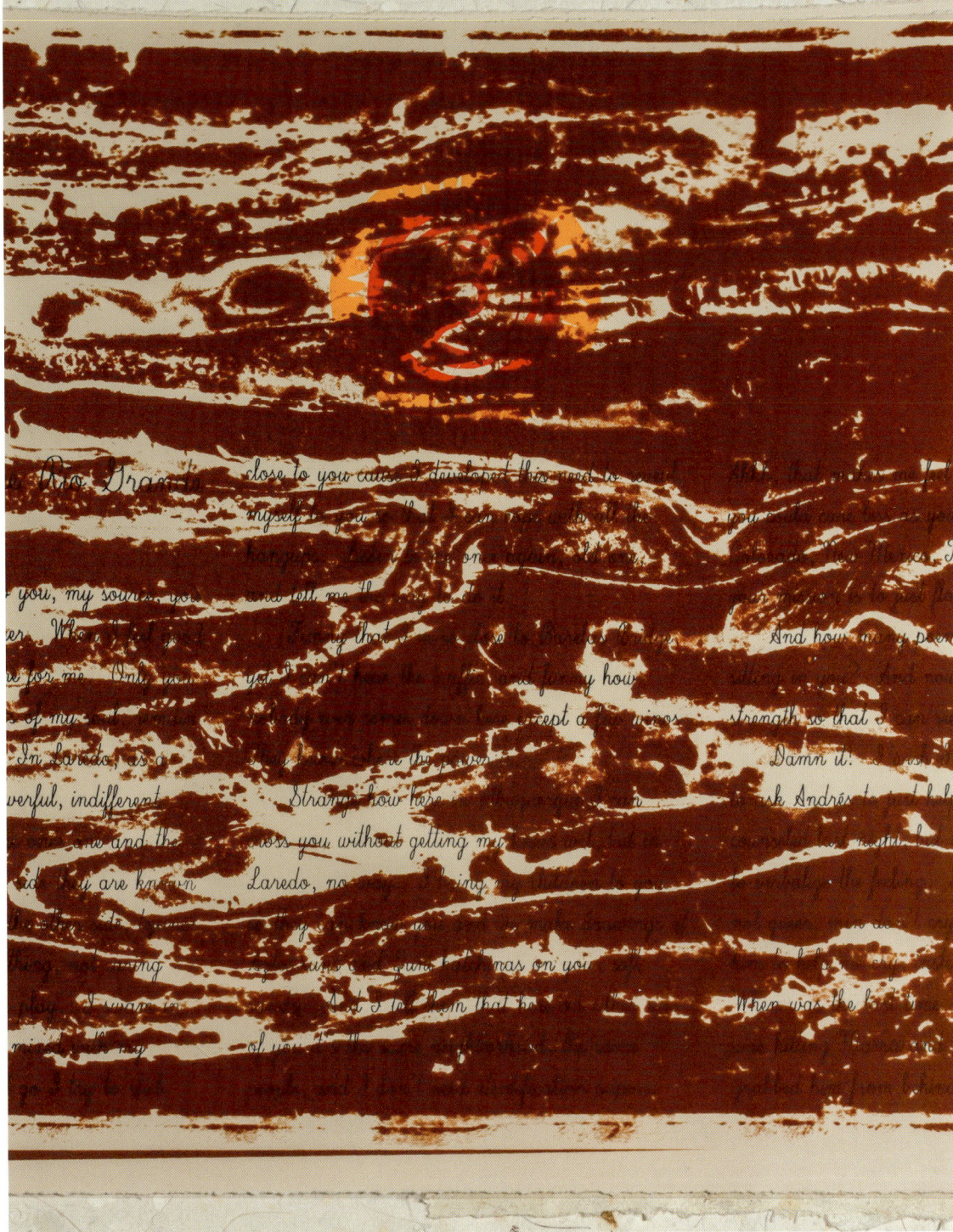

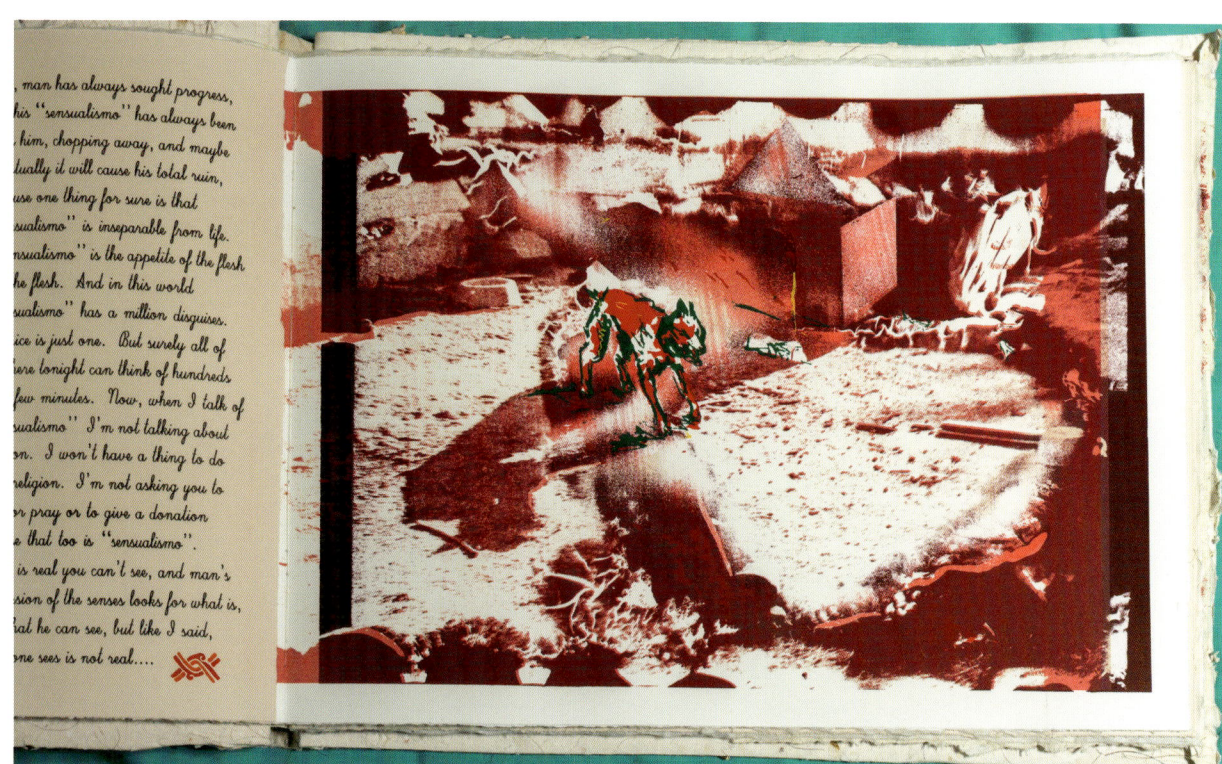

, man has always sought progress,
his "sensualismo" has always been
him, chopping away, and maybe
dually it will cause his total ruin,
use one thing for sure is that
sualismo" is inseparable from life.
ensualismo" is the appetite of the flesh
he flesh. And in this world
sualismo" has a million disguises.
ice is just one. But surely all of
ere tonight can think of hundreds
few minutes. Now, when I talk of
sualismo" I'm not talking about
on. I won't have a thing to do
religion. I'm not asking you to
r pray or to give a donation
e that too is "sensualismo".
is real you can't see, and man's
sion of the senses looks for what is,
at he can see, but like I said,
ne sees is not real....

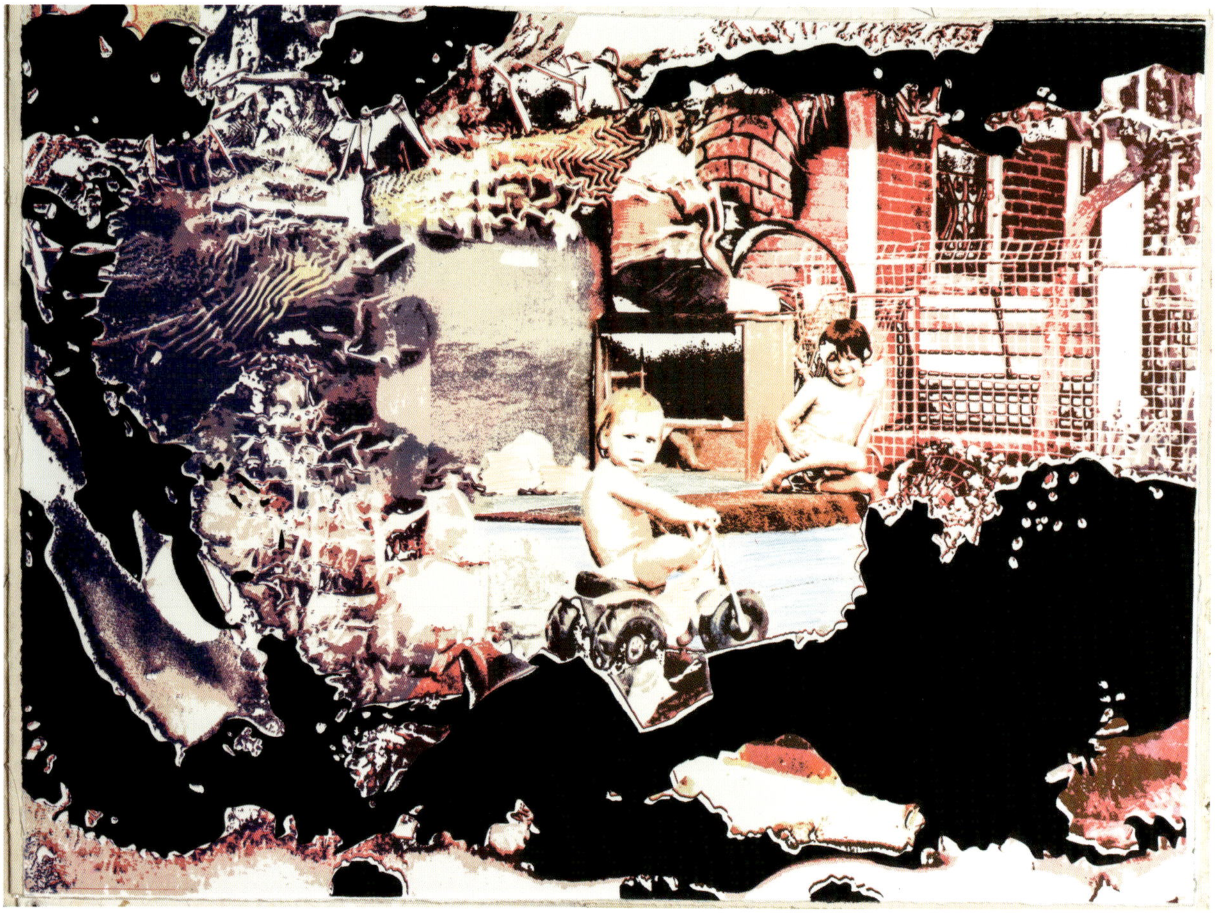

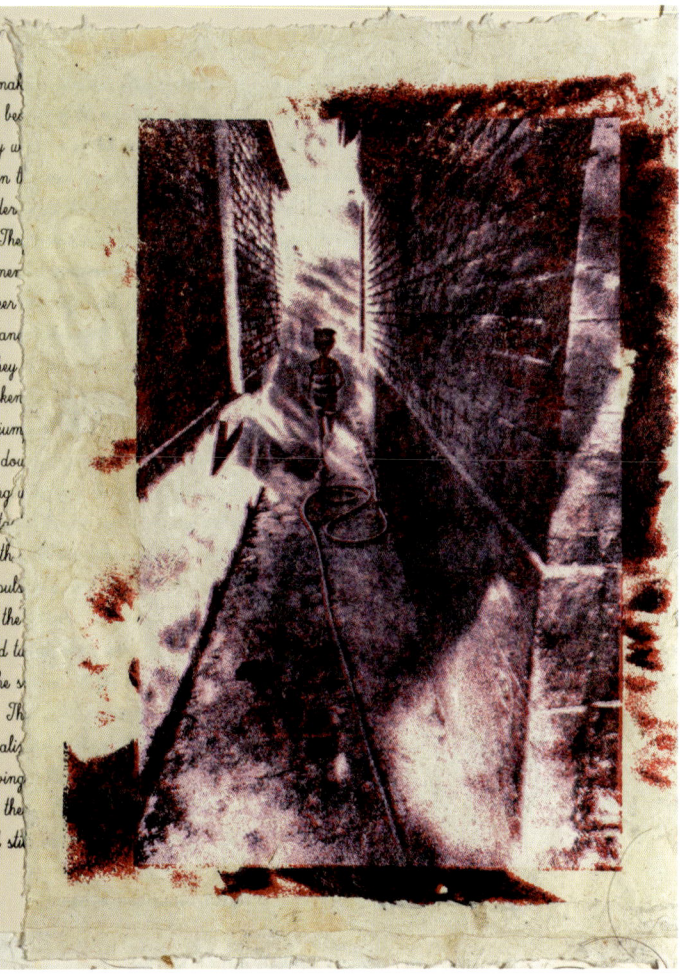

(*opposite page, top*) Delilah Montoya and Cecilio García-Camarillo
Crickets In My Mind, page 9 (from the series *Inca Street*)
1992
Lithography and serigraphy on Arches Hot Press
20 × 14¾ in.
University of New Mexico University Libraries, Center for Southwest Research and Special Collections

(*opposite page, bottom*) Delilah Montoya and Cecilio García-Camarillo
Crickets In My Mind, page 27 (from the series *Inca Street*)
1992
Lithography and serigraphy on Arches Hot Press
20 × 14¾ in.
University of New Mexico University Libraries, Center for Southwest Research and Special Collections

(*above*) Delilah Montoya and Cecilio García-Camarillo
Crickets In My Mind, pages 33 and 36, *Boy Running* (from the series *Inca Street*)
1992
Lithography on amate and Fabriano
32¾ × 15¾ in.
University of New Mexico University Libraries, Center for Southwest Research and Special Collections

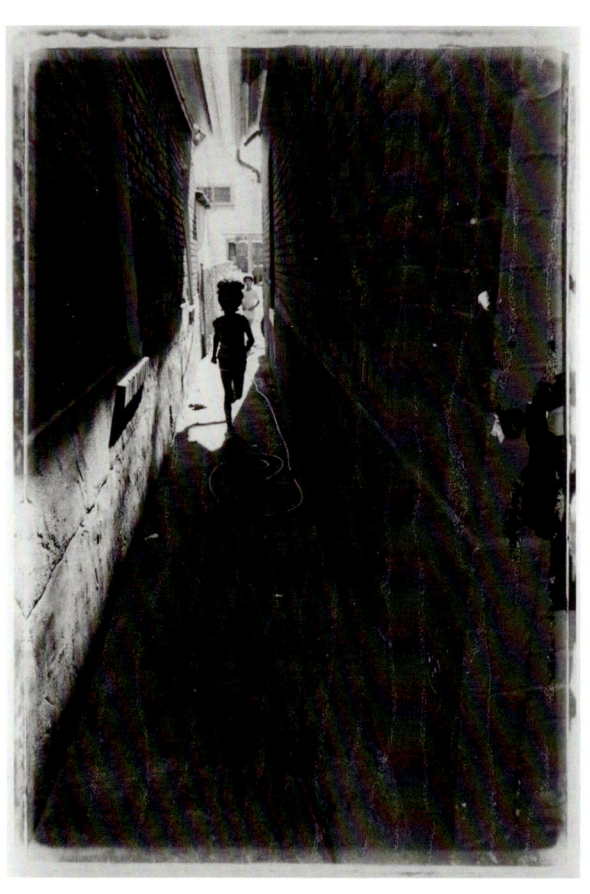

(*left*) Boy Running (from the series Inca Street)
1978, print date 1982
Silver gelatin print
16 × 20 in.
Collection of the artist

(*bottom*) Delilah Montoya and Cecilio García-Camarillo
Crickets In My Mind, page 37
1992
Paper pulp, hair, organic material, string, arrowhead, and wasp paper
20 × 14¾ in.
University of New Mexico University Libraries, Center for Southwest Research and Special Collections

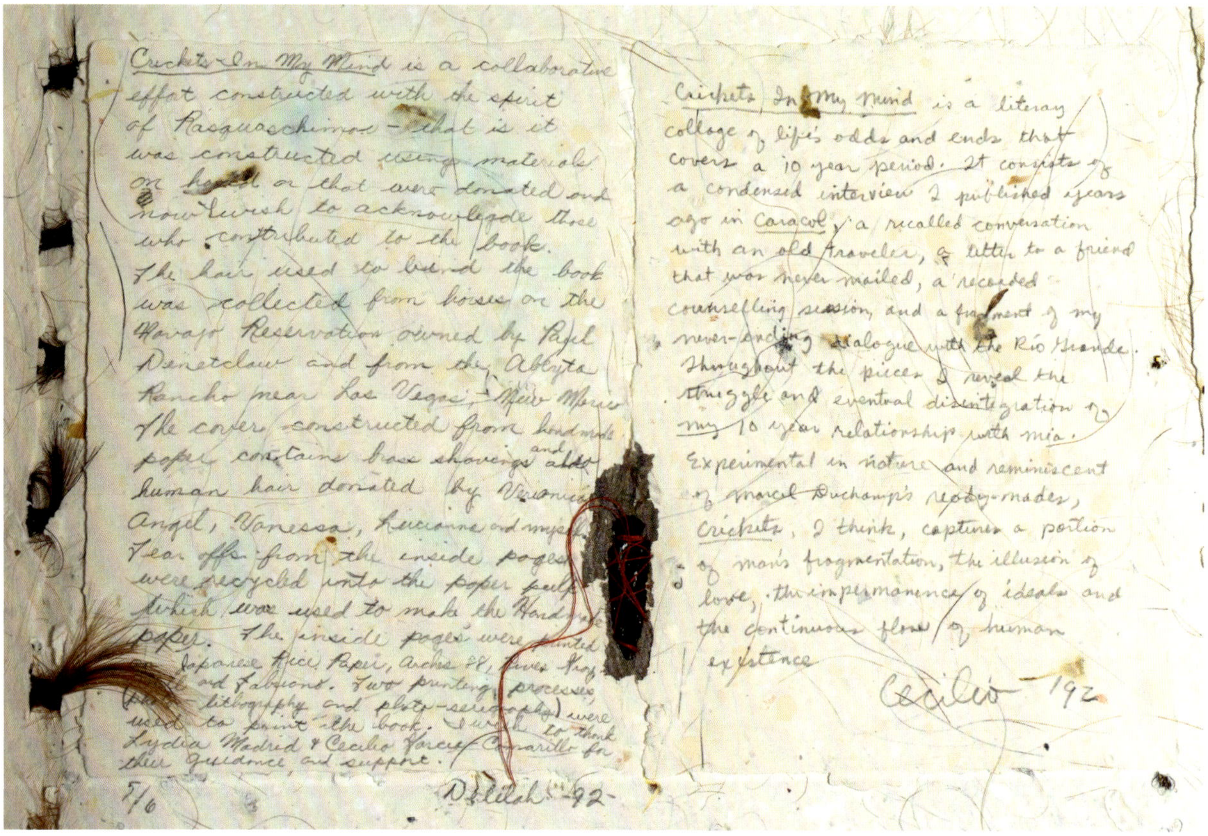

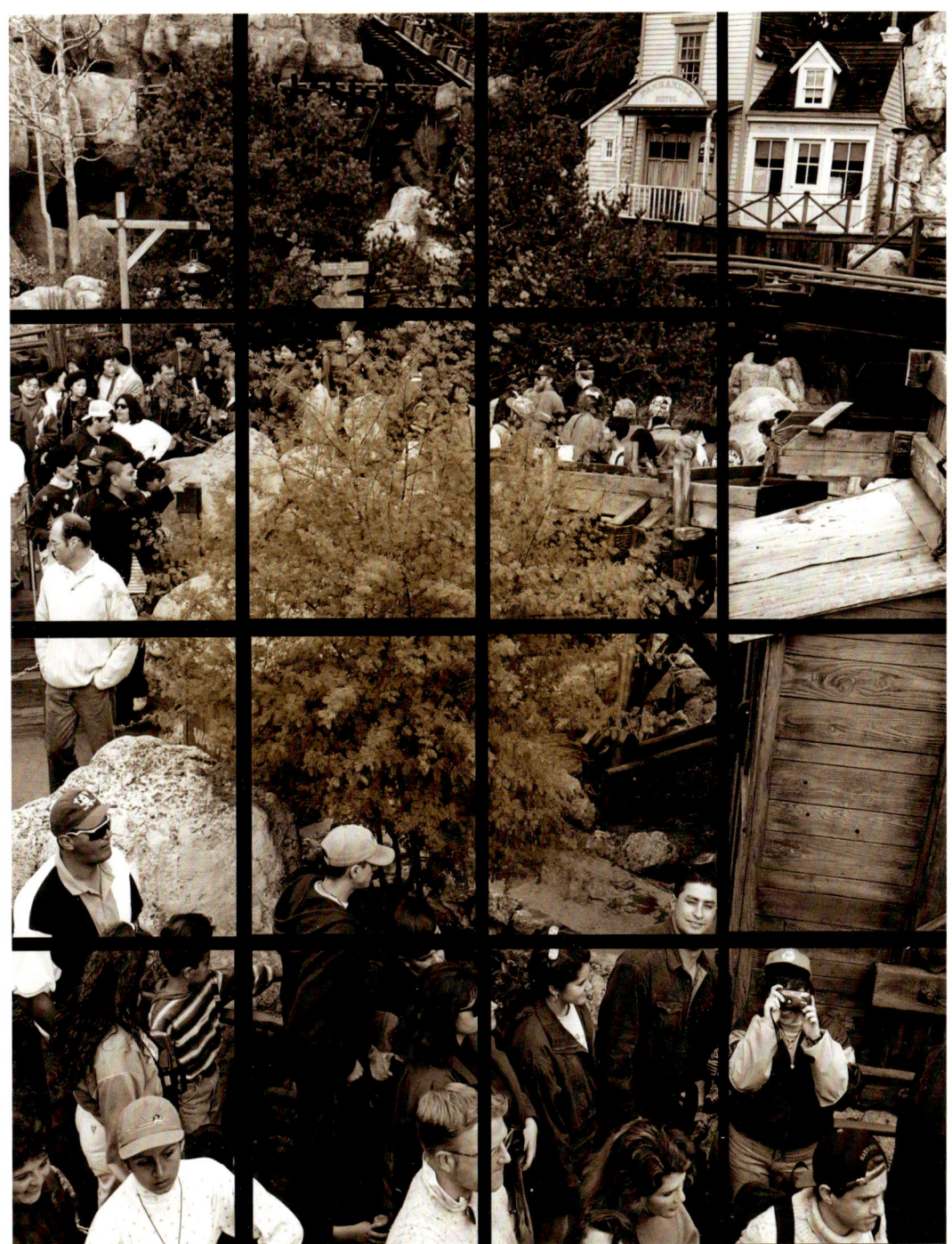

Delilah Montoya
Thunder Mountain (from the series
Shooting the Tourist)
1995
Photomural
96 × 80 in.
Collection of the Mexican Museum,
 San Francisco

In July of 1994, Montoya received a letter from curator and art historian Chon Noriega inviting her to participate in *From the West: Chicano Narrative Photography*, which opened at the Mexican Museum in San Francisco and traveled to other venues. The exhibition included six photographers, each commissioned to develop a narrative series. Noriega elaborates that the West is prominent in many art forms, from the visual arts to film and literature. Still, the act of looking west implies an Anglo perspective, an imaginary and a privileged way of looking. Noriega asks, "But what has the notion of the 'west' meant for Chicano artists in terms of ways of looking?" The exhibition sought to interrogate the history of the West embedded in Chicano history, the history of photography, and the history of the colonial conquest of land and culture.

In her project proposal, Montoya provided a detailed description of the questions she wanted to explore. She turned her attention to the tourist, arguing that tourism has produced particular ways of picturing and seeing the other. Rather than seeking land or riches, the tourist is looking for authenticity, which is related to the myth of the vanishing Indian. The desire to consume and witness Indigenous culture is part of a mystique and an exoticized folklore of the West. Ironically, the so-called authentic engagement is filtered through a European or tourist lens, and therefore, authenticity itself is a fragmented notion. As Edward Said discussed in his seminal book *Orientalism*, the privileged view also reflects back an image to the communities being pictured, advancing another element in the process of colonization. Tourists collect and consume objects, photographs, culture, and foods but ultimately, these items lose their authenticity when taken out of context. According to Montoya, "The tourist believes their gaze goes undetected as though they are an invisible presence in the land and assume that this reflectiveness, searching for the self within the territories of the other cannot be perceived by the other. To contest these notions, I propose to document the tourists as they move through Aztlán, accumulating and peeking at the interiors of the West."

Montoya referenced Dean MacCannell's book, *The Tourist: A New Theory of the Leisure Class* to inform an organizing methodology that she used to frame a series of seven accordion fold postcard books and a photo mural she created from the photographs she took in New Mexico and California. The primary actions that defined tourism were collecting, staging, syncretizing, going native, looking, and preserving. In addition to postcard books, the installation included a photo mural, *Thunder Mountain*, and a series of photographs. As Montoya describes, "Around the turn of the twentieth century, photographic postcards were actually collotypes or lithographs printed to look like photographs. They were produced using printing presses despite the fact that there was a photographic negative. In *Shooting the Tourist*, Montoya's postcards are silver gelatin photographs made to look like printed postcards. Montoya says, "My interest was to mimic the expectations of the tourist industry, and it was the postcard that I believed was essential to that process."[5]

In the catalog for the exhibition, Chon Noriega describes how there are many Wests and that the concept itself is a construct. He describes Montoya's *Shooting the Tourist* as an interrogation of the history of photography

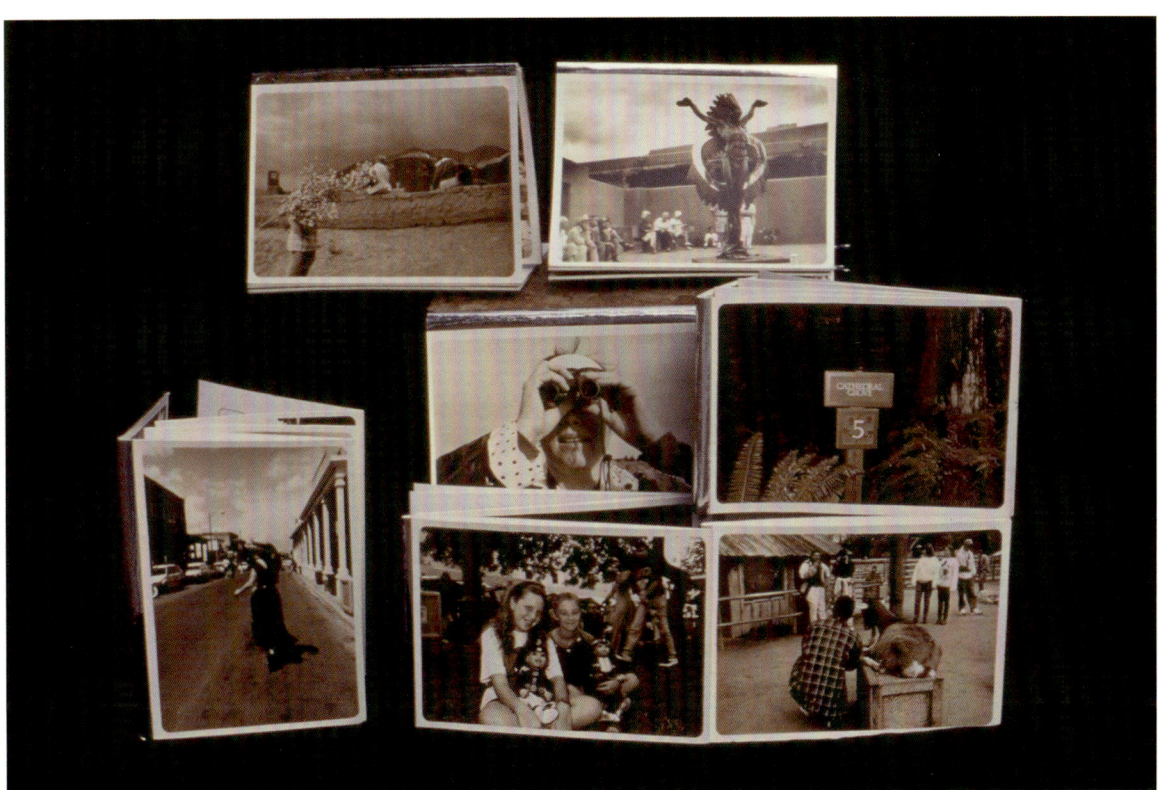

Delilah Montoya

From the West: Shooting the Tourist

Collection of seven accordion-fold postcards

1995

Sepia-toned silver gelatin print, amate paper, and foil

Collection of the artist

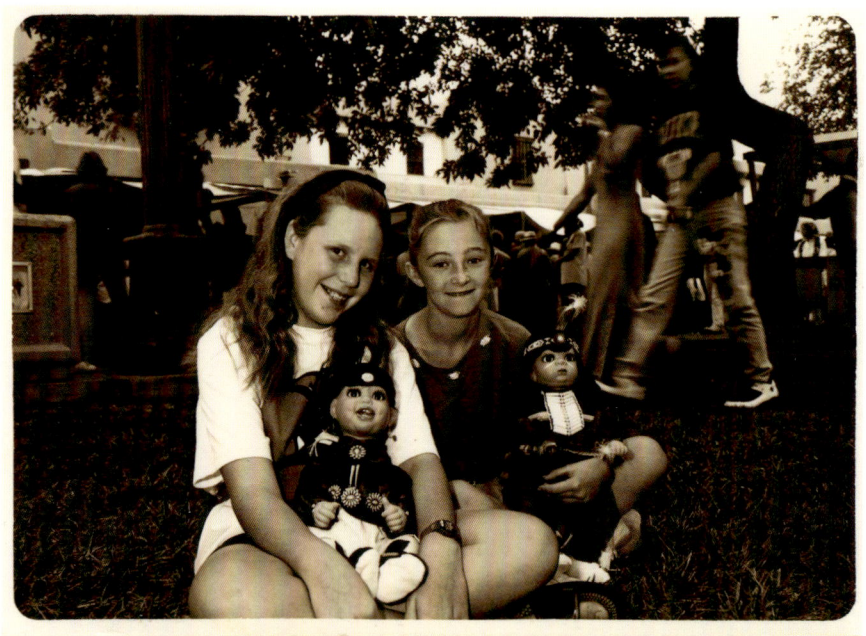

From the West: Shooting the Tourist

Tarjeta
Postal

Delilah Montoya
From the West: Shooting the Tourist: Imaging
(front/back details from the accordion-fold
postcard book)
1995
Sepia-toned silver gelatin print, amate paper, and
foil
4¼ × 36½ in.

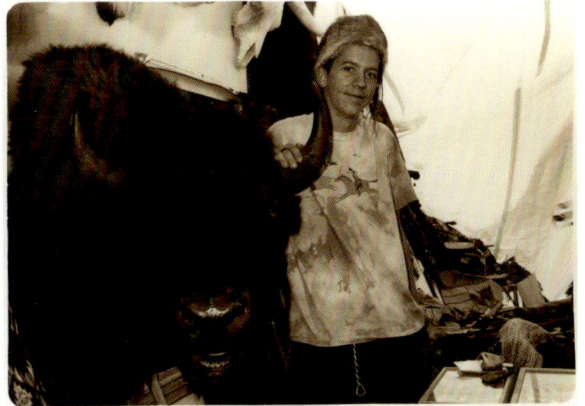

Imaging the last of its kind.
Santa Fe, NM

Tarjeta
Postal

From the West: Shooting the Tourist

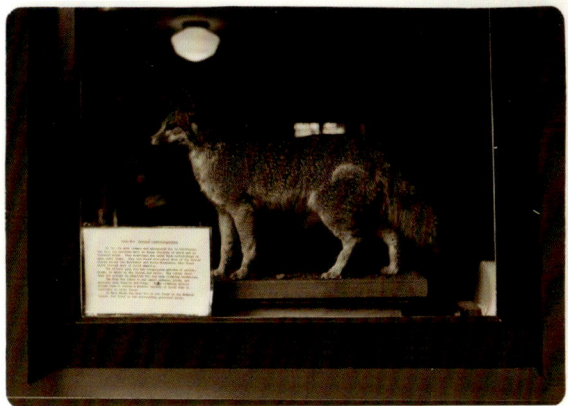

Imaging by placing an official boundary
around it. Muir Woods, CA

Tarjeta
Postal

From the West: Shooting the Tourist

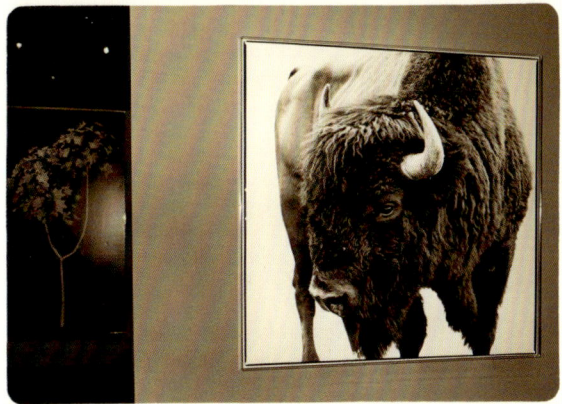

Imaging an authentic western
reconstruction. San Francisco, CA

Tarjeta
Postal

From the West: Shooting the Tourist

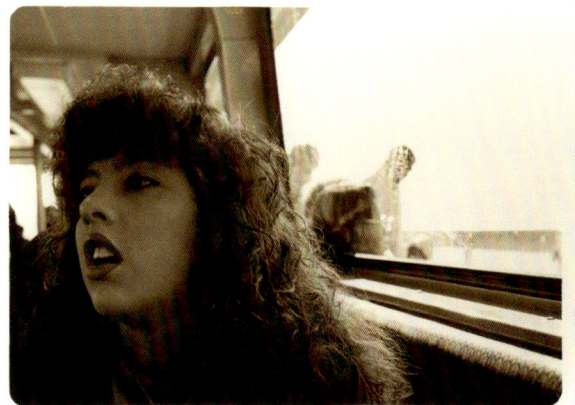

Imaging a world filled with people who know they are just passing through.   San Francisco, CA

From the West: Shooting the Tourist

© 1995 Photo by Delilah Montoya

Imaging an atmosphere of disinterest to convey objectivity. Alcatraz, CA

From the West: Shooting the Tourist

© 1995 Photo by Delilah Montoya

Tarjeta Postal

Tarjeta Postal

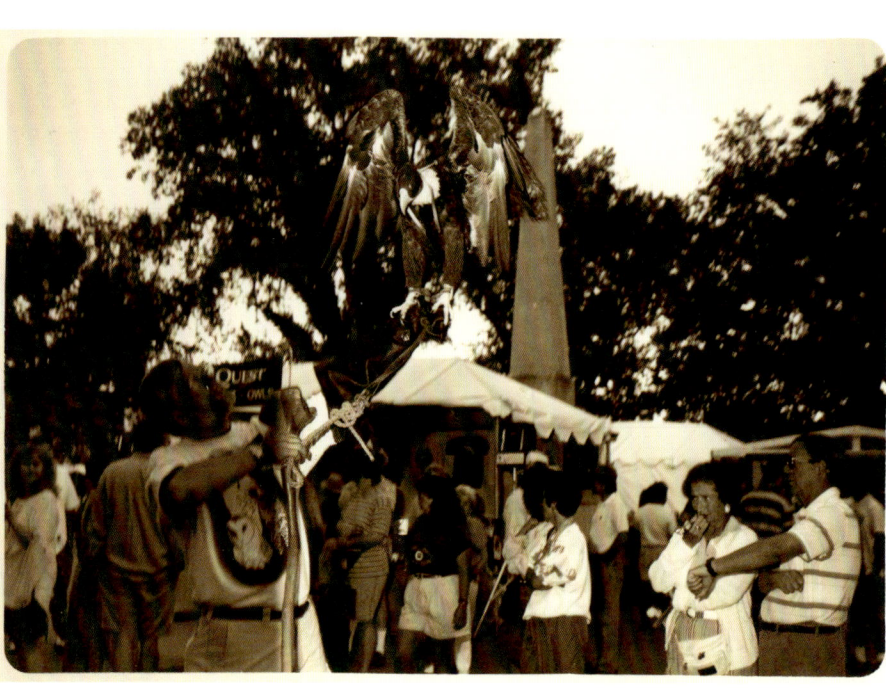

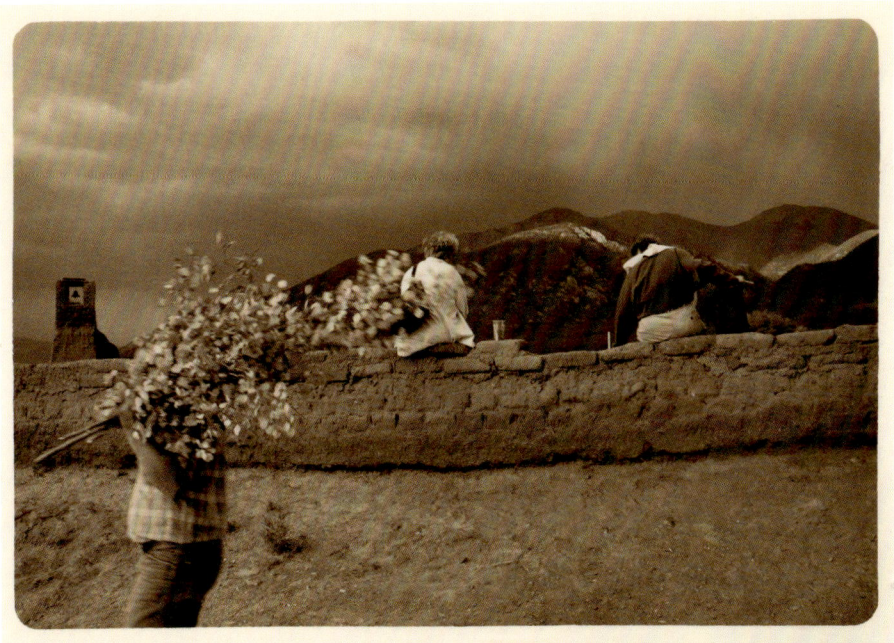

Collecting the souvenir to mark the experience.
Taos, NM

Tarjeta Postal

From the West: Shooting the Tourist

© 1995 Photo by Delilah Montoya

Delilah Montoya
From the West: Shooting the Tourist: Collecting
(front/back details from the accordion-fold postcard book)
1995
Sepia-toned silver gelatin print, amate paper, and foil
4¼ × 36½ in.
Collection of the artist

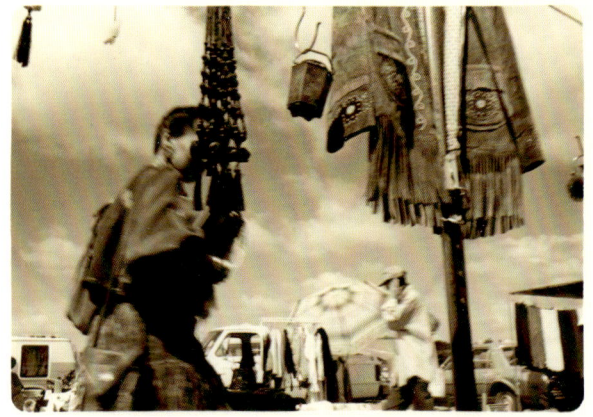

Collecting alternatives prompts the consumption of the *other's* object. Santa Fe, NM

From the West: Shooting the Tourist

Tarjeta Postal

© 1995 Photo by Delilah Montoya

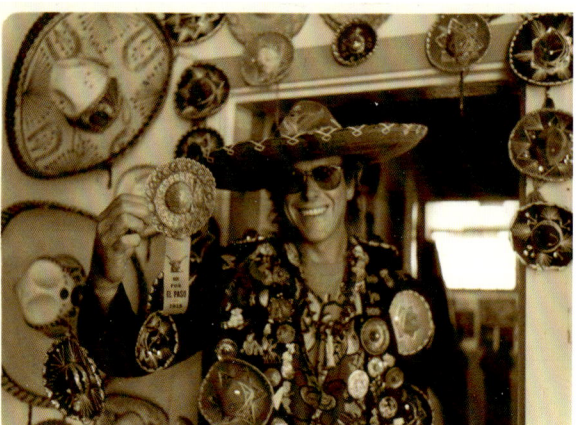

Collecting generates a communion with the object, not the culture. Santa Fe, NM

From the West: Shooting the Tourist

Tarjeta Postal

©1995 Photo by Delilah Montoya

Collecting an invented western symbol. Santa Fe, NM

From the West: Shooting the Tourist

Tarjeta Postal

© 1995 Photo by Delilah Montoya

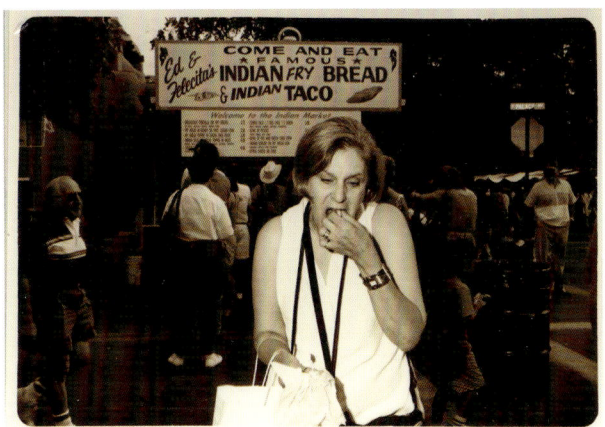

Collecting and consuming promised
experiences. Santa Fe, NM

From the West: Shooting the Tourist

© 1995 Photo by Delilah Montoya

Tarjeta
Postal

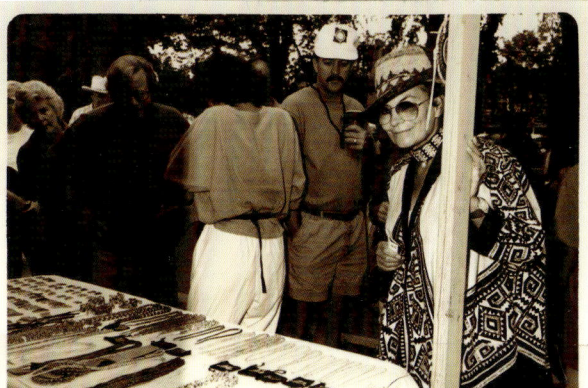

Collecting the fetish for reasons
beyond material needs.
Santa Fe, NM

From the West: Shooting the Tourist

© 1995 Photo by Delilah Montoya

Tarjeta
Postal

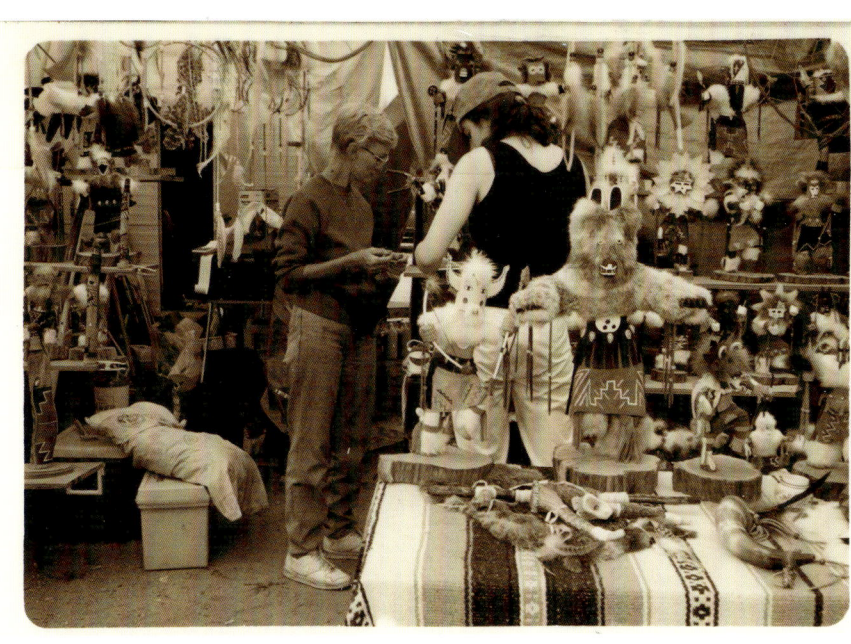

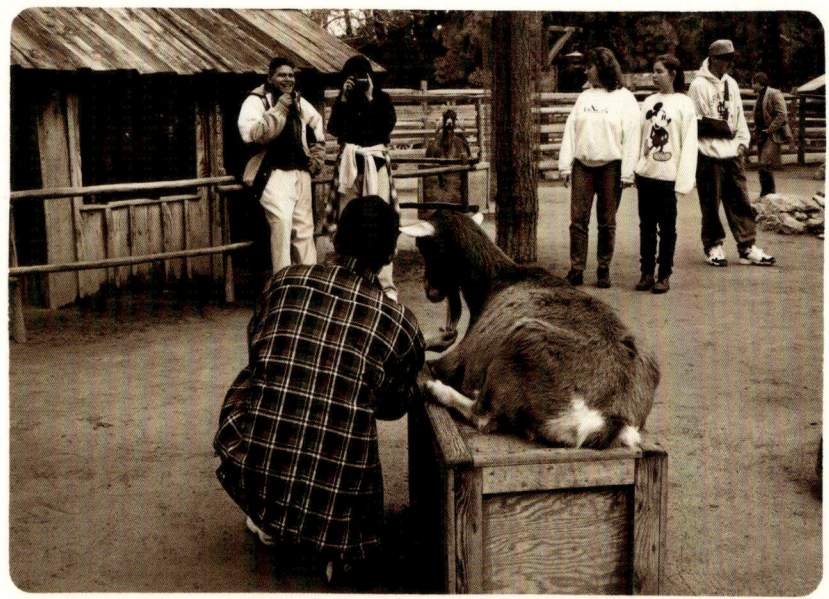

Staging a public *pseudo-event* for personal entertainment. Disneyland, CA

From the West: Shooting the Tourist

Tarjeta Postal

© 1995 Photo by Delilah Montoya

Delilah Montoya
From the West: Shooting the Tourist: Staging
(front/back details from the accordion-fold postcard book)
1995
Sepia-toned silver gelatin print, amate paper, and foil
4¼ × 36½ in.
Collection of the artist

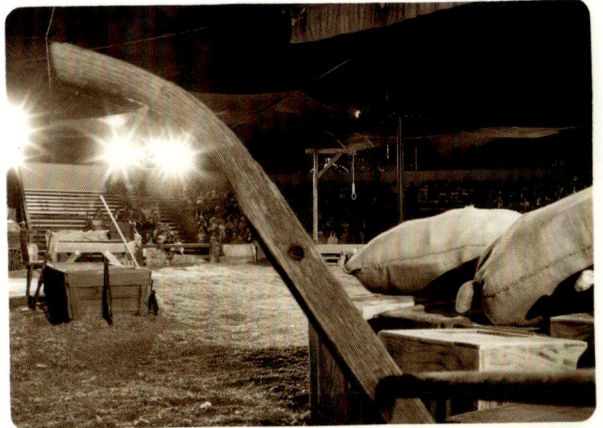

Staging a heightened reality, the staple motif of Wild West Tourism. Los Angeles, CA

Tarjeta Postal

From the West: Shooting the Tourist

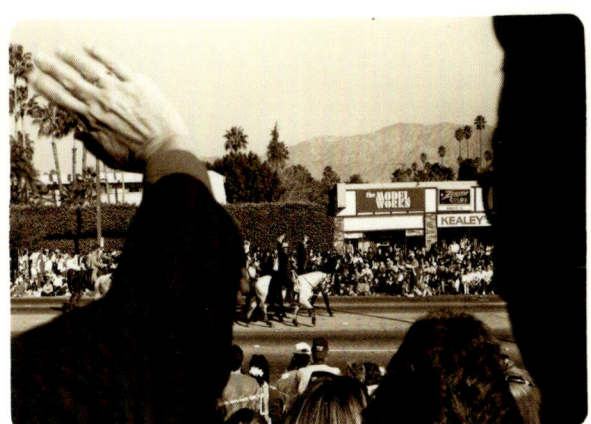

Staging a historical encounter provides a sense of unity. Pasadena, CA

Tarjeta Postal

From the West: Shooting the Tourist

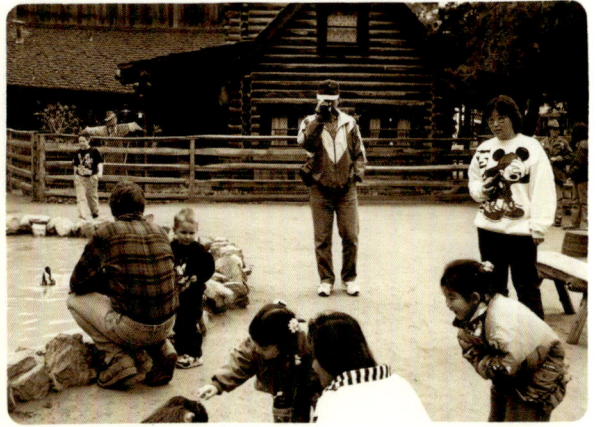

Staging the *Real Experience* with western props. Disneyland, CA

Tarjeta Postal

From the West: Shooting the Tourist

128

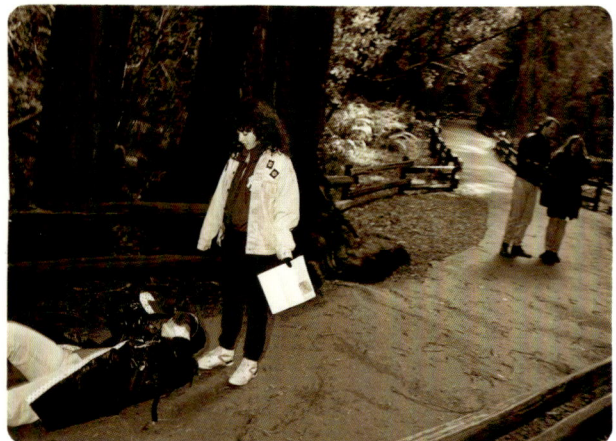

Staging inside the tourist attraction. Muir Woods, CA

From the West: Shooting the Tourist

© 1995 Photo by Delilah Montoya

Tarjeta Postal

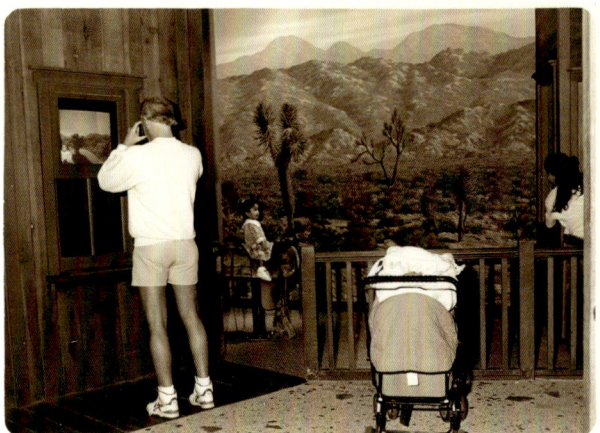

Staging at the center of a great moment. Los Angeles, CA

From the West: Shooting the Tourist

© 1995 Photo by Delilah Montoya

Tarjeta Postal

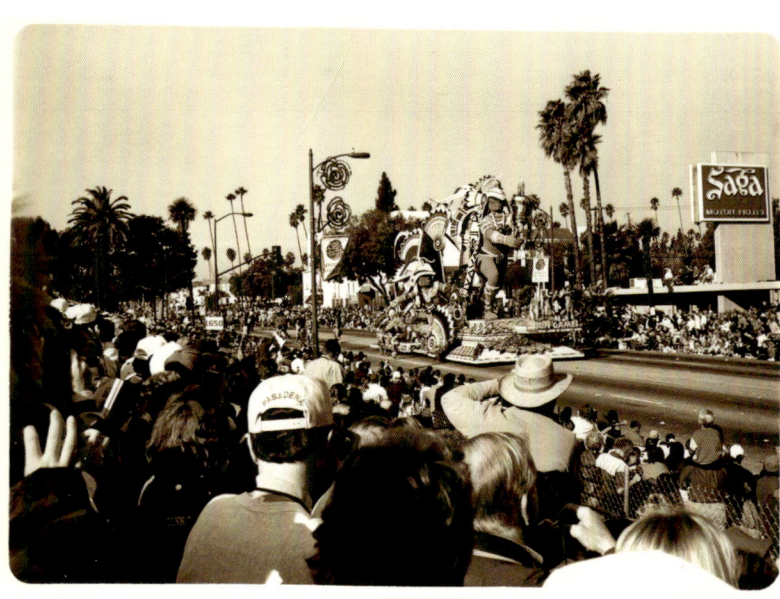

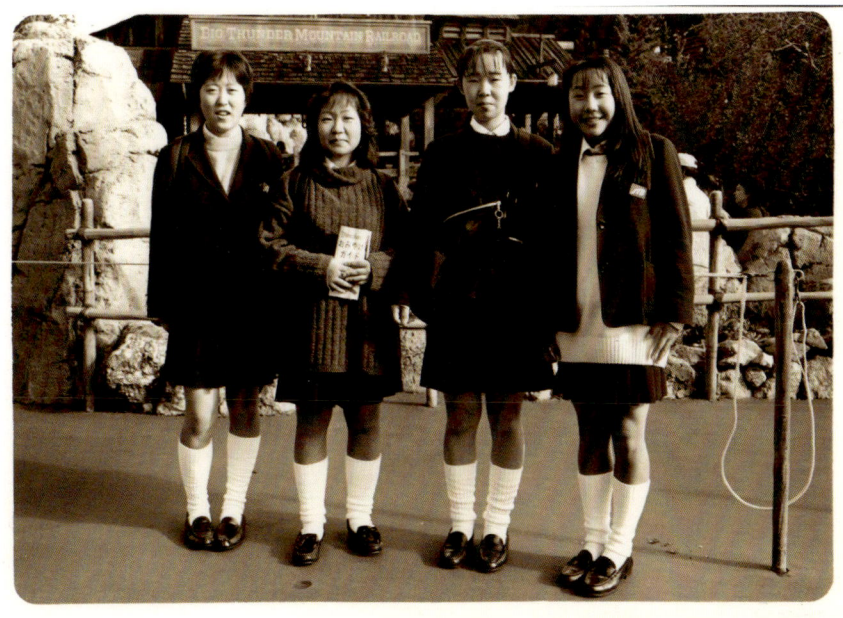

Syncretizing the *East* with the *West*
- a convergence of the Occidental.
Disneyland, CA

From the West: Shooting the Tourist

Tarjeta
Postal

© 1995 Photo by Delilah Montoya

Delilah Montoya
From the West: Shooting the Tourist: Syncretizing
(front/back details from the accordion-fold
postcard book)
1995
Sepia-toned silver gelatin print, amate paper, and
foil
4¼ × 36½ in.
Collection of the artist

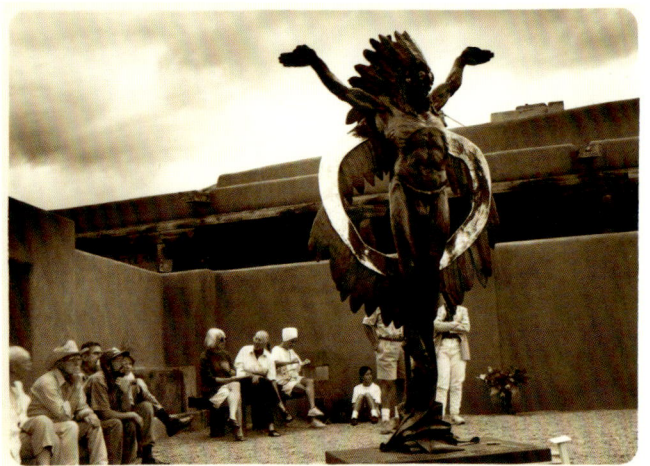

Syncretizing *civilized* cultures to convey a message of humanism. Disneyland, CA

From the West: Shooting the Tourist

Tarjeta Postal

© 1995 Photo by Delilah Montoya

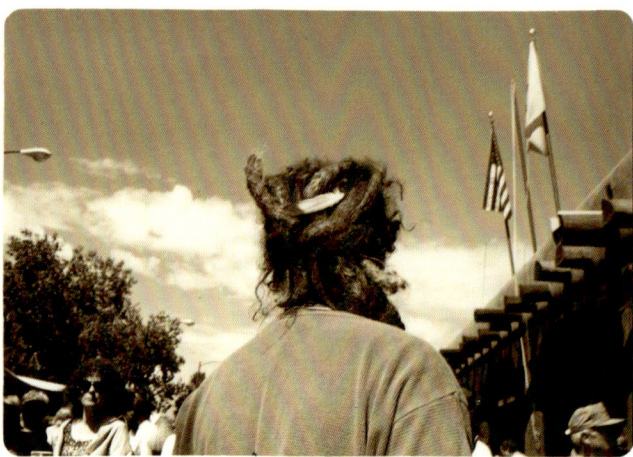

Syncretizing to glimpse at the authenticity of noble *other*. Santa Fe, NM

From the West: Shooting the Tourist

Tarjeta Postal

©1995 Photo by Delilah Montoya

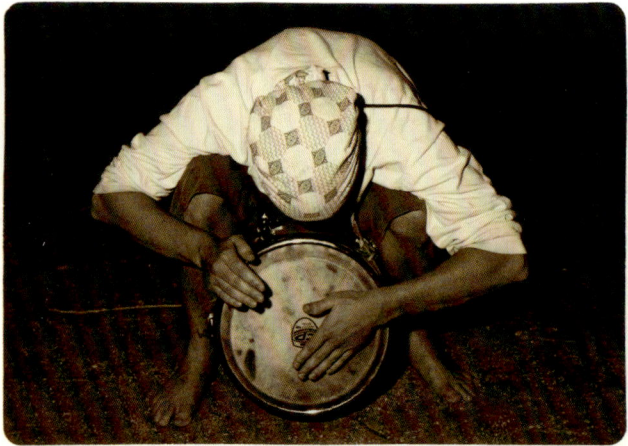

Syncretizing to incorporate the cultural activities of the *other*. Albuquerque, NM

From the West: Shooting the Tourist

Tarjeta Postal

© 1995 Photo by Delilah Montoya

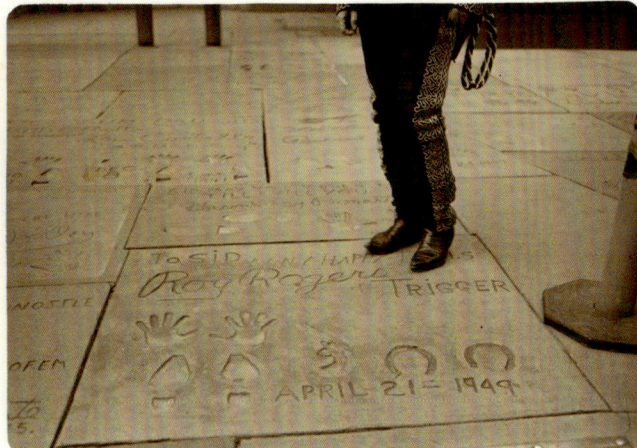

Syncretizing cultural heritages to form an identity. Los Angeles, CA

© 1995 Photo by Delilah Montoya

From the West: Shooting the Tourist

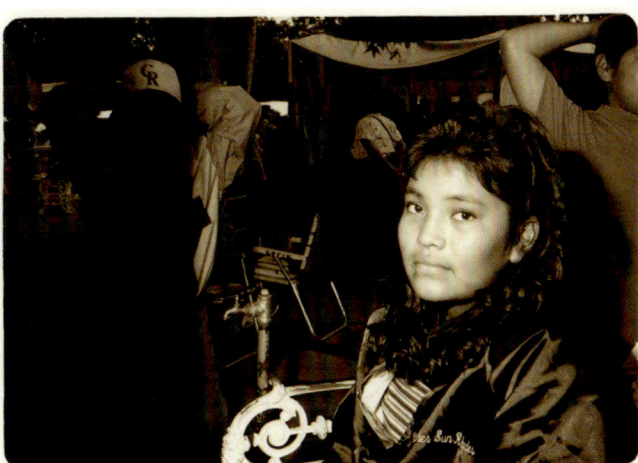

Syncretizing non-western people with modernity. Santa Fe, NM

© 1995 Photo by Delilah Montoya

From the West: Shooting the Tourist

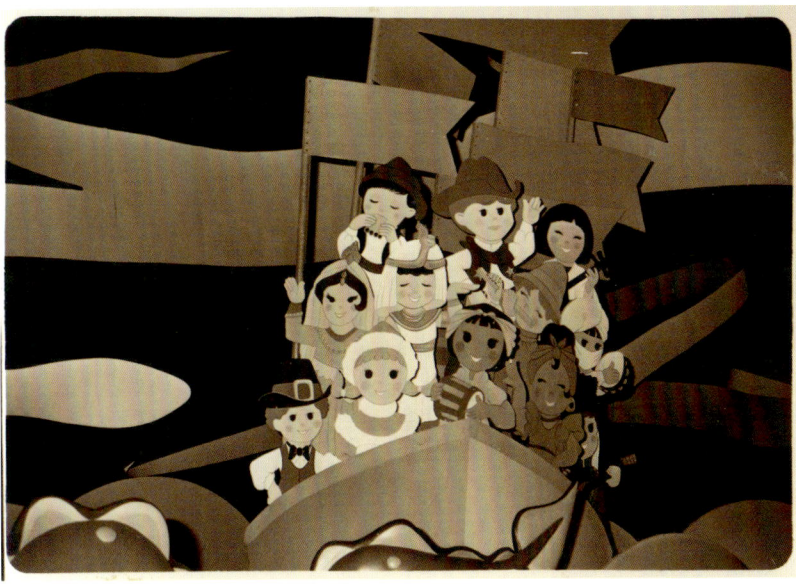

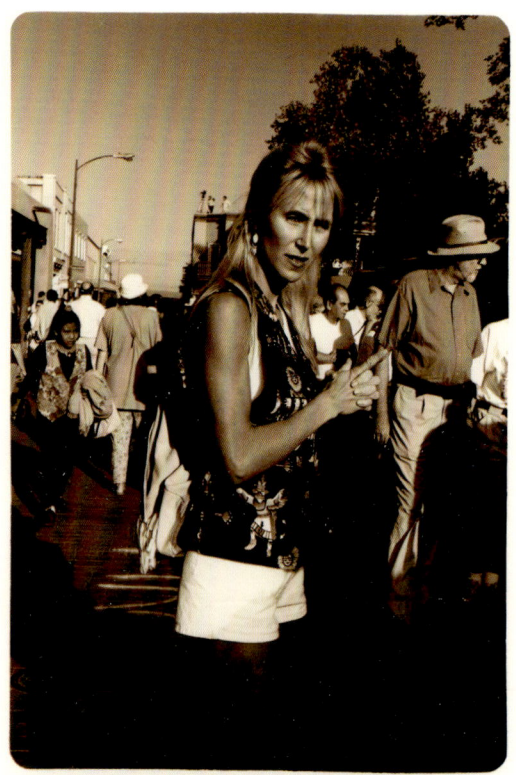

Going Native is only skin deep.
Santa Fe, NM

From the West: Shooting the Tourist

Tarjeta
Postal

©Photo by Delilah Montoya

Delilah Montoya
From the West: Shooting the Tourist: Going Native
(front/back details from the accordion-fold
postcard book)
1995
Sepia-toned silver gelatin print, amate paper, and
foil
4¼ × 36½ in.
Collection of the artist

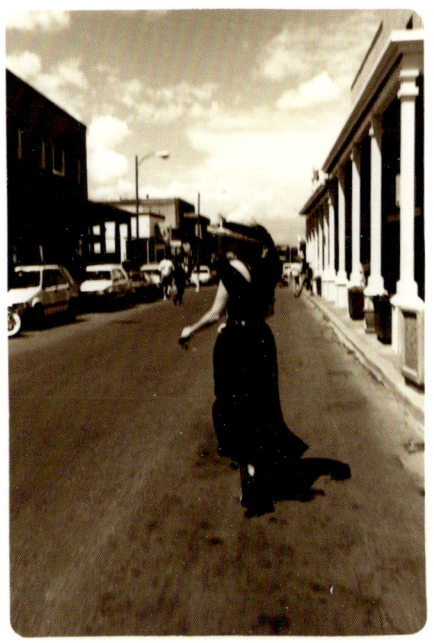

Going Native out of a desire for
the authentic mystified event.
Santa Fe, NM

Tarjeta
Postal

From the West: Shooting the Tourist

© 1995 Photo by Delilah Montoya

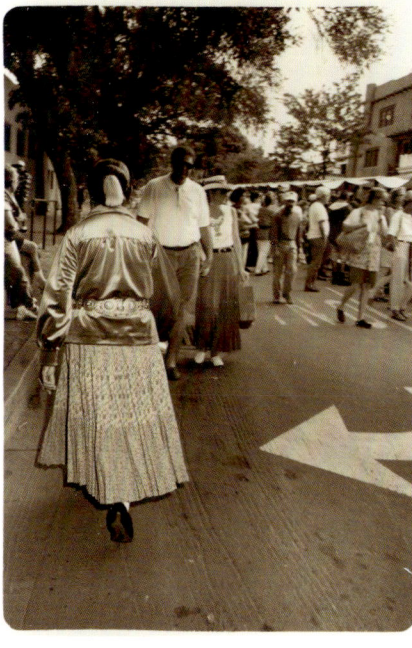

Going Native - to be or to be
perceived? Santa Fe, NM

Tarjeta
Postal

From the West: Shooting the Tourist

© 1995 Photo by Delilah Montoya

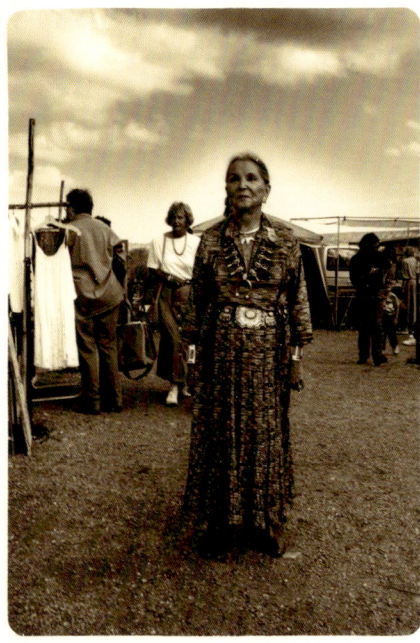

Going Native - the appropriation of
the *other's* aesthetic. Santa Fe, NM

Tarjeta
Postal

From the West: Shooting the Tourist

©1995 Photo by Delilah Montoya

134

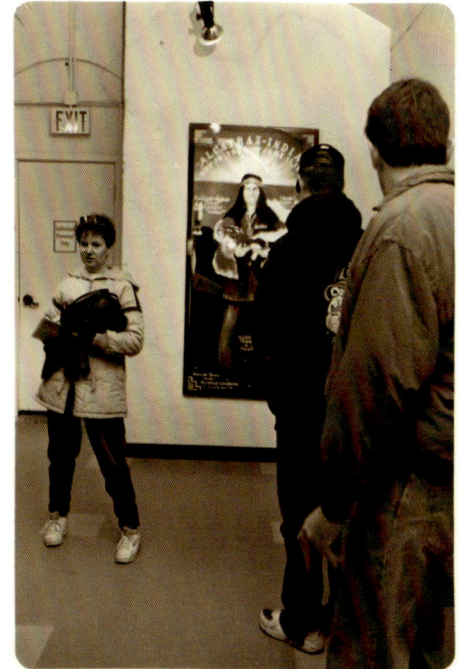

Going Native - self-identification
through sight recognition.
Alcatraz, CA

Tarjeta
Postal

© 1995 Photo by Delilah Montoya

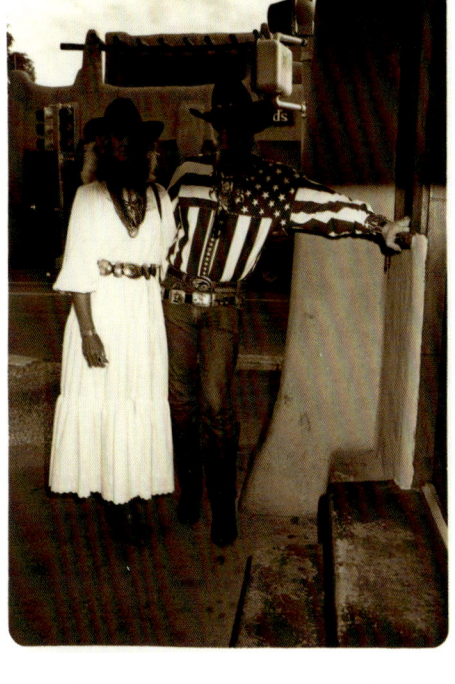

Going Native with style.
Santa Fe, NM

Tarjeta
Postal

© 1995 Photo by Delilah Montoya

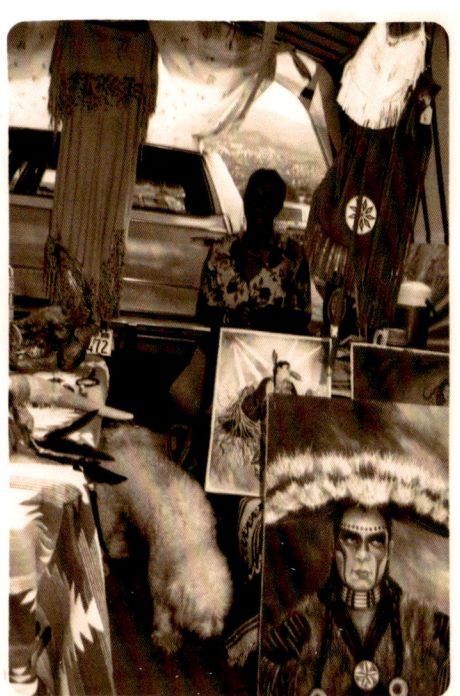

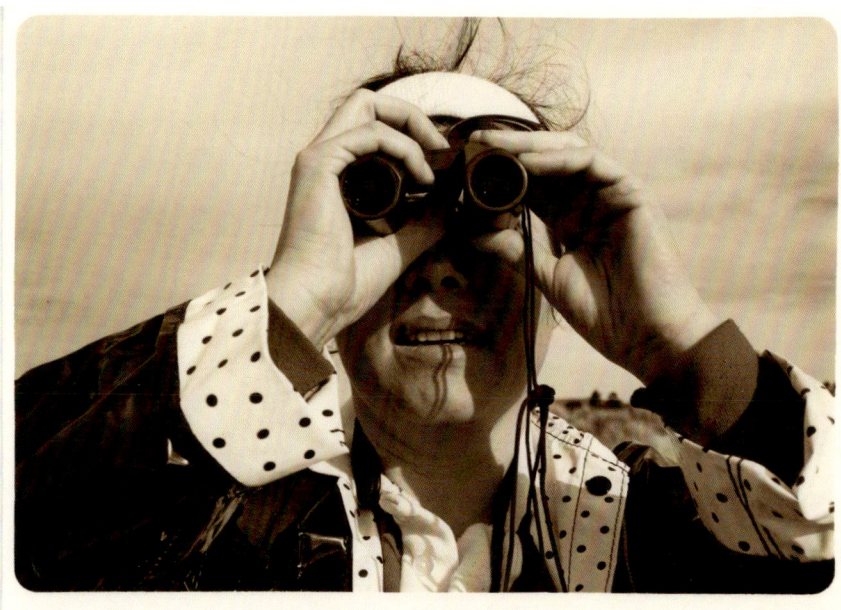

Looking at it for the first time.
Point Reyes, CA

Tarjeta Postal

From the West: Shooting the Tourist

© 1995 Photo by Delilah Montoya

Delilah Montoya
From the West: Shooting the Tourist: Looking (front/back details from the accordion-fold postcard book)
1995
Sepia-toned silver gelatin print, amate paper, and foil
4¼ × 36½ in.
Collection of the artist

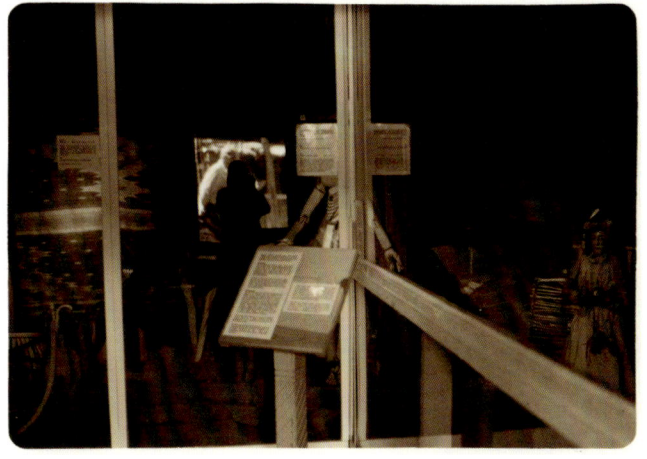

Looking to jump into where
the action was. Taos, NM

From the West: Shooting the Tourist

Looking to explore the
differences. Disneyland, CA

From the West: Shooting the Tourist

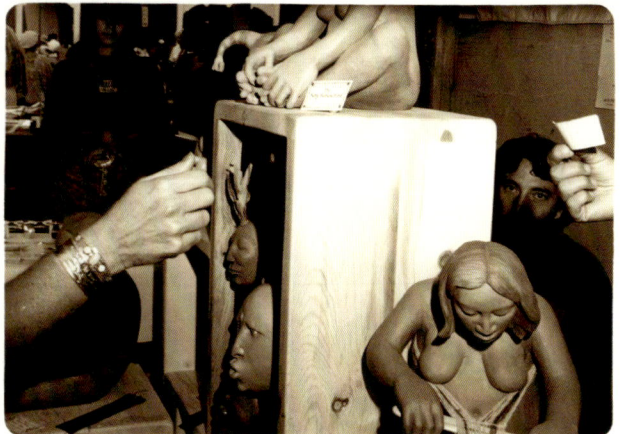

Looking at the primitive.
Santa Fe, NM

From the West: Shooting the Tourist

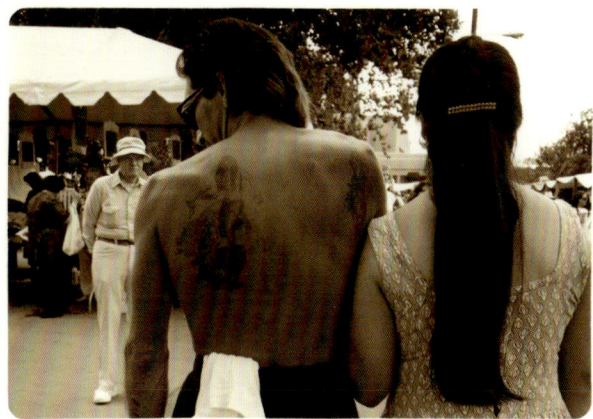

Looking at the local color.
Santa Fe, NM

Tarjeta
Postal

From the West: Shooting the Tourist

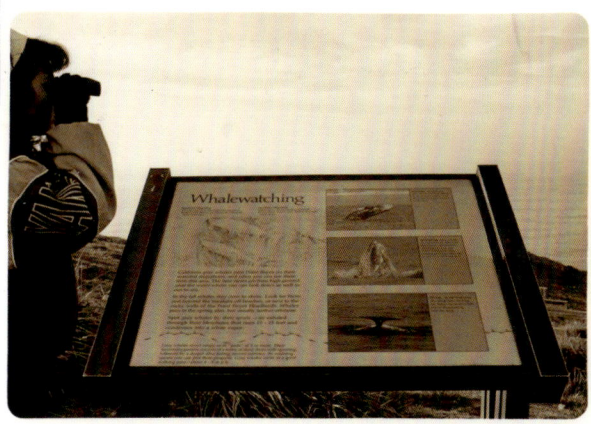

Looking to find the true object.
Point Bonita, CA

Tarjeta
Postal

From the West: Shooting the Tourist

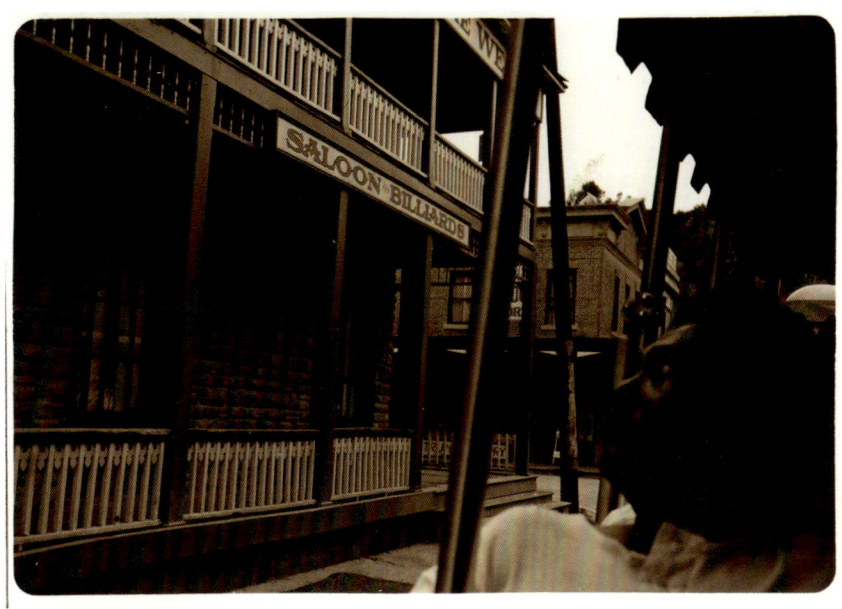

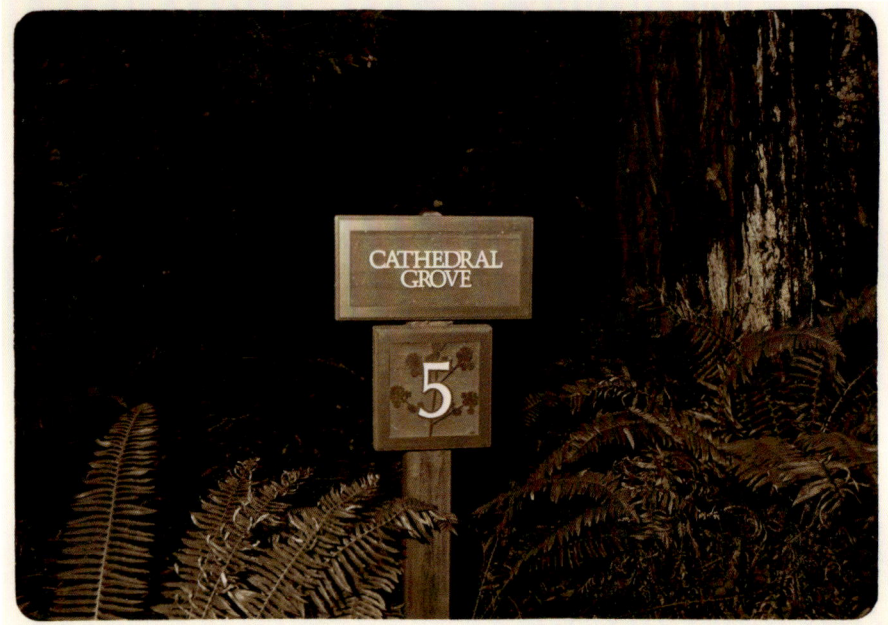

Preserving the sight with a marker.
Muir Woods, CA

From the West: Shooting the Tourist

Tarjeta
Postal

© 1995 Photo by Delilah Montoya

Delilah Montoya
From the West: Shooting the Tourist: Preserving
(front/back details from the accordion-fold
postcard book)
1995
Sepia-toned silver gelatin print, amate paper, and
foil
4¼ × 36½ in.
Collection of the artist

139

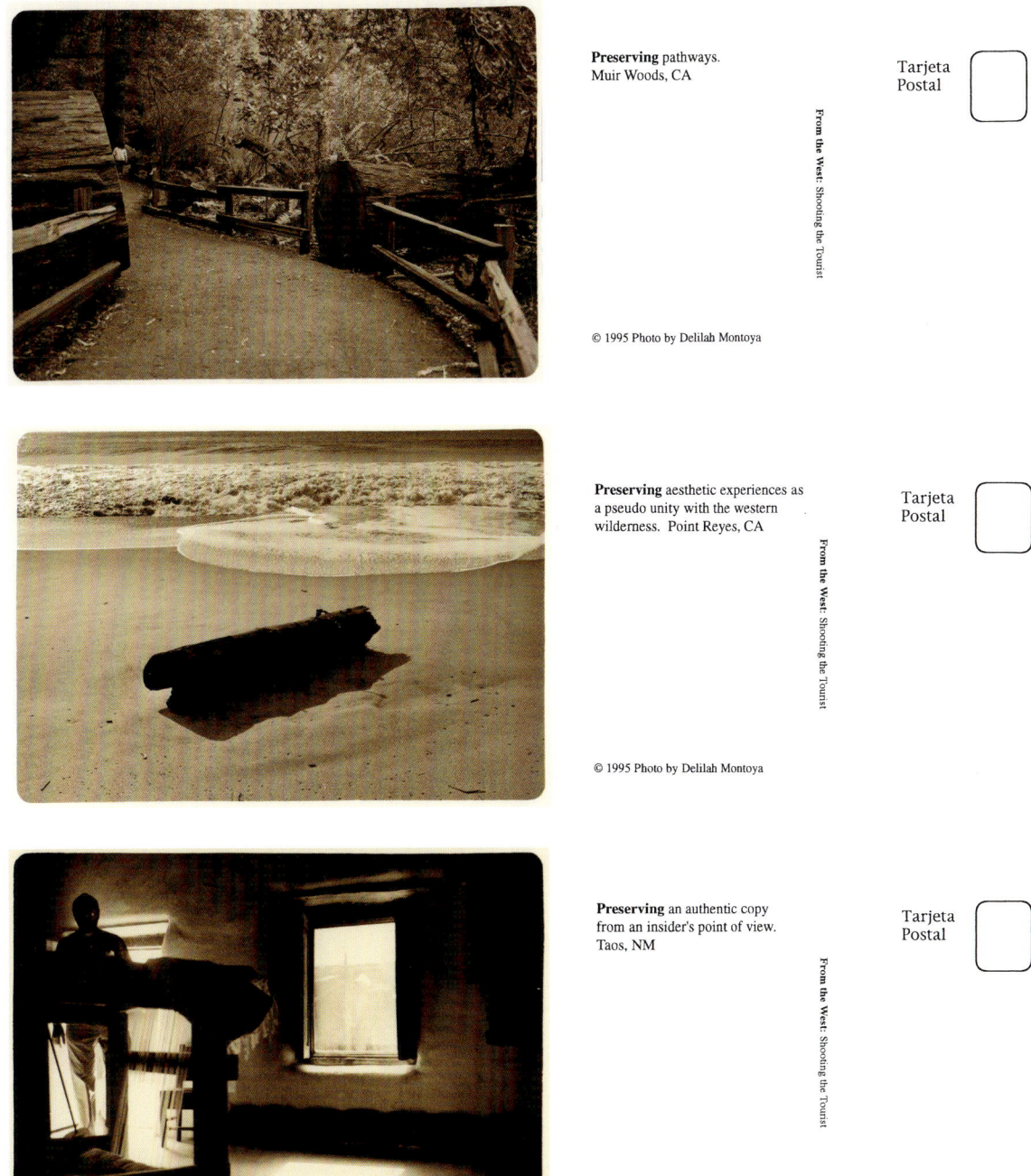

Preserving pathways.
Muir Woods, CA

From the West: Shooting the Tourist

Tarjeta
Postal

© 1995 Photo by Delilah Montoya

Preserving aesthetic experiences as
a pseudo unity with the western
wilderness. Point Reyes, CA

From the West: Shooting the Tourist

Tarjeta
Postal

© 1995 Photo by Delilah Montoya

Preserving an authentic copy
from an insider's point of view.
Taos, NM

From the West: Shooting the Tourist

Tarjeta
Postal

© 1995 Photo by Delilah Montoya

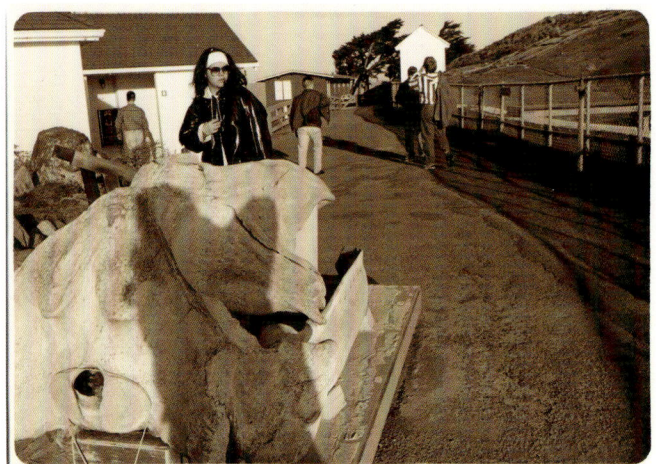

Preserving the tourist position
of seeking his own alienation.
Point Bonita, CA.

© 1995 Photo by Delilah Montoya

From the West: *Shooting the Tourist*

Tarjeta
Postal

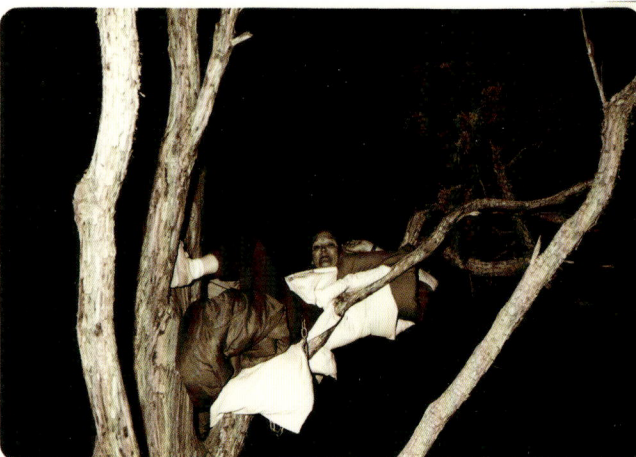

Preserving a tree with a chain.
Albuquerque, NM

© 1995 Photo by Delilah Montoya

From the West: *Shooting the Tourist*

Tarjeta
Postal

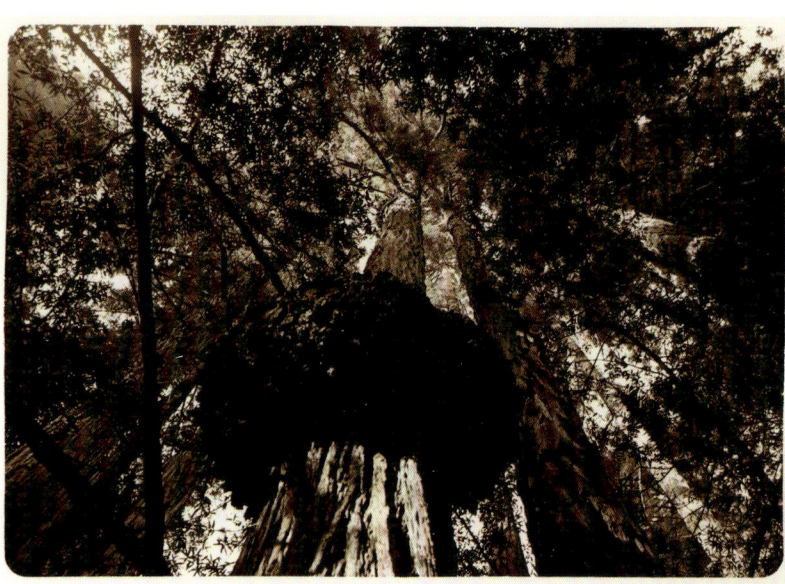

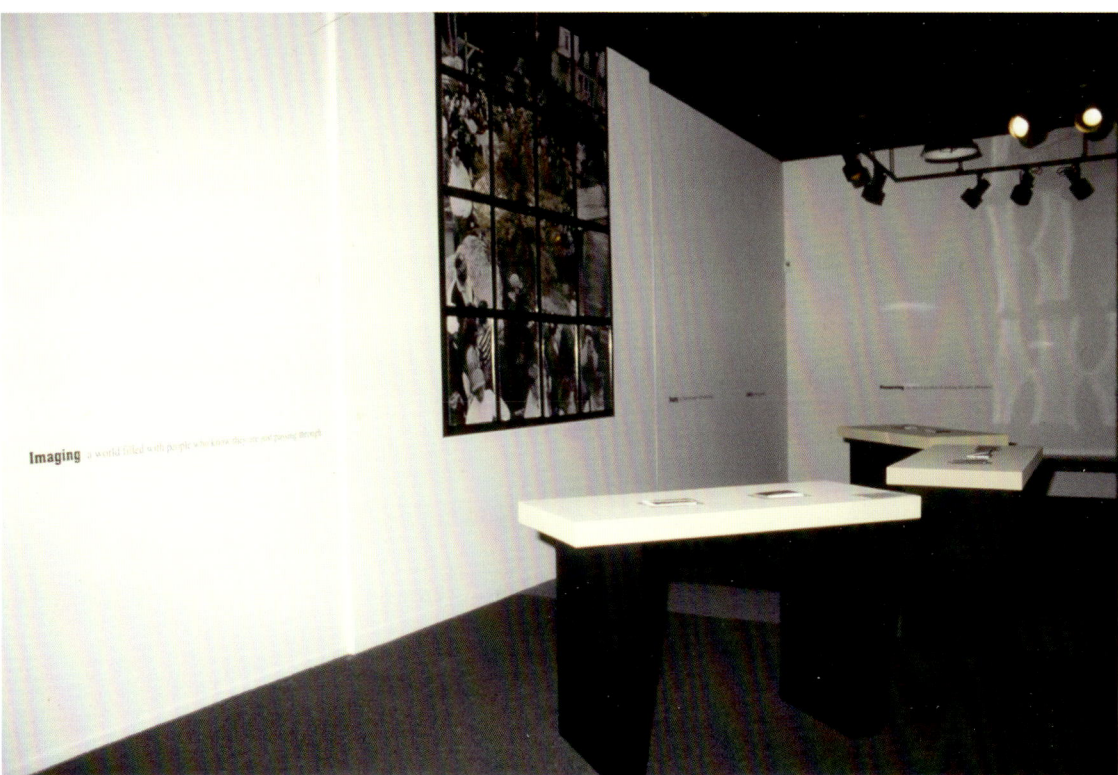

From the West exhibition installation of *Shooting the Tourist*, Mexican Museum 1995

that pushes against an ethnographic approach to capturing her subjects. By photographing tourists in spaces that were constructed for them, Montoya reveals the underlying complexities of the contested places that are the West and asks, "Who is looking at who?"[6] According to Jennifer Gonzalez, Montoya makes her audience aware of its role in a system of looking.[7] Returning the tourist gaze was central to Montoya's project from the outset; however, as she reflects in her conversation with Demetria Martinez, the meaning of the gaze is different when it is directed back on the group who is accustomed to being the voyeur.

In Conversation with Delilah Montoya and Demetria Martinez: *Shooting the Tourist*

Demetria: I loved the double meaning of your series, *Shooting the Tourist*, shooting as in a symbolically violent act and shooting as in taking a picture. It brought to mind the years I lived in Old Town Albuquerque, a stone's throw from this museum. I was always appalled by the way tourists took pictures of Indigenous craftsmen and women who sold their jewelry under the portal—usually without asking permission. The tourists wanted pictures of "real Indians." Not to mention the times they took pictures of darker-skinned Chicanos—again, to capture what they believed to be a "real" Indian. *Shooting the Tourist* is an indictment of how New Mexico has been sold as a tourist's paradise—in other words, a place of exotic, primitive others—the wild, wild West. You expose the racist underpinnings of tourism. You're the one doing the shooting. As a Chicana, how do you understand the West? How did you unpack that in your series?

Delilah: When I photographed *Shooting the Tourist*, I was asked by Chon Noriega to be part of an exhibition titled *From the West: Chicano Narrative Photography* at the Mexican Museum in San Francisco. It was based on the idea of many Wests and explored how Chicanos have their own particular perspective on the West. The exhibition expanded on the idea that there was more than one truth and asked what viewing the West from a Chicano lens would look like. I remember thinking very clearly when they asked me to do this, *How would I approach it? What would I want to do?* It dawned on me: *Who's West is this? The West is something that has been manufactured. Why is it West? Why is it not center? Or why is it not east of Asia? Why is it always west of Europe?* I thought that the term itself was awkward and didn't make sense. I began to think about how superficial the idea of the West is.

I had taken a class that explored the history of tourism in New Mexico. We talked about the Harvey Houses and how our tourist items were manufactured. There was a certain amount of exoticism involved ina creating the tourist industry, which was very marketable in New Mexico. I was also reading a book titled *The Tourist: A New Theory of the Leisure Class*, written by Dean MacCannell in 1979. He emphasized the idea that tourism is performative. And he broke it down into different performative actions. I visually captured these actions and turned the images into postcards. I wanted to capture the tourist gaze and send it back. Oftentimes, people come to New Mexico and see a culture and place that is different from what they know. So we have a whole group of people who moved here trying to find themselves, and the book talks about how the tourists are in search of their own identity. The project also expanded beyond New Mexico because I was teaching at Cal State LA. I thought it would be great to look at California, which also held a mystique of the West. I was interested in places like the Jean Autry Museum. Disneyland was perfect because it has an Old West theme park.

Delilah Montoya
From the West: Shooting the Tourist: Imaging
(back/front of accordionfold postcard book)
1995
Sepia-toned silver gelatin print, amate paper, and foil
4 1/2, x 36 1/2, in.
Collection of the artist

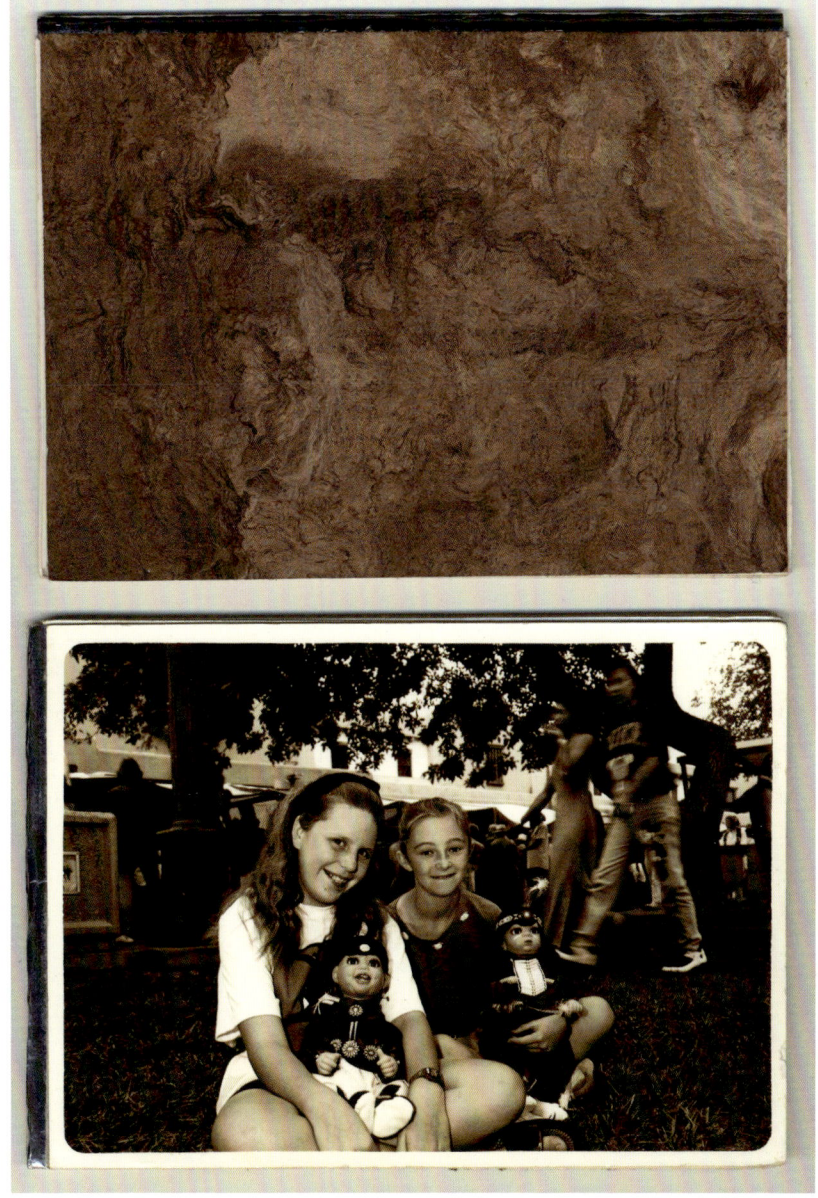

There were specific themes in MacCannell's book, including collecting, going native, preserving, and so on. At times, the categories overlap, but they became the organizational structure for the project. One of the images was taken after a performance at Taos Pueblo. The dancers were using leaves and branches in the ceremony. Strangely, tourists were collecting those items. So I took a picture of that kind of collecting.

Consumption was another important theme. I went to the Indian

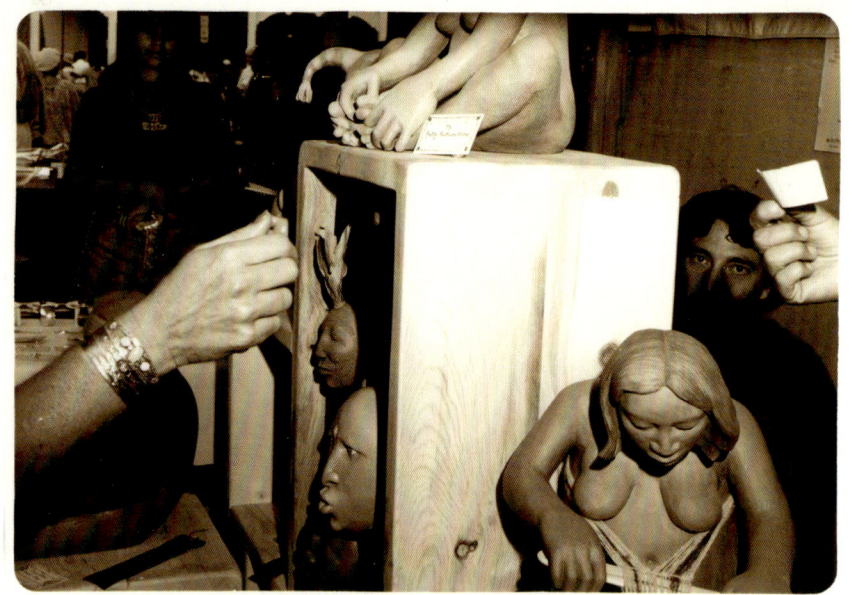

Delilah Montoya
From the West: Shooting the Tourist #4: Looking at the Primitive (excerpt from the accordion-fold postcard book)
1995
Sepia-toned silver gelatin print
4 × 6 in.
Collection of the artist

Market, and there would be tourists just drenched in Native American apparel. I went to the Santa Fe Flea Market, and sure enough, there was a lot of Indigenous art that people were trying to sell. I also encountered a man who would walk around the plaza wearing as many sombreros as he could, and he was obviously not from New Mexico. I asked him if I could take his picture. He was excited to take me to his house so I could see all of the sombreros he had collected.

There was so much of the same that was going on. I was photographing the superficial, but ultimately, everything seemed to become superficial. In hindsight, there was a certain amount of frustration. How do you set yourself apart from that? I was doing the exact same thing that they were doing, but I was just using a different subject. Them.

The process ended up being more like documentation, which is different from the documentary. The documentary approach looks at particular subjects in a way that is related to anthropology because it looks at the other from the perspective of being the First World looking at the Third World. I was looking at the First World to create a documentary on the First World as a leisure class. But it was problematic because the first world is looking at themselves; they don't see the separation or the exoticized other. I was documenting something that was in front of you with little composition involved. I have a picture of my sister Page taken in Point Reyes. She is holding binoculars, being the perfect tourist. I realized in this project that I was looking while the subject was looking.

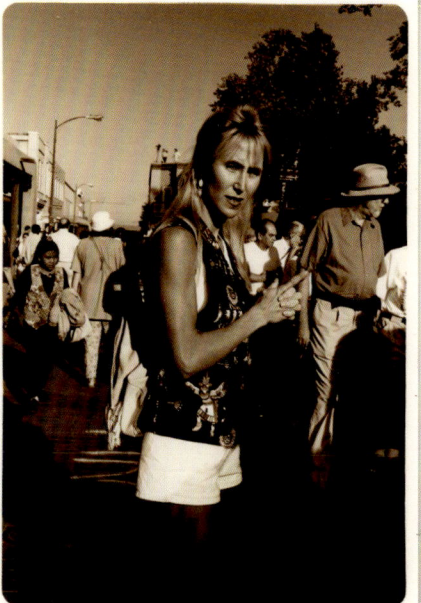

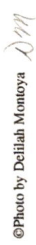

Tarjeta
Postal

From the West: Shooting the Tourist

Going Native is only skin deep.
Santa Fe, NM

©Photo by Delilah Montoya

(*top*) Delilah Montoya
From the West: Shooting the Tourist: Going Native #4
(front/back details from the accordion-fold postcard book)
1995
Sepia-toned silver gelatin print, amate paper, and foil
4¼ × 8½ in.
Collection of the artist

(*bottom*) Delilah Montoya
From the West: Shooting the Tourist #5: Looking at the Local Color (excerpt from the accordion-fold postcard book)
1995
Sepia-toned silver gelatin print
4 × 6 in.
Collection of the artist

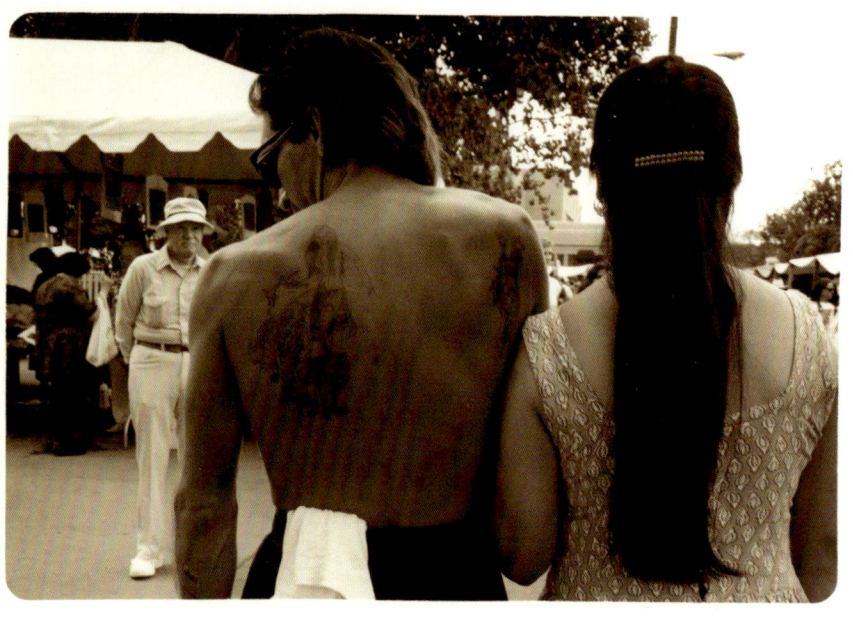

In another postcard, a man is walking with his woman. He seems to be a Chicano or cholo. But not a current cholo, because I was photographing this in 1996. In the postcard, there is an older man who is obviously a tourist wearing his tourist hat, white pants, and white shoes. He is looking at the cholo, and I was looking at him right over the back shoulder of the cholo accompanying his woman. He was just staring down the cholo. Of all the images I did for this series, this one shows what I was trying to capture. It really returns the gaze.

I was interested in staging. I was interested in the idea of preserving. Tourist attractions maintain some kind of mythic West, and generally, it's done with a visual marker. The notion of syncretism was all around us in terms of the West. What you see in some of my images is how the people are from all over, and what they are looking at is preserved or witnessed or looked at. One example of syncretism that I particularly liked was a photograph of a group of young Asian girls. You can tell that they were schoolgirls and giddy to be in the United States, particularly Disneyland, because they had heard so much about Disneyland. They witnessed and were part of the West, although it was staged and manufactured. But for them, there was a sense of authenticity, which I found really interesting, a kind of the East giving veracity to the West.

The large photo mural was taken in Disneyland. You can see this massive line of people. They're snaking around, waiting to get onto the attraction, and then there is a couple looking at me, and one of them is taking my picture. That was my daughter and, at that time, her boyfriend, who soon became her husband. So my family always tends to become collaborators as well. After producing *Shooting the Tourist* postcards, I proceeded to sell them back to tourists visiting Santa Fe at the Hispanic Market. Some of those cards did sell, which I thought was hysterical, but I also received a threatening phone call to cease selling them.

The exhibition brought important ideas and artists together. I was thrilled to be included with artists like Harry Gamboa, Miguel Gandert, and Robert Buitrón. Buitrón's work was interesting in that it was creating parodies of the West, and I was thinking about that as I developed my series. He had this whole thing called *El Corrido and the Happy Trails* starring Pancho and Tonto, which was really great. Kathy Vargas was also in the show, and she focused on the Alamo. Her family had been on the other side of the Alamo. Christina Fernandez's work *Maria's Great Expedition* was also powerful. It was a strong group of Chicano/a artists.

(*opposite page*) Delilah Montoya
Installation photograph of Chicano Postcards Promotion stand displayed at 1996 Hispanic Market, Santa Fe, NM
1995
Sepia-toned silver gelatin print, amate paper, and foil
Collection of the artist

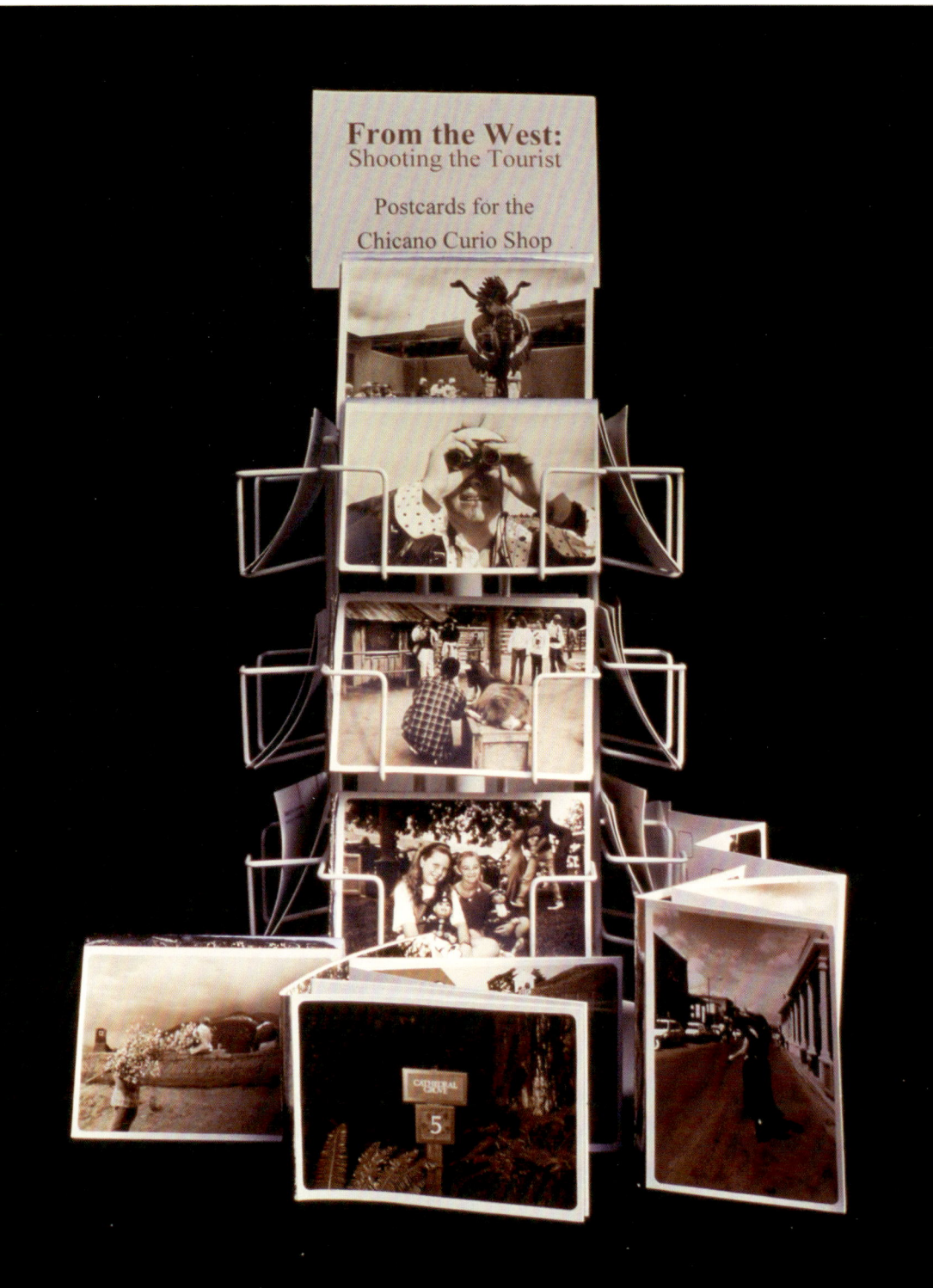

According to the Catholic tradition, the Virgen of Guadalupe, mother of Jesus Christ, first appeared on the hill of Tepeyac in Mexico in 1531. Juan Diego, who was of Aztec descent, saw a glowing figure on the hill. She identified herself and asked Juan to build a shrine for her in that same spot. Afterwards, Juan Diego visited Juan de Zumárraga, who was the archbishop of what is now Mexico City. Zumárraga dismissed him and asked for proof of his story. Juan Diego returned to the hill and encountered the Virgen again. She told him to climb to the top of the hill and pick some flowers to present to the archbishop. Although it was winter and nothing should have been in bloom, Juan Diego found abundant flowers. The Virgen bundled the flowers into Juan's cloak, known as a *tilma*. When Juan Diego presented the tilma and flowers to Zumárraga, they fell out, and he recognized them as Castilian roses, which are not found in Mexico. The tilma was miraculously imprinted with a colorful image of the Virgen herself. This story appeared in a Nahuatl manuscript written by Antonio Valeriano sometime after 1556.

The Virgen appears surrounded by the sun's rays, and her foot rests on a crescent moon. Her head is lowered, and her hands are clasped together in prayer. Stars appear on her blue mantle, which is worn over a rose-colored dress that is adorned with flowers and references the map of Mexico. She wears a black cross and a black Aztec maternity belt. Images of the Virgen of Guadalupe are ubiquitous across Mexico, Latin America, and Latinx communities in the United States. Her image operates far beyond the religious symbol that she embodies. She is central to Mexico's national identity and standing in the Catholic Church. Her appearance in the Americas asserts a connection directly related to God that legitimized Mexico within the colonial context. She also serves as the site of religious syncretism that Montoya is interested in exploring through several of her series. The hill that the basilica was built on was the site of the temple of Tonanzin, the Aztec goddess whose Nahuatl name means "our mother." As Montoya points out, Juan Diego's vision was not a coincidence.

The Virgen of Guadalupe would have been a legible icon to the Indigenous peoples of Mexico, and she was used to frame Christian teachings designed to evangelize them. She carried meaning that intersected both belief systems and was ultimately taken back to Europe. In the *Guadalupana* series, Montoya engages explicitly with the Virgen of Guadalupe and how her image is manifested within the visual language of tattoo art.

SIX

La Guadalupana

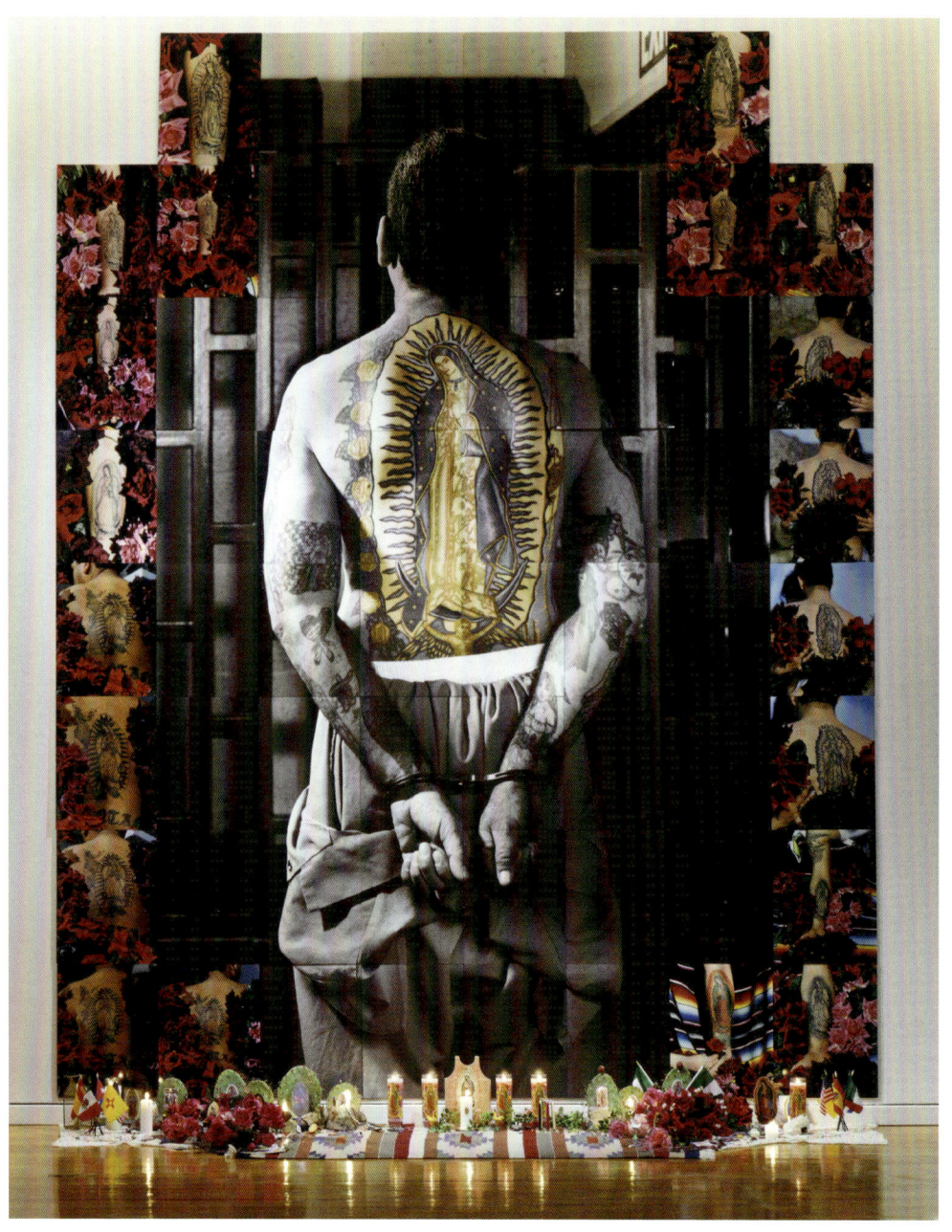

Delilah Montoya
La Guadalupana, Imagenes E
Historias Chicana Altar-Inspired Art
Tufts Museum
1999
Serape blanket, white lace fabric, candles,
flowers, and Virgin of Guadalupe para-
phernalia
176 × 144 in.
Williams College Museum of Art, Muse-
um purchase, Kathyrn Hurd Fund
M.2008.5

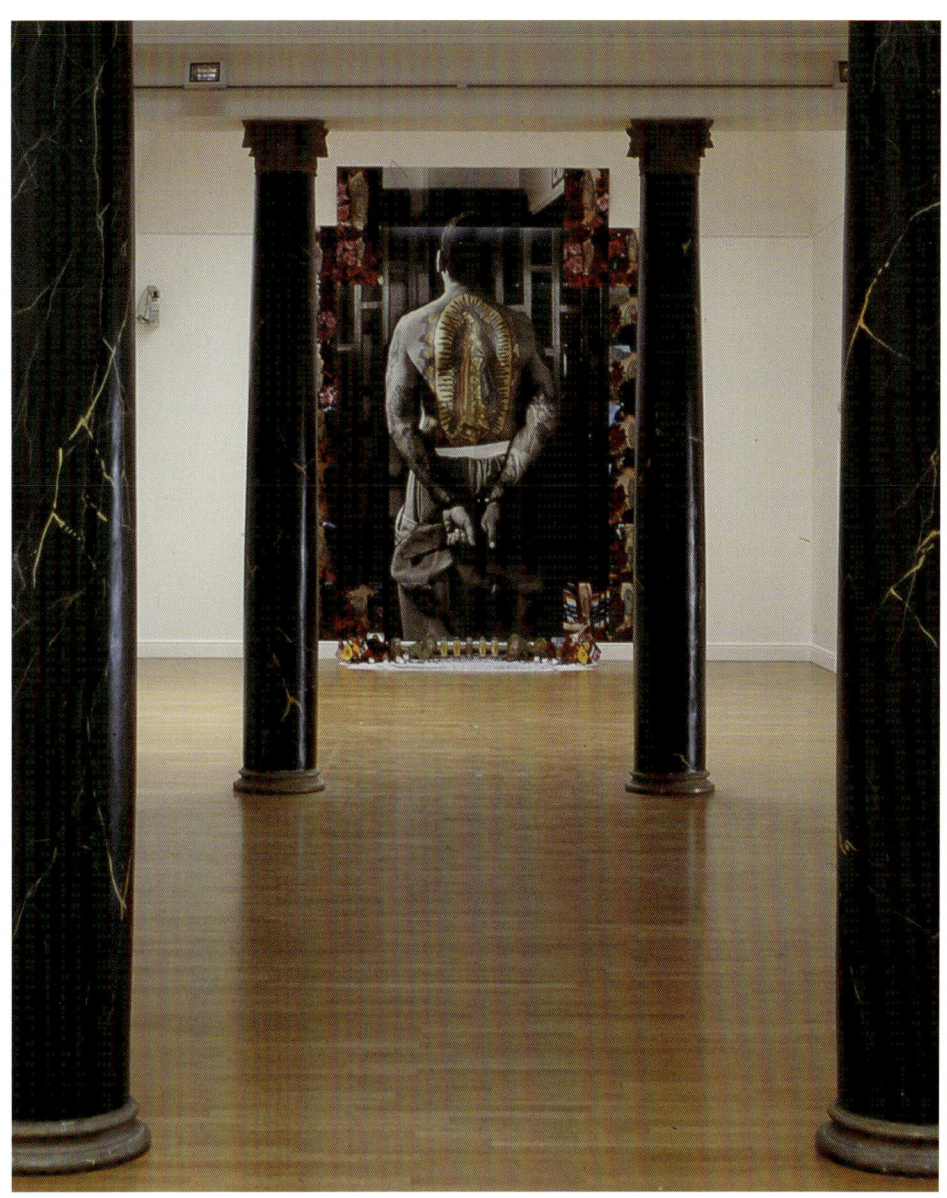

Delilah Montoya
La Guadalupana, Ida Y Vuelta
Musée Rodez installation
1998
Photomural installation, serape blanket, flags,
white lace fabric, candles, flowers, and Virgin of
Guadalupe paraphernalia
176 × 144 in.
New Mexico Museum of Art, museum pur-
chase with finds from the I. A. O'Shaughnessy
Foundation and Helen Kornblum, 1999
1999.7.1

For the *Guadalupana* series, Montoya created prints, photographs, and a large photo mural that also functioned as an altar after Felix Martinez, who is pictured in the mural, was killed in an Albuquerque detention center. This series reveals stories of incarceration, oppression, and the sacred/profane dichotomy that is displayed directly on the body, mirroring the wearing of the tilma. The Virgen of Guadalupe is a revered figure in Chicano culture and history. Still, in this case, she becomes not only a figure of devotion but a symbol of protection, forgiveness, and continued connection to faith and family. It delves into the cultural and spiritual dimensions of skin as a medium, drawing connections between Aztec rituals and contemporary expressions of Chicanx identity. Martinez's story, sadly, became a real example of the reverberations of history in everyday lives.

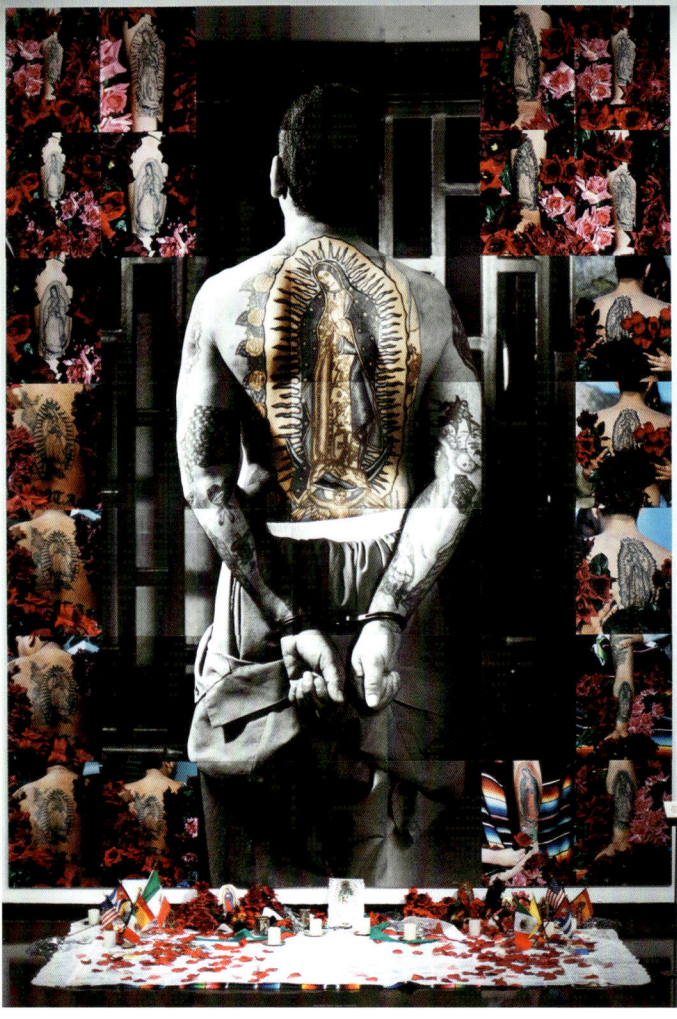

Delilah Montoya
La Guadalupana, Case Studies from the Bureau of Contemporary Art
New Mexico Museum of Art, Santa Fe, NM, 2011
1998
Photomural installation, serape blanket, flags, white lace fabric, candles, flowers, and Virgin of Guadalupe paraphernalia
150 ½ × 119 in.
New Mexico Museum of Art, museum purchase with finds from the I. A. O'Shaughnessy Foundation and Helen Kornblum, 1999
1999.7.

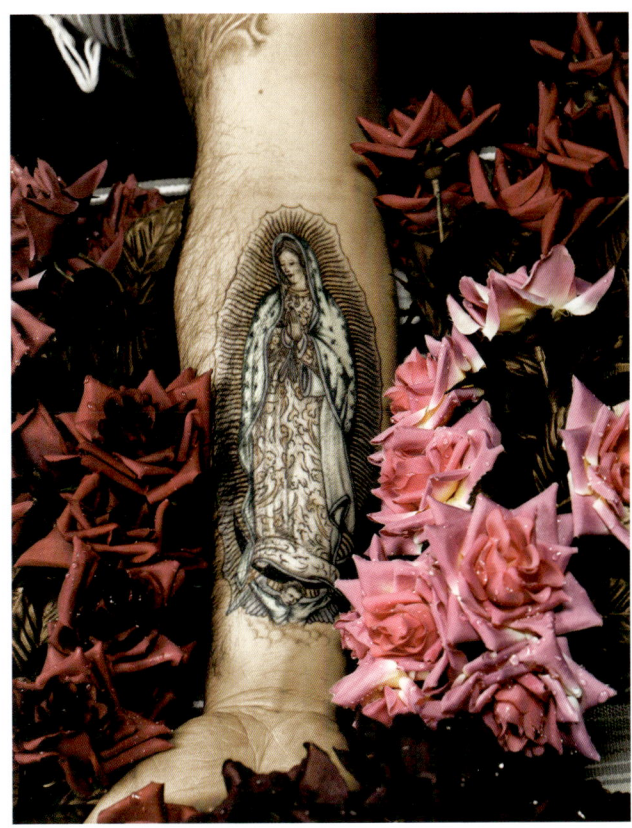 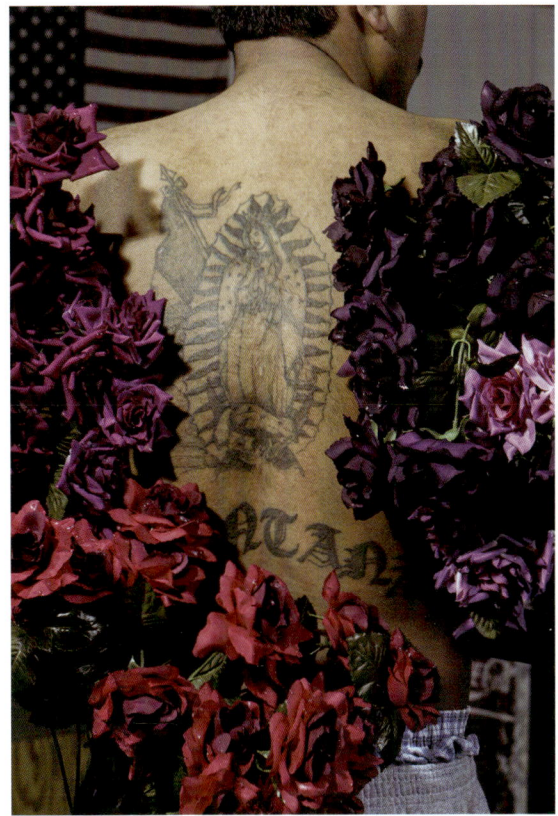

(*left*) Delilah Montoya
Jaramillo
1999, print date 2002
Dye sublimation on aluminum
32 × 24 in.
Collection of the artist

(*right*) Delilah Montoya
Laurence Quintana #1
(Guadalupana mural detail)
1998
Chromogenic print on Fuji-
color Crystal Archive type
C paper
24 × 20 in.
Collection of the artist

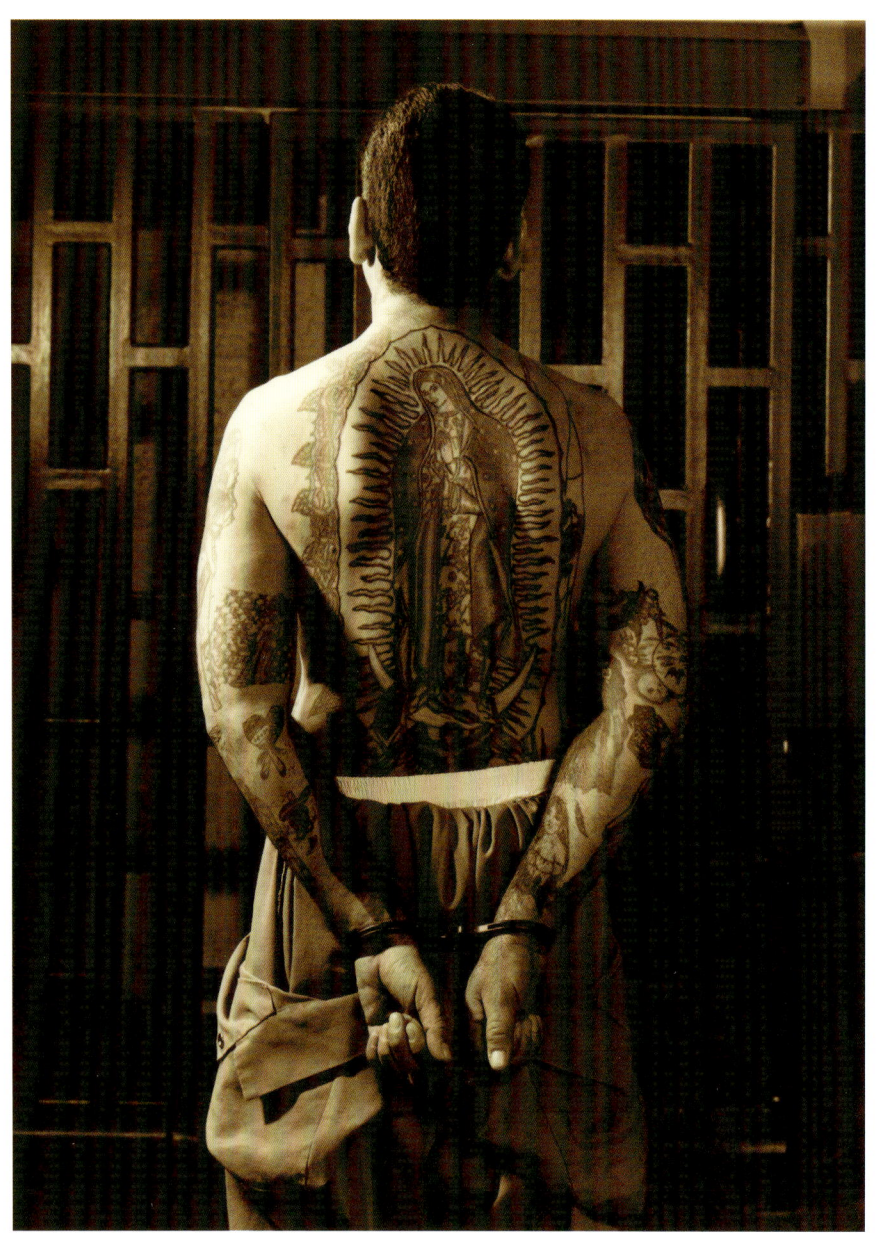

Delilah Montoya
El Guadalupano (from the series *Guadalupe Tattoo*)
1998
Sepia-toned gelatin silver print, A/P
23⅛ × 18½ in.
Albuquerque Museum, museum purchase and gift of the artist
PC2022.32.17

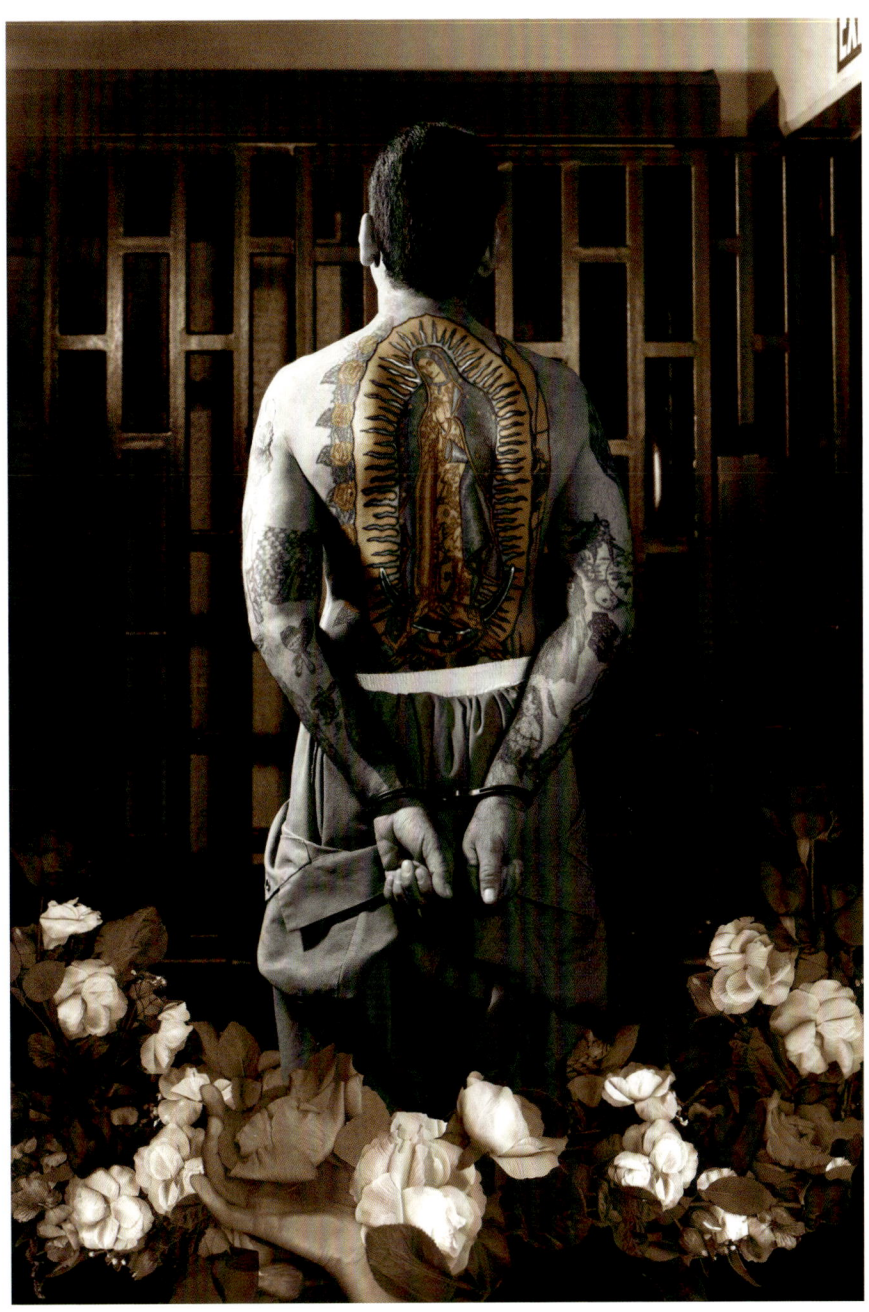

Delilah Montoya
La Guadalupana (from the
series *Guadalupe Tattoo*)
1999, digital composition
Printed 2024
Archival inkjet on
Hahnemuhle photo rag
ultrasmooth paper
17 × 22 in.
Collection of the artist

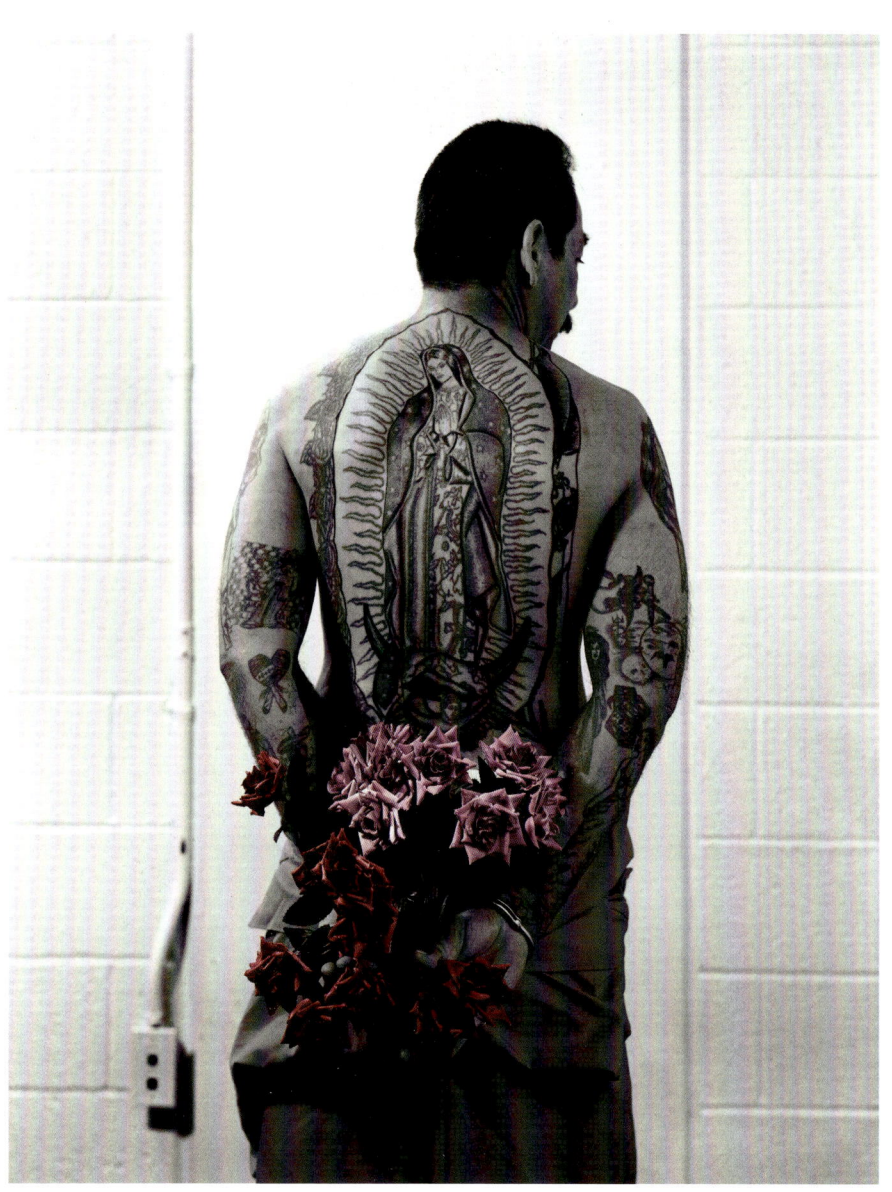

Delilah Montoya
El Guadalupano #3 (from the
series *Guadalupe Tattoo*)
1999, digital composition
2024
Inkjet on eSatin paper
17 × 22 in.
Collection of the artist

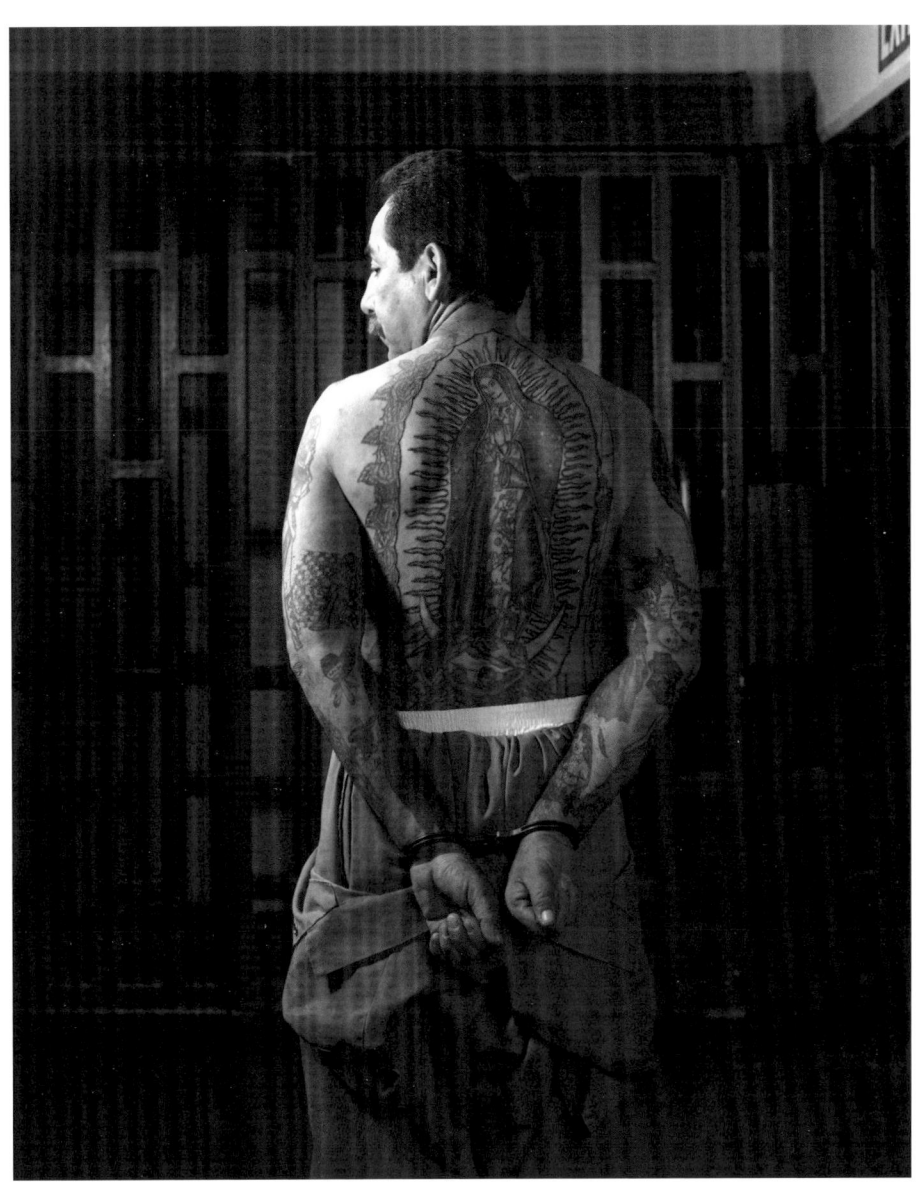

Delilah Montoya
El Guadalupano #4 (from the
series *Guadalupe Tattoo*)
1999
Gelatin silver print
20 × 24 in.
Collection of the artist

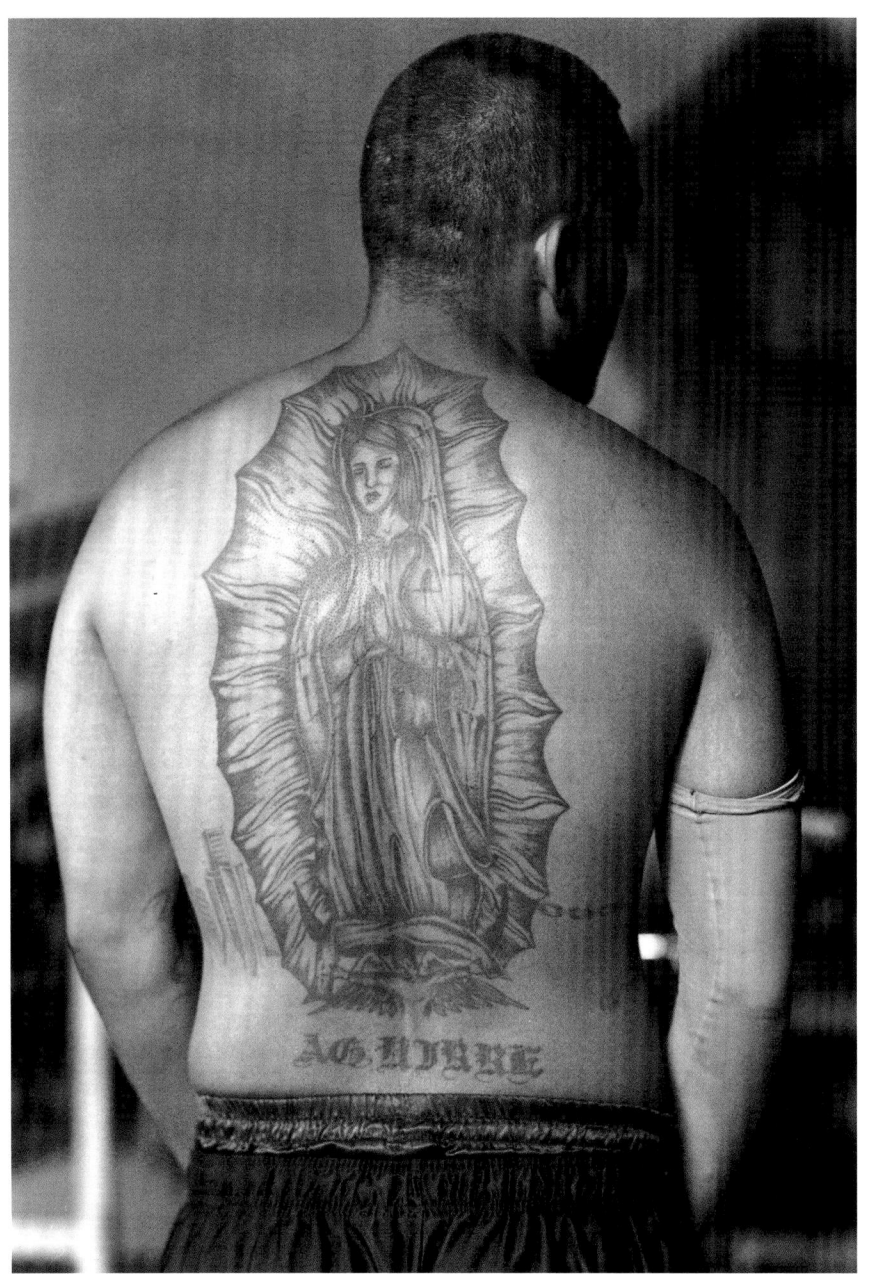

Delilah Montoya
Aguirre #2 (from the series
Guadalupe Tattoo)
2005
Silver gelatin
5 × 7 in.
Collection of the artist

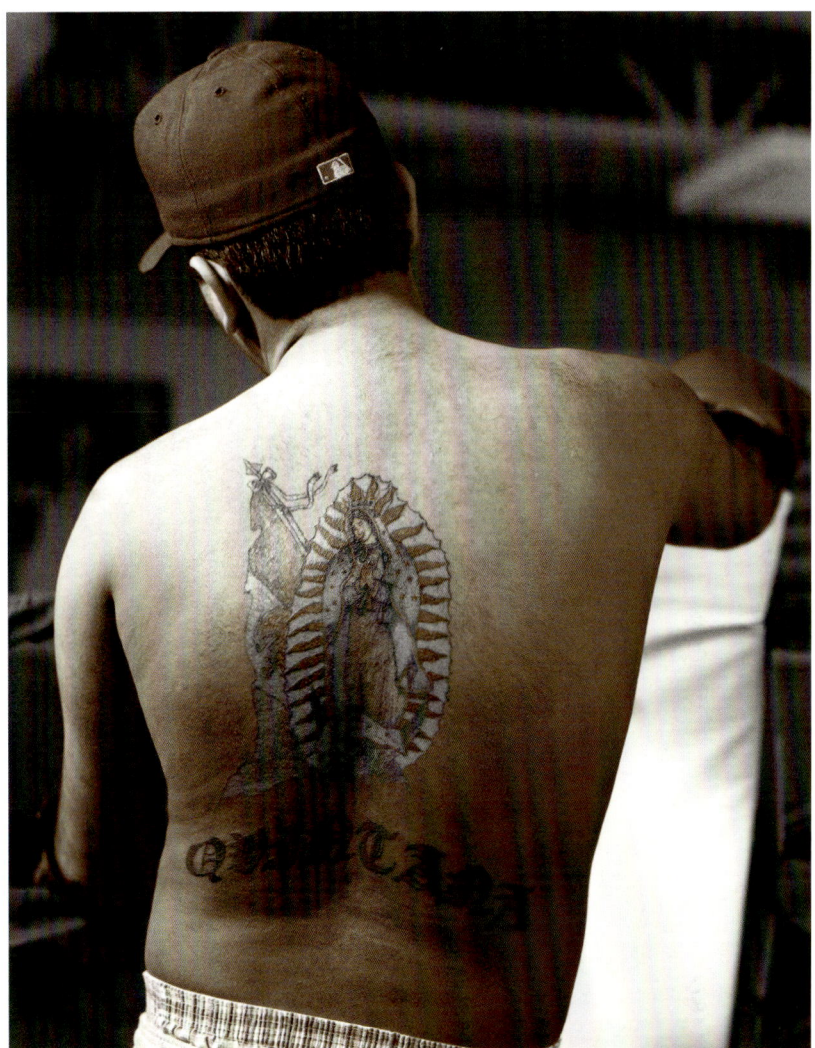

Delilah Montoya
Quintana (from the series
Guadalupe Tattoo)
1999, print date 2014
Archival inkjet on eSatin
paper
32 × 24 in.
Collection of the artist

In the *Guadalupe Tattoo* and *Guadalupe en Piel* series, Montoya continued photographing women and men with tattoos of the Virgin. Because her subjects were not necessarily prisoners or previously incarcerated, the cultural and spiritual meaning of the Virgen is tied to a broader Chicanx identity, though she still embodies the ideas of spirituality, protection, and care that also reference Tonanzin, the earth mother. The photographs were set in different sites. *La Virgen* and *La Virgen and Diego*, for example, were taken at a remote site that features the landscape of New Mexico. These images reference the original encounter between Juan Diego and the Virgen of Guadalupe. The figures wear garments that evoke the tilma, and they are looking away from the camera, expressing a sense of spirituality.

In *Guadalupe en Piel*, Montoya furthers the visual experience by depicting the body in fragmented forms. The viewer can see multiple perspectives simultaneously. For *Guadalupe en Piel*, Montoya digitized her process in part to explore the possibilities of large-scale printing, which provided the opportunity to create images with a higher resolution and clarity.[1]

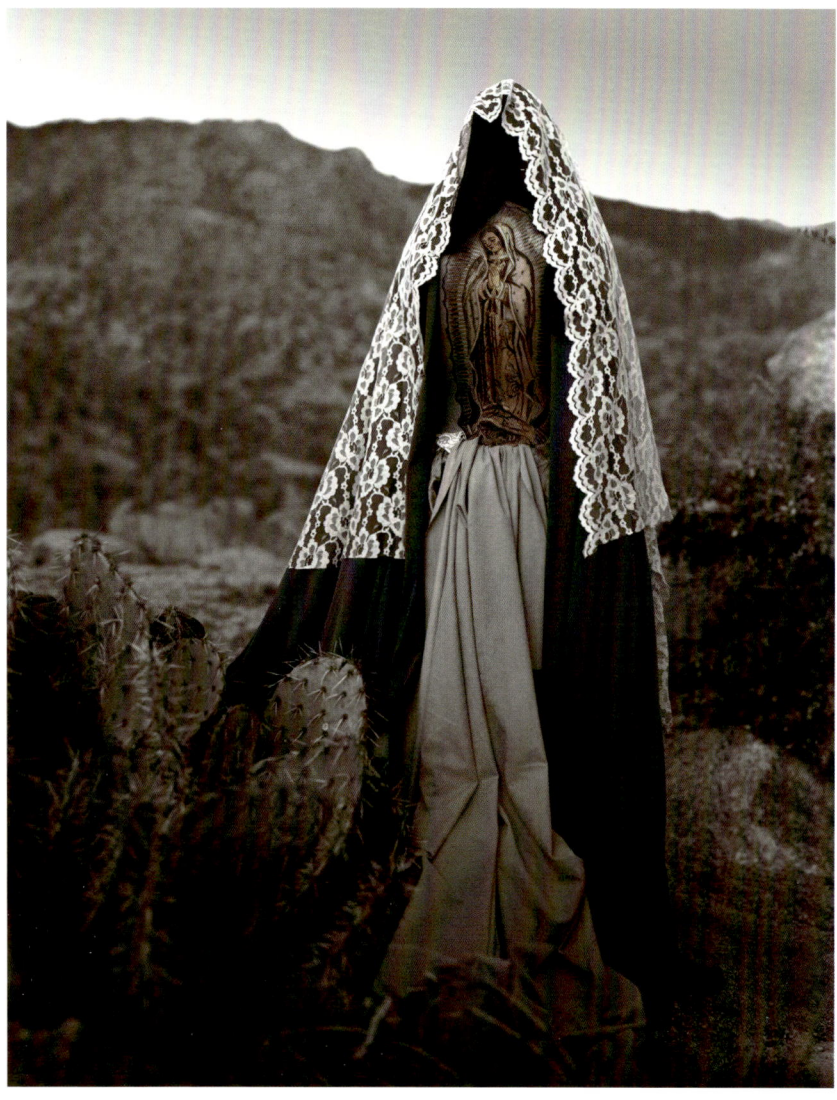

Delilah Montoya
La Virgen (from the series
Guadalupe Tattoo)
1998, digital print 2002
Inkjet on rag paper 1/2
22 × 27½ in.
Collection of the artist

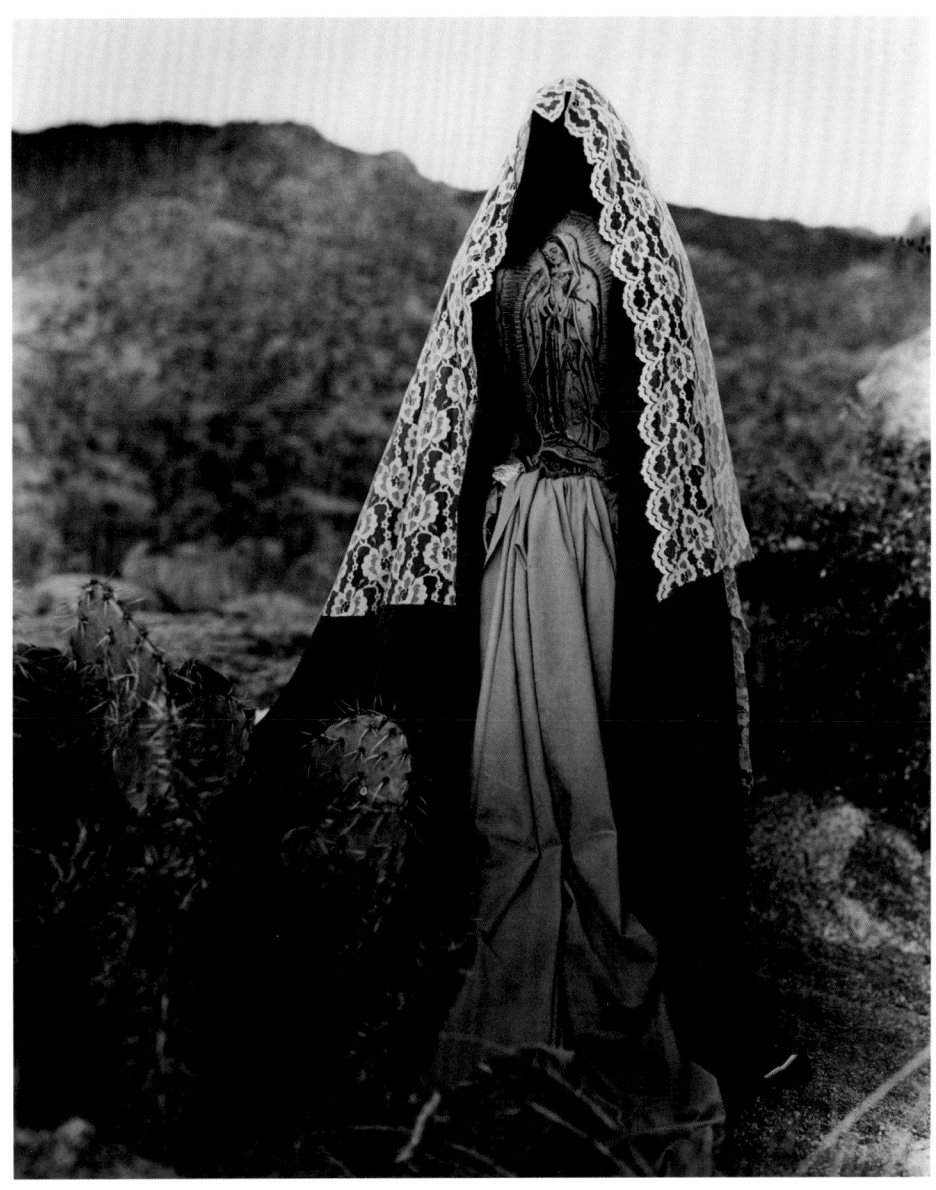

Delilah Montoya
La Virgen (from the series
Guadalupe Tattoo)
1998
Gelatin silver print, ed. 2/2
20 × 24 in.
Albuquerque Museum,
museum purchase and gift of
the artist
PC2022.32.18

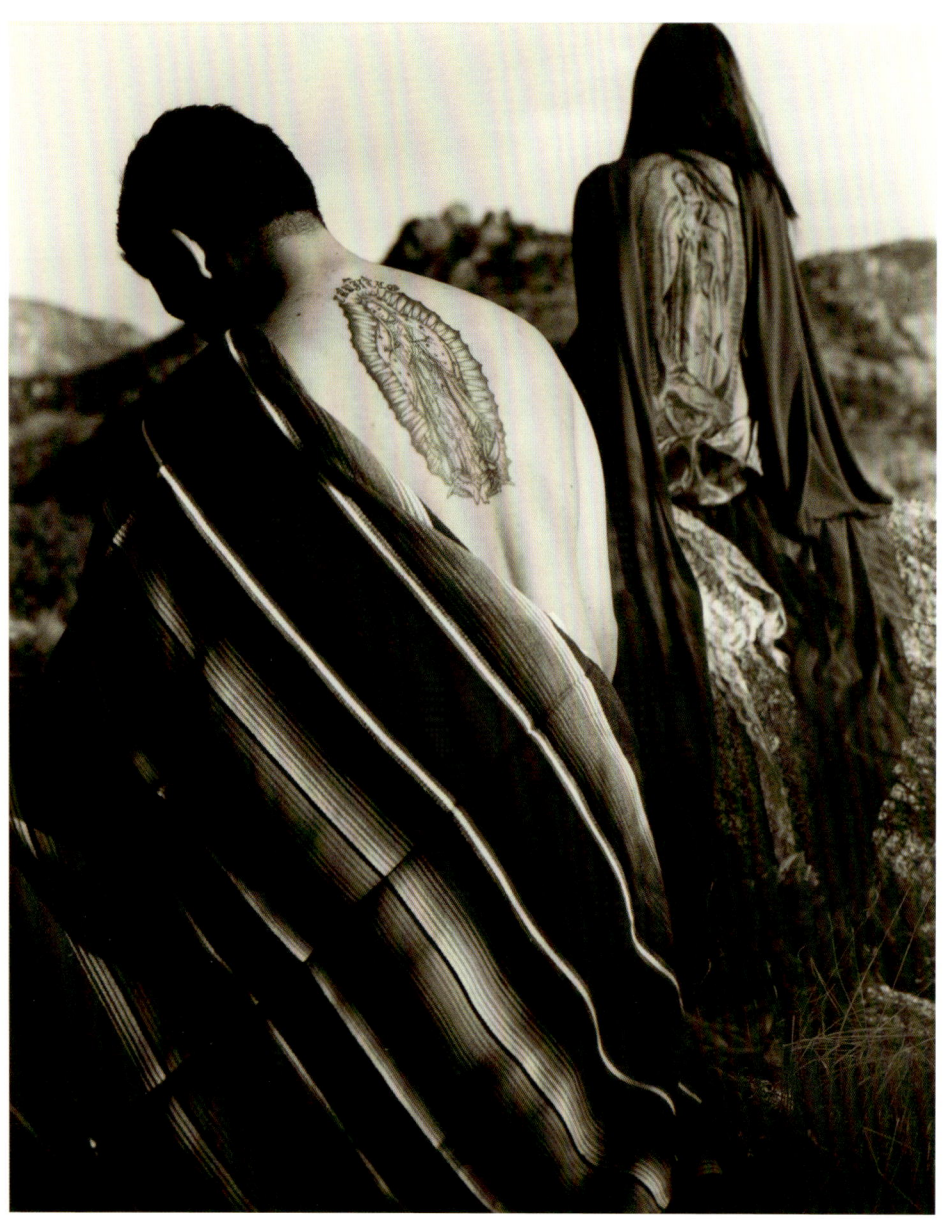

Delilah Montoya
Diego y la Virgin #2 (from the
series *Guadalupe Tattoo*)
1998
Gelatin silver print, ed. 2/2
23 × 18⅝ in.
Albuquerque Museum,
museum purchase and gift of
the artist
PC2022.32.16

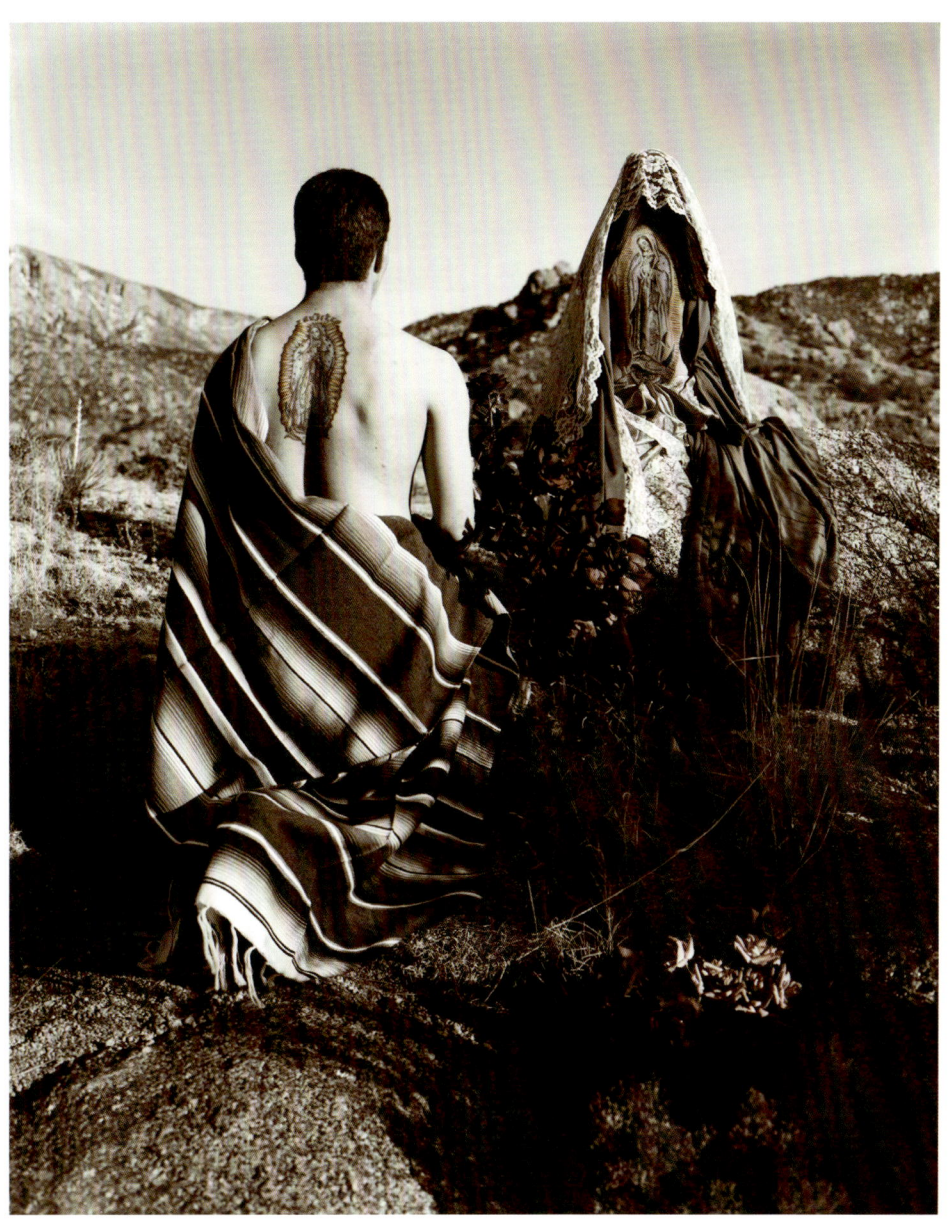

Delilah Montoya
Diego y La Virgen #3 (from
the series *Guadalupe Tattoo*)
1998, digital print date 2014
Archival inkjet on eSatin
paper
32 × 24 in.
Collection of the artist

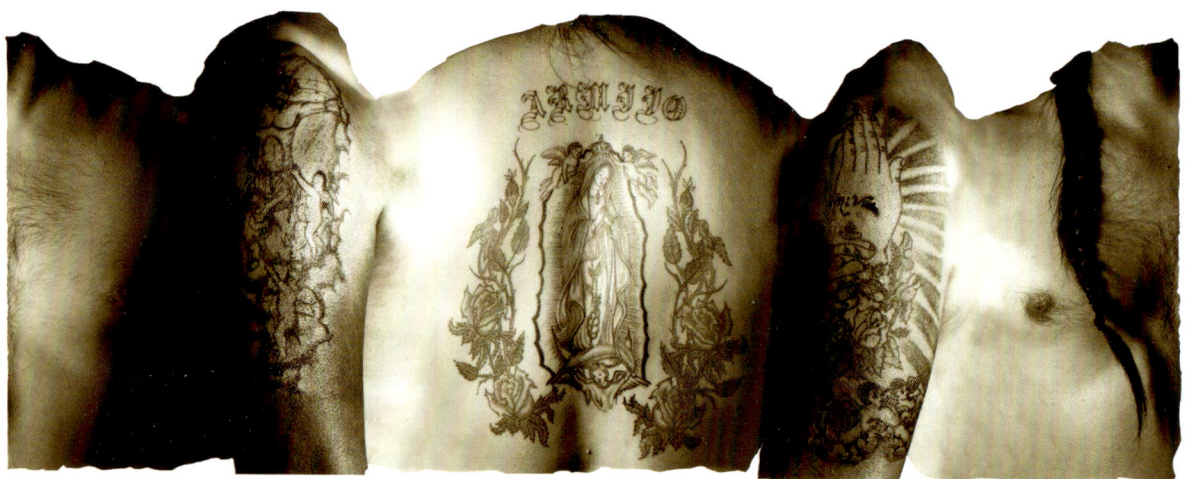

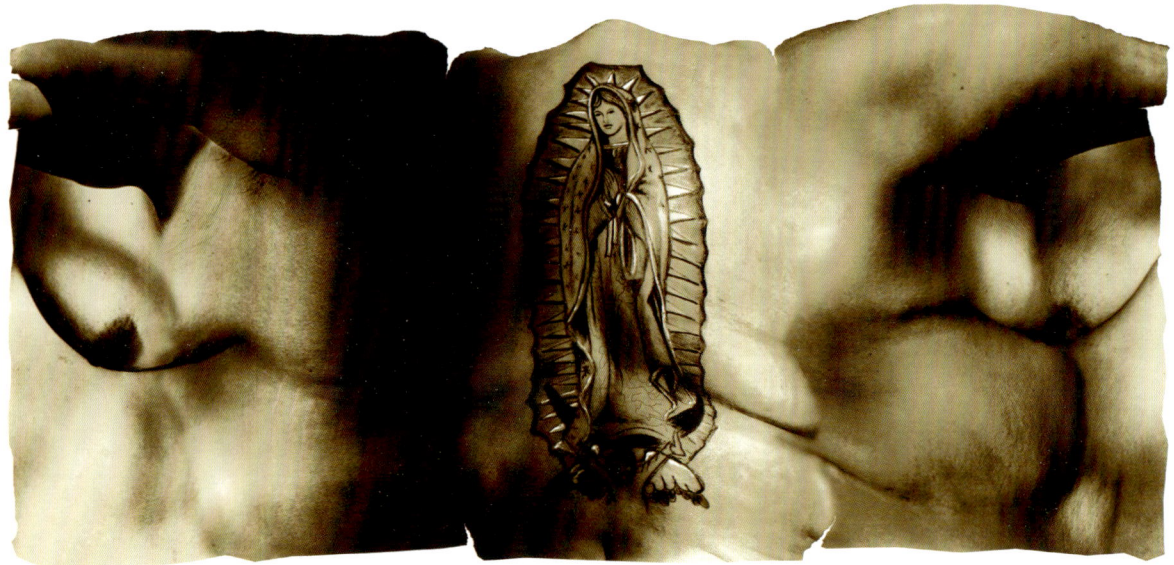

(*top*) Delilah Montoya
Guadalupe en Piel—Armijo
2000
Installation LightJet on film
24 × 60 in.
Collection of the artist

(*bottom*) Delilah Montoya
Guadalupe en Piel—Earth Mother
2000
Installation LightJet on film
24 × 60 in.
Collection of the artist

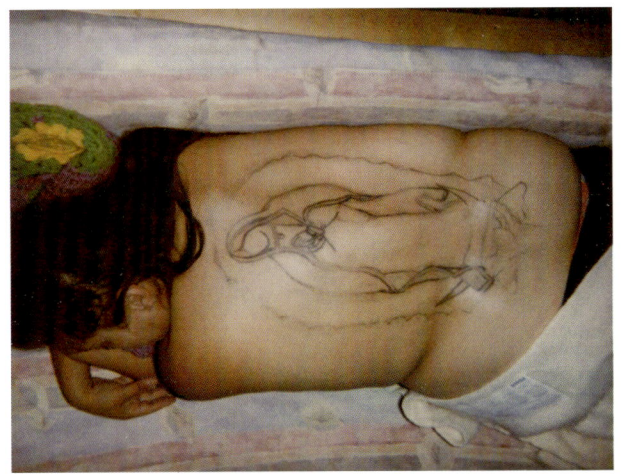
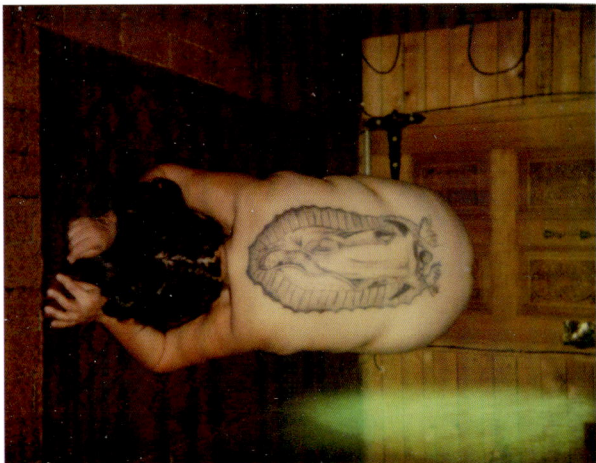
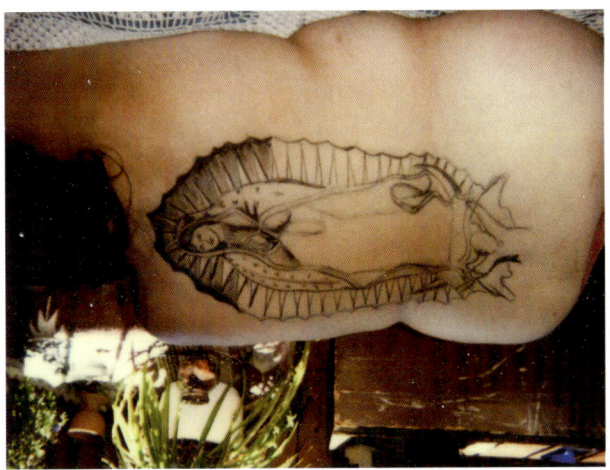
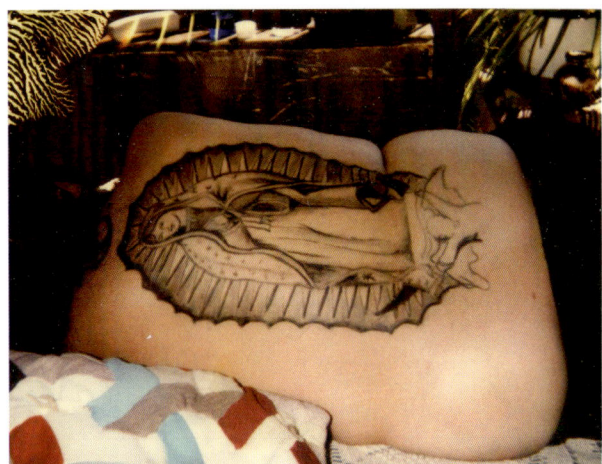

Delilah Montoya
Laura's Back (drawing the
Guadalupe)
2000
Suite of four prints
Polaroids
2⅛ × 2⅞ in.
Collection of the artist

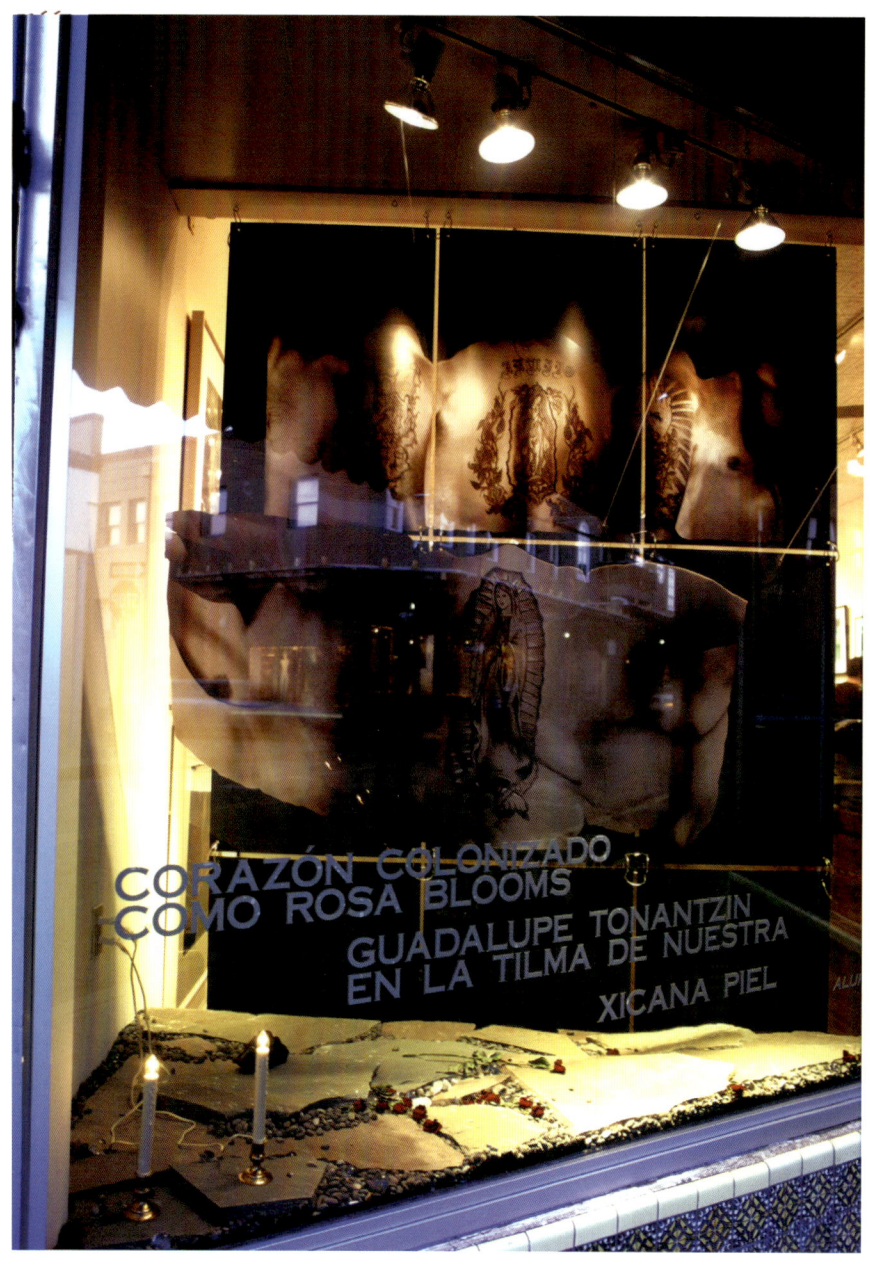

Delilah Montoya
Guadalupe en Piel (installation front view)
2000
Andrew Smith Gallery, Santa Fe, NM
Inkjet on Sintra and acetate, vinyl lettering, stone, and electric candles
8 × 4 × 3 in.
Collection of the artist

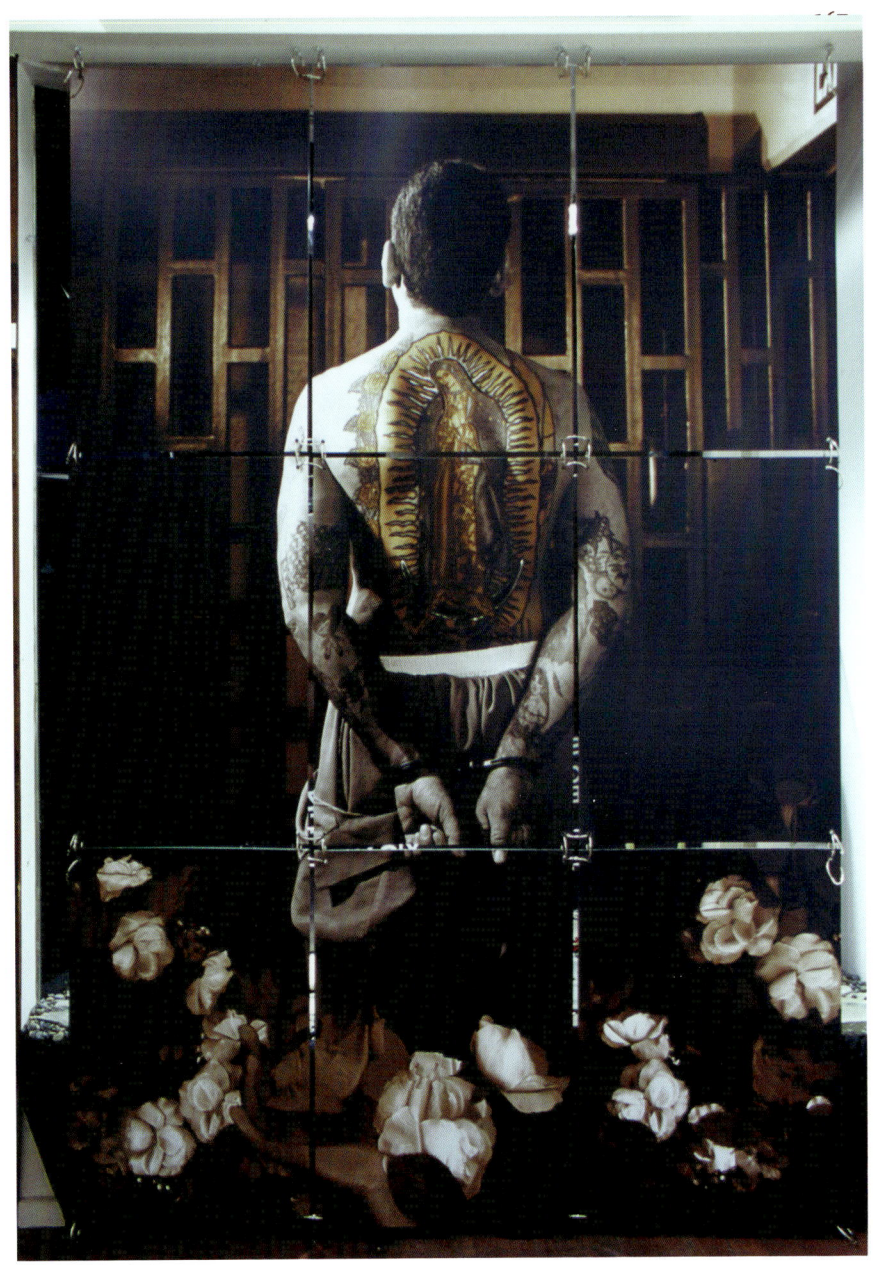

Delilah Montoya
Guadalupe en Piel (installation
back view)
2000
Andrew Smith Gallery, Tucson,
AZ
Inkjet on Sintra and acetate,
vinyl lettering, stone, and electric
candles
8 × 4 × 3 in.
Collection of the artist

In Conversation with Delilah Montoya and Demetria Martinez: *La Guadalupana* **Series**

Demetria: The *Guadalupana* series works on so many levels. She appears as a tattoo—a brown woman on brown bodies. You have Chicanos literally embodying the Divine—and not a male god but a goddess. The brown body, the colonized body, is uplifted in your work. What inspired you to undertake this project?

Delilah: Sometimes, these projects develop from requests to participate in exhibitions with a specific theme. That is what happened with the Chicano codices, *Shooting the Tourist*, *Detention Nation*, and the *Guadalupana*. I was always interested in doing something involving Guadalupe because she was so important, but I hadn't really thought about what, specifically. Musée de Beaux-Arts Denys-Puech organized this show in Rodez, France, with Francisco Benitez and his wife negotiating the project. I was asked to do something related to the Guadalupe because in Rodez, the basilica in the central plaza houses one of the first easel paintings of the Guadalupe. I wondered if other artists were asked to make something specific like that.

I had about a year to put it together, and I knew it would be expensive, so I applied for some grants. At that time, I was teaching at Hampshire College in western Massachusetts and felt far away from home. I remembered a lecture by Flora Clancy where she talked about pre-Columbian art and transculturation, the process by which European ideas, goods, and systems came to the New World, but also what the Old World got from the New World, which is very seldom talked about. And then she says, "I'm not just talking about tomatoes. There was more than just tomatoes that went in the other direction."

The Guadalupe is one of those examples of something born in the Americas and transferred over to Europe. I began to ask, "What does that mean? Why would that particular image be important to take back? What does that say about the Americas?" The Guadalupe is a colonial image, and she was a perfect example of the idea of syncretism. She was revered as an Aztec goddess, Tonantzin, in Tepeyac, where there was an Aztec temple dedicated to her. She was the earth goddess, and I don't think it was a coincidence that Diego saw her there.

She was needed for the continuation of Indigenous existence. The rupture of colonialism meant the people had to find a way to survive. The

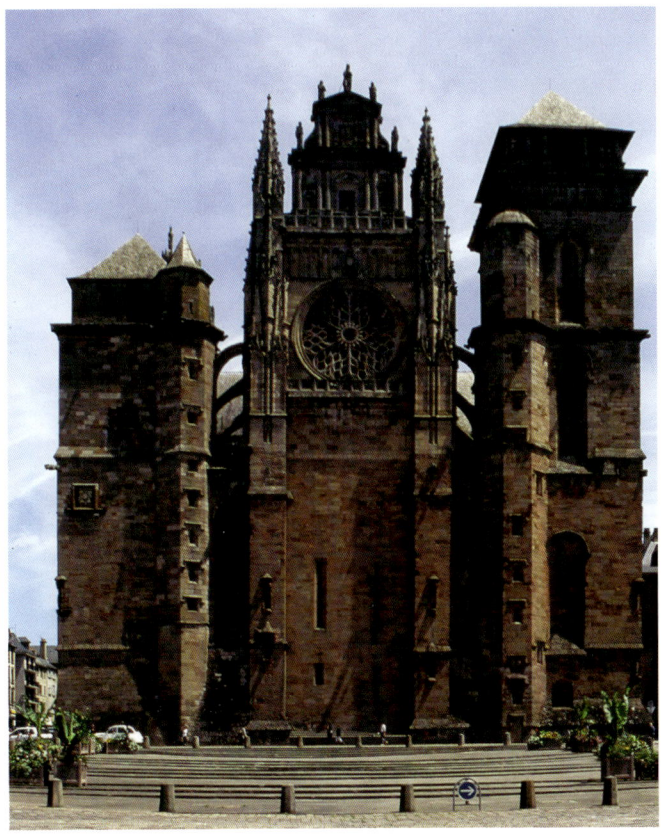

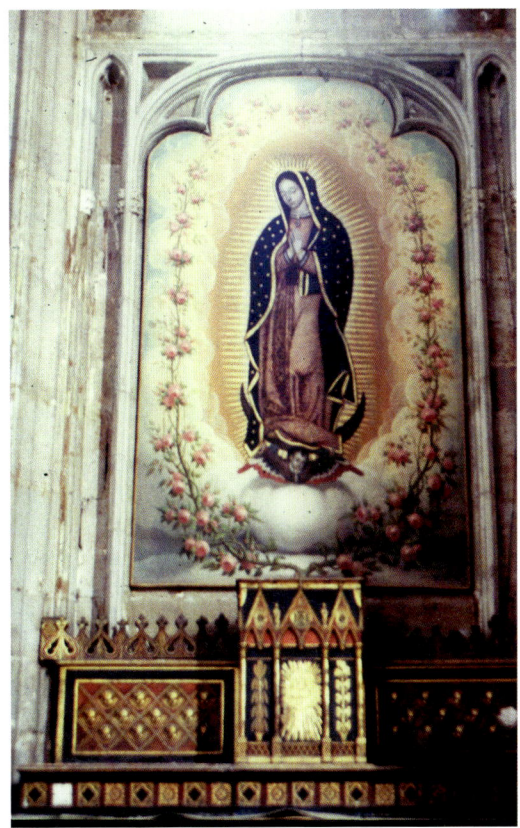

Rodez Basilica, where an easel painting of Guadalupe was brought from Mexico by Franciscans in the seventeenth century
Photo courtesy of Delilah Montoya

fact that she was brown, and she spoke Juan Diego's language, and she persisted, and her image never went away. She became the goddess of the Americas. She was the image that César Chávez carried. She was carried in all of the Mexican civil wars, and she's carried across the border. She's in all our homes. I remember going to New York, and she was in Saint Patrick's Cathedral. I began to think about how she's used as a tattoo, particularly on bodies who have been incarcerated. Why are they placing her on their back? Is it because they're staunch Catholics? I don't think so.

I was interested in the connection between the tilma being worn with her impression and the Guadalupe being worn as a tattoo directly on the backs of cholos. The wearing of her image was important because it goes back to Mesoamerica. This act just didn't go away—the wearing of her references Tonantzin and the association of wearing a tilma to evoke her presence.

My idea was to photograph her being worn as a tattoo, and I wanted to create a large-scale mural. I started to call tattoo parlors and boxing rings. I called Cecilio, and he said that he was doing some work with prisoners in his role as a cultural attaché at the Mexican Consulate. When I returned to Albuquerque, I had lists of people to photograph.

I wanted to photograph a woman with a Guadalupe on her back, but I couldn't find anybody. I collaborated with my cousin, Darlene Madrid, who agreed to have the Guadalupe drawn on her back. I included Diego in the shot. He had a tattoo on his back inked at a local tattoo parlor. I thought it was interesting that his name was Diego, but he didn't know of Juan Diego's historic relation to the Guadalupe. The shoot was located in the Sandia Foothills. Diego was positioned as Juan Diego at the point of encountering the Virgin. An 8 × 10 camera was used to take the photograph. This shoot turned out to be really strong. Diego's girlfriend came along, and I thought it'd be really interesting to have some shots with roses around Diego's back, so I asked her to hold the roses, and there was an intense chemistry between them. Those photographs were used to frame the *La Guadalupana* mural.

Felix Martinez, the model for *La Guadalupana*, was photographed at an Albuquerque detention center. He was awaiting trial for a drive-by shooting. The police didn't know if he had done it, but, as a *veterano* who just got out of prison and went back to his hood, they figured that the *cholitos* told him who did it. So they arrested him on the charge, hoping that he would point out the shooter. When I looked at the tattoo on his back, I knew that was the right tattoo. It covered his full back from the top down. I realized the Guadalupe on the back of a *pinto* (inmate) was conceptually the right image to represent the colonized Guadalupe in France. It spoke clearly of colonialism, revealing the servitude and the violence, and it spoke clearly about the issues the Chicanx community faces. The French would understand what I was trying to say with that image. Felix agreed to the shoot, and Michael Esfera touched up the tattoo, deepening the lines so that I could get a clean shot.

Around that time, I went to a party with Cecilio in Santa Fe as part of his work with the Mexican Consulate. This guy came up to me, Michael O'Shannessy, and he owned a publishing house called Red Crane. He said, "Delilah Montoya, I never want to hear that you could not get the shot you needed because you didn't have the equipment, and he handed me his card." It was perfect timing. I called him up, saying I needed an 8 × 10 camera with lights to take to the detention center. And he said, "Sure,

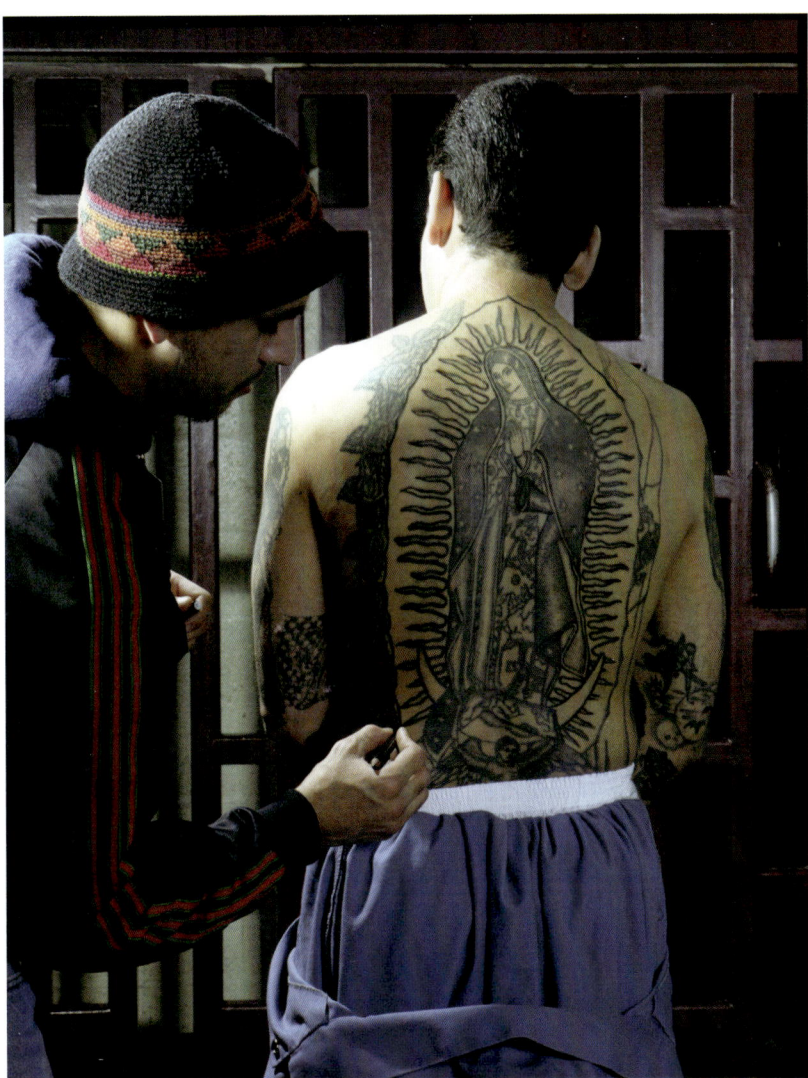

Michael Esfera touching up
Felix Martinez's back (from
the series *Guadalupe Tattoo*)
High-resolution digital file
from color negative
1998
Collection of the artist

come on down." He generously took me to this locker, asking, "What
do you need?" I held a lens to the light, and it was like a diamond, so
beautiful. Tripod, electronic flashes—I mean all of it. I put it into my car
and drove it to the detention center. While I was setting up the camera
and lights, Felix was brought in, and Michael began to work on his back.
I positioned Felix in front of the bars. I remember asking him if it was
OK to handcuff him. I felt bad about cuffing him, but he was fine with it,
and we made sure the cuffs were loose. Everything looked great, and after
about eight shots, nothing was working. The lights were really strong,
and they tripped the breaker. At that point, I said, "We're done here," and

loaded everything back in the laundry cart and said, "Thank you very much." When the film was processed, I looked at it and knew that it was the image for the mural.

I wanted to put an altar below the mural using nopales and little Chicanx kitsch things and ship it to France. Believe it or not, the cactus made it. It was really something; they didn't pull it out at customs. The mural was larger than the wall, so it slanted onto the ceiling, but it worked in the sense that the mural consumed the space.

Demetria: Beautiful. What a gift to France! You know a picture of a cell that is transformed into a sacred space. And a man, an inmate, whose body becomes an *ofrenda*.

Delilah: I was able to make my point in terms of the colonized body and how colonialism created the calamity that we are still feeling. Colonialism in the Americas was devastating. It is the largest holocaust, genocide that this planet has ever seen. It went on for centuries, literally centuries, with stolen land and free labor. That's what the wealth was built on. Truth is truth, they can try to change the narrative. But that was the truth.

Demetria: Physical violence as well as, you know, psychic, spiritual violence.

Delilah: Exactly, it's just part of the everyday. I paid Felix for the photograph; I paid him half when I shot it. And I told him I'd pay him the other half after I returned from France. I wanted to show him pictures of what it looked like installed. I contacted his counselor, and he said, "Well, I got some bad news for you. Felix was killed in the Detention Center." Apparently, he had decided to point out the shooter . . . the gang took him out. It was at this point, all of this theory, like colonialism and violence, got real. I mean, it's not just theories. And these are people's lives. You know, it's real. At this point, it became an ofrenda because he was no longer with us. And so all of those things that I put down, all of those kitsch items. I don't know how I ever really felt about it. It just was never right—the underpinnings on all of that.

In her project of recasting iconic female spiritual and folkloric figures, Montoya centers women who have been seen as monstrous, traitors, evil antagonists, and the embodiment of the treacherous female. Montoya's malcriadas include Doña Sebastiana, La Llorona, Malinche, and Lilith.

In her presentation of *La Sebastiana* at the Museum of Spanish Colonial Art in Santa Fe in 2003, Montoya quoted her mother Amalia Garcia: "Sebastiana never wanted to be Death. Really, all she wanted was love—if not love, at least respect. As the story goes, God needed someone to collect the souls of the dead, and he decided Sebastiana was the woman for the job. She begs him to reconsider because people would despise and fear her for bringing death onto them." Montoya collaborated with Mónica Sánchez to create a photo series and film to rewrite Sebastiana's story. The *Sebastiana* series was one of the bodies of work in which Montoya waded into the world of digital photography. *Women Boxers, Sed: Trail of Thirst, Guadalupe en Piel* were also forays into the rapidly changing medium of photography.[1]

In 2004, Montoya collaborated with Christina Hernandez on a site-specific installation, *La Llorona in Lillith's Garden*, which consists of two photographic murals printed on canvas created for El Museo Cultural de Santa Fe. The rich photographic installation brings together two archetypal figures thought to have betrayed their husbands and murdered their children. According to folklore, both Lilith and La Llorona continue to haunt the living world as evil spirits. These women were presented as monsters and constructed to teach young girls how to behave and how they should feel about these sorts of "monstrous women." This work was also included in the *Contemporary Art Houston* exhibition in Shanghai, China. These series and installations depicting Malinche, La Llorona, and Lilith explore the traditional double standards defining women's roles and imbues these female archetypes with new meaning and Montoya's continuing exploration of the colonial body.

SEVEN

Malcriadas

Malinche, Doña Sebastiana, and La Llorona

In Conversation with Delilah Montoya, Mónica Sánchez, and Demetria Martinez: Malinche and Sebastiana

Demetria: Bad Girls, *Las Malcriadas,* is a perfect title for your series celebrating La Malinche, La Llorona, and Doña Sebastiana. These women embody what patriarchy fears—intellectual prowess, sensuality, and death itself. La Malinche, a Nahua Indian, was sold or given as a slave to conquistador Hernan Cortez, and she ended up as his interpreter. Particularly after Mexican independence from Spain, many intellectuals condemned her as a traitor to the Indigenous race. An idea popularized in the 1900s by Octavio Paz. But feminists have been reimagining her as an embodiment of female power and celebrating her as the mother of Mestizaje, the mother of our *raza*. How are you reimagining her in your work?

Delilah: Malinche was part of a number of series, including *Codex Delilah,* where she is presented as Llora-Llora-Malinche. This association happened early on with the Chicano movement; this was Cecilio's influence on the narrative. Llora-Llora-Malinche describes the conquest; in her character, she is both Malinche and Llorona. It had to do with her being the mother of the first mestizo. In Chicanx minds, the first mestizo child was from Hernán Cortés and Malinche. In the codex Llora-Llora cries for her lost children, but she is also aware of the New Race and Malinche as the mother. The next time I represent her in the *Sagrado Corazón*, she is a young girl in a First Holy Communion dress. This is very New Mexican. All the other Chicanxs from outside of New Mexico wonder why she is a little girl in a First Holy Communion dress! But that is how she appears in the Matachin Dances, which are colonial baroque dances where she brings the tribes into Christianity. So she is also the first New World Christian. The dance is performed throughout Latin America. For some reason, in the United States, a lot of the Chicanx communities have forgotten that traditional dance. I wanted to start thinking about how she was considered a traitor who was also the first Christian and mother of the Mestizos. She is surrounded by the whore/Madonna syndrome. Octavio Paz demonizes her, yet she is revered as a Christian. Malinche was a complicated figure. Like Sebastiana, her humanity is overwhelming. Malinche has always been at the forefront of my thoughts in terms of the malcriada. Chicana women are misunderstood, not clearly understood for our importance of what we have done and we can do.

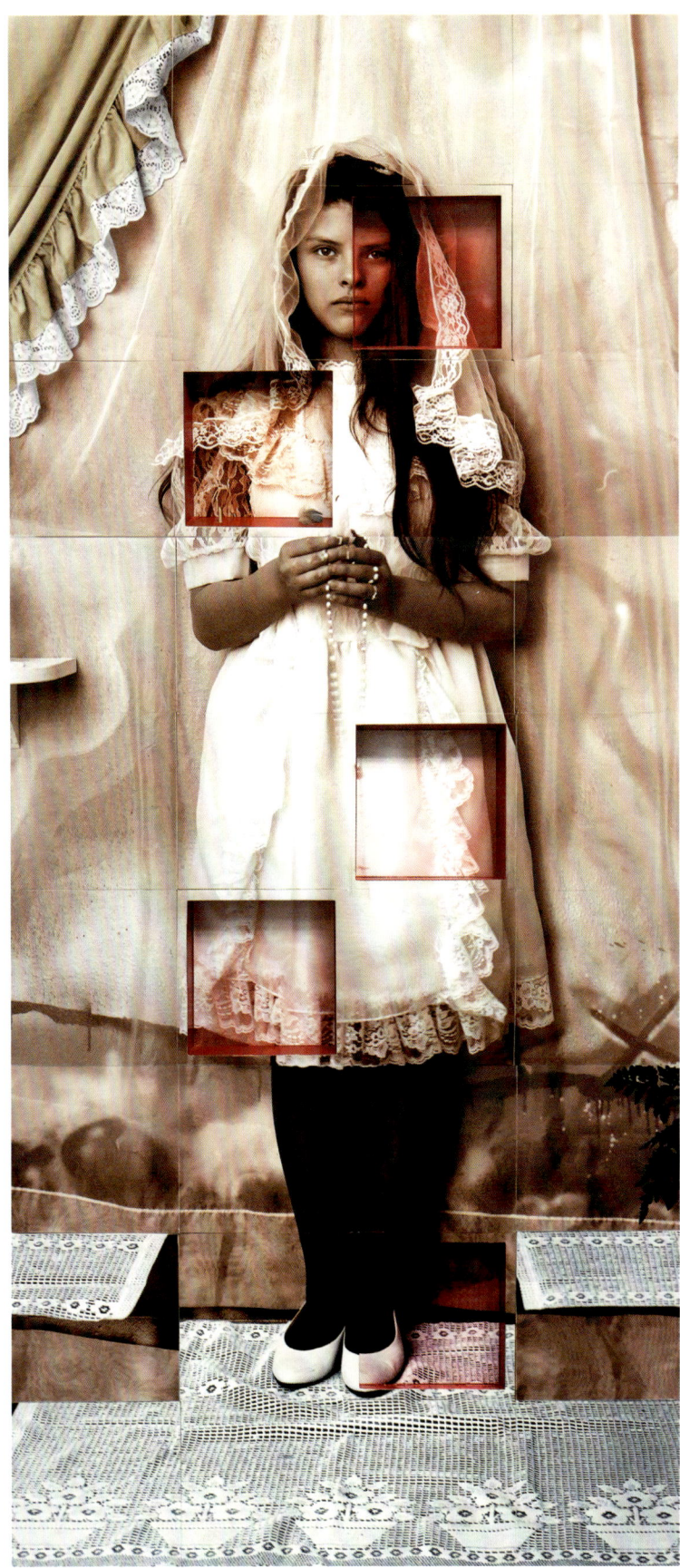

Delilah Montoya
Malinalli: La Lengua Como Poder
1993/2022
Wood, inkjet on eSatin paper, one feather, gold leaf, and enamel paint
32 × 72 in.
Collection of the artist

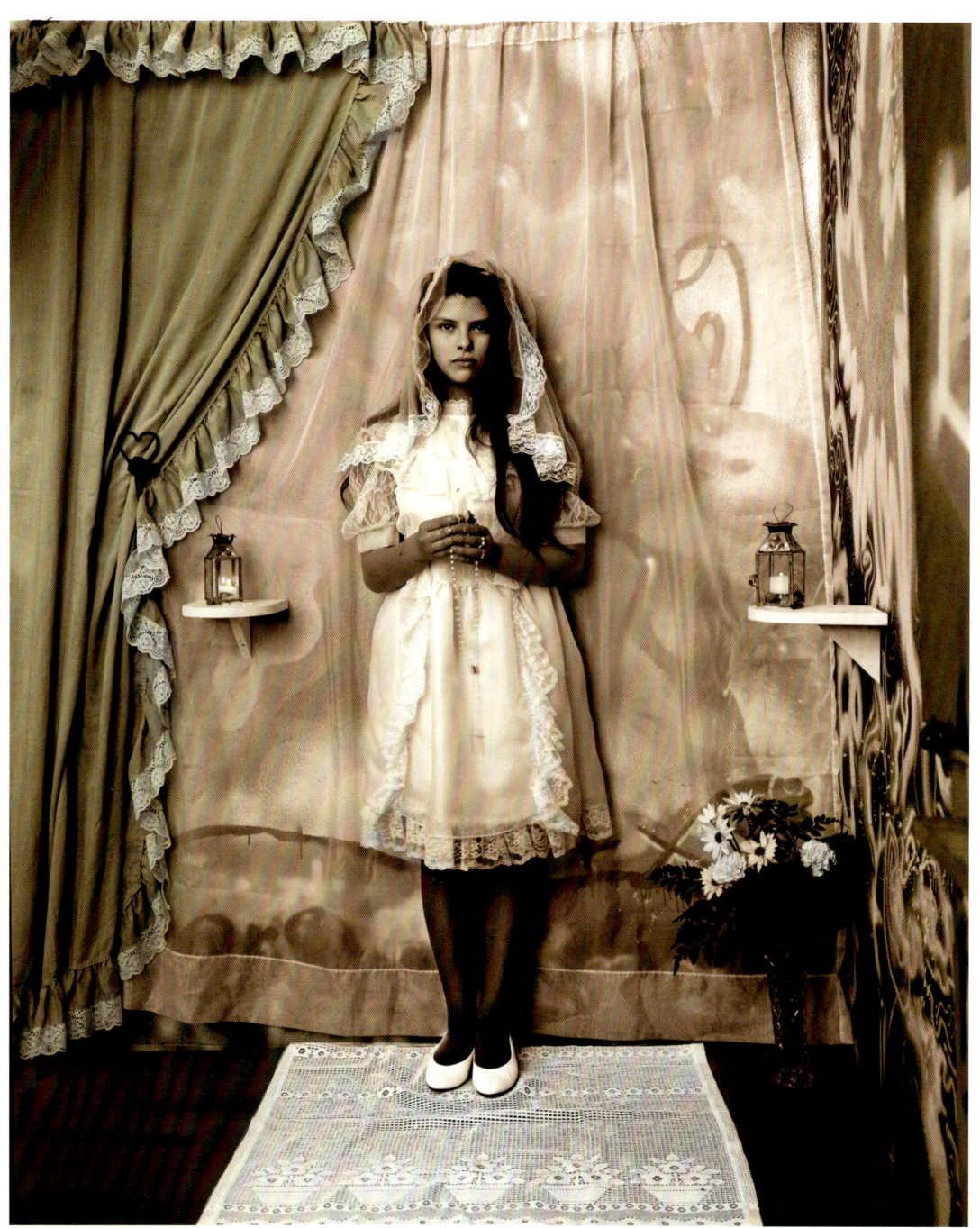

Delilah Montoya
La Malinche from the portfolio (*El Sagrado Corazon*)
1993/2000
Colorized digitally, Lysonic ink on luster paper
37 × 30 in.
Collection of the artist

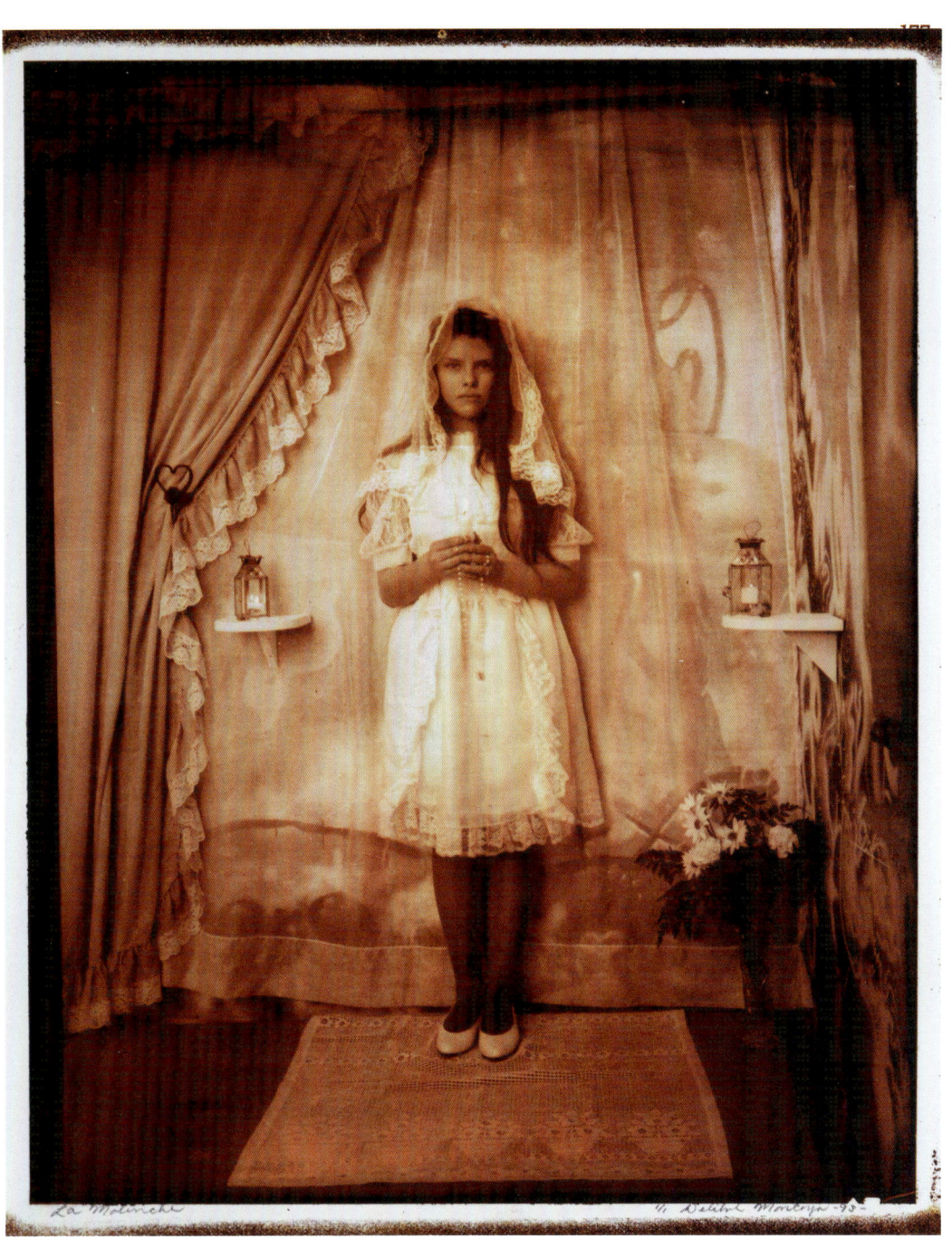

Delilah Montoya

La Malinche (from the portfolio *El Sagrado Corazón*)

1993

Collotype, ed. 1/1

10 × 8 in.

Albuquerque Museum, museum purchase and gift of the artist

PC2022.32.21

Mónica: Well, here's the thing about las malcriadas. The word "malcriada" literally means "brought up badly," which by definition, exonerates said malcriada of any blame! Another way to see the "malcriada" is someone who does not obey, someone who breaks the rules. But if the rules are not just or they go against the better, more vital, creative and self-possessed parts of our nature, they *should* be broken! Delilah, I see your "malcriadas" as heroic agents of liberation, subverting the limitations and judgements imposed by the vestiges of colonialism and patriarchal culture.

I've been wondering for a long time about the representation of La Malinche in our New Mexican tradition of Los Matachines—when, how, and why was she infantilized? How did "La Malinche" go from a young woman slave/translator/consort to the prepubescent initiate of the Holy Communion ritual? Interestingly, the initiate's role in the Catholic rite of passage (First Holy Communion) is passive, in stark contrast to the role of the Malinche in the Matachín dance ritual.

This is one question that I'm addressing in my new play, *Voy*. The dramatic narrative posits that the child-Malinche of the Matachines is a vessel for innocence lost to trauma. Some believe that Malintzín, aka La Malinche, was between eight and eleven years old when she was taken into captivity. Perhaps our Malinche depicts a child's psyche frozen in time, resulting from a cataclysmic personal and cultural *susto*. The inner child, if you will, of the feminine collective is now given agency in this dance ritual of Los Matachines.

Delilah: I know the dance has something to do with the idea of the Moors and how Christianity tamed the Moors and brought them into Christianity. The headdress that the tribes wear in the dance is very Moorish, which was intentional to associate the tribes as pagan.

Mónica: Yes, but we're talking about the Malinche, the child, and the name Malinche; we do not know her real name. So I'm fascinated.

Delilah: She is definitely a person of consequence. She was the translator. I wrote this about her: *Malinalli: La Lengua Como Poder*. So little is known about Malinalli. It is not certain when she was born or died nor her name or even how she felt about being Cortez's tongue. Yet her presence is still felt. Her mind authored the first contact between two powerful worlds. Her survival is her truth. Because there's so little known about her, the artists are left to find creative ways to fill in that void.

Demetria: It is important to remember the oversimplification of the narrative that she helped Cortez conquer the indigenous race. But the fact of the matter is, her own people, Indigenous people, wanted to see an end to the Aztecs because they were a brutal Imperial force.

Delilah: The first time I heard the word "Malinche" was when my mother used it. Two of my aunties were desperate to find jobs in Omaha, and they found employment as sewing machine operators. When they came on board, many of the women were from Latin America, and couldn't speak English, and the supervisor couldn't speak Spanish! The supervisor soon realized that my mother was bilingual, so she wanted her to translate her ugly directives. She would pull my mother away from what she was doing to translate, and still she wanted her to make the quota. My mom told her, I'm not going to be a Malinche. Either pay me to translate or lower my quota. As a northern New Mexican woman, she knew who Malinche was. Malinche's story is our story.

Demetria: In our society, we are taught to fear death. Enter Doña Sebastiana. Female skull faces appear in our homes as candles, as sculptures, or emblazoned on Day of the Dead costumes. You can't help but love her even as she scares us. Monica, how did you become involved in this project? And how did you take on Sebastiana's persona?

Mónica: Growing up in Albuquerque, I had seen Delilah's work, and in the late 1980s, she photographed a play I was performing in with La Compañía de Teatro de Alburquerque. I was playing El Diablo, and the malcriada in Delilah would not limit the photo shoot to the confines of the dark theater; we went out to various locations in downtown Albuquerque and posed the Diablo in a number of shenanigans. I told Delilah how much I loved her work and would love to collaborate again, not knowing how or if it might ever be possible.

Fast forward to 2001. Delilah calls me and tells me about a project she's conceiving about *Doña Sebastiana El Angel de La Muerte*, and she invites me to portray El Angel herself! The timing could not have been better. This was a telephone conversation, so she had no way of knowing that at the time I happened to be completely bald. I had just finished working on an independent film written and directed by Octavio Solis, adapted from his play, *Prospect*. I played a cancer patient and shaved my head bald and lost a lot of weight. Basically, I was a Calaca . . . with a gap in my schedule. I came to New Mexico, and we began the project. She

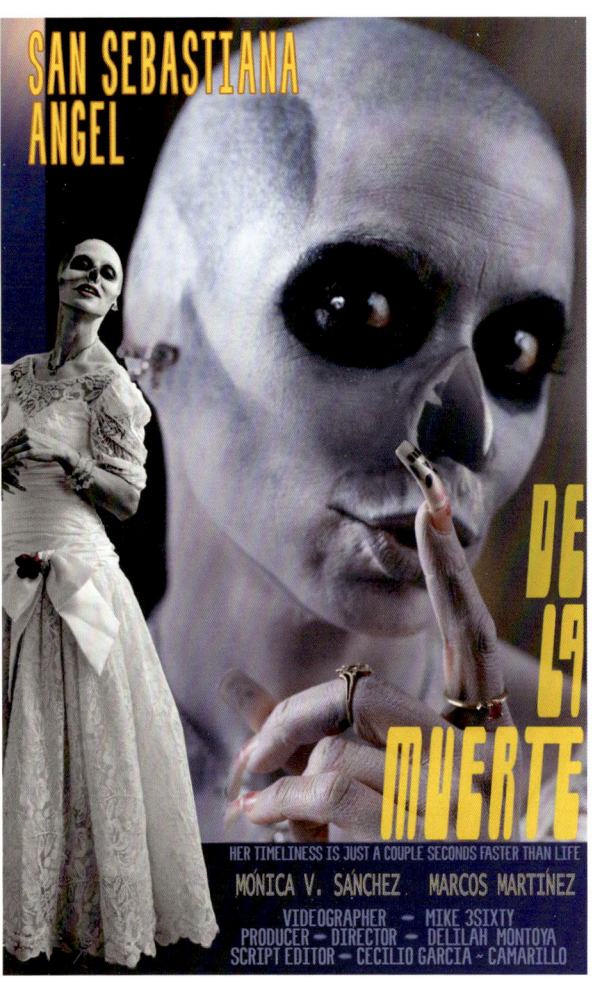

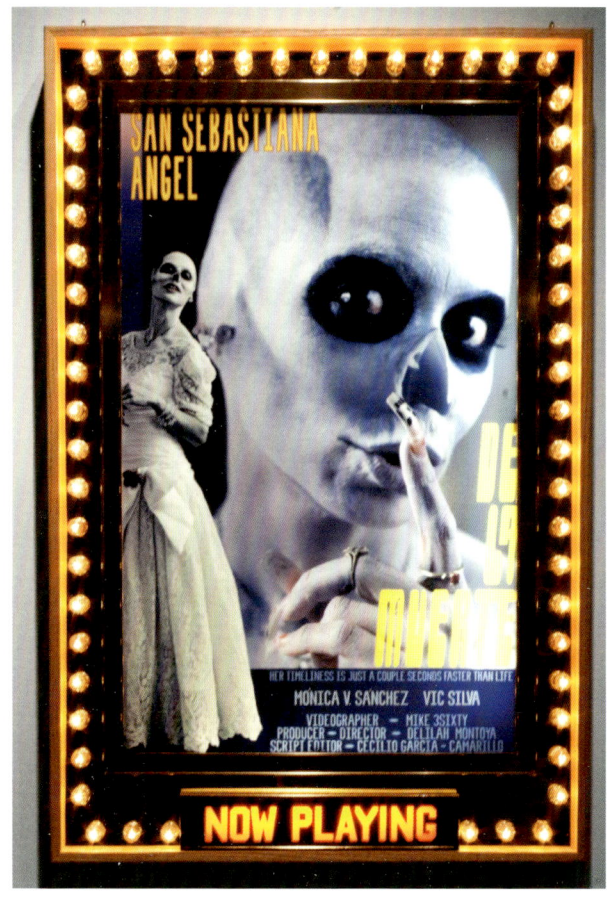

(*left*) Delilah Montoya
San Sebastiana: Angel de La Muerte,
poster
8-minute video with installation
2001, updated 2008, 2014
24 × 28 in.
Collection of the artist

(*right*) Delilah Montoya
San Sebastiana: Angel de La Muerte
2002
Inkjet on mylar
4½ × 3 ft.
Collection of the artist

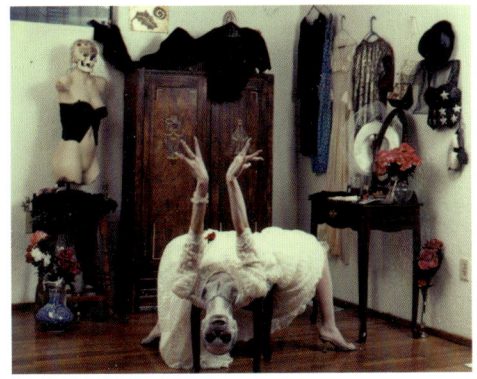
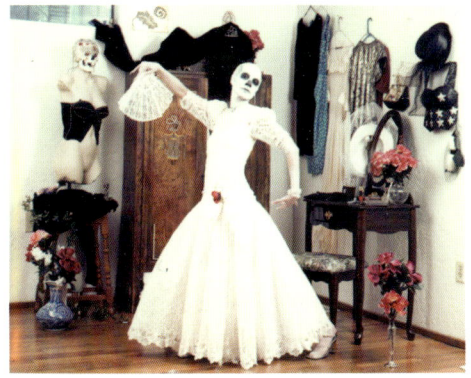
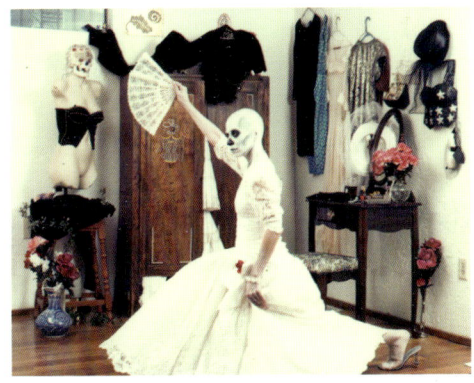
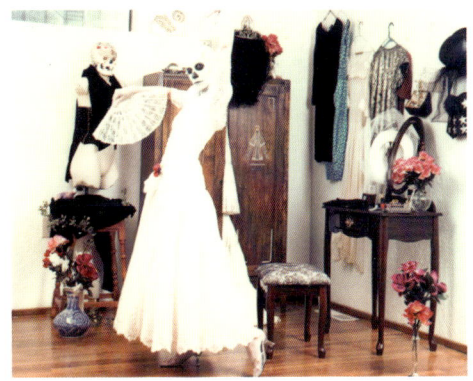
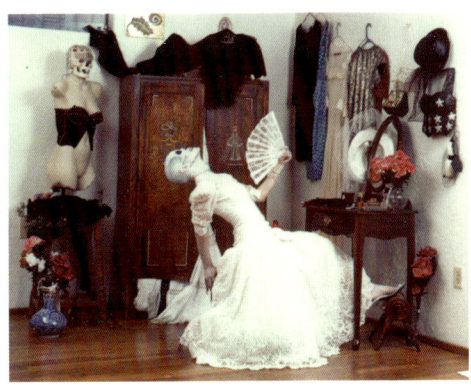
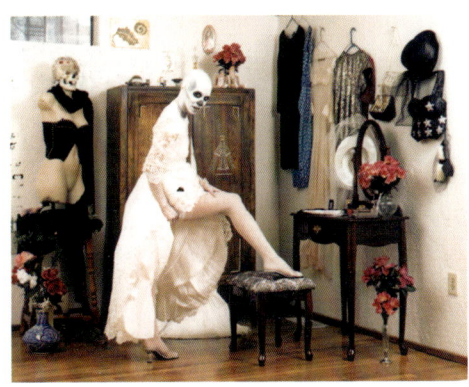

Delilah Montoya
Suite of seven Polaroid studies
(from the series *Doña Sebastiana*)
2001
4½ × 3½ in.
Collection of the artist

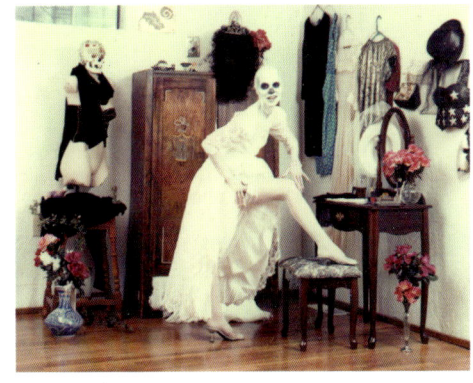

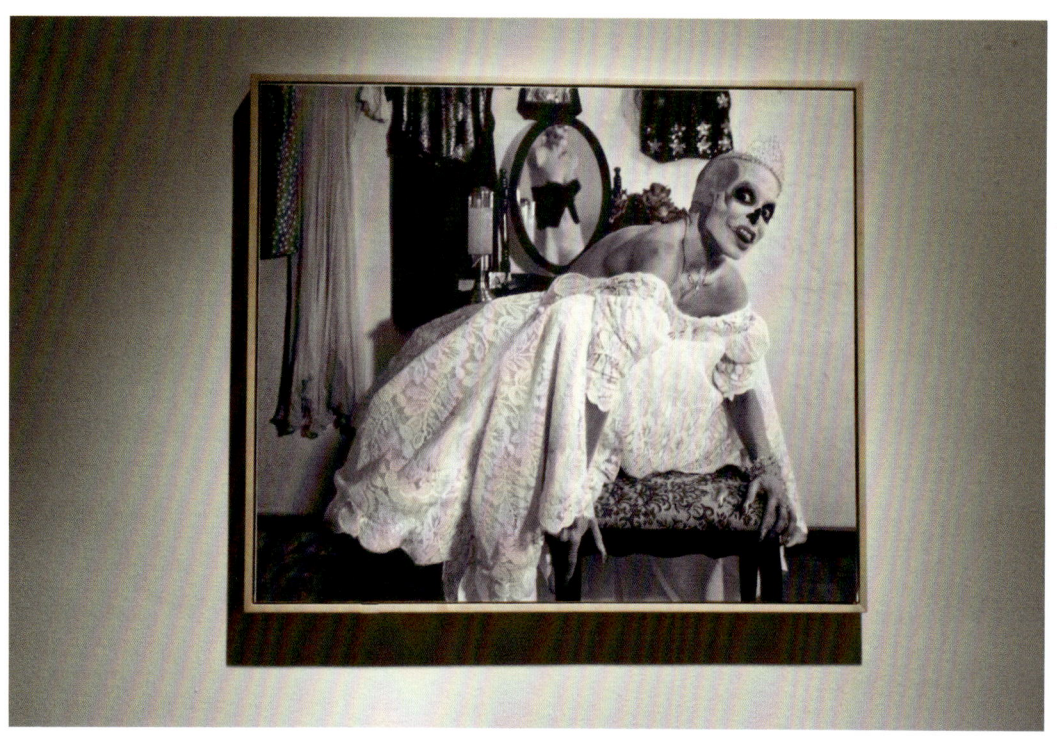

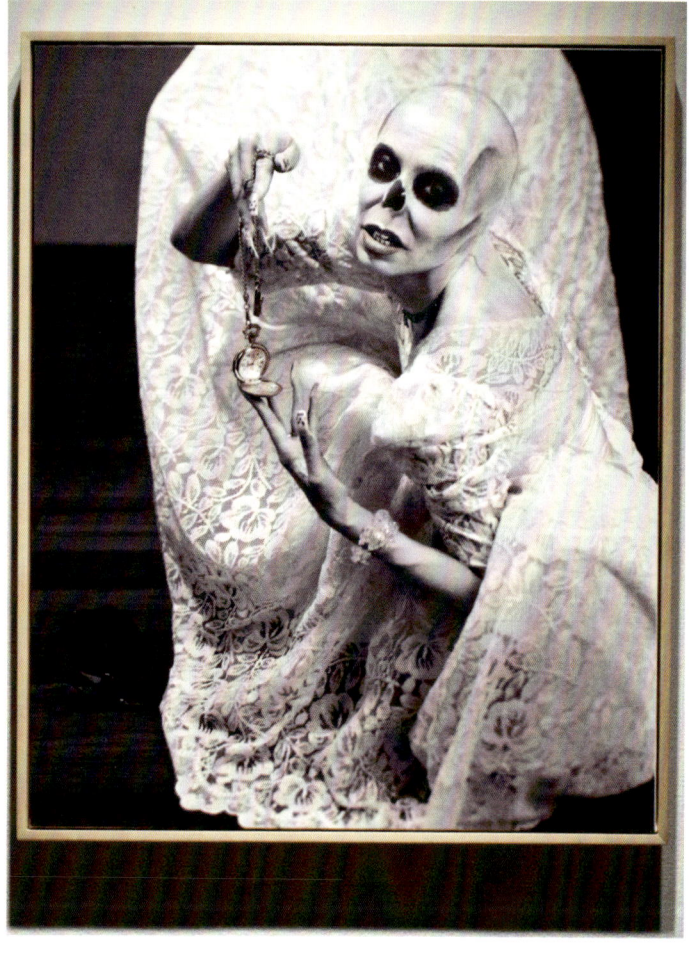

(*left*) Delilah Montoya
La Lengua Negra (from the series
Doña Sebastiana)
2002
Digital colorized archival inkjet
print on canvas
20 × 24 in.
Collection of the artist

(*right*) Delilah Montoya
Ahora (from the series *Doña Sebastiana*)
2002
Digital colorized archival inkjet
print on canvas
20 × 24 in.
Collection of the artist

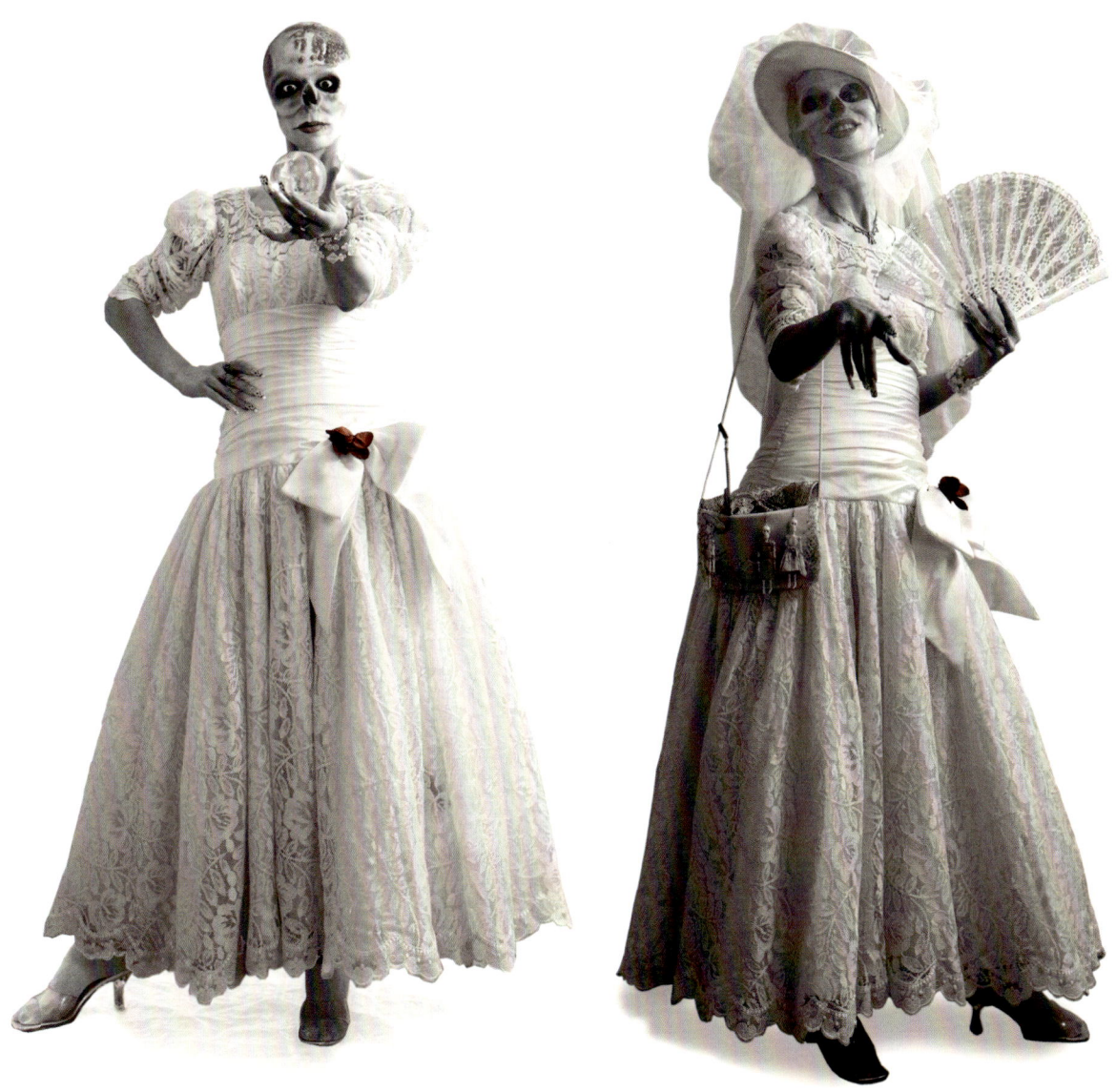

(*left*) Delilah Montoya
Gitana (from the series *Doña Sebastiana*)
2006
Inkjet on canvas
60 × 24 in
Collection of the artist

(*right*) Delilah Montoya
Te Quiero (from the series *Doña Sebastiana*)
2001
Inkjet on mylar
66 × 24 in.
Collection of the artist

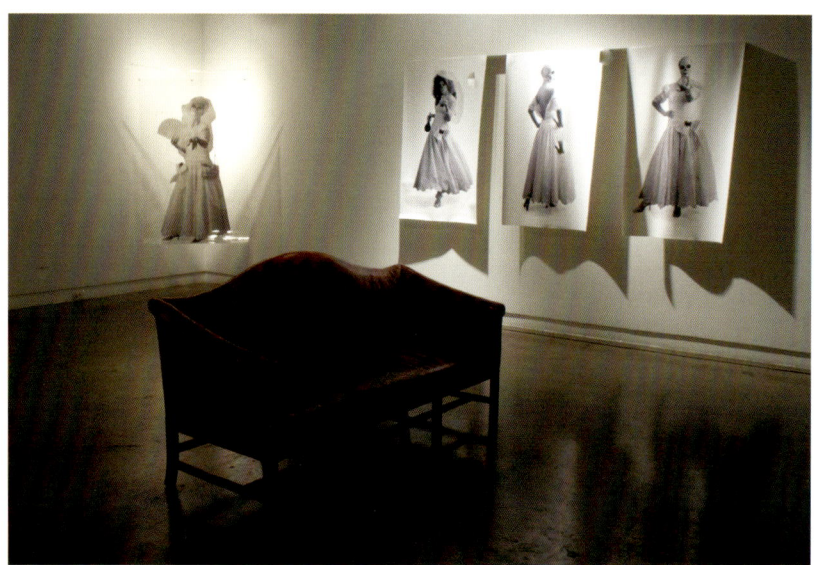

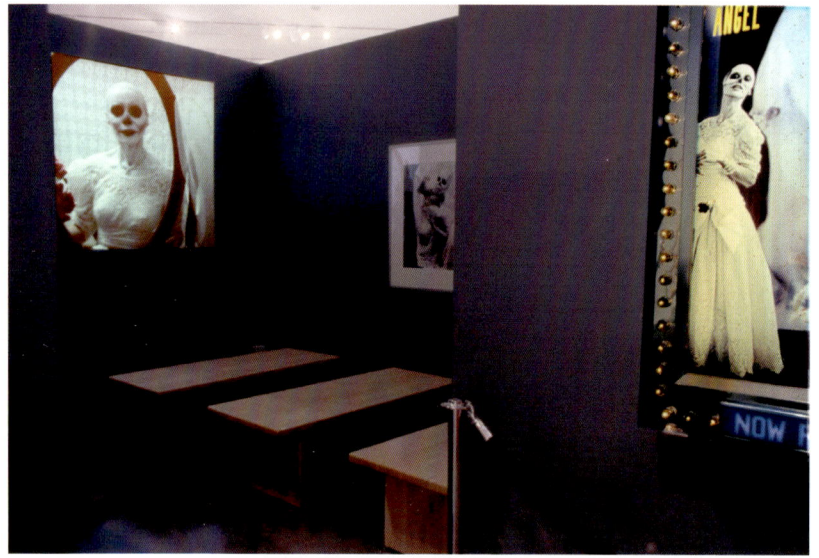

(*top*) Delilah Montoya
San Sebastiana: Angel de La Muerte
Las Malcriadas exhibition, MacKinney Avenue Contemporary Arts
Center, Dallas, TX
2006
Installation
Collection of the artist

(*bottom*) Delilah Montoya
San Sebastiana: Angel de La Muerte
Ahora: New Mexican Hispanic Art
exhibition, National Hispanic Cultural Center, Albuquerque, NM
2002
Installation
Collection of the artist

handed me the costume to try on, a vintage wedding dress that went on and fit like a glove.

Delilah: The dress just zipped right up. The hat was great, it had the purse, it had the gloves, it had everything! My grandmother had passed on my father's side. She was from Poland, so the family actually came to work at the Omaha packing houses. It had been decades since the last time I was in Omaha, but I found myself in a thrift store, and there was this dress with a slender waist and the bottom flared out as though it was a flamenco dress, but it was obviously a wedding dress. So I brought it back with me, and I didn't know what I was going to do with it. I started thinking about Sebastiana because of my grandfather's death. My grandfather on my mother's side, Reyes Garcia, died, and my mother saw this little note in the paper about Ilfeld's will that, after forty years, was finally executed. My mom thought that because the last surviving heir had passed, the will could be opened. She concluded it was because her father died, and he was the last person who could contest the will. $1.5 million were donated to Highlands University and the University of New Mexico. The family always said that my grandfather was Charles Ilfeld's illegitimate son.

Mónica: Ilfeld Auditorium at Highland University

Delilah: Yes, so they say

Delilah: I have a pedigree, the Ilfelds. But the thing was, my grandfather's mother would never say who the father was. Everybody knew it was Ilfeld. My mom tells how her mother could shop in the Ilfeld hardware store and never had to pay for merchandise. My auntie says that when the old man Ilfeld died, his two sons came down to talk to my grandfather and then walked away. The two legitimate sons never married. My grandfather had five children, but eleven were born. Half his children died because of poverty. I was thinking of all this. And who could tell that story? There's only one person who could tell that story, and that was Sebastiana, because she was at all the deathbeds. And that's how it started. I started thinking about Sebastiana and her power.

I wanted to do a character sketch of her and understand who she was. Another story my mother told me is how she didn't want to be Death. God had to convince her to do this. She could talk back to God. This is a woman *con ganas*. God bargained with her and told her so people will know that death doesn't come from you. It comes from me; I will make you my handmaiden. I realized she's a Doña! She thinks of herself as beautiful. Everything just started unfolding. I was telling Cecilio Garcia about this and how I wanted to make a short film. He really liked the whole idea and offered to write the script. I wanted *dichos* brought into the script because in the old days, they spoke in dichos. When the script was written, I took it to you, Mónica. And Mónica, you changed it all. Well, not all of it, but I mean it was your dialog. It actually sounded more comfortable once you put your magic to it. Do you remember doing that?

Mónica: Honestly, I don't clearly remember rewriting, and in retrospect, I feel very badly about changing the original text, especially from a poet like Cecilio García-Camarillo. I can only hope and surmise that we had his blessing. I do vaguely recall an impetus to make changes in service of activating the text more as dialogue versus a narration. The "bones" of the text, though, are all Cecilio!

Delilah: You can feel Cecilio in the script. At that time, he had been diagnosed with cancer, sensing that he could die. You can hear him wrestling with that with lines like "death is not a period, but a comma in life." The unfortunate thing was that he never lived to see the film's completion. That saddened me.

Sebastiana was quite the lady. And you did a really beautiful job with her. I remember I asked you to be both the Doña and a Calaca. The idea was that when we look at Sebastiana, we see a Calaca, and as she looks at herself in her mirror, she sees a beautiful, voluptuous woman. You blocked your movements perfectly. Michael Esfera was working with a single camera, one mic, one light, and one talented actress. Everything was being done on a shoestring, and you blocked your motions so well that the edits between Doña and Calaca were seamless. When you brought your hand up to your hair as a Calaca where there was no hair but the same dialog as the Doña allowed the edits to cut back and forth producing a mesmerizing visual experience. I was like, wow, Monica is a professional.

Mónica: Well, you know, a couple of things helped. One was getting into that makeup. Patricio Tlacaelel Trujillo y Fuentes did a beautiful job applying shadows and highlights until zaz! The *calavera* magically appeared before us. And then, of course, the day before, Delilah, you had taken me to the nail salon, where they applied these two-inch acrylic nails, complete with the stencil of a skull you had made! So, I had these new claw-appendages, this incredible makeup, and a dress that could have been tailor-made for my measurements. Some actors consistently work from the inside out or the outside in. For me, it depends on the role. With this character at that time, it was helpful to work from the outside in. When I looked in the mirror and did not see myself, La Doña's voice was somehow liberated to perform without premeditation or self-consciousness. The truth was in the text. And then, of course, I had just come off a twenty-day shoot, my biggest lead role on film, and was primed for the demands of maintaining consistency between each take in service of the final edit.

You asked a question earlier about how I might approach the character differently. At the time, it was definitely a process of working from the outside in. The makeup and costume were so distinctive, they created a mask of sorts that lent an incredible freedom for the character to emerge and "fill in the cover." At this time in my life, I think my process would be more from the inside out, perhaps a deeper, more existential take on power, delusion, regret, and desire.

Delilah: Well, the other thing you pointed out was that there was no background score in the earlier versions. I didn't even think about using background sound. At that time in 2014, the film was going to go to the Fulton Museum for the exhibit, and I realized that you were right. You got me in contact with a musician who recorded a sound score. With that score, it came together as a little movie. I always knew there was something off. I had no idea what it was. But, Monica, because of your experience in theater and film. The film pulled together brilliantly.

Mónica: You've offered many opportunities to collaborate, but not just with me. You often invite interdisciplinary collaborators with an incredibly generous creative spirit. The late theater director Bill Ball would say that a good director never says "no," because the minute you say no to an actor you will shake their confidence, or they won't feel secure in sharing any more ideas or fully committing to their instincts. A bad idea can lead to a good idea, and if it's a really bad idea, the dead weight of it will eventually fall off on its own. That's just something that you, Delilah, innately know; you organically invite the input and alchemize it to best serve what you want to say, how you want to say it.

Delilah: Thank you for that insight. The best thing that you can do is listen. Sometimes, within the listening, as you are learning, your own creativity ignites, and you can see the vision, and then creative momentum flows. As the artist, we get to watch it. The artist is the first witness to any creative practice. We are witnesses. I don't know if you felt that.

Mónica: In my process, I'm the Creator and the audience at the same time, which can sometimes be problematic because we can also be our own worst critics. But then, again, that all speaks to another benefit of having collaborators, trusted collaborators.

Delilah: I know one thing for certain: I'm never too sure about anything. Trusted collaborators can help guide through this. When I become too confident in anything, it doesn't seem to work out well. I start getting really worried. Oh, my God! I'm too confident, and this thing is gonna crash!

Mónica: Recently, viewing the video after many years, the sexuality and the sensuality were more evident to me than I remembered. Looking at it almost twenty-five years later, with the perspective of time, now beyond my middle-aged years, I had another feeling about Doña Sebastiana, her desire to be desired, and her desire to remain beautiful. I think Sebastiana's mirror is an intriguing invitation for us to reverse an experience or an expectation we may have when we look into the mirror and see only or mainly the "flaws." Sebastiana looks in the mirror, and she sees only beauty; Death can see the beauty. How do we see the beauty before we reckon with La Doña? Perhaps she is offering us a feminine gaze, where memory and desire meet in the glass. Where do we find our own true reflections?

Delilah: She was a powerful woman. What she's been asked to do gives her the power of time. She can grab the time away, or she could give more time. One of the things that I was thinking about was her narcissism. She was a bit of a narcissist, but that is okay; it got her through what needed to be done. Everybody else saw this frightful image. But in her mind, she couldn't understand their fear—she was beautiful. She knew that she could hold back time to give a person a bit more time to say or do what needed to be done. That was her humanity. She could pause death for the deathbed confessions. Sebastiana liked community gossip. That was Sebastiana's humanity; she wasn't perfect. She wasn't God, and she knew that and was OK with that.

Mónica: I was on the verge of asking you why God himself would not take the job that he offers to Sebastiana. What you just said, I think, answers the question for me in that it takes somebody to have been human, of the flesh . . . almost like the flip side of the Jesus story. Christ offers eternal life, and she offers the exact opposite: death, in order to get to that "eternal life." She has an innate understanding of what it is to be a human being; it's important that to do her job, one must know what it is to be alive, in order to honor the taking of life.

Delilah: You know, life with all its beauties and all of its flaws. So in many ways, she held the balance. We were changing the narrative to identify her power. And what she delivers and gives to humanity itself.

In Conversation with Demetria Martinez, Delilah Montoya, and Christina Hernandez: La Llorona

Demetria: Perhaps the ultimate malcriada is La Llorona. The Mexican legend tells of a monstrous mother who drowns her children. Her children are illegitimate; she drowns them so that their father cannot take them away to be raised by a new wife. She turns into a wailing ghost, forever haunting bodies of water. The Rio Grande in the New Mexico version that many of us heard growing up. I am particularly struck by the very sensual ways in which you depict her. In one image, she has a breast exposed, and in another, she's wearing a transparent veil. I'm thinking of the poet Audre Lorde's seminal essay, the "Uses of the Erotic," in which she uplifts female desire as a source of self-knowledge and power. Delilah, why don't you start by talking about the sensuality of the Llorona pieces that you did with Tina.

Delilah: I have to give Tina credit. I never thought of La Llorona as being that sensual until I met Tina. I had just started teaching at the University of Houston. Tina, you were in my first class, and you were talking about how Lilith was Adam's first wife. I was taught that Adam was married to Eve. I was ready to argue with you and damn it, you were right. Through research, I learned that Lilith was first mentioned in Babel, pre-dating Christianity and Judaism. The story of Lilith as Adam's first wife was very sensual. I realized that La Llorona was also sensual. She was a beautiful woman who lured in men. She shows up every once in a while in the back of a man's car as it crosses a bridge. Especially an evil man, and she scares him straight. And later, I found out there's a persona called Deer Woman. She is part of Native American storytelling and is kind of like Lilith or Llorona.

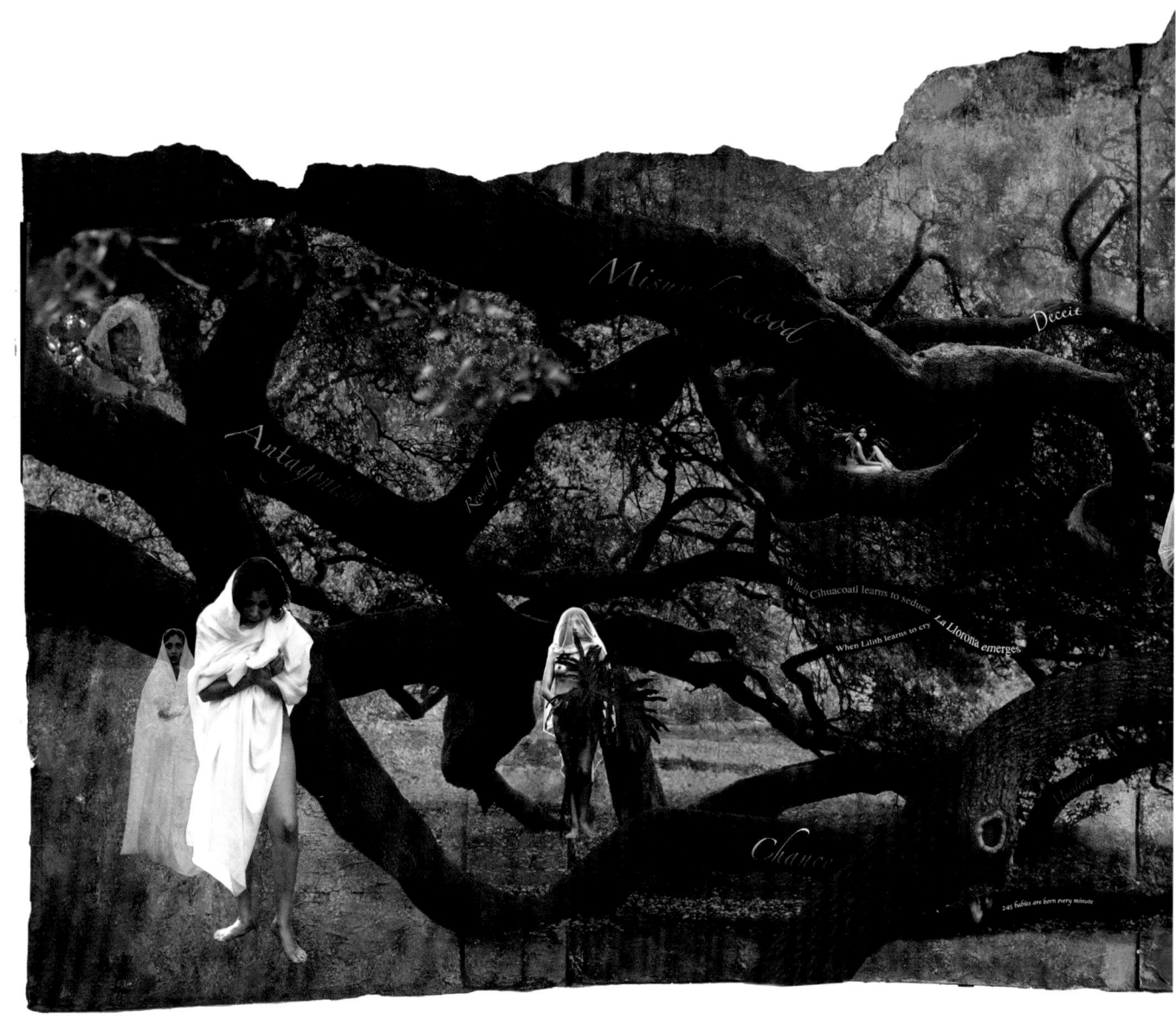

Delilah Montoya in collaboration
with Christina Hernández
La Llorona in Lillith's Garden #2
2004
Photographic mural printed on
canvas
96 × 240 in.
Collection of the artist

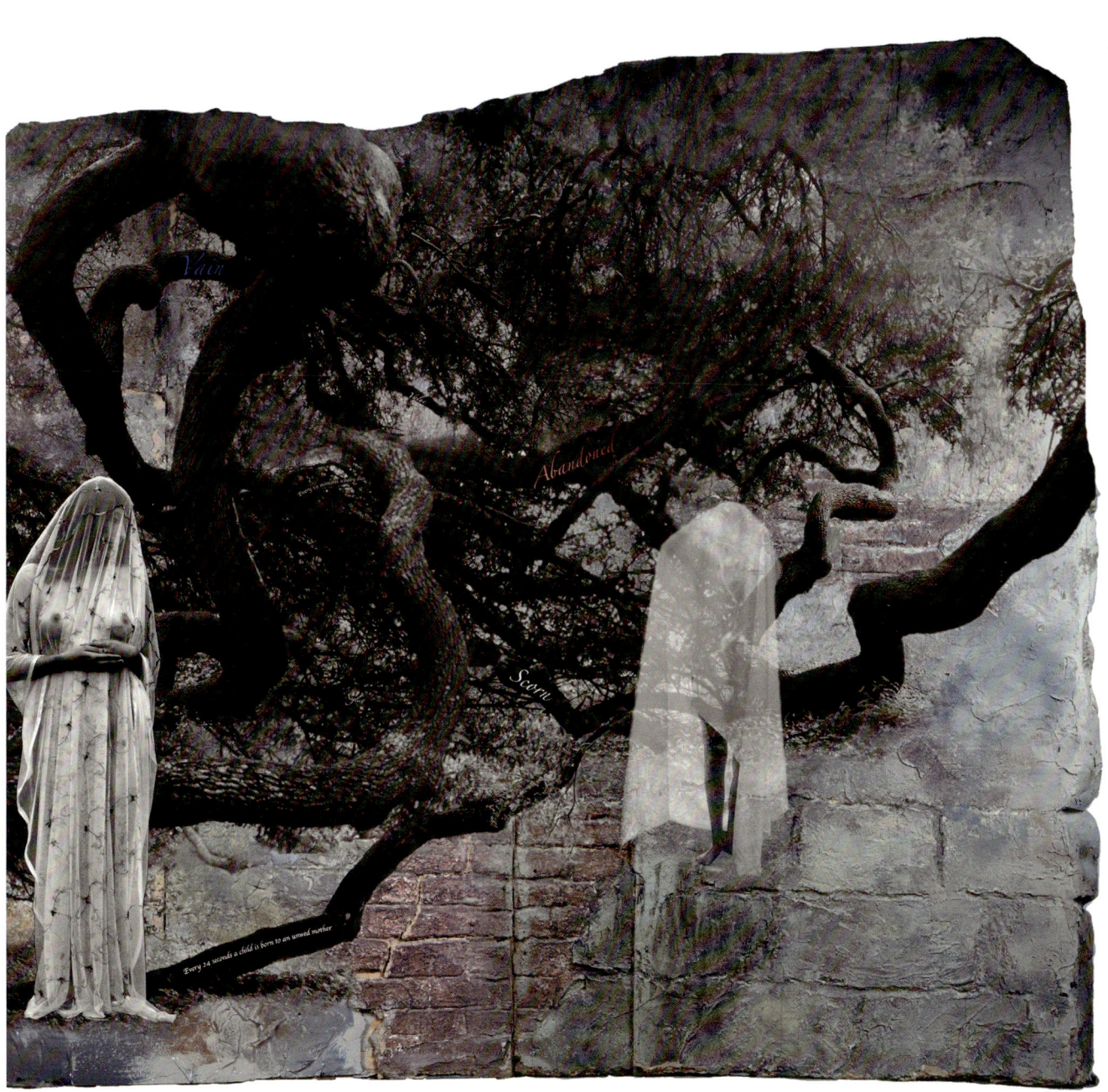

Vain

Abandoned

Scorn

Every 24 seconds a child is born to an unwed mother

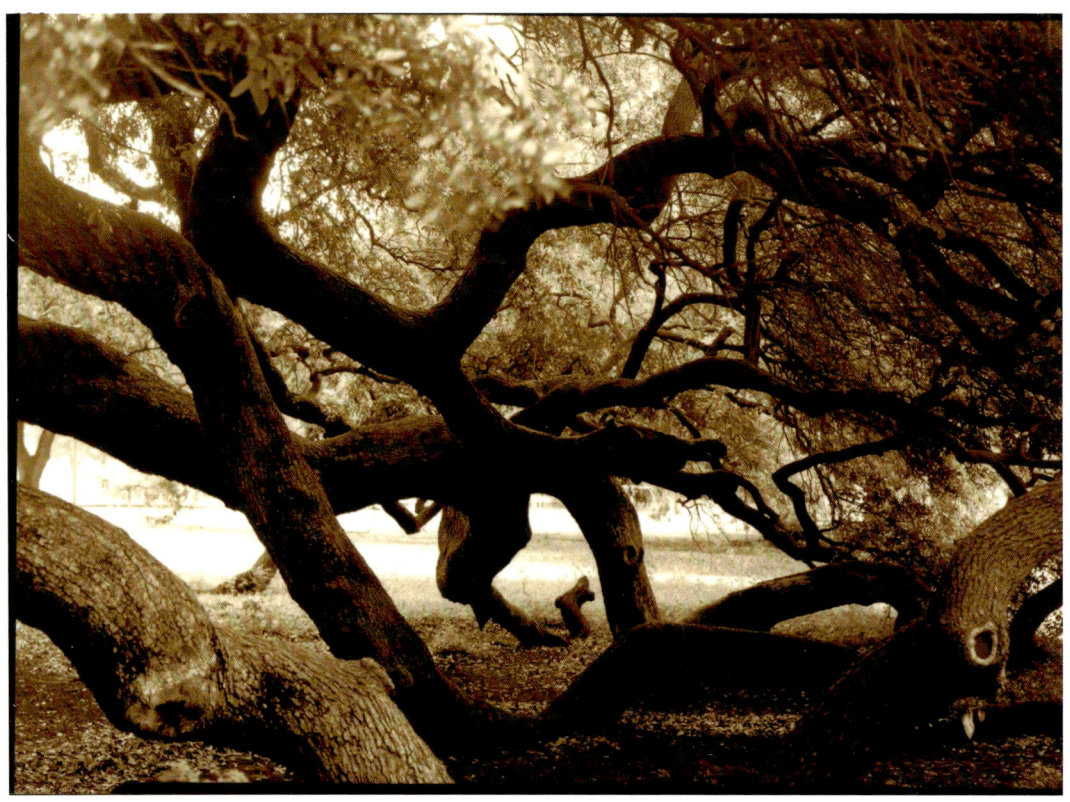

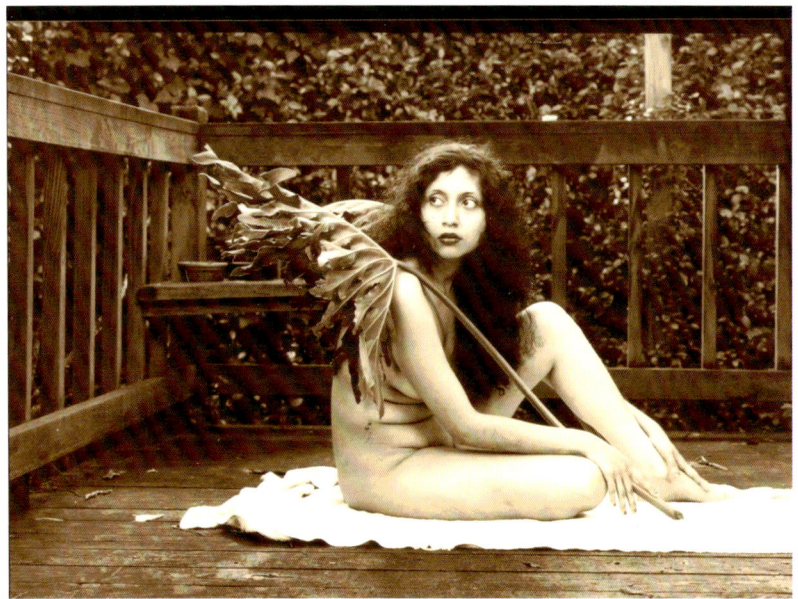

(*top*) Delilah Montoya
Background Study for La Llorona in Lillith's Garden
2004
Sepia-toned silver gelatin
5 × 7 in.
Collection of the artist

(*bottom*) Delilah Montoya
Lilithan Study for La Llorona in Lillith's Garden
2004
Sepia toned silver gelatin
5 × 7 in.
Collection of the artist

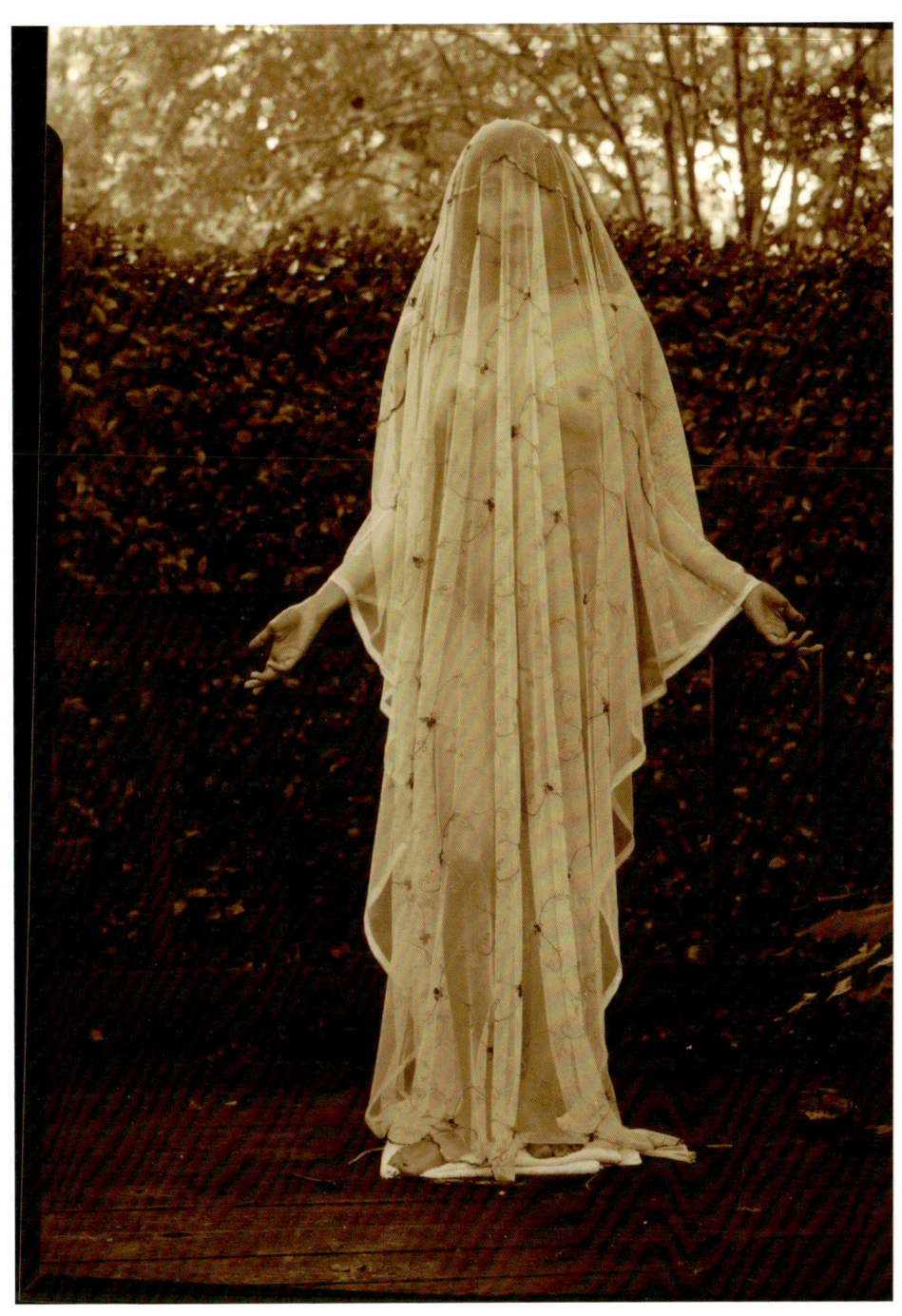

Delilah Montoya
*Lillith Study for La Llorona in Lil-
lith's Garden*
2004
Sepia-toned silver gelatin
5 × 7 in.
Collection of the artist

When I started thinking about the sixth omen of the Aztecs, the goddess Cihuacoatl is later thought to be Llorona. Cihuacoatl was not sensual, she's a crier. Thinking of La Llorona as we know her with the qualities of sensuality, which Lilith definitely has. But she was also a crier and a baby snatcher like both Chihualcoatl and Lilith. Clearly, evidence of cultural syncretism, the joining of two powerful worlds' storytelling. The European world came and met the indigenous world. If you take off your colonial lenses, the world is never the same. I wanted to portray La Llorona as a syncretic malcriada.

So Tina, you have always photographed your own body very well, much like Laura Aguilar who understood her own sensuality. I did not see myself as the one photographing you Tina. It was your practice to portray yourself as various personas. You brought Llorona to Lilith's garden.

Cristina: I think a lot has to do with how much knowledge of our own bodies has been denied through generations past. Whether it started with colonialism, I don't know. I can't say how much even Mexicana women knew about their bodies. I would like to investigate that myself later on, but I always felt that even as a little girl you're always taught that "You can't do this. You can't do that." And you observe how males have all this freedom, and of course, you grow up with, "Oh, we're not allowed to talk about sex or enjoy sex like that?" and so all that comes together. I think later on, as a young woman, you're exploring your sexuality and your body. Nobody told me; I had to figure that out. Nobody told my mom, and nobody told my grandma, so that kind of knowledge has been denied, and I think it also has been weaponized against us so we could stay ignorant of how our bodies work and about sex. So when you're that age and you get to know your body, that was a way of me exploring that, and also coming into terms with my own self-esteem, with myself, and with my body. But look at the way it can occur throughout the world, right? And you could see how it's been similar throughout different societies, that repression of women with their lack of knowledge of their bodies and their sexuality. So art was a way for me to explore that, you know, because it wasn't my mom's fault or her mom's fault that they didn't know. So I had a privileged opportunity, right, because I'm a first-generation Chicana, and my mom wasn't able to go to school. But now that I'm a college girl and I have books here,

I have art to look at and photography, so I went to town with all that stuff, including even being into like the bad girl stuff that I remember. I was so into the bad girl stuff because you grow up with oh, that we're supposed to grow up a certain way, right. And the bad girls that they were, they served as examples to morally not be like, "You don't be like that!" But I was just so curious about them, because to me they seem like someone that must know something that I don't. What do they know? What happened to them? And I know they've been misjudged. When Delilah said that La Llorona is misunderstood, I believe all that because I think about the La Lloronas of today, especially Andrea Yates.

Are y'all familiar with Andrea Yates? She's like the modern La Llorona, and she suffered from extreme postpartum depression because everybody misunderstood, and they didn't know and didn't take her life or her mental illness seriously. For me, getting to know about my body was just a way for me to learn to become comfortable with myself, and also pass down that knowledge even through art.

Delilah: When we started putting *La Llorona in Lillith's Garden* together, it was for an exhibition in Santa Fe at El Museo Cultural. They asked me to create an installation on two fake rock walls that faced each other. I photographed the walls with 8 × 10 transparency film. And did extensive photo shoots of with Tina in a variety of poses. I had a large 45-inch inkjet in my office that could print the panels on canvas. We started thinking about how to put these murals together and get the message across about cultural syncretism. We had a couple of long nights, remember, over at the university block lab computers. You designed your portraits into the mural's composition and also helped with the text. I was compositing a live oak tree into Lilith's garden. You remember the tree was at Baldwind Park. The tree had a branch that wound to the ground and then came back up like the head of a snake. It was a rainy day, which is why the garden feels very wet and shiny. The photo mural was designed to fit back onto the manufactured walls. We talked about what we wanted to explore. Why was Lilith considered a bad woman? And we came up with a lot of different words that make women bad, words like "knowledge."

Demetria: Knowledge. That was, that was Eve's sin.

Delilah: Yeah, you're right. It was Eve's sin.

Cristina: And why should it be sin? Again, tying back to how many decades that women have been denied knowledge of their own bodies? That's why I was so attracted to Lilith because she was the opposite of what I was reading, and I was telling Delilah that Lilith was someone who questioned. She's like "Hell no! Why are things that way? Why can't I? What about what I think and what I want?" And when she complained, that's when Adam supposedly had an issue, and she was kicked out.

Delilah: As the story goes. Adam was in the garden of Eden by himself, and all the other animals had partners and were happy. Adam didn't, but the other animals didn't want him hanging around either. So he was lonely and went to God, and asked for a mate. God brought down Lilith, and they got along beautifully. They were having a great time loving each other. Adam decided he preferred the missionary position, and Lilith didn't want it. She said that she will never be beneath him, and so they got into a big fight. Lilith called God down to straighten this out, and when she called God using the nameless god's actual name, energy surged through her body, and she flew out of the garden to the Red Sea where the demons resided. She was having a good time there having baby Lilithans. Adam got really sad and depressed because Lilith wasn't around and asked God to bring her back. God sent three angels to tell Lilith that she had to go back to Paradise, but she said, "No." "If you don't go back, God's going to kill you," said the angels. "No, no, God cannot kill me because he put me in charge of all the newborn babes." So, God made a pact with her. That's her connection as a baby snatcher. According to the Judeo tradition, if you put a medallion on your child, Lilith will not come and snatch your baby. When I read this, I began to understand how close her story correlated to Llorona, but Lilith was never a crier. What we put into the mural is when Cihuacoatl learns to seduce, when Lilith learns to cry, and Llorona emerges. These two badass women merge together as Llorona. What we also thought about were words that make women frightful. Some of the words listed are misunderstood, antagonism, resentful, deceit, scorn, and abandonment. We also inscribed that 255 babies are born every minute, and every twenty-four seconds, a child is born to an unwed mother. Tina, you insisted on those quotes.

I remember imagining what it would be like if a woman had as many babies as her body could contain. We would bear hundreds of babies just pushing out baby after baby after baby. But that's not what we do. We lose our babies, not all our babies live. It is impractical for women to have all the babies they could conceive. We can't do it, it's impossible. Think about every month, a woman loses a child. Are we biological murders? The body will reject fetuses. Does that make us an automatic murderer of all of our children? Tina, you were really thinking about what it meant for a woman to make that choice of having their child or not having their child. Using contraception or abortion.

Cristina: I am actually getting into it again because of the overturn of *Roe v. Wade* that I didn't think was ever going happen. It was always threatened. And with these words, they just ring to some a woman that's been demonized and so many women have been demonized throughout history.

Delilah: Right now at this moment abortion is banned in Texas yet I remember when you worked or volunteered at Planned Parenthood.

Cristina: I worked at an abortion clinic and The Cause after I graduated. Part of also getting to know your body and your own sexuality is a part of reproductive justice, whether you want to be pregnant or not, and also the right to have a healthy child, too. To me, it's all interconnected. And La Llorona lost her children for whatever reason. Lilith, too, making those decisions for her autonomy that they tried to deny her, well, from what I was reading. So that has happened throughout history to women, over and over and over again the attack on her autonomy. So we still have to make work about it, because it's still going on, and I think art helps make those connections. So when we were doing that, you were finding those connections; I was making those connections because that's what art does. It makes you think it, makes you draw those parallels.

Demetria: No, this is just fascinating, and it makes me think, too, of all the women who were burned at the stake as witches. I mean, there have always been opportunities throughout history to demonize women.

Delilah: The words written in the mural were in 2004, So that is twenty years ago.

Cristina: Twenty years ago. Yes, I like these words better. Free will, independence, ambition.

Delilah: Temptress, independence, acquire, so bad to acquire things right, we threw Goddess in. Pleasure, you're not supposed to find pleasure, especially sexual pleasure right? Selfish! You can't be selfish. These were all the words that make women malcriada! Bad girls and dangerous.

Cristina: Yeah, love, these words.

Delilah: There was a lot in there. I'm really glad that we were able to collaborate. When this piece installs, I always put your name down as a collaborator. You are very much a part of it, and thank you.

Cristina: No, thank you.

Delilah: Prior to the mural I was in a show with Alma Lopez at Pola Lopez's studio. It was a reactionary show when Alma's Guadalupe was in controversy. Pola Lopez wanted to give Alma support at her Santa Fe Studio.It was kind of nostalgic that La Llorona first showed in Santa Fe. Remember. I remember how excited you were when the image hit the local paper. We stopped at all the newspaper stands and pulled copies.

Cristina: Yeah, that was fun. And it was my first time in New Mexico as well. So it was awesome to participate as a young Chicanita.

Delilah: That's right. We worked really hard to get the canvas up. We were stapling, stapling it all together. Your friend Eva came along. It's always collaborative. And, you know, my community is always with me.

Cristina: And Demetria, may I ask you when you first saw this? Because I mean me and Delilah were making those connections. So once you put this kind of work into the universe, you don't know how people will react, but I have heard positive things. May I ask you what you think about it?

Demetria: I think it's interesting to see the generational differences between you and Delilah. I'm kind of envious of the sort of freedom that your generation has had, as far as being introduced to so many of these concept at a relatively young age, and, you know, being able to think about issues like abortion and the demonization of women. And rethinking La Llorona and what bad girls even mean. I'm lucky, because about twenty years ago, you know, I started reading Audre Lorde and other *mujeres*. You know, Anzaldúa.I was thinking deeply about these kinds of issues, and that's just made all the difference in my own intellectual and even spiritual development.

Cristina: And what did you think when you saw these pieces?

Demetria: I thought they were so on target and considering when you guys made the pieces and what's happened in our country since then. You hate to think about it, but it's true. It's relevant all over again. We are living in frightening times.

Cristina: We did those photographs after I graduated college. Now, I'm in my mid-forties. I'm not young; I'm not at that age to worry about getting pregnant and stuff like that, even though I still can. But it just seems like we gotta go back into the trenches now. So I don't know. Maybe, Delilah, maybe we can collaborate on another piece.

Delilah: You're doing some really great work right now. I'm always in your court. Demetria, Tina does these tabloids of herself as a Chicana allegory. And they're really strong, amazing work. I would love to see an exhibition of just your work. I would like to do another collaboration in the future. I think that would be wonderful. I would like that.

When we were working on the mural, at the time, very few people were doing digital work correctly. You know, that was 2004. So, Photoshop was still a bit clumsy. Printing to mural size was still experimental. The piece was twenty feet across on canvas. I was trying out new materials. Canvas really worked out well for us. It stores great, because it rolls it up and doesn't crease like paper. You could roll it back out and staple it back to the wall. So, yeah. It was all experimental for us.

Delilah Montoya's *Women Boxers: The New Warriors* is a profound visual engagement with the world of female boxing. Through striking black-and-white photographs, Montoya captures the intensity, resilience, and dignity of female fighters, portraying them as modern warriors who challenge entrenched gender norms and redefine cultural narratives of strength and femininity. Focusing on fighters in Colorado, Texas, and New Mexico, the series not only honors and celebrates women boxers but also serves as a disruption of the historically male-dominated arena, positioning female athletes as protagonists who defy the sport's historical narrative.

Montoya's decision to work in black and white echoes the photographic tradition of Larry Fink, who extensively documented male boxing. By employing this aesthetic, Montoya places female fighters within a historical lineage, emphasizing their legitimacy within the sport.[1] According to Montoya,

> There are various stories for each of the women, but still, all of them like taking the challenge to participate in a combat sport. The boxing ring is the bastion of masculinity, and for that moment, that brief moment, they are taking control of the ring—they take control of the game. I wanted to do something to honor them. I intentionally shot the series with black-and-white film because this is how famous boxing images . . . like the ones by Larry Fink, those bastions of masculinity . . . they are all in black and white.

The stark contrast and deep shadows in her images accentuate the athleticism and expressive determination of the boxers, drawing parallels between their physicality and the visual language of earlier documentary photography.

Boxing, as Montoya describes, is both brutal and elegant. It is like ballet, a dance of strategy, force, and response.[2] Her images capture this physical engagement, revealing the artistry and the aggression that play out in the ring. The movement of her subjects, their stances, and their focused gazes speak to a discipline that transcends gendered expectations of violence and sport.

In addition to celebrating the fighters, Montoya captures the energy and culture of the events themselves. Many of the matches were held

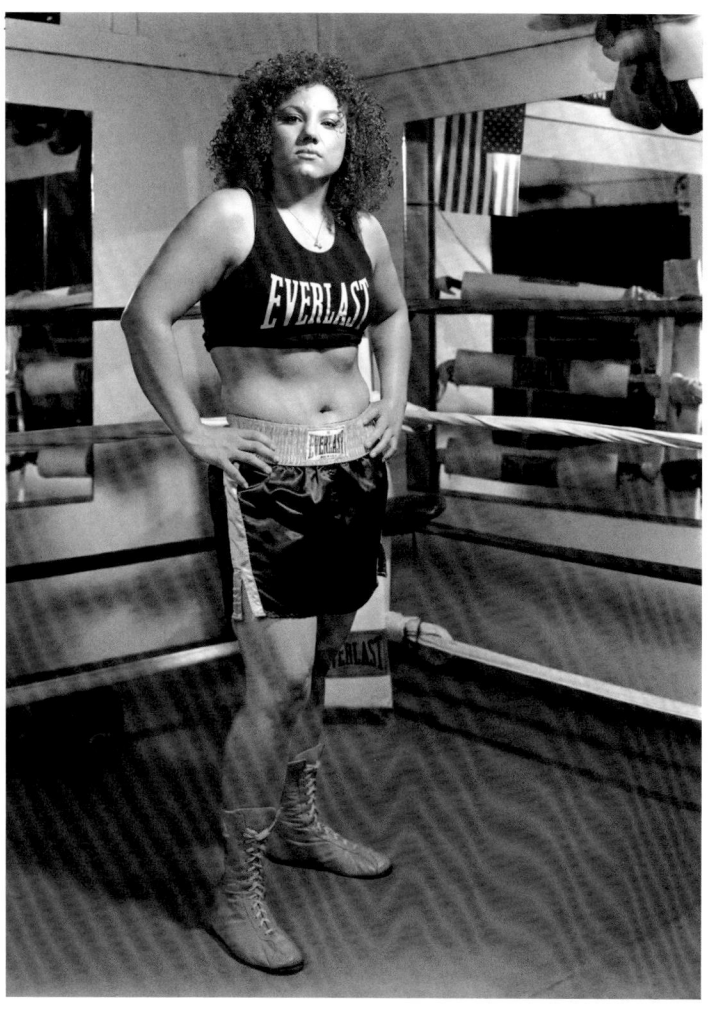

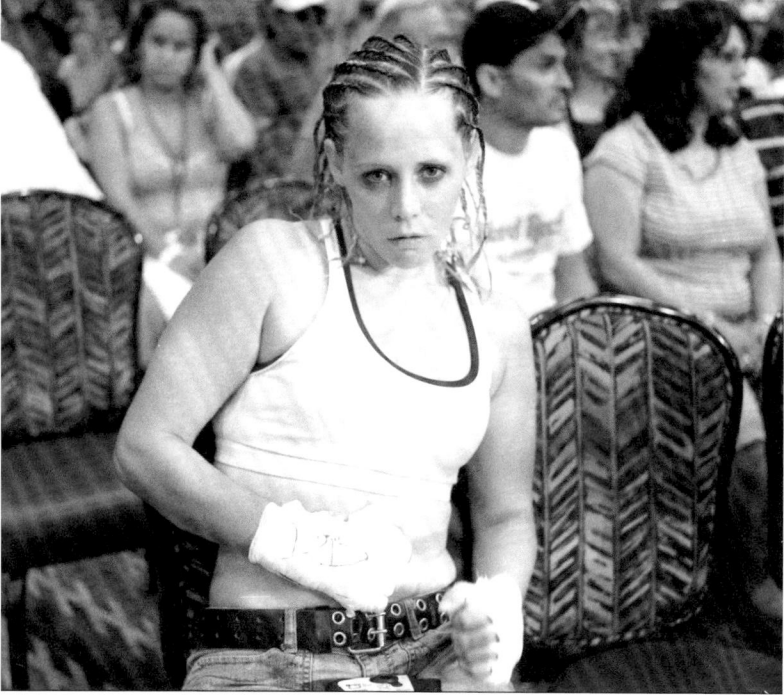

(*top*) Delilah Montoya
Stephanie "Golden Girl" Jaramillo
2005, printed 2006
Piezograph on Hahnemuhle photo
rag 310 paper, ed. 1/3
30 × 22 in.
Albuquerque Museum, museum
purchase and gift of the artist
PC2022.32.6

(*bottom*) Delilah Montoya
Doreen Hilton
2004, printed 2006
Piezograph on Hahnemuhle photo
rag 310 paper
30 × 22 in.
Sheldon Museum of Art, Univer-
sity of Nebraska–Lincoln, Olga N.
Sheldon Acquisition Trust
U-5590.2010

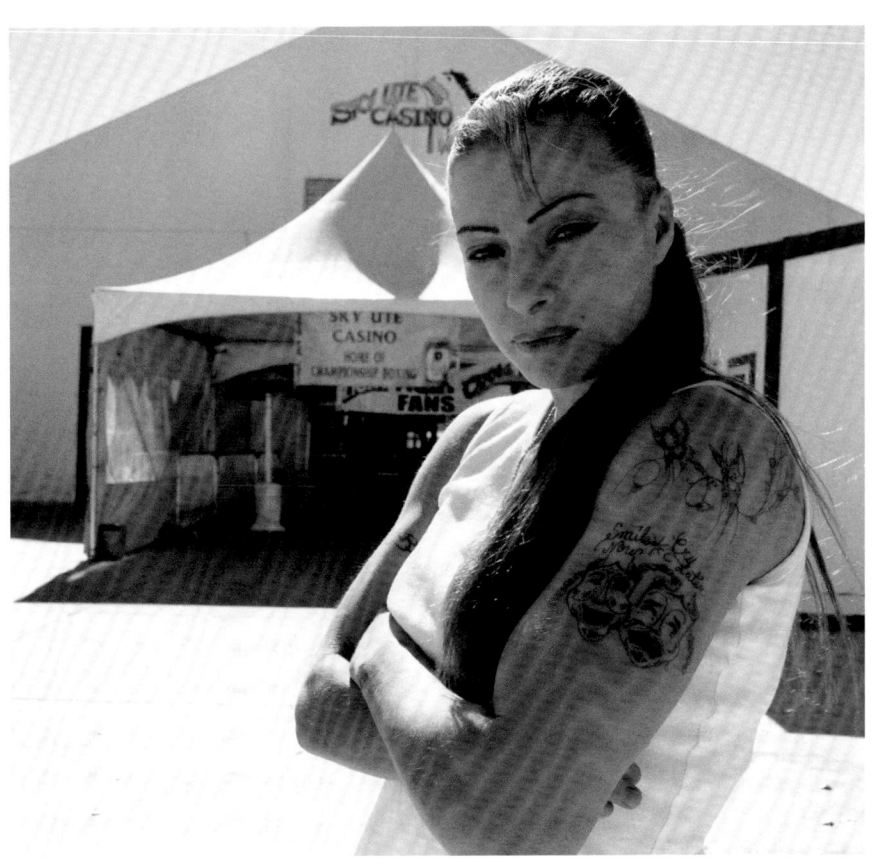

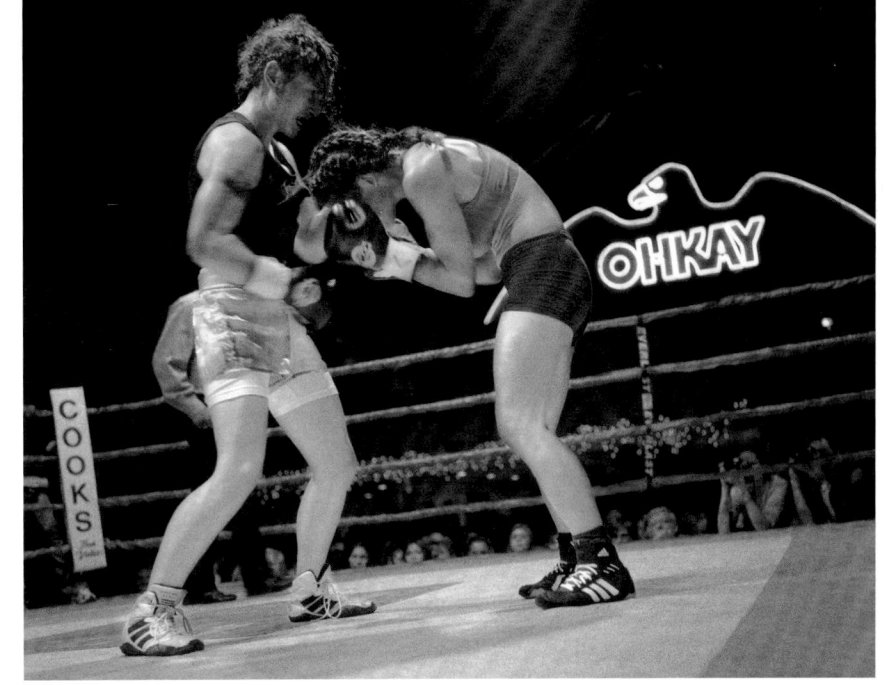

(*top*) Delilah Montoya
Teri "Lil Loca" Cruz
2005, printed 2018
Dye sublimation print on aluminum, A/P
32 × 40 in.
Albuquerque Museum, museum purchase and gift of the artist
PC2022.32.9

(*bottom*) Delilah Montoya
Jackie vs Audrey
2004, printed 2006
Piezograph on Hahnemuhle photo rag 310 paper
23¼ × 28¼ in.
Collection of the artist

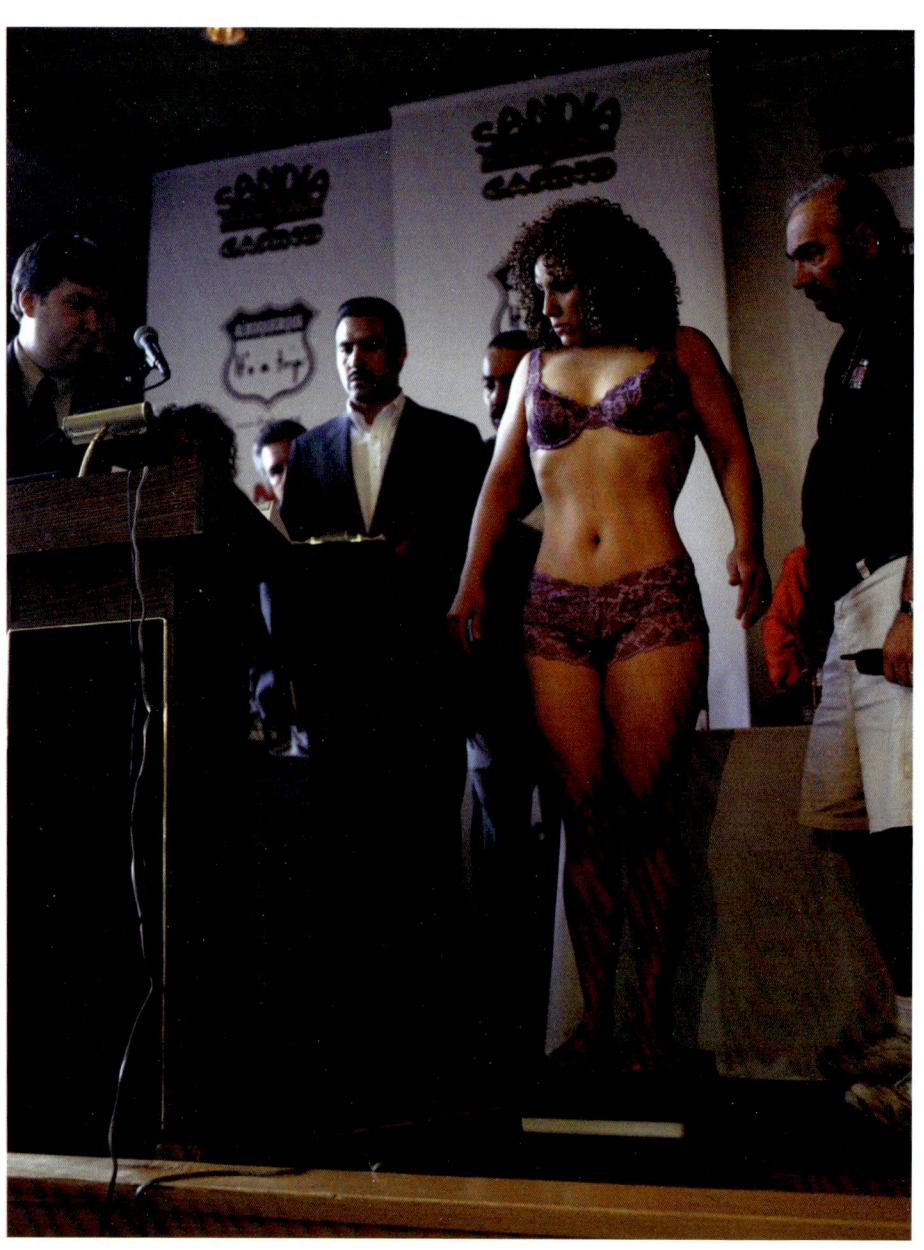

Delilah Montoya
Stephanie Jaramillo: Weigh In
2005
Color c41 print Endura, ed. 4/4
19¼ × 15½ in.
Albuquerque Museum, museum
purchase and gift of the artist
PC2022.32.7

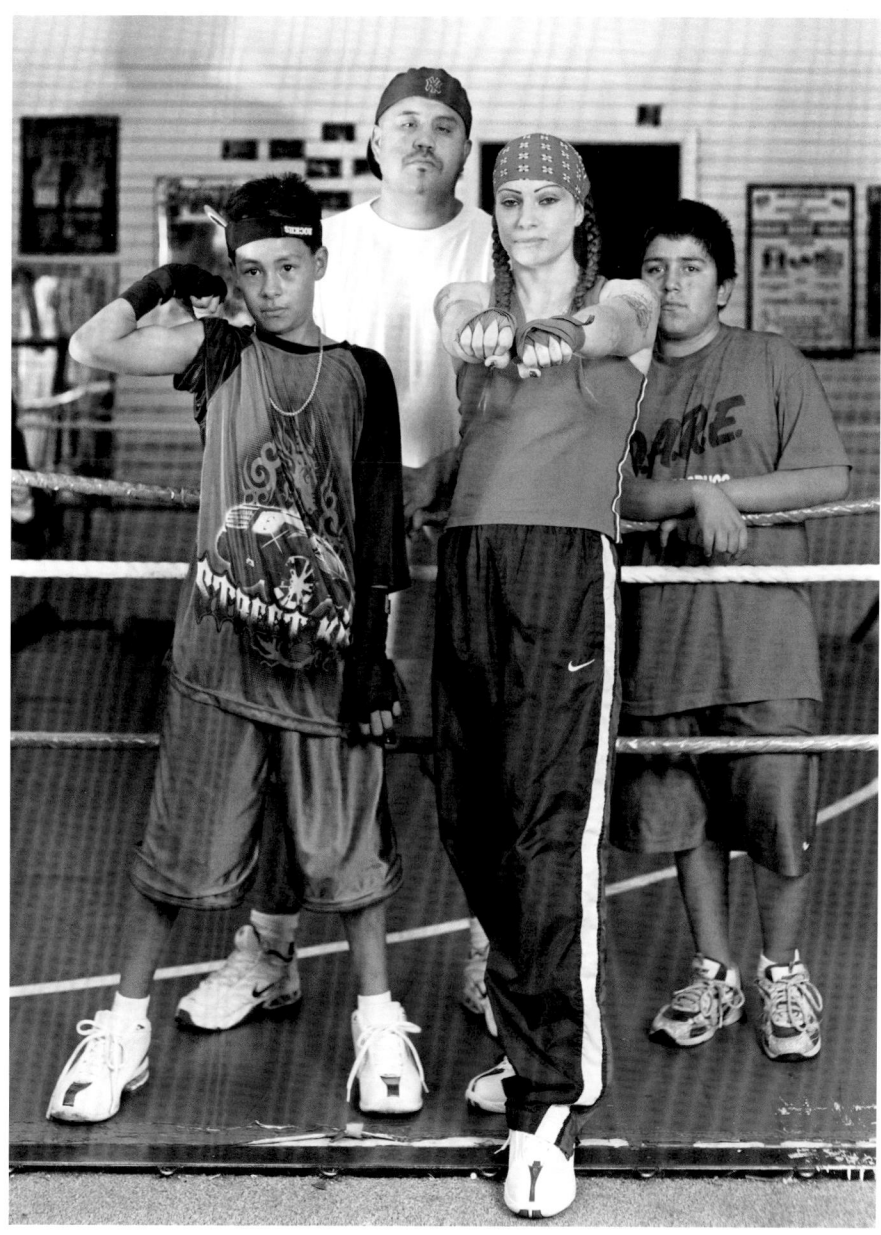

Delilah Montoya
Teri "Lil Loca" Cruz with Her Trainer
2003, printed 2006
Piezograph on Hahnemuhle photo rag 310 paper
35 × 25¾ in.
Collection of the artist

at casinos. Scantily clad ring girls act as provocateurs, holding up cards announcing each round. Coaches and trainers shout out instructions to the fighters sitting in their corners. Partners and children are depicted back at the hotel as their mothers prepare to enter the ring. Montoya juxtaposes the spectacle of the fight with personal behind-the-scenes moments, exploring the complex overlapping roles that each athlete negotiates.

Terri 'Lil Loca' Lynn Cruz encapsulates this dynamic interplay. Cruz's intense focus is evident as she listens to her coach offering guidance between rounds. The directness of her gaze, coupled with the tension of the moment, underscores the mental and emotional endurance required

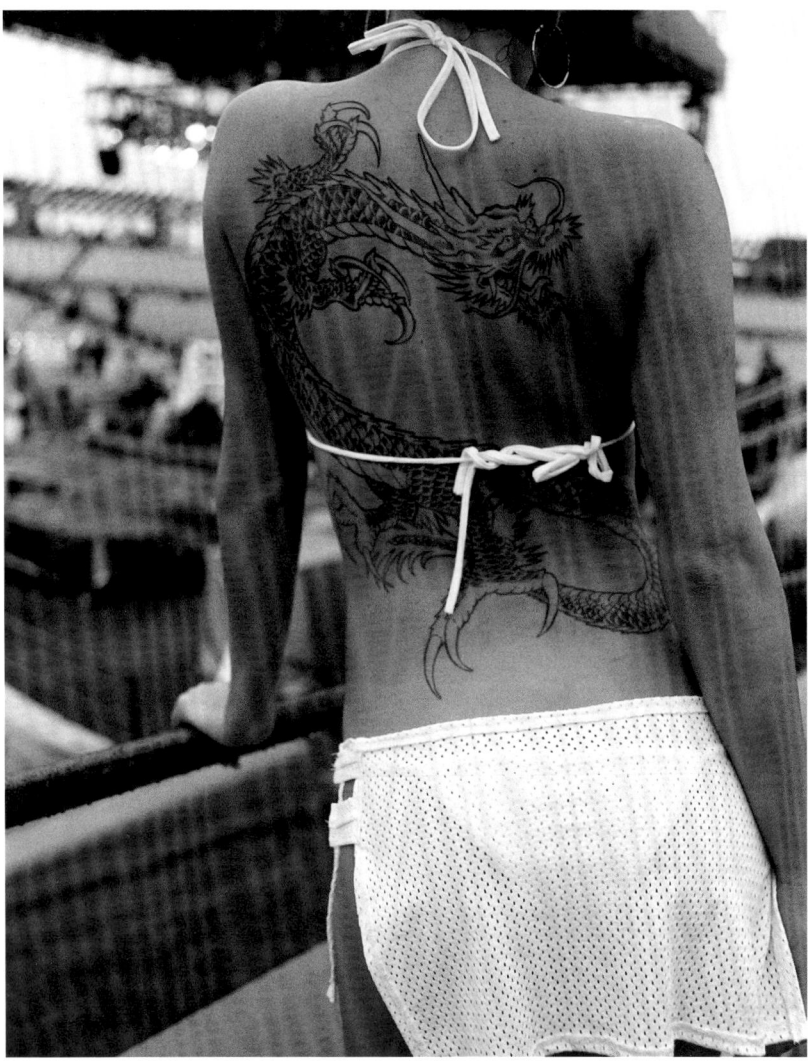

Delilah Montoya
Dragon Lady
2004, printed 2006
Gelatin silver print, ed. 2/4
23⅜ × 18½ in.
Collection of the artist

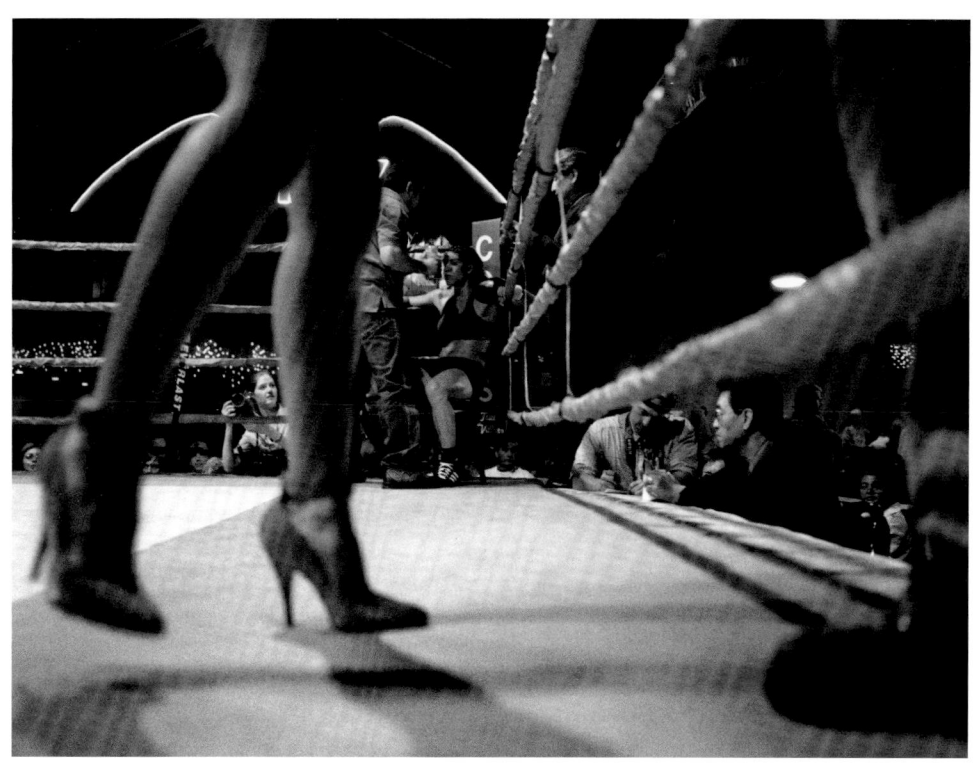

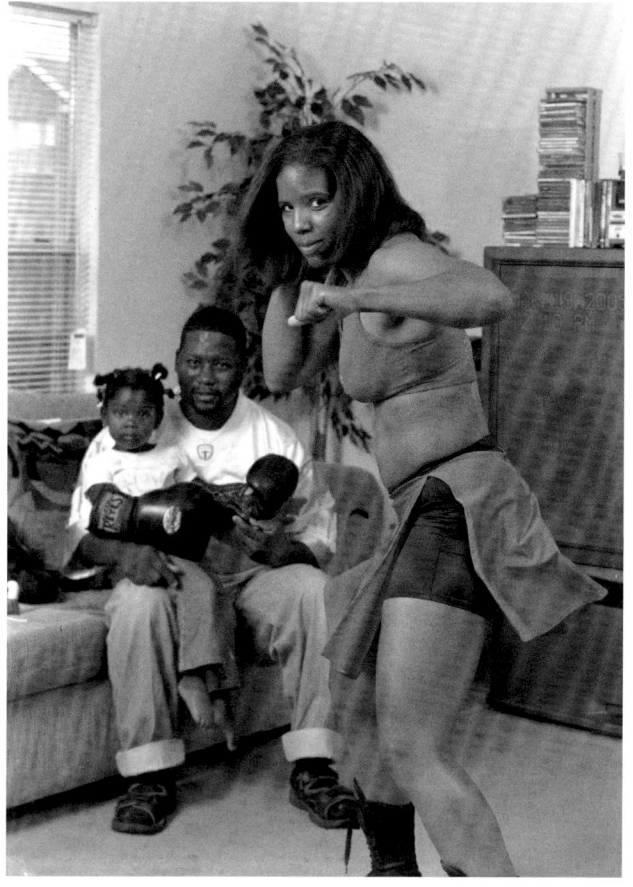

(*top*) Delilah Montoya
Audrey Vela Resting in Her Corner
2005, printed 2006
Gelatin silver print, ed. 2/5
8 × 10 in.
Collection of the artist

(*bottom*) Delilah Montoya
Akondaye with Family
2006, printed 2018
Dye sublimation on aluminum,
A/P
19 × 13½ in.
Collection of the artist

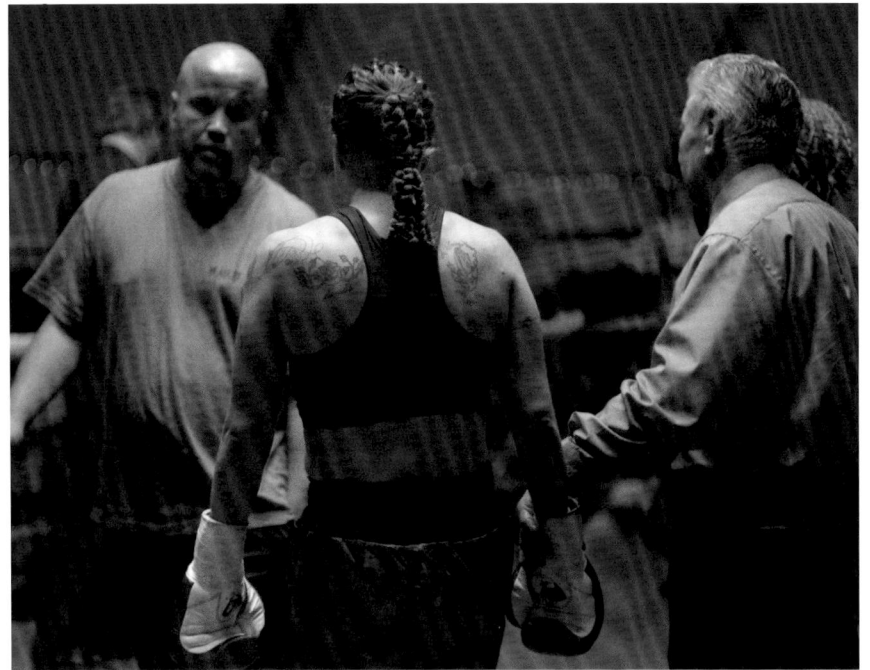

Delilah Montoya
Teri Waits for the Decision
2003, printed 2006
Piezograph on Hahnemuhle
photo rag 310 paper
23 × 28½ in.
Collection of the artist

in the sport. Montoya's triptych captures Stephanie Jaramillo and Holly Holm in action, similar to a series of film stills. The images show the power, strength, and grace of these two athletes as they exchange blows. Jaramillo and Holm met in the ring twice. In their first match, Holm won with a majority decision, and in their second meeting, it was a draw (this match took place at Sandia Casino on October 3, 2003). Jaramillo and Holm are from central New Mexico—Jaramillo is from the South Valley in Albuquerque, and Holm is from Los Lunas.

This series also fits within Montoya's conceptual framework embodied by malcriadas, women who reject societal constraints and carve their own paths.[3] The female boxer, in stepping into the ring, disrupts deeply ingrained ideas about femininity, propriety, and physicality. Historically, women in combat sports were viewed as anomalies, often sexualized or dismissed as spectacles rather than serious athletes.[4] Montoya's work challenges this perception, depicting these fighters as self-possessed, determined, and skilled.

This theme resonates with broader Chicana feminist discourses that interrogate the intersections of race, class, and gender. While Montoya's series includes women from across different races, ethnicities, and socioeconomic circumstances, many of the fighters are Latina and women of color. Many of them come from working-class backgrounds. Montoya's

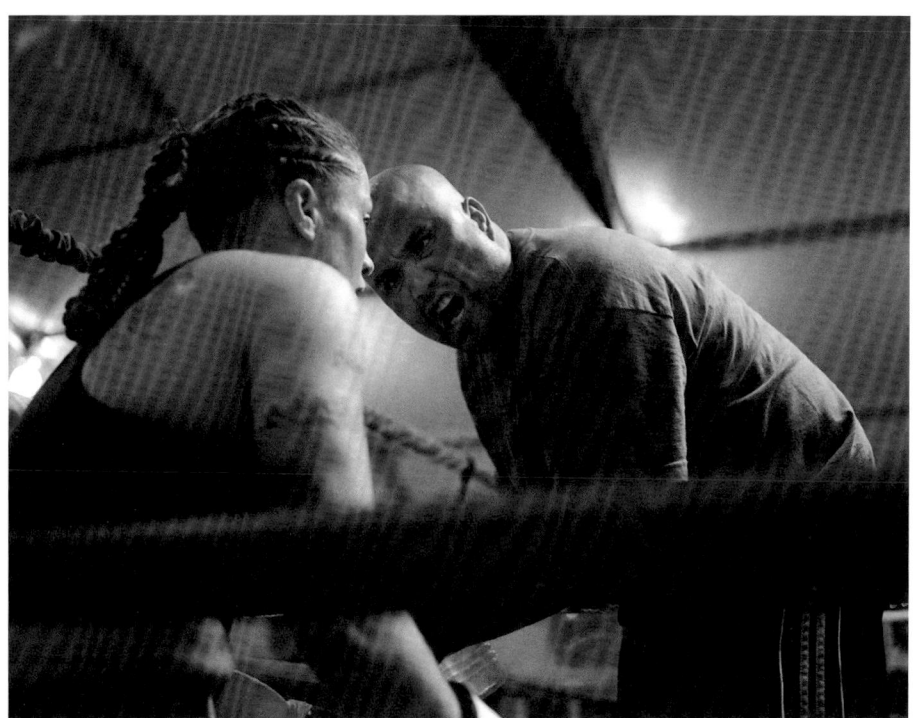

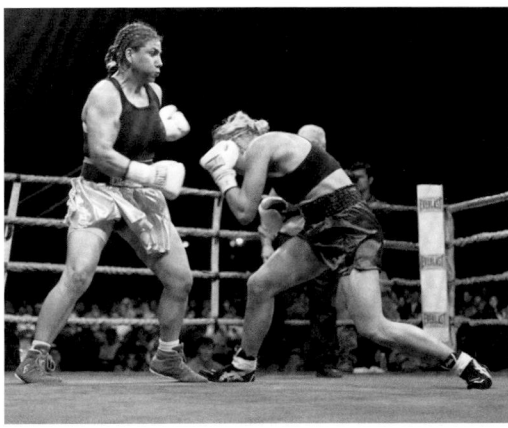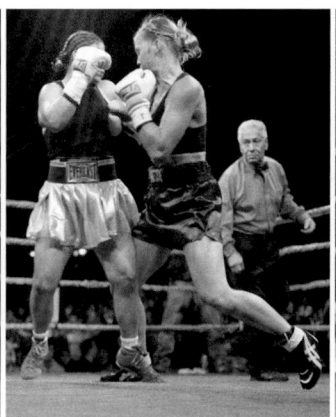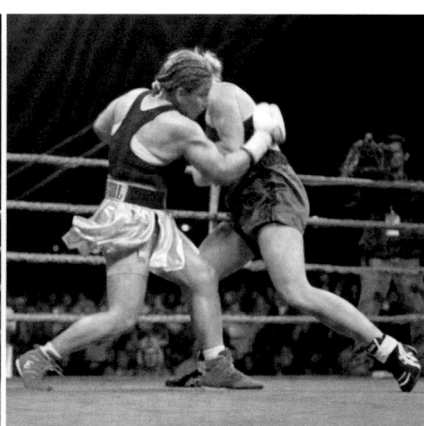

(*top*) Delilah Montoya

Lil' Loca with her Trainer

2003, printed 2006

Piezograph on Hahnemuhle photo rag 310 paper

22⅕ × 27½ in.

Collection of the artist

(*bottom*) Delilah Montoya

Stephanie vs. Holly; Sandia Casino

2003 negative, printed 2006

Piezograph on Hahnemuhle photo rag 310 paper, ed. 2/3

23⅜ × 18½ in.

Albuquerque Museum, museum purchase and gift of the artist

PC2022.32.8

series underscores how these athletes navigate multiple layers of marginalization. Their presence in the ring is not just about claiming space or advancing their careers; it's about visibility in a cultural landscape that has historically excluded them.[5]

The history of women's boxing is fraught with resistance and struggle. As María Teresa Márquez notes, female boxers have historically been regarded as "monstrous." In their quest to compete in a male-dominated system, in and out of the ring, they also have to fight against notions that it is unnatural for women to be strong, aggressive, and confident. From the eighteenth-century fights of Elizabeth Stokes and Ann Field to the struggles for Olympic inclusion in the twenty-first century, women in boxing have continually fought to disrupt societal restrictions and gender bias.[6]

Montoya's series documents a pivotal moment in this history, capturing boxers who trained for the 2012 Olympics, when women's boxing was finally recognized as an official event.[7] These fighters embody the perseverance and defiance that have characterized the sport's evolution, transforming it from a marginalized spectacle to a recognized discipline.

Photographs such as *Jackie Chávez* illustrate how these women are in possession of their own bodies and stories in and out of the ring. Chávez, a super bantamweight champion, sits in her corner poised and ready, the ropes of the ring framing her as an empowered athlete. The image's composition reinforces the actions of these athletes as they challenge the historical constraints placed upon female boxers. The photographs collectively represent ongoing efforts to break free from these limitations.

Montoya does not merely document her subjects; she engages with them to learn about their motivations, struggles, and aspirations. She resists suggesting that the women share a monolithic cultural experience and clearly states that each boxer has their own motivations and their own personal stories. While this series may appear more documentary than some of the other series, Montoya is utilizing the medium to act as an ally in the boxers' fight for visibility and legitimacy.

This methodology aligns with Montoya's broader worldviews prioritizing community engagement and activism. As seen in her other projects, Montoya's work is not simply about representation but about creating dialogues that challenge dominant narratives and empower her collaborators. Montoya critically reimagines women's roles, harnessing their potential and resisting historical exclusion. Her strategies move beyond mere

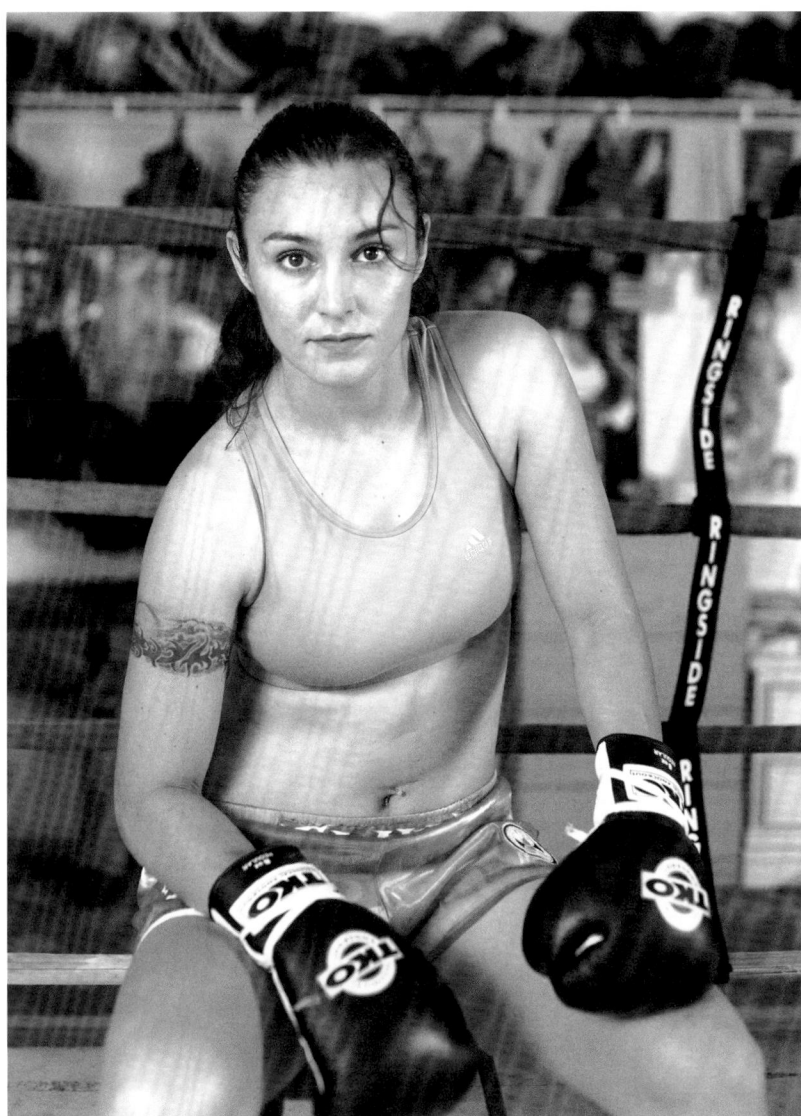

Delilah Montoya
Jackie Chavez
2005, printed 2008
Gelatin silver print, ed. 2/4
23⅜ × 18½ in.
Albuquerque Museum,
museum purchase and gift of
the artist
PC2022.32.4

observation, presenting women boxers not as anomalies but as integral figures in a redefined cultural and athletic landscape.

Women Boxers: The New Warriors is a testament to the power of photography as a tool for social commentary and historical documentation. Montoya's series captures the beauty and brutality of boxing while foregrounding the agency and resilience of female fighters. In doing so, she not only expands the visual archive of boxing but also contributes to a larger discourse on gender, power, and representation.

Through her lens, Montoya elevates the female boxer from the margins of sport and culture to the center of a dynamic and evolving narrative. In doing so, she ensures that these athletes are not merely recorded but celebrated, their stories woven into the broader fabric of resistance and transformation in contemporary visual culture. Many women boxers are fierce fighters and loving mothers. Montoya's series shows how these women exist in multiple roles that society may perceive as contradictory. These images affirm Montoya's commitment to capturing the depth and complexity of her subjects.

In Conversation with Delilah Montoya and Demetria Martinez:
Women Boxers: The New Warriors

Demetria: Delilah, you've talked about how Teresa Marquez, a librarian

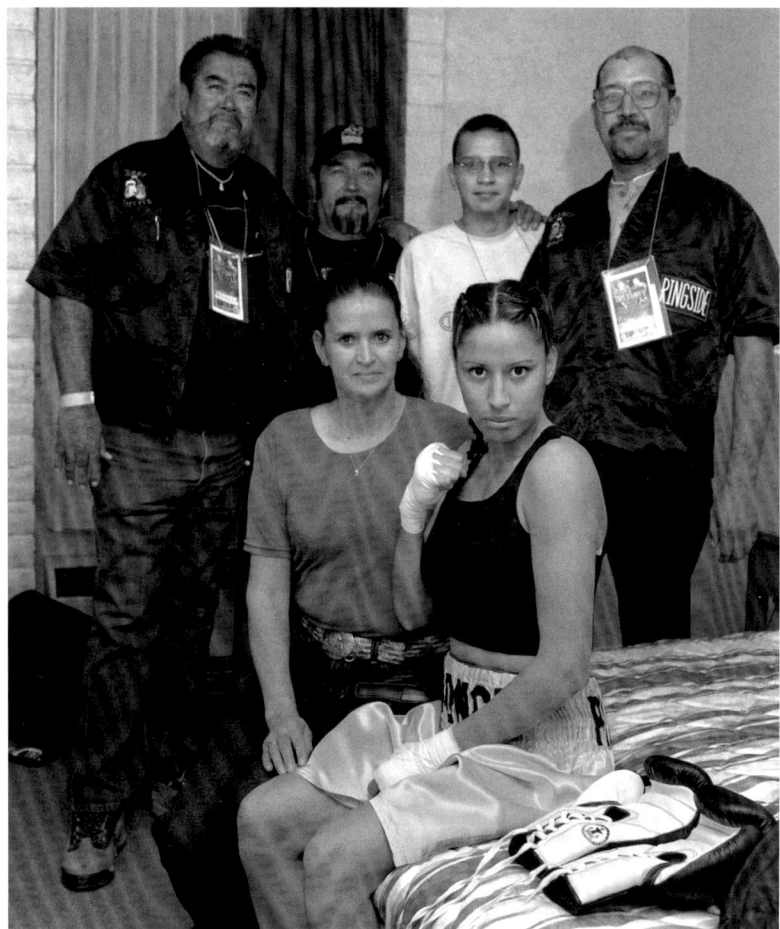

Delilah Montoya
Pink Panther and her family
2003, printed 2006
Piezograph on Hahnemuhle
photo rag 310 paper
16 × 14 in.
Collection of the artist

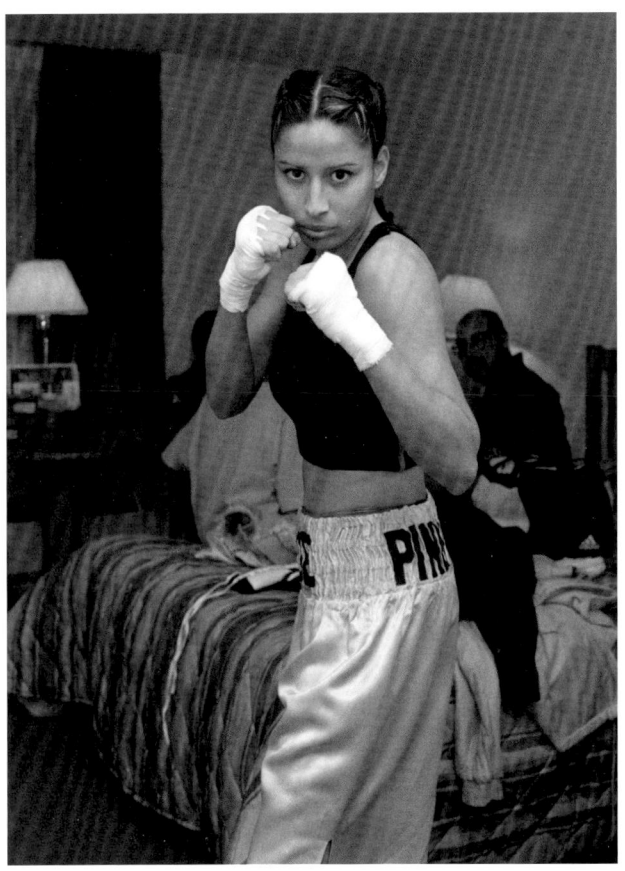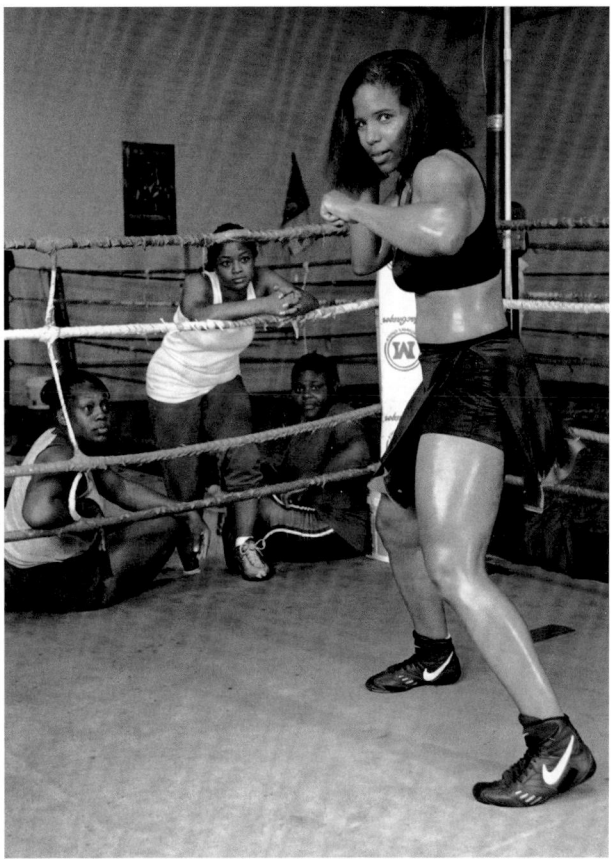

(*left*) Delilah Montoya
Pink
2003, printed 2006
Gelatin silver print, ed. 1/5
10 × 8 in.
Albuquerque Museum, museum
purchase and gift of the artist
PC2022.32.5

(*right*) Delilah Montoya
Akondaye "Storm" Fountain
2005, printed 2006
Piezograph on Hahnemuhle photo
rag 310 paper, ed. 2/2
13⅝ × 10 in.
Collection of the artist

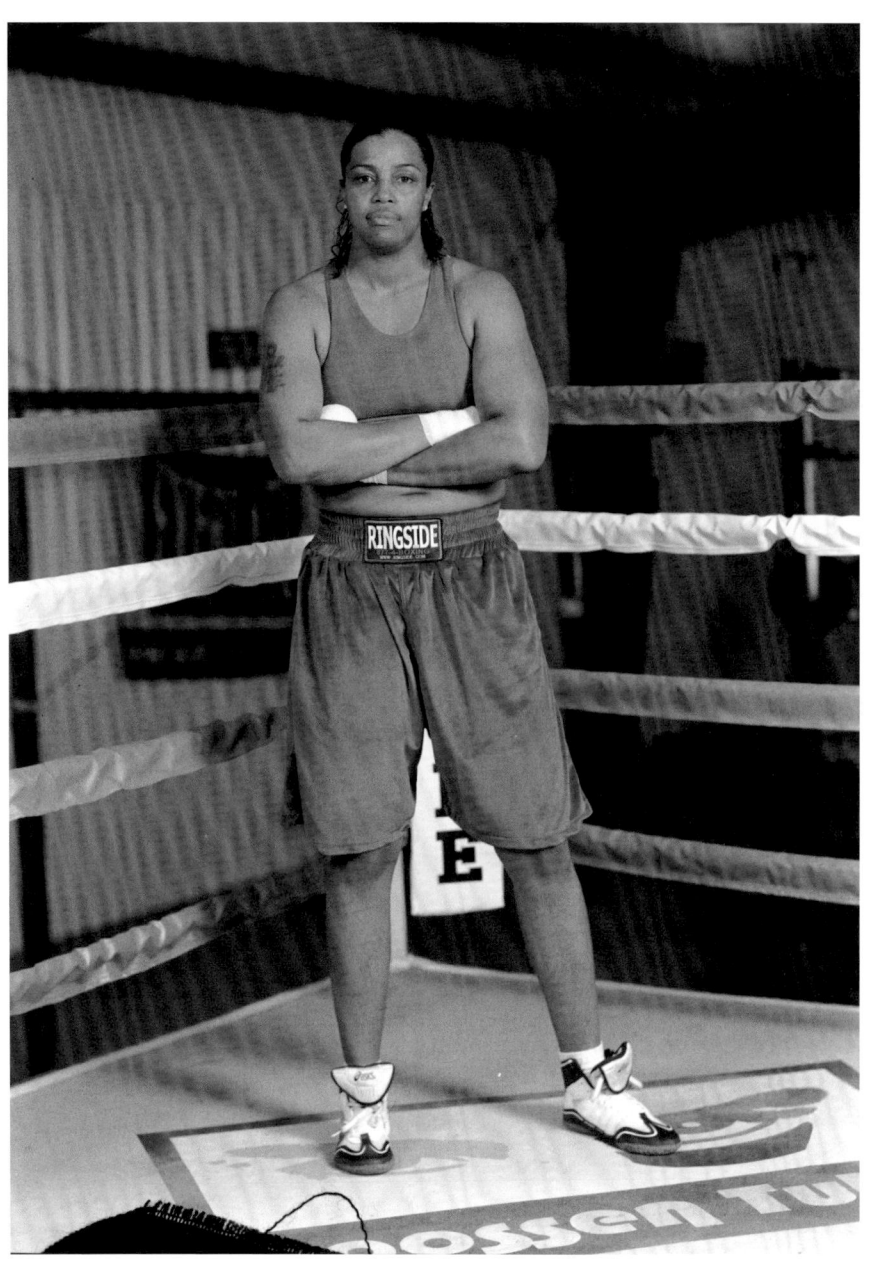

Delilah Montoya
Yolanda "Stone Hands"
Swindell
2005, printed 2006
Piezograph on Hahnemuhle
photo rag 310 paper, ed. 1/2
36 × 28 in.
Collection of the artist

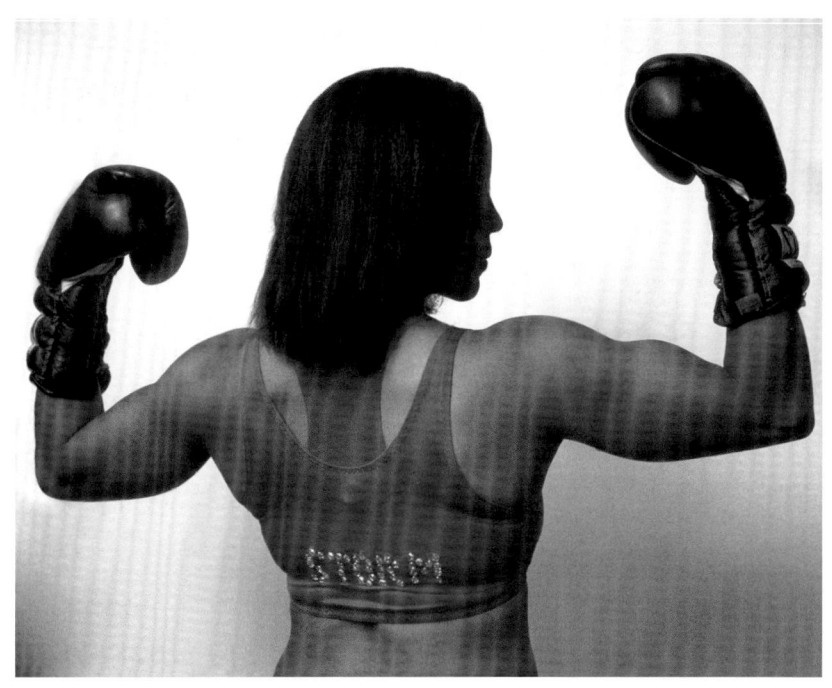

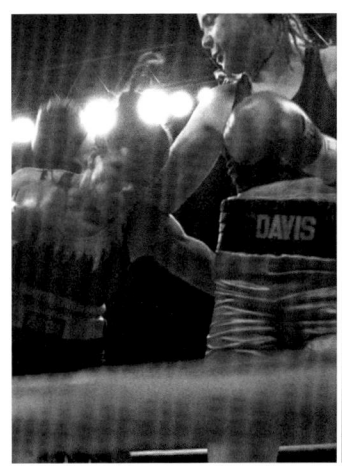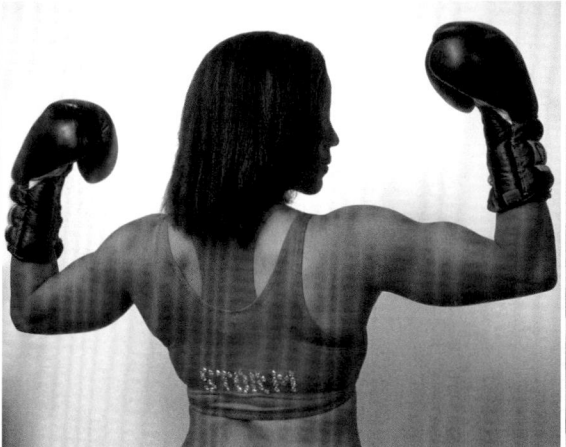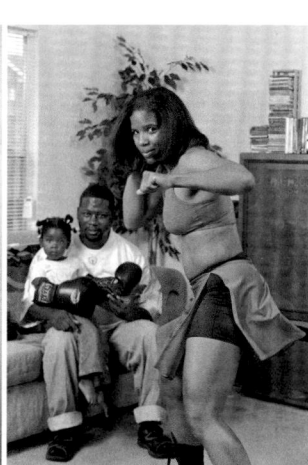

(*top*) Delilah Montoya
Akondaye "Storm" Fountain
2005, printed 2006
Piezograph on Hahnemuhle photo rag 310 paper, ed. 1/3
26 × 34¼ in.
Collection of the artist

(*bottom*) Delilah Montoya
Quiet Before the Storm
2005, printed 2006
Piezograph on Hahnemuhle photo rag 310 paper, ed. A/P
16¾ × 36 in.
Collection of the artist

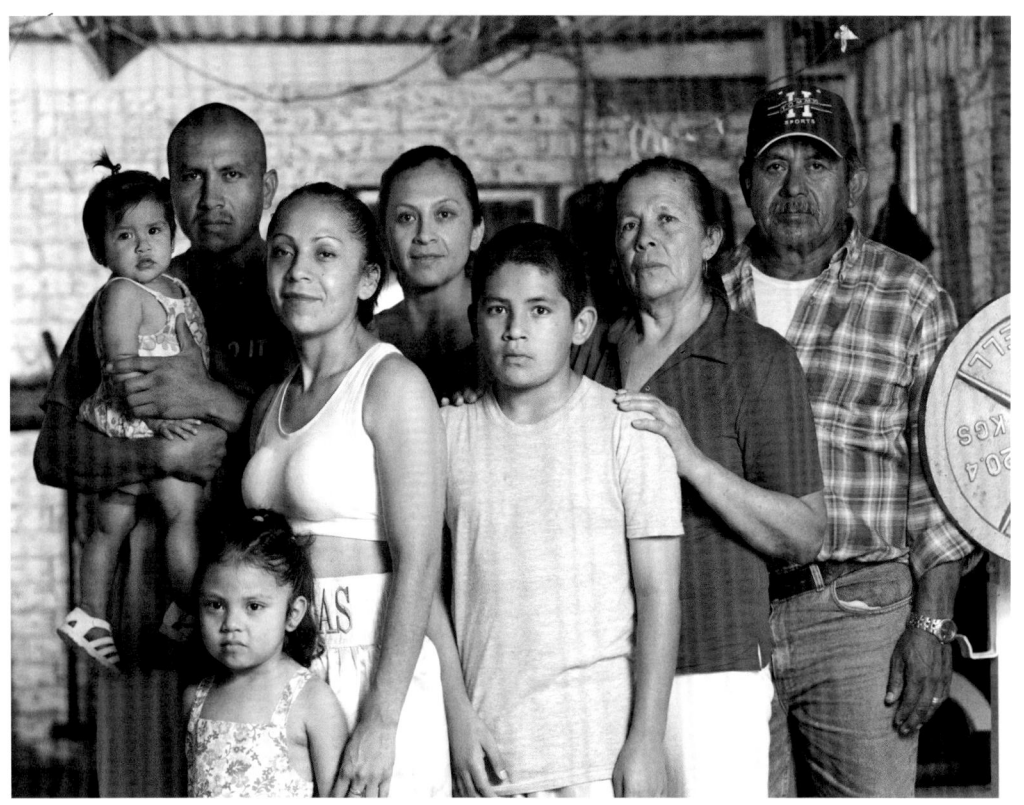

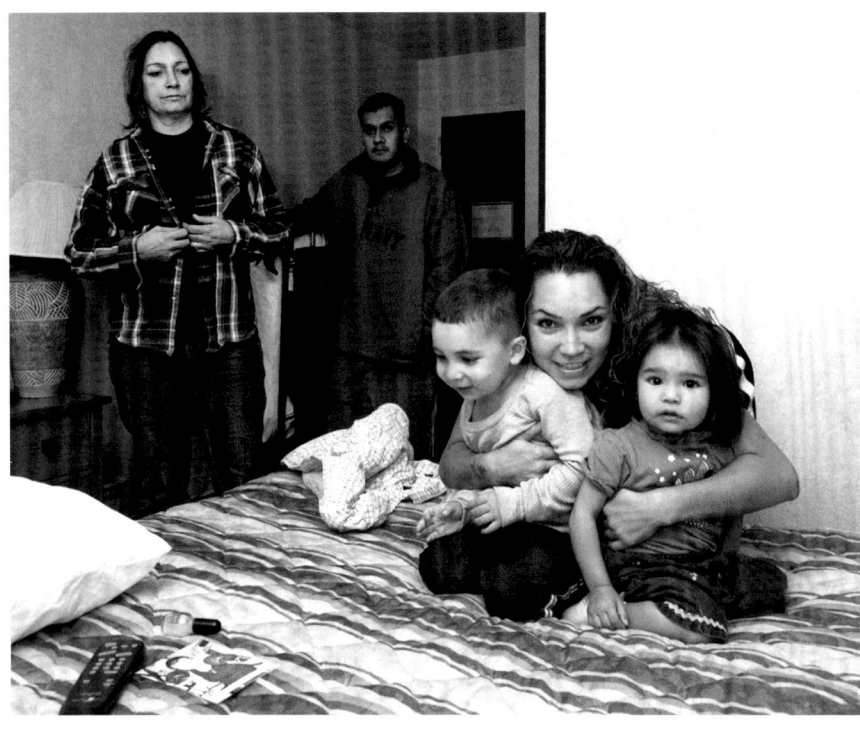

(*top*) Delilah Montoya
Lucy and Family
2006, printed 2018
Archival inkjet on eSatin, ed. 1/2
24 × 32 in.
Collection of the artist

(*bottom*) Delilah Montoya
Elisha Olivas With Her Mom, Two Children, and Friend
2005, printed 2006
Piezograph on Hahnemuhle photo rag 310 paper, ed. 2/3
30 × 35 in.
Collection of the artist

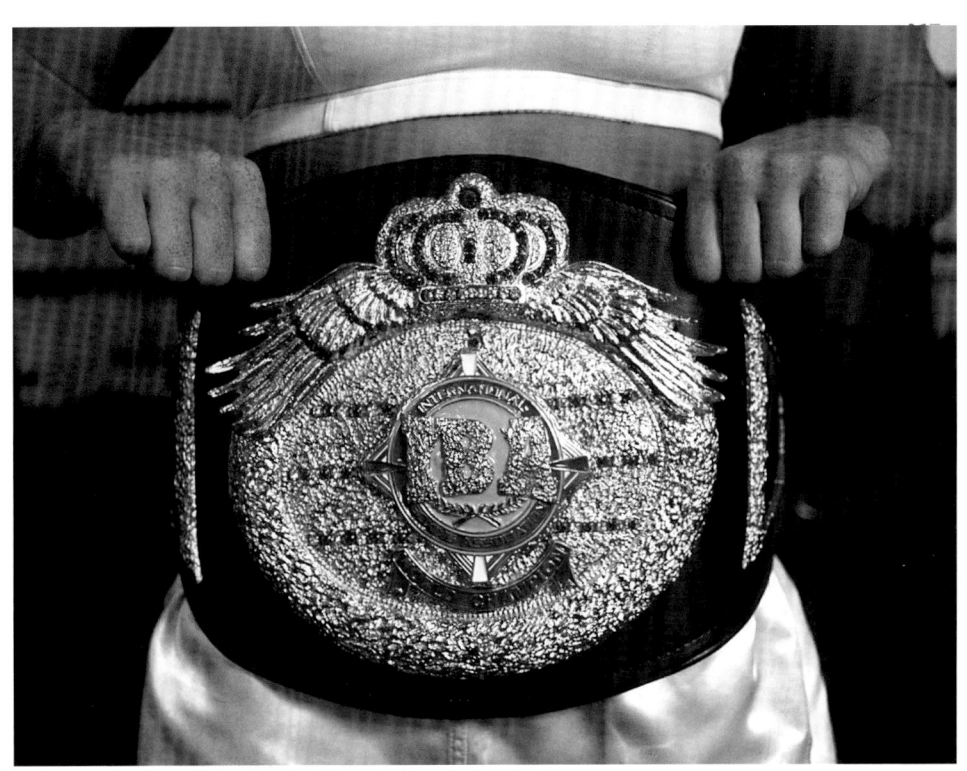

(*top*) Delilah Montoya
*Holly Holm with her IBA Junior
Welter Weight Belt*
2005, printed 2006
Piezograph on Hahnemuhle photo
rag 310 paper, ed. 1/3
17½ × 23 in.
Albuquerque Museum, museum
purchase and gift of the artist
PC2022.32.2

(*bottom*) Delilah Montoya
Holly in the Gym (at Ringside)
2005, printed 2006
Gelatin silver print, ed. 1/4
10 × 8 in.
Albuquerque Museum, museum
purchase and gift of the artist
PC2022.32.3

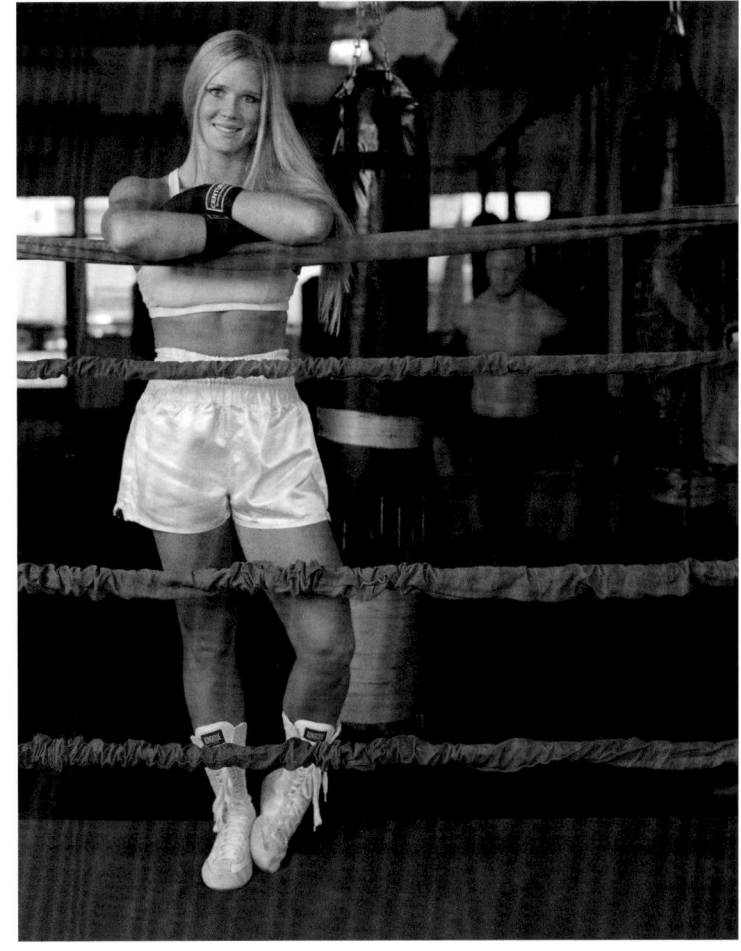

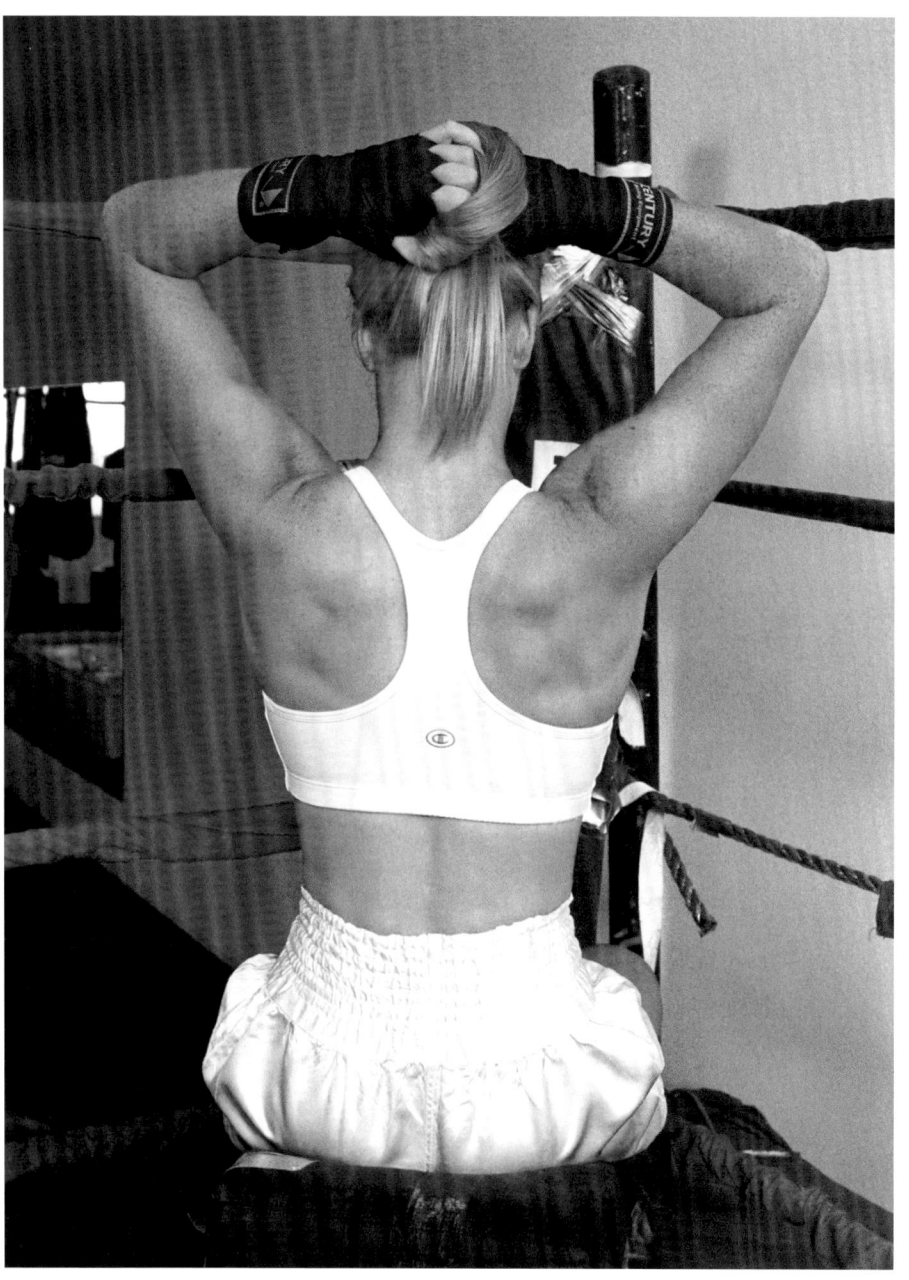

Delilah Montoya
Holly Holm
2005, printed 2006
Gelatin silver print, ed. 2/5
10 × 8 in.
Albuquerque Museum, museum
purchase and gift of the artist
PC2022.32.1

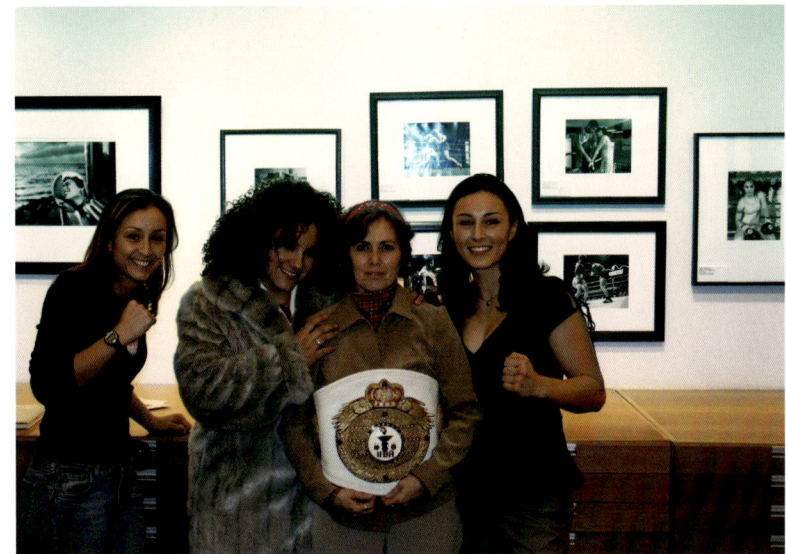

Delilah Montoya
Monica Lovato, Stephanie Jara-
millo, Delilah Montoya, and Jackie
Chavez
Women Boxers: The New Warriors
Andrew Smith Gallery, Santa Fe,
NM
2006

who took up boxing in her 60s, helped you identify some of the women that you ended up photographing. You have women in the ring doing what men do: fighting. At the same time, you show them mothering. The other ring, so to speak, that they inhabit is that of *familia*.

Delilah: I first started thinking about women boxers around the time I was making work about La Llorona and Sebastiana. I wondered, "How does one describe the contemporary Malcriada, and who is she? I couldn't help but think about Teresa Marquez. As an Albuquerque community activist who brought people together, especially as a librarian, by hosting talks at Zimmerman Library. She kept a finger on the pulse of the community. She had an interest in boxing and would promote it. I remember these newspaper images of her with gloves on, training at a local gym. At that time, Cecilio was not doing well, and she approached me about acquiring his papers for the library. I worked with her and Cecilio to archive his collection. She sparked an energy about women boxers in the back of my mind. So when I started thinking about modern-day malcriadas, I thought about Teresa. She was very malcriada and just didn't stop. Teresa would move things to their limits, and then it occurred to me that modern-day malcriada are women boxers.

One of my first jobs as a photographer was shooting sports for a small-town newspaper. At the time, I couldn't afford a professional camera with autofocus and a motor drive. I learned to pull focus and shoot with anticipation. That means you anticipate the action, and when you hit the shutter at the point of action, you don't see the action because the mirror flips up so you can't see what is being captured on film. What I did was follow the subject as it was moving with the camera focus and then click on the anticipated height of action. I was working decisively.

Because I only had one fixed lens, I learned to get really close to things and pull back quickly to get out of the way of players, refs, and the ball. I would shoot a roll of film quickly, pop it out of the camera, and reload film as fast as I could. I actually got some good shots that way. At first, I felt a little intimidated about getting in there, but there was this sports photographer who came up to me and said, "Well, you've got to act like you own the place." And I thought, *Oh, I can do that.* So I would just go in there and act like I own the place, and it worked. Holding a camera somehow commanded a certain amount of respect. All these skills came in handy because I used a 6 × 9 medium format film camera to film the fights at the boxing ring. All the other sports photographers were using digital cameras with all the latest bells and whistles. The medium format camera had no auto focus, motor drive, and only shot twenty frames at a time, but I had the skill and got some good shots.

I wanted to photograph female boxers but knew I needed to collaborate with Theresa to gain insights. We talked about doing a book of her writings and my photographs. I found this approach helped to solicit professional boxers because I could give them something in return for their photographs—a copy of the book. That was really important because it gave them not only press coverage but permanency.

Teresa shared contact information, and I would follow up with their promoters or coaches to see if the boxers might be interested in participating in the project. The promoters and the trainers saw this as helping the boxer's career. Upon reflection, I may have been biased in my thinking that their permission should be mediated through male handlers.

Another bias that I had to confront was the expectation that the boxers came from the streets. That they were cholas. That's what I was thinking. I thought that they came from lower middle-class families. As I started getting to know the women who were boxing on a professional level, I found that wasn't true. I had to rethink my own biases. What I found was that these women were athletes. First and foremost, they were athletes who came from many types of backgrounds. They were not confined by a particular background, economic status, or ethnic identity. They were athletes who wanted to excel in a combat sport. I found that they were serious about what they were doing and had overcome many stereotypes and biases in order to just get in the ring.

Women physically do not necessarily have excessive upper body strength. They had to work twice as hard to develop that upper body strength. They had to work twice as hard even to find a fight. To get into the ring, they had to find a match, which is harder for women because there are fewer athletes. Many fights would get canceled because they didn't match up at the weigh-in. It is difficult for them to find a sparring partner or a trainer who is willing to train them.

They also had to confront biases within their own community. I remember hearing a fighter ask if another woman was really a woman. There were rumors of fighters using steroids. Within the sport of women's boxing, there were questions on how to modify the rules for the woman boxer. There were rules about whether they could even be boxing. All the women had to take pregnancy tests before each fight.

Many boxing matches were held at casinos. I remember going up to the Ute casino near the Four Corners area for a big match. All the women were in hotel rooms. And I was going through with my camera to see whether or not I could get in and take pictures of them before they went into the ring. I was struck by one fighter in particular. She had two babies, her mother was there, and her boyfriend was in the background. Her mother was there to help with the kids when their mom went into the ring. You assume that the kids would be elsewhere, but in this case, she had her babies with her. It was a real celebration of the female body and female power. She was both a fighter and someone who gave birth, which is its own kind of fight. Elisha Olivas was also a soldier who had just come back from Iraq. Her mom had been watching her babies while she was deployed. She was a soldier, and that's where she picked up boxing.

There was another athlete, Akondaye, who was getting her PhD in social work. I asked her, "Why boxing?" She said, "I can do it solely by myself. I don't have to be part of the team. I can do it on my own time. I'm an athlete who engages in combat sports." She had a young child and a husband who was very supportive.

Later, I was talking about getting matched up. She said, "I was ready to go in the ring." She had to take a pregnancy test, and she found out she was pregnant. These encounters opened up my mind about gender. And how gender and the demands it puts on us but also how it is not binary. I learned a lot about gender and how, biologically, it is a spectrum. I remember talking with my daughter, who was in med school at the time, and she confirmed that it is more complex than we often assume. Now, she's a doctor.

The women boxers taught me a lot about being a woman but also about just being a person in our world. A person who had dreams and desires. A person with the strength and the willpower to negotiate a world that many do not think is for them. They have to be willing to punch and hit. They have to be willing to take it too.

I wanted to find out more about what made them tick and what led them to boxing. I wanted to see what violence looked like when women were the ones delivering it. What does that violence look like? Does it look the same on a man as it does on a woman? This was an early question when I still had not fully understood my own biases. That question is loaded with biases. I realized violence is violence.

There are some people willing to engage in a violent sport, and there are many that just can't. I think we all have a little bit of malcriada in us, but some of us are willing to take it to a whole other level of physicality.

Sed: Trail of Thirst (2004) is a photographic installation by Delilah Montoya in collaboration with artist Orlando Lara and contributing artists Beatrice Briones, Mario Arosemena, and Gwen Thompson. The project reveals the underlying truths related to migration through perilous routes across the Arizona-Sonora desert, which the US Border Patrol calls the Tucson Sector.[1] The project is an activist intervention aimed at revealing the humanitarian crisis at the US-Mexico border. Through panoramic landscape photography, the series captures traces of migrant journeys, often without directly depicting human subjects. Focusing on the artifacts and environmental markers that bear witness to the perilous journeys of undocumented border crossers, the series underscores the horrific experiences that individuals and families face. According to Montoya, the harsh realities are a continuation of the historic reverberations of layers of colonialism.

One of the defining images in the series, *Humane Borders Water Station*, presents an isolated water station placed in the desert by the nonprofit group Humane Borders. The photograph features an expansive desert landscape with three large water tanks marked by a blue flag—a beacon of survival for migrants traversing the harsh terrain. The composition of the photograph evokes the aesthetics of nineteenth-century expeditionary photography, a technique Montoya deliberately subverts. By referencing the visual language of Manifest Destiny–era depictions of the land, the artists critique the historical framing of the American Southwest as an empty frontier while simultaneously drawing attention to the contemporary humanitarian crisis at the border.[2] According to Montoya,

> In *Sed: Trail of Thirst*, I merged multiple negatives as a panorama. Now, smartphones can automatically construct a pano, but in 2004, it was done with photoshop masks and image reconstruction. I used color and black-and-white large format negatives to construct the largest possible images using Photoshop and an Epson printer. My desire was to make those tragic landscapes epic like the Western paintings and photographs that represent "America." The migrant trails are an "American Experience" just like those the pioneers traversed seeking new lives.[3]

The juxtaposition of the expansiveness of the sky and the stark desert terrain force the viewer to imagine a crossing filled with relief and hope accompanied by looking out at the clouds and seeing the life-saving resource emerge in the distance. The photograph simultaneously evokes an understanding that crossing the harsh landscape in excruciating conditions has taken the lives of many migrants.

In *Desire Lines, Baboquivari Peak, AZ*, Montoya photographs an arid landscape with white plastic gallon water jugs scattered among cacti. The image captures a lone figure with a wheelbarrow traversing the Tohono O'odham Nation's land, which is bisected by the border. The shared histories of displacement experienced by both indigenous communities and migrants are starkly evident.[3] The photograph tells the stories embedded in the land. Natural elements like cacti, shrubs, dirt, and rocks represent the inhospitable. The plastic jugs, however, serve as a reminder of the human quest for safety and a better life. They also point to the humanitarian efforts and empathy that could be employed to confront the inhumane immigration system that creates the crisis.

Migrant Campsite, Ironwood, Arizona is an image of an abandoned migrant campsite, capturing the remnants of human presence in an otherwise desolate desert setting. Among the scattered belongings are a pink backpack and a single black leather boot, stark reminders that among those making the crossing are women and children. The image provokes an unsettling question: What became of the individuals who left these items behind? The absence of human figures intensifies the sense of loss and precarity, making the viewer confront the harsh reality of undocumented migration without the sensationalism of direct representation. The shadow in the right foreground connects with the idea that the land carries the stories of those who have passed. The land remembers.

In *Powerline Trail, Ironwood, AZ*, Montoya contrasts the landscapes traversed by migrants with the visible infrastructure of contemporary American life. The photograph features utility poles stretching into the distance, visually dividing the landscape. Montoya talks about the poles as markers that will eventually lead to a city. In that way, they also become beacons of hope and directional guides. White plastic water jugs dot the foreground, emphasizing again the life-and-death necessity of hydration and the humanitarians who also risk their safety to provide help.

While in Ironwood, Orlando Lara engaged with members of the humanitarian group Samaritans, who support migrants with food and water as they cross dangerous terrains. They also collected some of the artifacts they found, including personal hygiene items, backpacks, clothing, and shoes that were later included in the exhibition of the *Sed: Trail of Thirst* series.

But there are also oases in the desert—the "running water" blue tanks placed by Humane Borders in over fourteen locations throughout the Arizona border provide 100,000 gallons of water per year. A group called the Samaritans drives near migrant trails and camps in order to dispense first-aid and food packets to border crossers. Mike Wilson, a Tohono O'odham tribal member, places 150 gallons of water every few weeks near Baboquivari Peak, which is used as a landmark by migrants. He does this despite frequent vandalism to his jugs. Some argue that these humanitarian acts encourage migration, but these activist groups believe that death should not be part of the migration experience."[4]

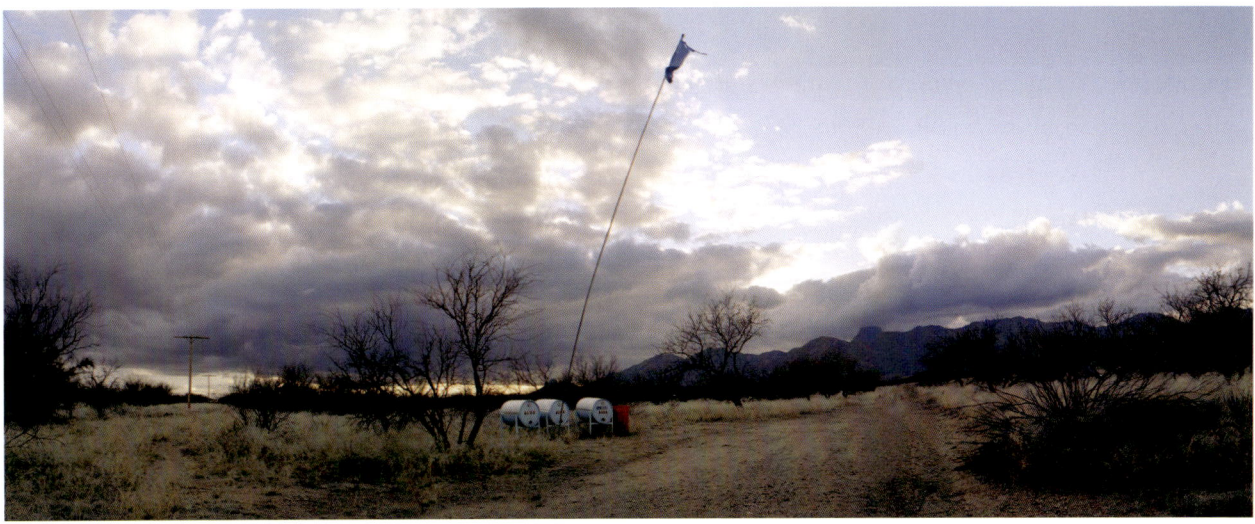

Delilah Montoya
Humane Borders Water Station, 2004
(from the series *Sed: Trail of Thirst*)
2004, printed 2008
Inkjet print on eSatin, ed. 1/5
19 × 47½ in.
Smithsonian American Art Museum, Gift of the Gilberto Cardenas Latino Art Collection
2011.52.2

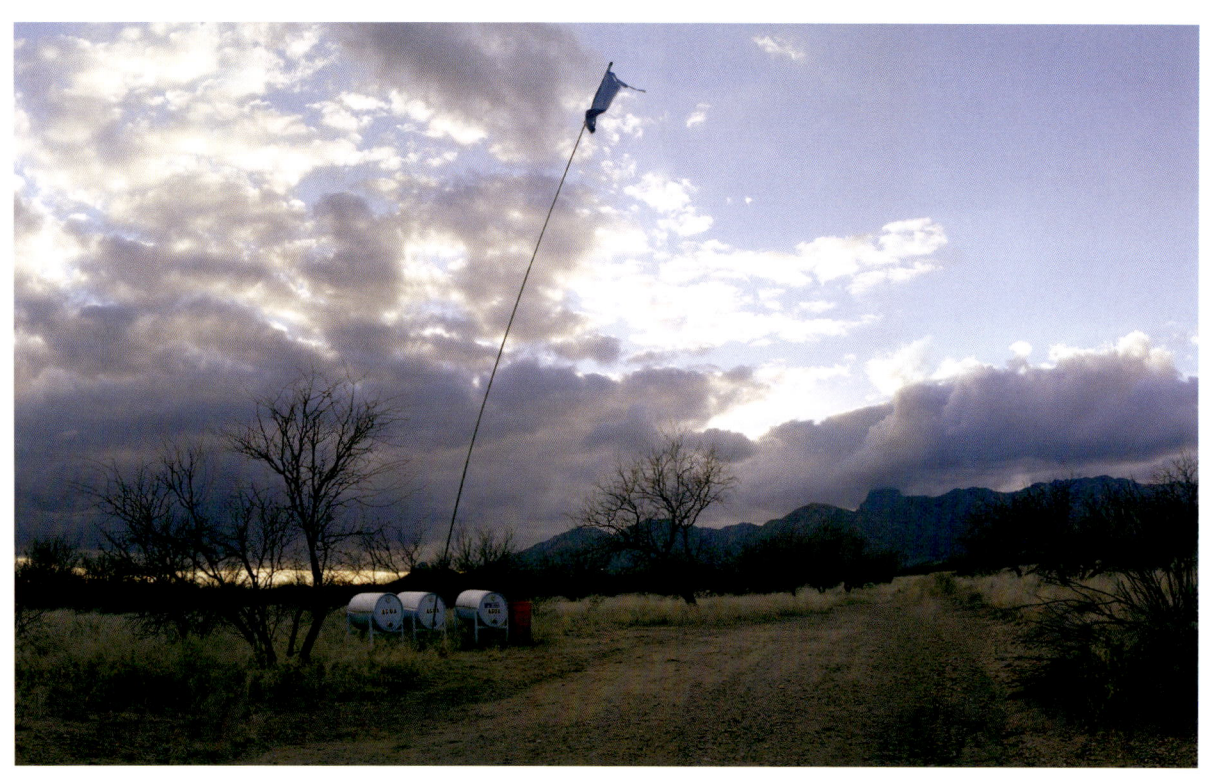

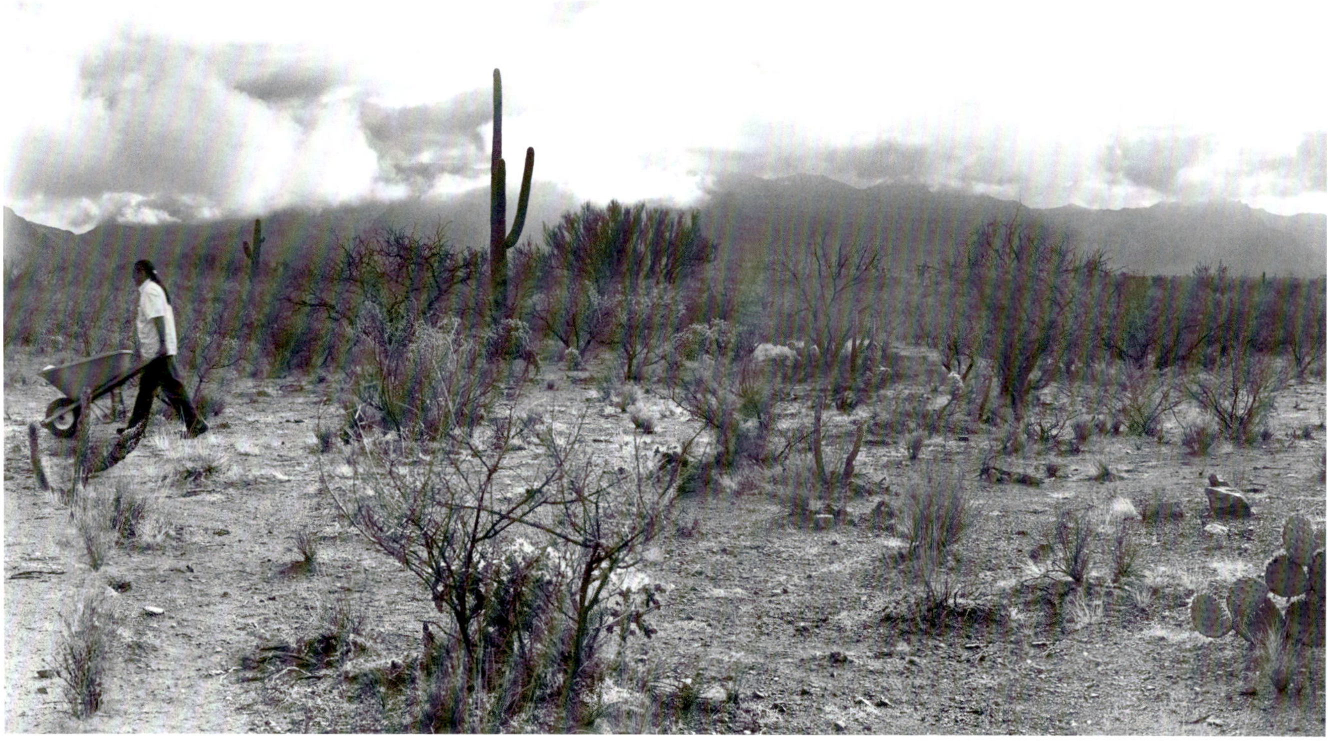

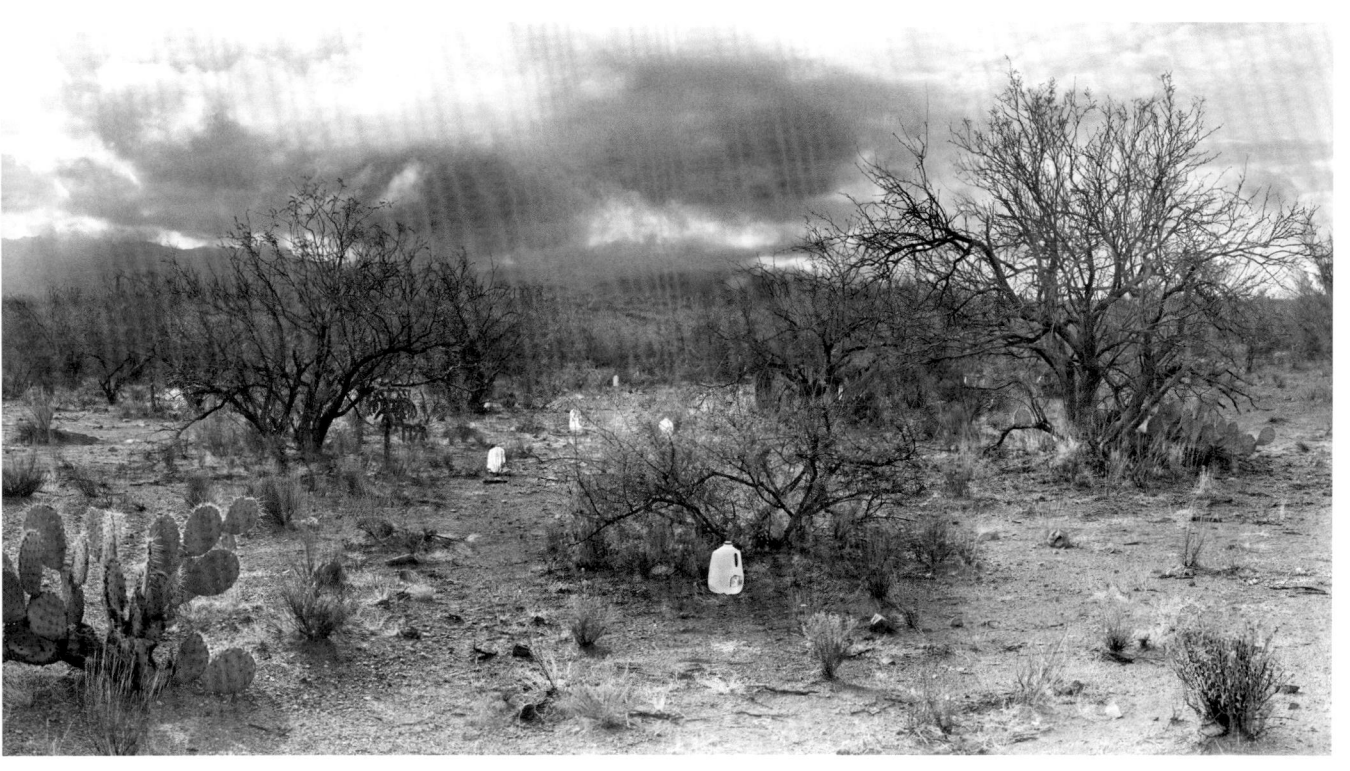

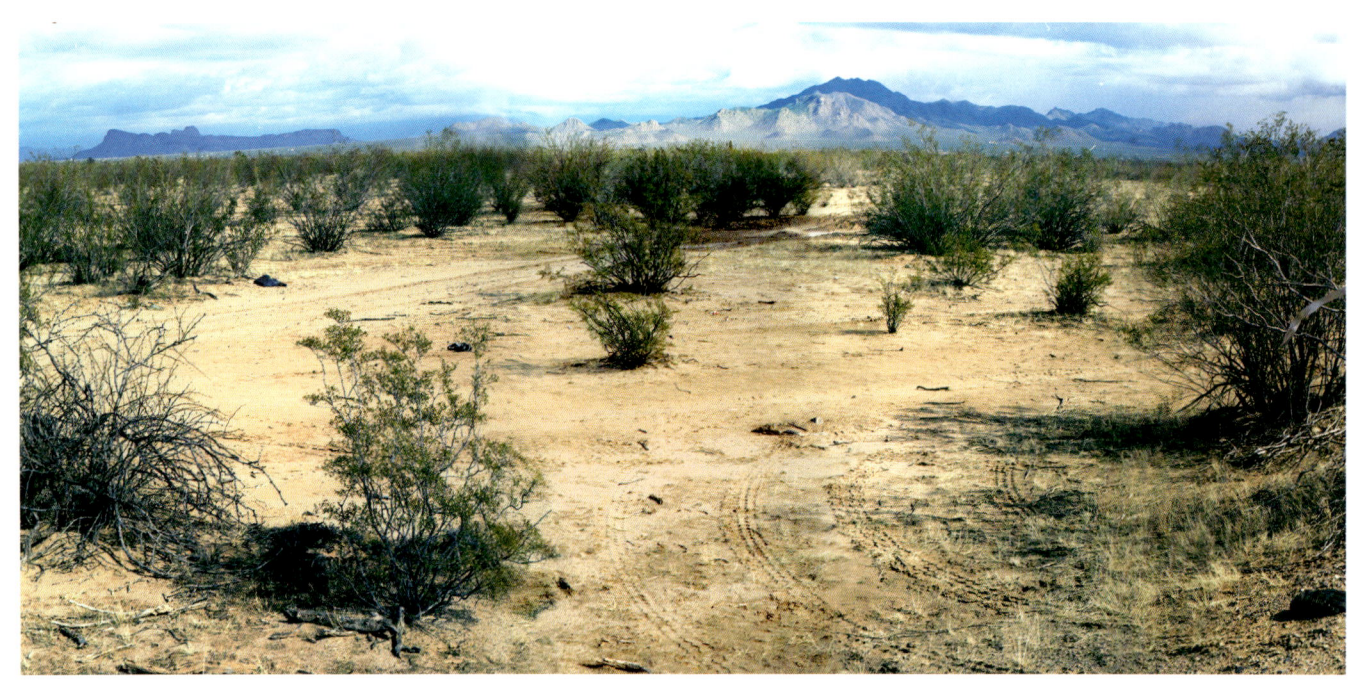

Delilah Montoya
Migrant Campsite, Ironwood, Arizona (from the series *Sed: Trail of Thirst*)
2004, printed 2008
Inkjet on eSatin with Dibond mount, ed. A/P
16⅛ × 69⅝ in.
Collection of the artist

(*opposite page, bottom*) *Migrant Campsite, Ironwood, Arizona*, detail (from the series *Sed: Trail of Thirst*)
2004, printed 2008
Inkjet on eSatin with Dibond mount, ed. A/P
16⅛ × 69⅝ in.
Collection of the artist

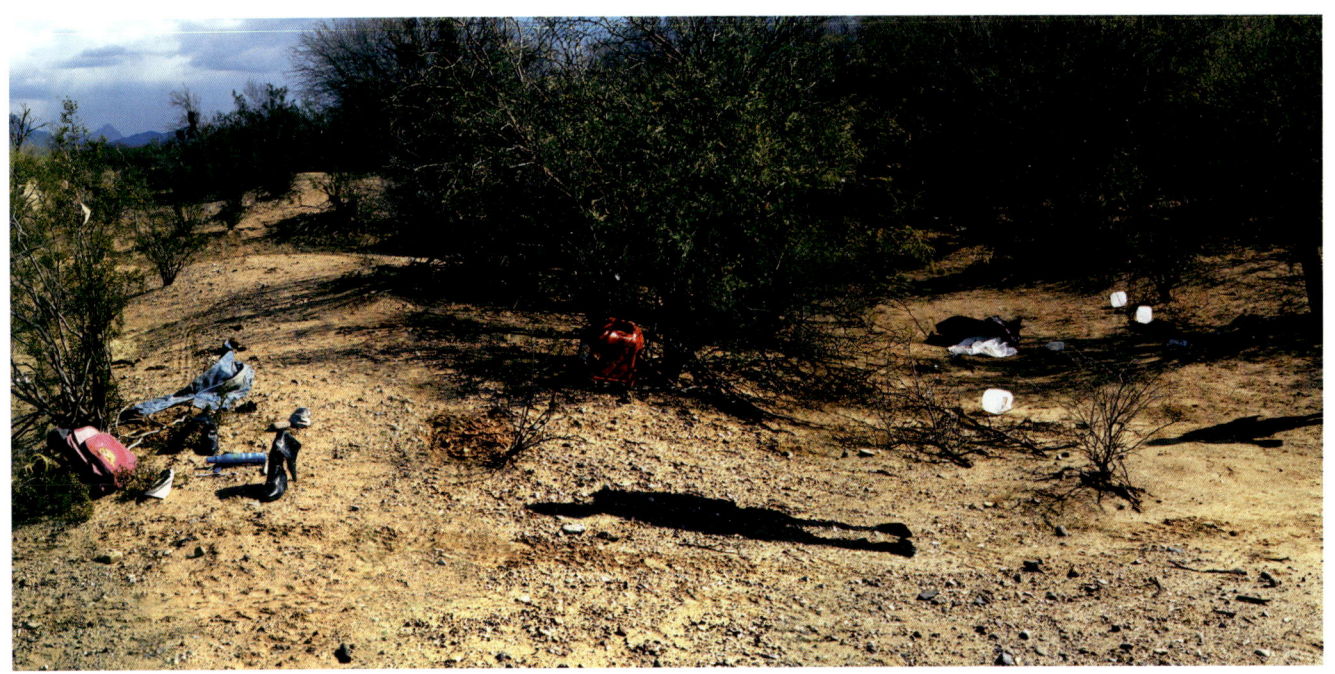

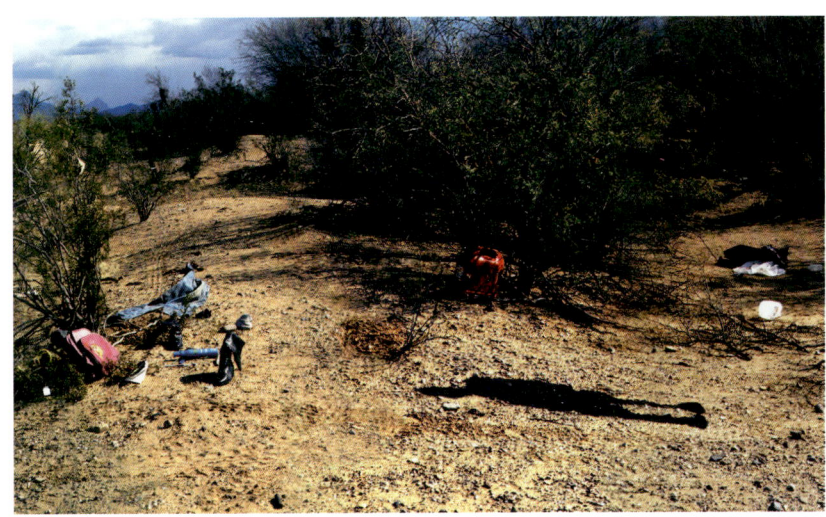

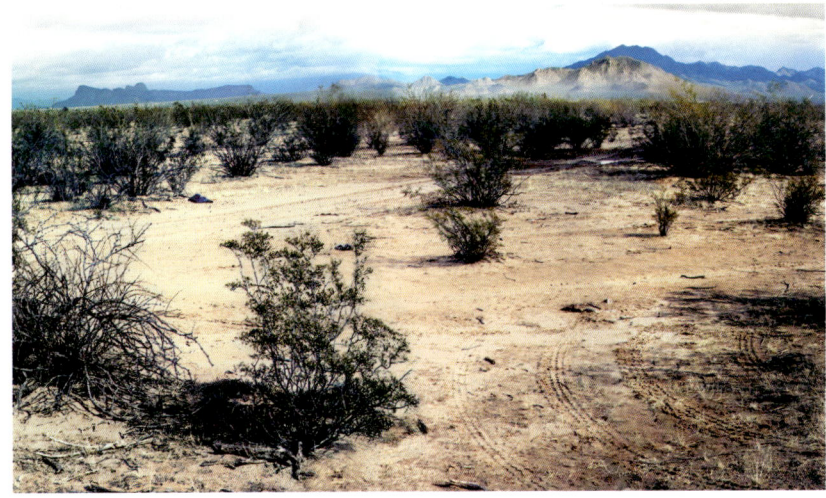

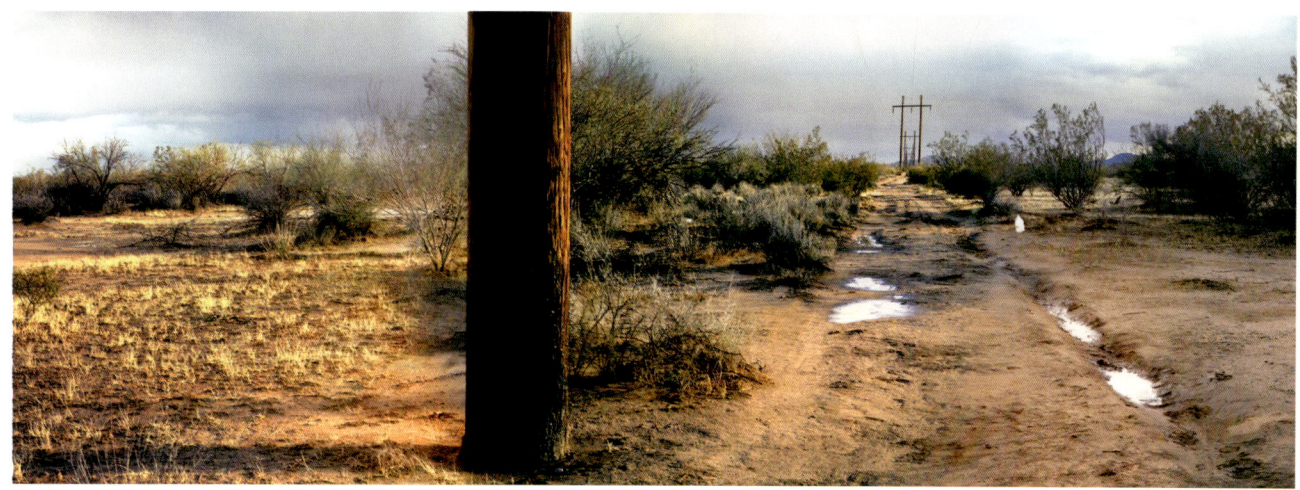

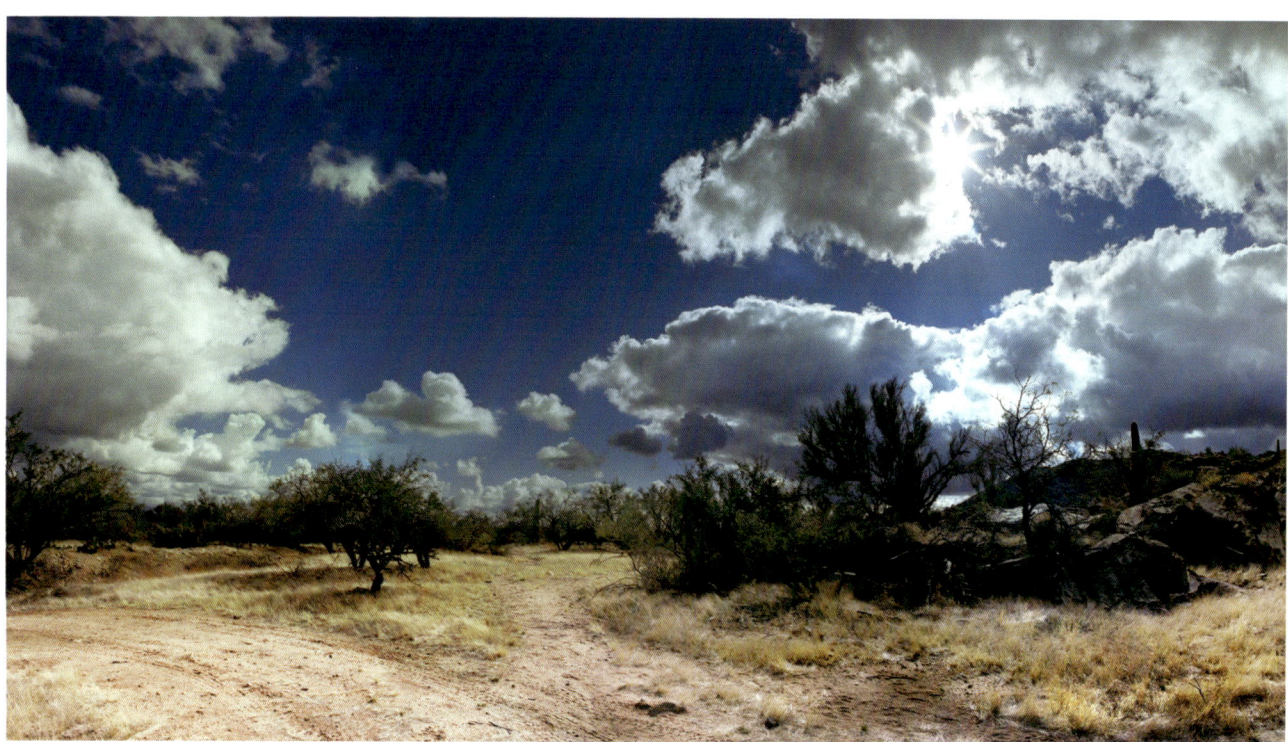

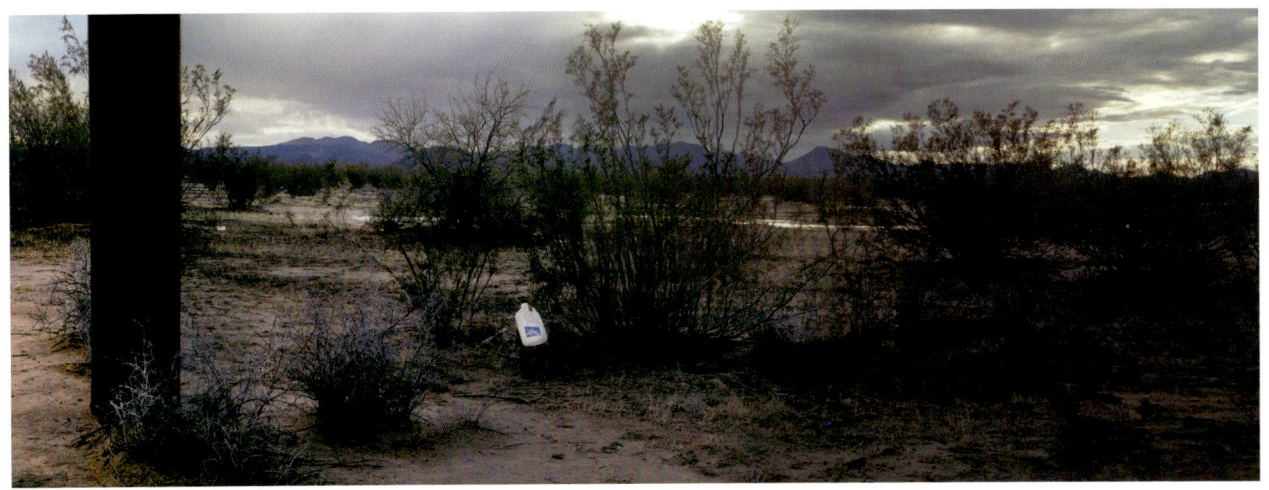

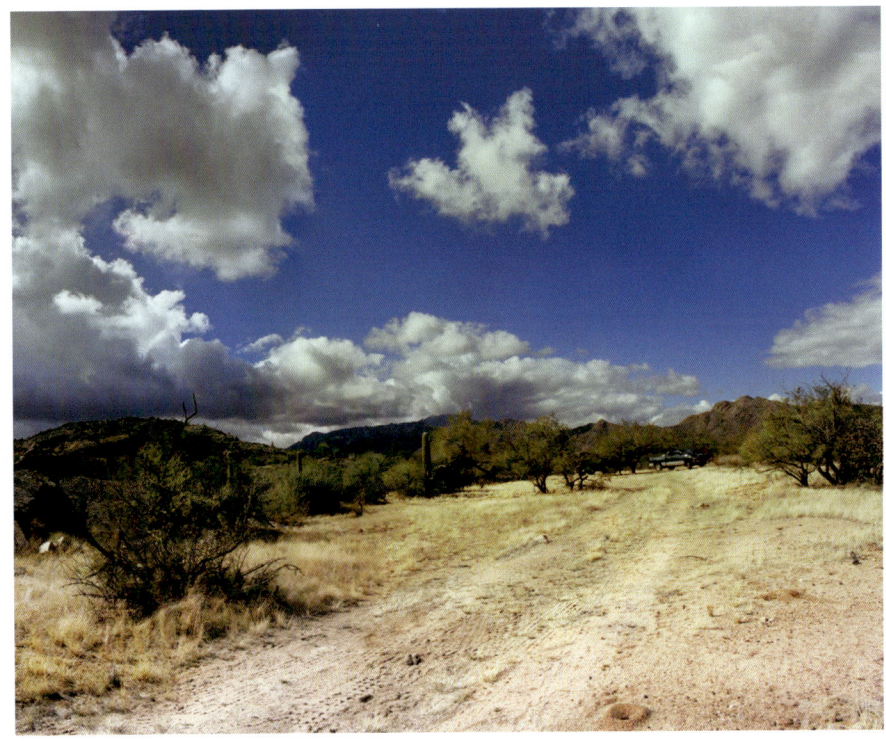

(*top*) Delilah Montoya
Powerline Trail, Ironwood, AZ (from the series *Sed: Trail of Thirst*)
2004, printed 2008
Inkjet on eSatin, ed. 1/5
19 × 58 in.
Blanton Museum of Art, University of Texas at Austin, Gilberto Cárdenas Collection, Museum Acquisition Fund
2022.114

(*bottom*) Delilah Montoya
El Paseo O'odham Nation 2004 (from the series *Sed: Trail of Thirst*)
2004, printed 2008
Inkjet on eSatin with Dibond mount
17 ⅞ × 55 ⅛ in.
Collection of the artist

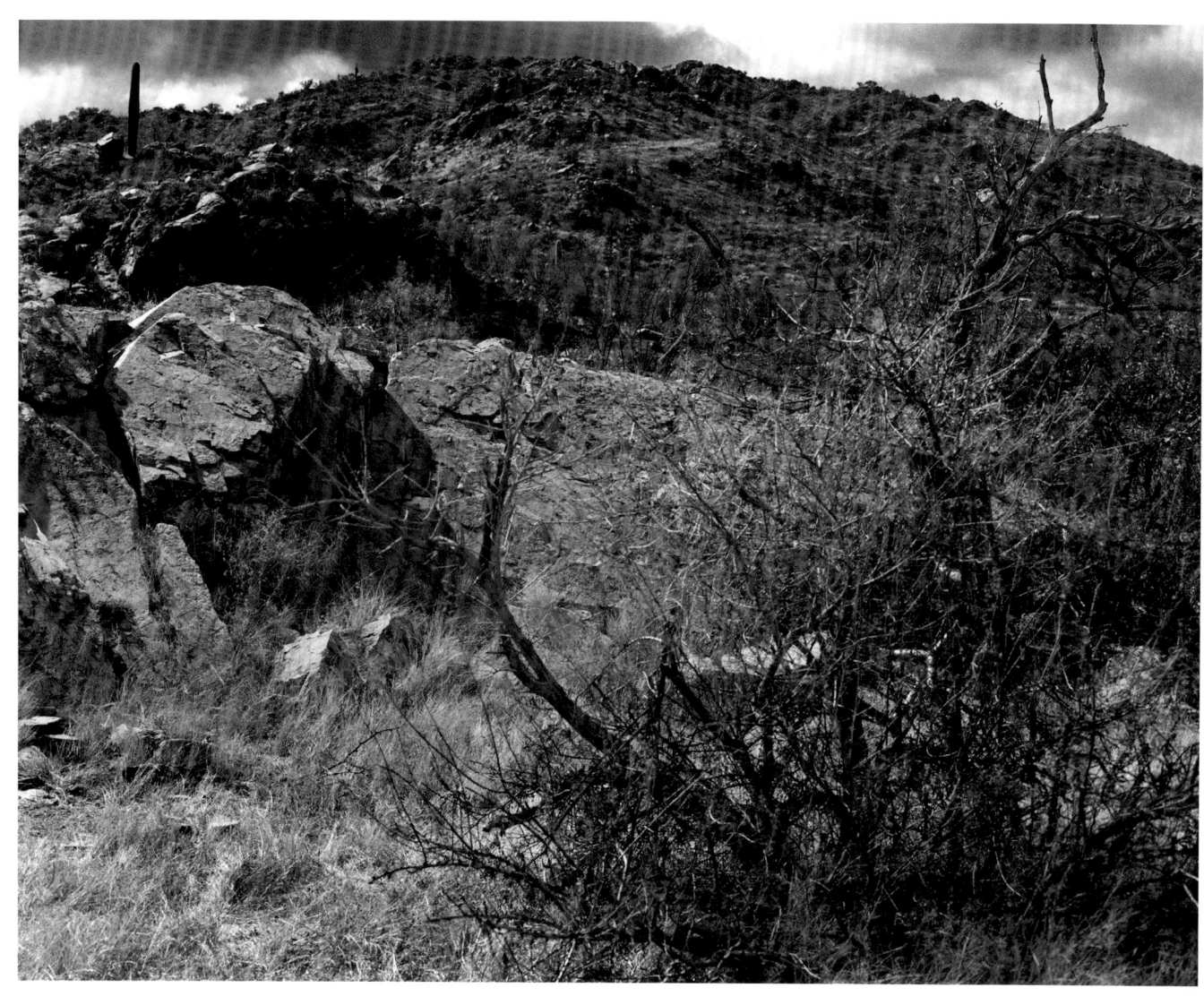

Delilah Montoya
Tribal Lands Sacred Space (from the series *Sed: Trail of Thirst*)
2004, printed 2008
Inkjet on Fibre paper with Dibond mount, A/P
21¾ × 54⅝ in.
Collection of the artist

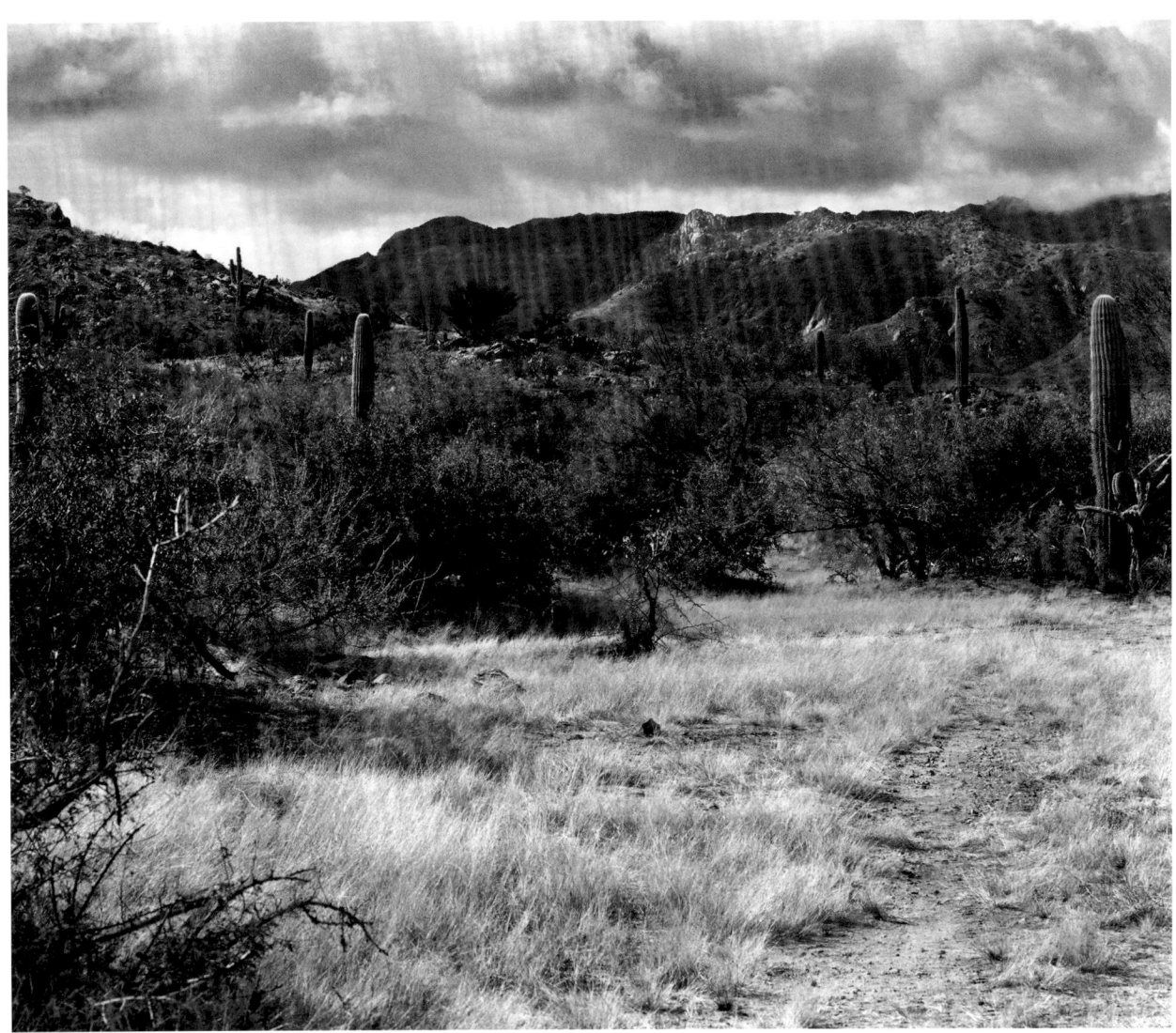

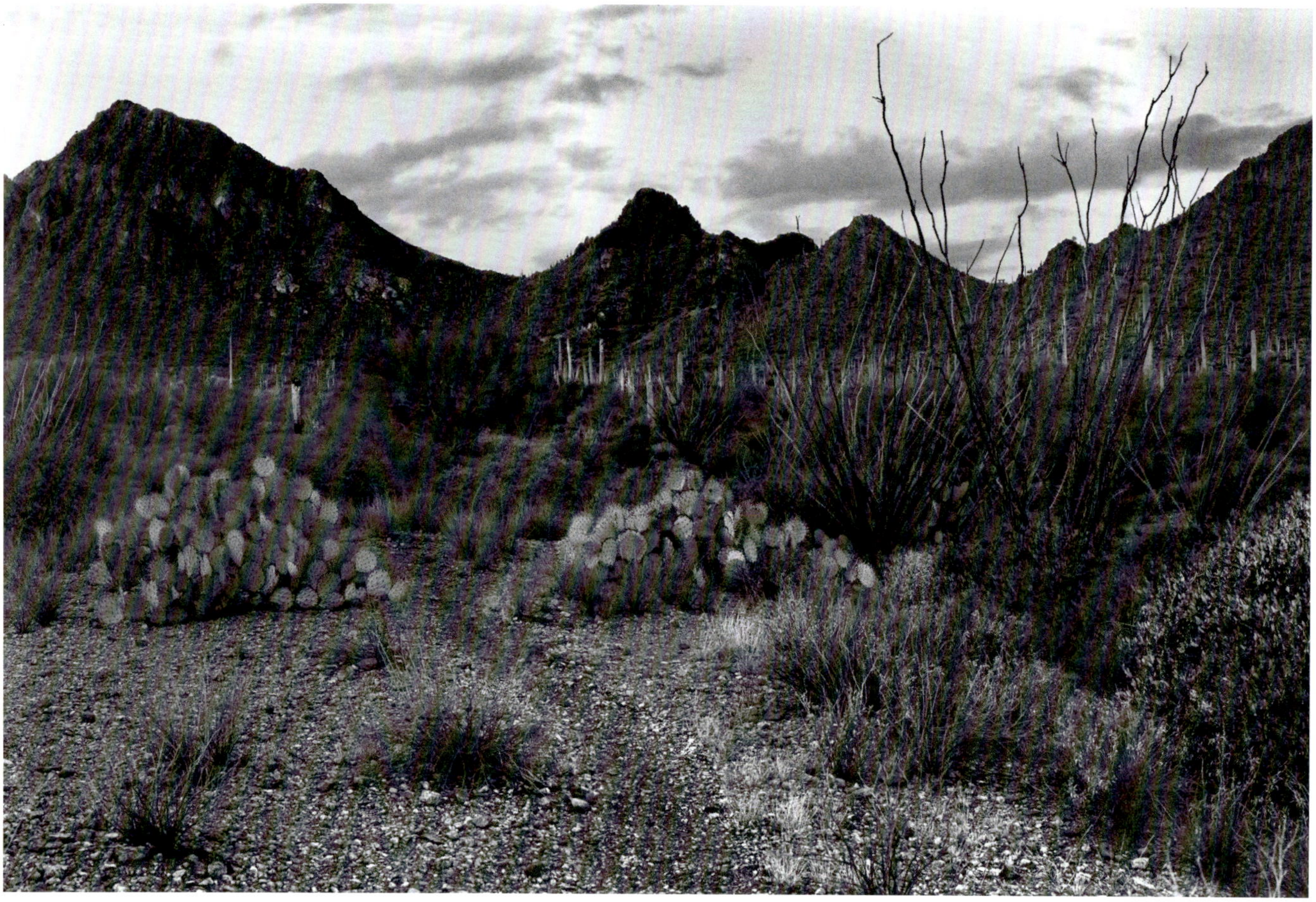

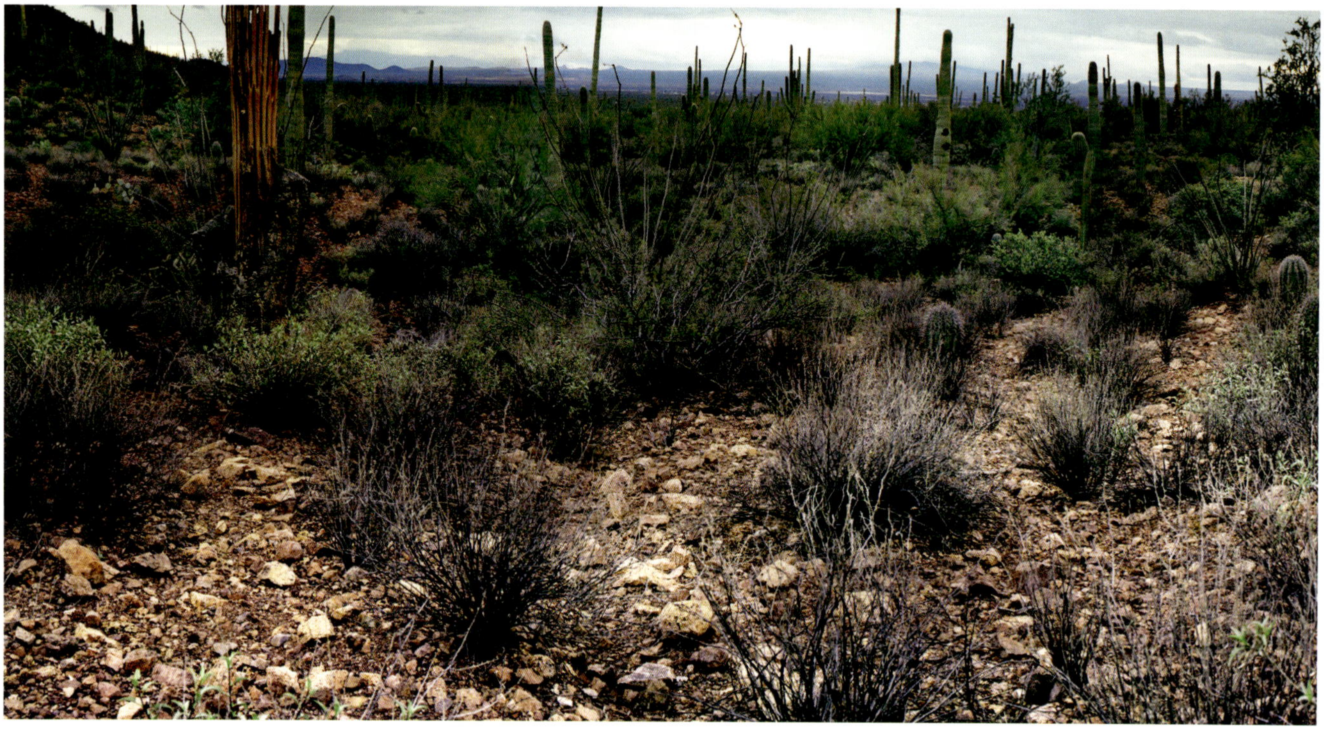

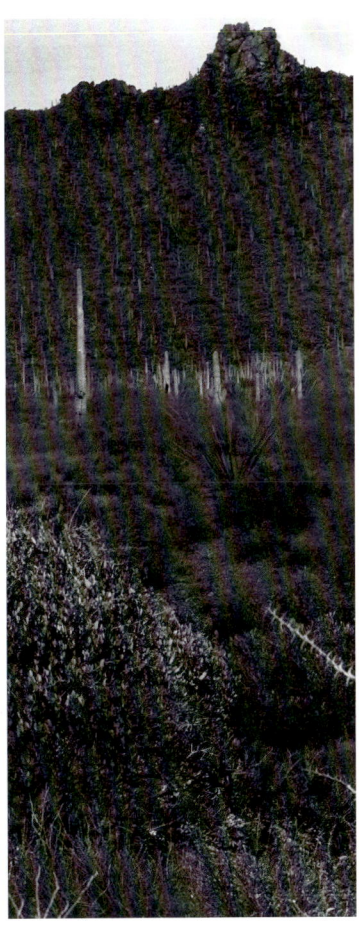

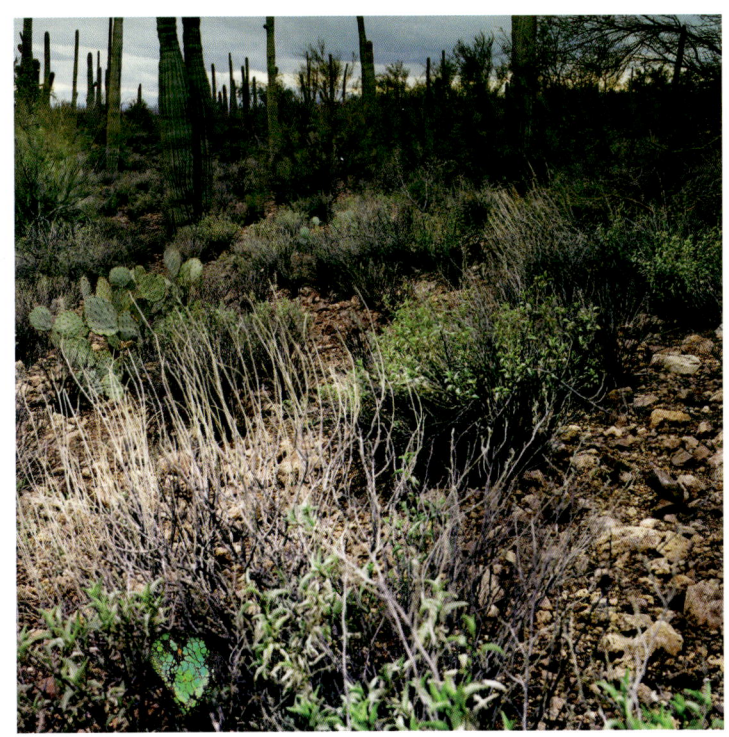

(*top*) Delilah Montoya
Saguaro Crossing, Arizona (from the
series *Sed: Trail of Thirst*)
2004, printed 2008
Inkjet on Fibre paper with Dibond
mount
22 × 43⅜ in.
Collection of the artist

(*bottom*) Delilah Montoya
Saguaro Crossing, Tucson (from the
series *Sed: Trail of Thirst*)
2004, printed 2008
Inkjet on eSatin with Dibond
mount
17⅝ × 53⅞ in.
Collection of the artist

Montoya and Lara employ a strategy of activism that bears witness to the tragic realities of crossing the border in the desert. Choosing to depict migrant trails, campsites, and water stations rather than the individuals themselves forces viewers to imagine the migrants' experiences and emphasizes the erasure of their stories in mainstream narratives. Art historian Ann Marie Leimer describes this technique as a "spectral aesthetic," where the material traces of migration—discarded belongings, footprints, and water jugs—serve as stand-ins for human presence.[5]

The project title, *Sed: Trail of Thirst*, evokes a historical parallel to the Trail of Tears, the forced removal of Native American tribes in the 1830s. By drawing this connection, Montoya and Lara underscore the cyclical nature of displacement and suffering tied to US territorial expansion and border enforcement policies.

The series portrays migration as an experience of liminality—a space between home and destination, legality and illegality, survival and death. The stark desert landscapes highlight the vulnerability of migrants, whose presence is sometimes only known or remembered through what they leave behind.

The *Sed: Trail of Thirst* series was first exhibited at Talento Bilingüe in Houston, Texas, in 2005. As part of the installation, found objects from the border, including backpacks, playing cards, baseball caps, scarves, and a white plastic water jug, were displayed. These items functioned as physical remnants of the project, reinforcing the absence-driven aesthetic of the photographs. A notable feature of the exhibition was a poster listing the names of 200 deceased migrants recently found along the border, confronting viewers with the human toll of border enforcement policies.

In 2008, a reimagined version of *Sed: Trail of Tears* was included in *Phantom Sightings: Art After the Chicano Movement*, a traveling exhibition by the Los Angeles County Museum of Art. The inclusion of *Sed* in this context positioned it within a broader discourse on Chicanx identity and the evolving role of art as political intervention.

Sed: Trail of Thirst is a profound visual meditation on the migrant experience. Through its strategic subversion of traditional landscape photography and references to historical trauma, the series compels viewers to engage with the crisis of undocumented migration in new and unsettling ways. The series disrupts the political spectacle of hate and the demonization of immigrants by shifting the focus to the stories told through

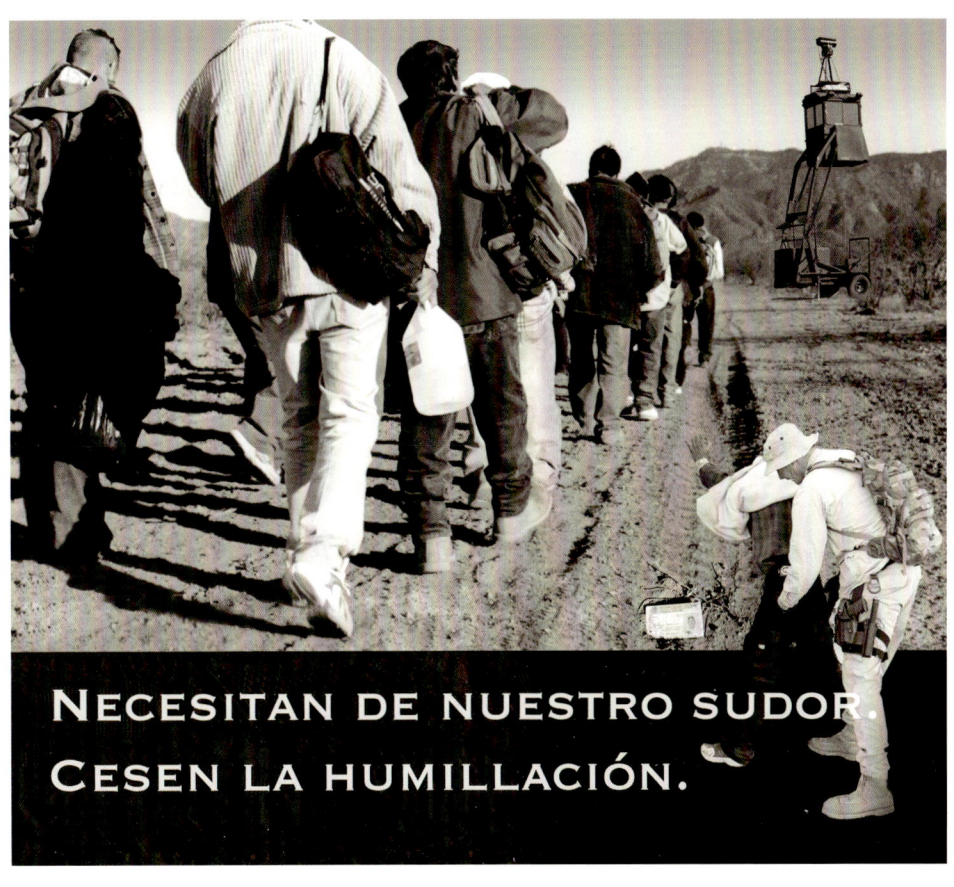

NECESITAN DE NUESTRO SUDOR.
CESEN LA HUMILLACIÓN.

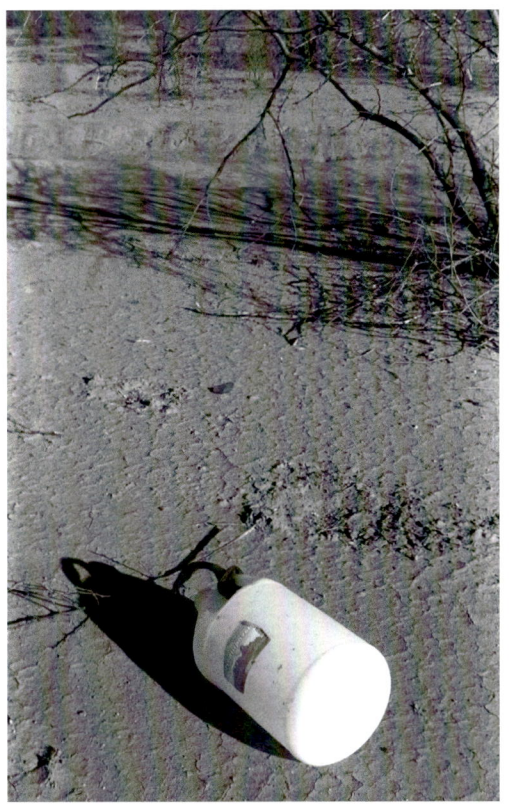

(top) Sed: Trail of the Thirst
Orlando Lara's contribution to the
first installation at Talento Bilingüe
de Houston for Fotofest 2004
Biennial

(bottom) Sed: Trail of the Thirst
Orlando Lara's contribution to the
first installation at Talento Bilingüe
de Houston for Fotofest 2004
Biennial

landscapes and objects that bear traces of human beings in need. Montoya and Lara challenge dominant narratives and reframe the borderlands as sites of both struggle and survival. Their work continues to resonate in contemporary discussions on immigration, making *Sed: Trail of Thirst* a critical contribution to the visual and political discourse surrounding the US-Mexico border.

According to Gloria Anzaldúa, "The border is the locus of resistance, of rupture, implosion and explosion, and of putting together the fragments and creating a new assemblage. Border artists *cambium el punto de referenda*. By disrupting the separation between cultures, they create a culture mix, *una mestizada*, in their artworks. Each artist locates her/himself in this border *lugar*, and tears apart and rebuilds the place itself.[6]

In these photographs, Montoya poses ethical questions about the nature of national borders, the dangerous conditions that migrants and refugees encounter, and the generosity and empathy that everyday people are compelled to act on. Reflecting on these photographs, Montoya says, "The land has a memory and anything that has passed on the land or is passing on the land—our stories, where we have been, what has occurred become scars on the land."

In Conversation with Delilah Montoya, Orlando Lara, and Demetria Martinez: *Sed: Trail of Thirst*

Demetria: *Sed: Trail of Thirst*, which is a collaboration with Orlando Lara, depicts a landscape turned graveyard thanks in large part to Operation Gatekeeper, which President Clinton instituted in 1994. The border was militarized—with more fences, walls, and a beefed-up border patrol—forcing people to cross into the United States in ever more remote and dangerous places. This has led to the deaths of thousands, thanks to a lethal journey that you have referred to as a "middle passage."

Especially striking is the way you depart from the usual photographic portrayal of this travesty. Your work focuses on a landscape absent of people—they exist as shadows or as abandoned objects—including a pink backpack, a child's boot, and plastic water jugs. What led you to use this approach?

You also took pictures of water stations left by human rights organizations. Members of some of these groups are also planting crosses where they find human remains. They look for clues as to the origins of the dead so they can inform families back home. The crosses become a way of honoring the dead. I feel like you, too, honor not only the dead but also those whose fate we know nothing about. Cold "objectivity" is not the approach you take.

Orlando: I went to the site about a week before Delilah showed up. I ended up staying at a church in Tucson that had been putting out water stations in the local desert. I had also recently gone through a death in the family. Something about staying in that church and the recent death that I was still processing. One night, I had a *pesadilla*—I felt the presence of a spirit. I mentioned this to Delilah, and we started talking about the feeling of ghostliness in the desert and the spiritual reality of death. Initially, I was thinking in terms of the materiality of place and landscape. I was thinking about what people leave behind. I wasn't thinking that we were going to photograph people or do interviews while people are trying to cross, so from the beginning, we knew that we were dealing with the landscapes and objects. However, the spiritual side emerged once we were there, and Delilah worked to figure out how to bring that in through the imagery.

Delilah: Orlando, I don't know if I've ever really thanked you enough for all that you contributed to *Sed*. Your efforts in going to the site earlier were invaluable. We shot this series in only three days. Unbelievable! We were able to capture the right landscapes. You met the right people. What's the name of the young man that took us around?

Orlando: His name is Mario Arosemena.

Delilah: Mario was amazing; he knew exactly where to take us. The landscape was magnificent. There was a beauty there, a spirituality. Amalia Mesa-Baines wrote that the landscape has scars, and the land has a memory. When we started looking across the landscape, there were objects scattered on the trails. Each item is a story, a memory that the landscape itself holds. We began to realize it was about photographing the landscape and allowing the land itself to speak.

I remember the day at the campsite, the sun raking down with a long shadow. It was your shadow, Orlando, and I realized it suggested people who were there. I decided not to show the person making the shadow. I photographed you and your shadow and then the same spot without you so that later I could experiment with compositing only the shadow into the landscape.

The expectation was that *Sed* was a documentary project, but our approach was more aligned with surrealist reality. The documentary photographer goes to photograph sensationalism as a perfect, unmanipulated shot. They want "speaking the truth" to shock people. Truth comes in many different forms, and I think with *Sed: Trail of Thirst*, we were looking for scars that were on the landscape where the land spoke the truth. Orlando, your studies regarding the border brought so much knowledge to what we were doing.

Orlando: I did some work with the Border Art Workshop in San Diego. I also did some trips with other undergraduate students and would do trips down to the border, and I started taking photographs. For this trip, I was thinking about the people who passed and didn't make it out of the border and whose spirits are still there. I definitely felt that, even though I'm not a spiritual or religious person. Maybe it is a cultural thing that even if you're not religious, the remnants of people's presence are there and what remains is their clothes and their items. So I think both of those presences are very much part of the project.

Demetria: You also shot photos of water stations left by human rights organizations, and members of some of these groups are also planting crosses where they find human remains. They look for clues as to the origins of the dead so they can inform families back home. The crosses become a way of honoring the dead. I feel like you, too, honor not only the dead but also those whose fates we know nothing about. A cold objectivity is not the approach that either of you takes.

Delilah: When we were down there looking at the trails running under the power lines, there were tracks where people walked and cars drove. I realized the power lines led them to a city. When you are out there, it is very disorienting. The trails cut right through a reservation. This brought up the legalities of the *migra* occupying that space and how the native community felt about that.

Mike Wilson was a humanist, and he was part of the Tohono O'odham Nation and willing to put the water out along the trail. But some vigilantes would shoot holes in the jugs and tanks to drain the water. It was 2004, fast forward to where we are now, twenty years later, and the level of hysteria at the border is unconscionable. We are talking about people's lives. We are talking about children and women trying to reunite with their families. These are people coming across just for a better education and to work. When I look back at that project, I am sad that all of those images are still relevant.

Demetria: And, of course, the irony is that migrants coming north are actually returning to their homeland, that of the mythical Aztec home of Aztlán.

The idea of Aztlán would become key to Chicano identity in 1968, with a political manifesto, *Espiritual de Aztlán*, which Rodolfo Corky Gonzalez introduced at the National Chicano Youth Liberation Conference in Denver artists enthusiastically embracing its revolutionary demands for social and economic equality. What has the idea of Aztlán meant to you, Delilah and Orlando, in terms of your own identity and art?

Delilah: I understand that this is my home. We've always been in New Mexico. So New Mexico has always been my Aztlán, and it is part of my identity. It also gives a sense of empowerment. It provides an opportunity to reinvent ourselves differently from how the mainstream sees us. This is all a reminder of where we came from. We were returning back to the North because my family came up the Chihuahua trail. Our ancestors were being pushed out into northern New Mexico. And so we walked up that trail and have been in northern New Mexico for hundreds of years, literally hundreds of years. We were separated from Mexico. When the United States came in and the Treaty of Guadalupe Hidalgo was made, we were left behind. We were the ones that the border crossed. And I've always had this kind of sense that we are still the same people. We were split, which is something I also understood in Tohono O'odham. Their tribe was split by the border, leaving some of them in the US and some in Mexico. Orlando, when you told me about this, I felt it was a perfect metaphor for what has happened to Latino communities in the United States. The border was fluid for hundreds of years. People went back and forth. There was communication and culture. Mexican movies would come up. I remember my grandmother would go see Maria Felix. Circuses from Mexico would come to the North. And now, it's just a political talking point that has brought suffrage to so many people and communities.

Orlando: The title, *Sed: Trail of Thirst*, echoes the Trail of Tears and other forced displacements and appropriations of land and Indigenous people. Often, these displacements are presented as if the people are all voluntary migrants. Yes, people are making certain choices that lead them to come through the border, but there are systems in place that create these social structures. There has been dispossession in Mexico, especially after the end of Ejidos and the infiltration of corn production. It is much harder for people to make a living, and Mexicans, especially Indigenous people, were pressured to sell their land. So, of course, they are going to be coming. I really relate to the idea of the decolonial imaginary that Emma Perez talks about. I see Aztlán as part of that idea that we need to remember that these are colonized territories, and there was a time before borders.

(*below*) Delilah Montoya
Road to Aztlán (from the series *Sed: Trail of Thirst*)
2008
Inkjet on Fibre paper with Dibond mount
18⅛ × 89⅞ in.
Collection of the artist

(*opposite page*)
Delilah Montoya
Road to Aztlán (from the series *Sed: Trail of Thirst*)
2008
Inkjet on Fibre paper with Dibond mount
18 × 89¾ in.
Collection of the artist

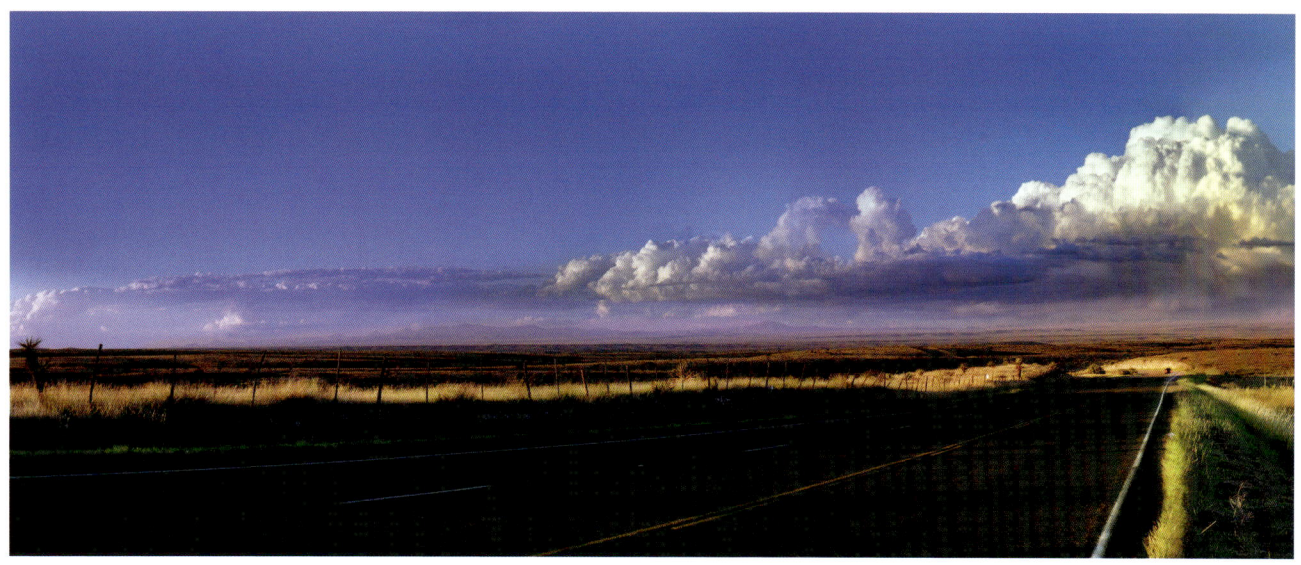

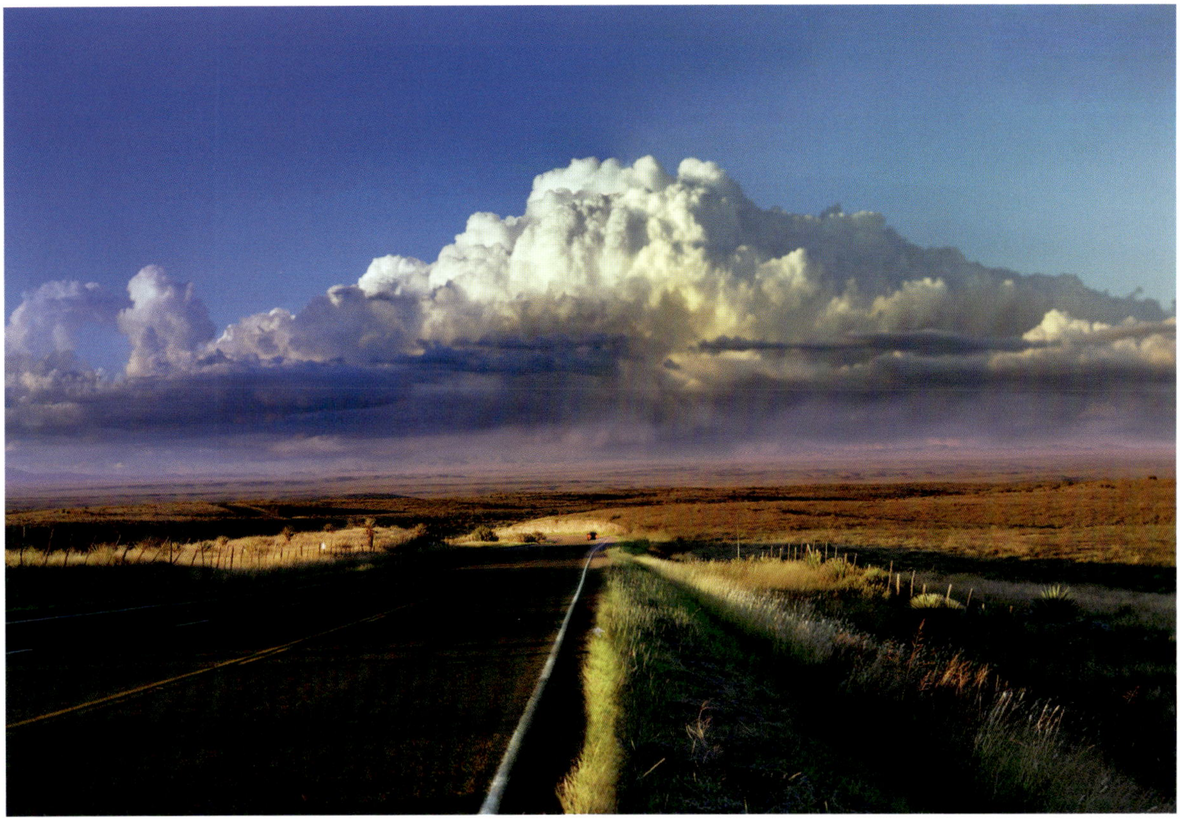

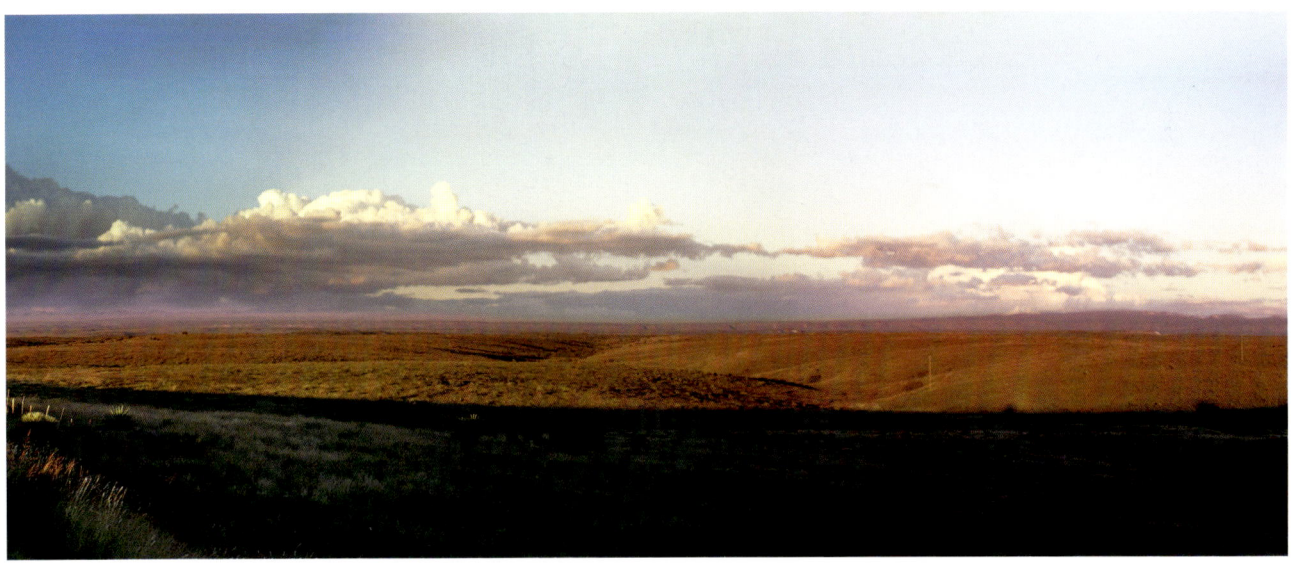

etention Nation is a multimedia art installation and activist project developed by the Sin Huellas Artist Collective. Through a combination of sculpture, photography, video, and text-based materials, the installation critiques the mass incarceration of immigrants in the US detention system. Initially exhibited in 2015 at the Station Museum of Contemporary Art in Houston, Texas, the project has since traveled to multiple venues, including the Museo de las Americas in Denver, the Mulvane Art Museum in Topeka, and the University of Houston. The project has evolved over time, particularly in response to the COVID-19 pandemic, which necessitated a shift to virtual formats while maintaining its core focus on the injustices of immigrant detention.[1]

The installation is designed to immerse viewers in a simulated detention facility. It includes cyanotype body prints of detainees and their families, life-sized plaster body casts wrapped in Mylar blankets, and video monitors embedded in bed frames. Testimonies of former detainees are also a central component of the project. The artists use these elements to evoke the dehumanizing conditions inside immigrant detention centers, which were invisible to the public, and to reveal systems of oppression, surveillance, incarceration, and erasure.

The visual strategy of *Detention Nation* is particularly compelling in its use of absence and materiality. As noted in previous exhibitions, the project "foregrounds the mass immigrant incarceration" while strategically omitting human figures, instead relying on their material traces—body prints, personal letters, and abandoned belongings—to stand in for their presence. This approach aligns with Sin Huellas's broader practice of using art as a means of political intervention.[2]

At its debut in the Station Museum of Contemporary Art in 2015, *Detention Nation* incorporated stark, prison-like bunkbeds fitted with cyanotype sheets bearing the silhouettes of detained individuals. These were accompanied by a prison toilet and a banner smuggled from a detention center with the plea: "President Obama, We Need Freedom." The installation also included a razor-wire fence at the entrance, reinforcing the idea of captivity.[3] Video monitors playing testimonies from detainees named Selene, Izzy, and Francisco were part of the exhibition.

The exhibition was shown at several additional venues including the Museo de las Americas in Denver in 2016, Landmark in Lubbock at Texas

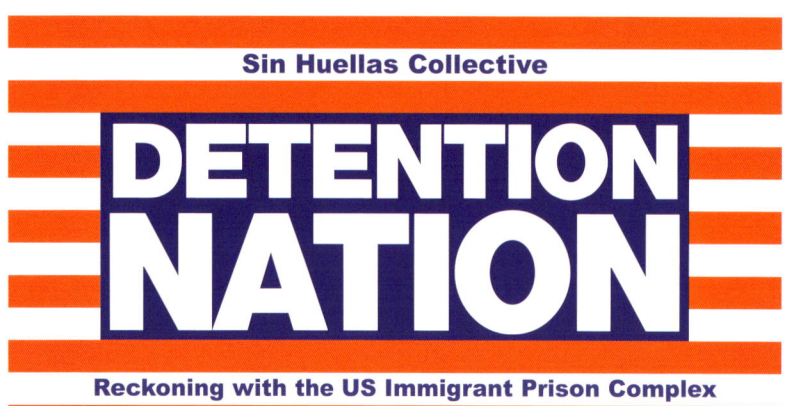

Sin Huellas Collective

DETENTION NATION

Reckoning with the US Immigrant Prison Complex

Sin Huellas Artist Collective
Detention Nation
2015–2021
Multimedia installation

Technical University in 2018, and Elgin Street Studios at the University of Houston in 2021.

By 2020, *Detention Nation* had evolved to address emerging concerns, such as the detention of minors and the rise of virtual court hearings. A funding campaign secured $30,000 to expand the project, allowing for new installations and collaborations, including an exhibition at the Mashburn Gallery at the University of Houston. However, the COVID-19 pandemic forced a dramatic shift. The physical exhibition was postponed, and a virtual platform, DetentionNation.com, was developed to provide an online experience replicating the themes of the installation.[4] This digital adaptation was launched alongside *Hostile Terrain 94*, a participatory art project visualizing migrant deaths in the Arizona desert. Together, these two projects presented a powerful critique of US immigration enforcement at the Blaffer Art Museum in 2021.[5]

Several key visual elements define *Detention Nation*:

> **Cyanotype Body Prints**: These blue-tinted images of detainees and their families resemble X-rays or surveillance images, reinforcing the themes of state control and the erasure of migrant identities.

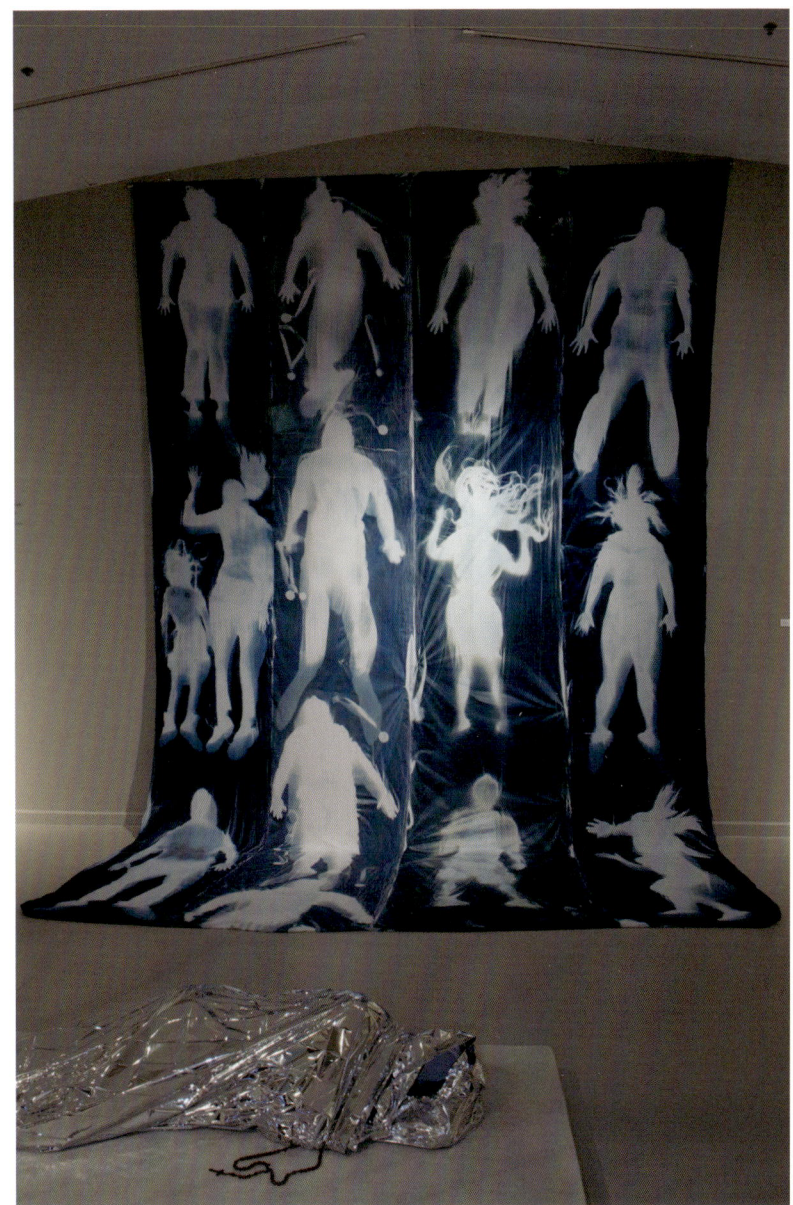

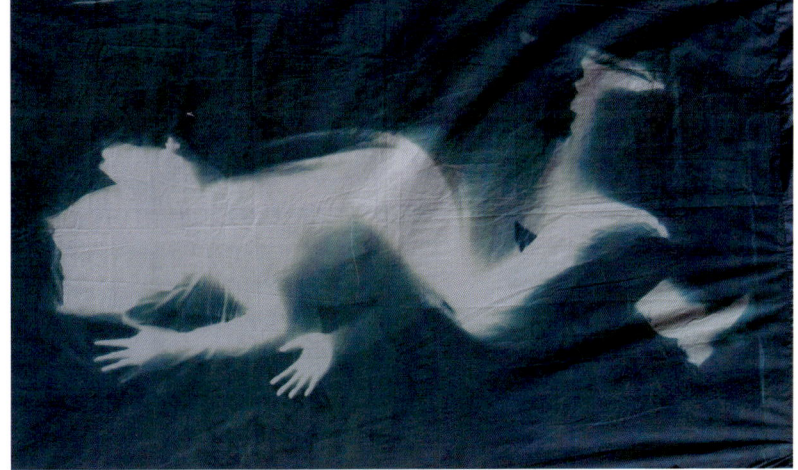

(*top*) Sin Huellas Artist Collective
The Rapture, Station Museum
Houston, TX
2015
Cyanotype on cotton gauze
168 × 144 in.
Collection of the artist

(*bottom*) Sin Huellas Artist
Collective
Elizabeth's Dream
2015
Cyanotype, body print
42 × 84 in.
Collection of Delilah Montoya

Plaster Body Casts Wrapped in Mylar Blankets: These ghostly figures evoke the vulnerability of detainees and reference the infamous *hieleras* (iceboxes), the freezing holding cells used by ICE to detain migrants.

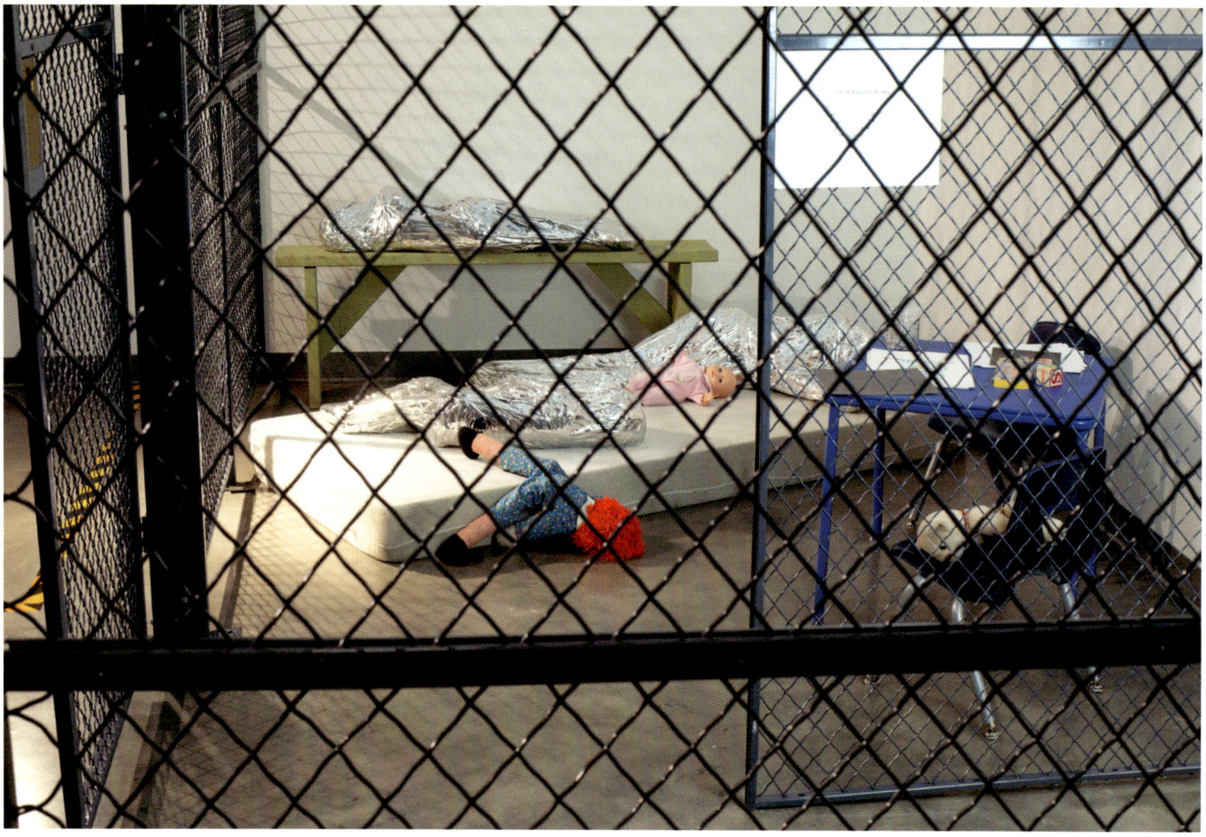

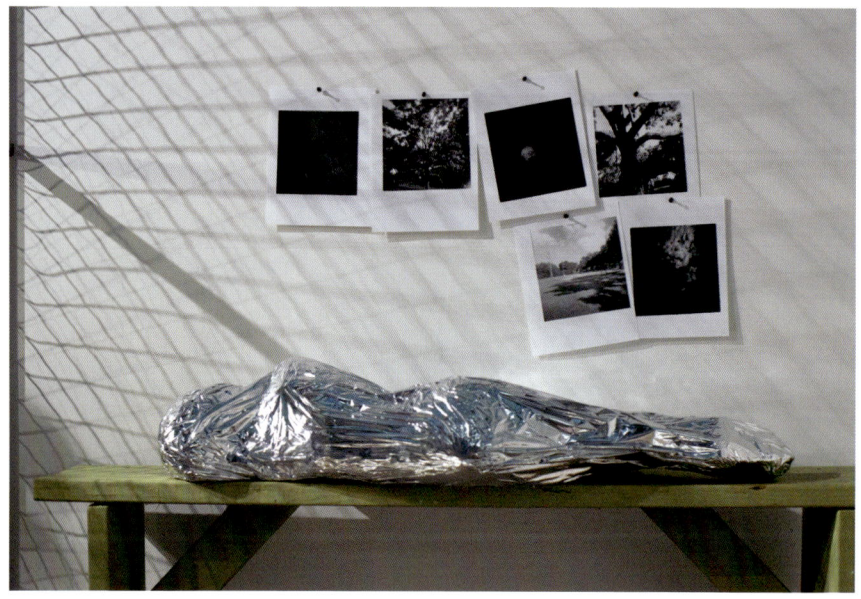

(*top*) Sin Huellas Artist Collective
Youth "Camp"—Detention Nation installation, Elgin Street Studio, University of Houston campus
2021

(*bottom*) Sin Huellas Artist Collective
Youth "Camp"—Detention Nation installation, Elgin Street Studio, University of Houston campus
2021

Through this communication, we, the detained at the Joe Corley Detention Center in Conroe TX, starting Monday March 17 2014, <u>declare a hunger strike</u> indefinitely as a way to pressure and protest the government of the USA and the Department of ICE for the following:

1. That deportations and the resulting separation of families cease immediately
2. That detainees be given a more just and fair treatment
3. That detainees be provided true and transparent information on each of the cases given that:
    a. Many detainees are forced to sign their deportations under pressure and lies
    b. Many detainees have been without resolution of their cases for more than a year
4, That the number of detainees per cell be reduced given that it is currently an unhealthy situation
5. That detainees should not be judged twice for things that happened before and were resolved in different state and county courts given that:
    a. Many of the cases already received final judgment and were closed several years ago, in some cases over 15–20 years ago.
    b. Many of the detainees are coming from local, state, and federal jails where they have completed their sentences and are handed over to immigration to be processed.
6. That local and state police stop cooperating with the immigration department

Attached are the signatures of those in the detention center.
All signatures were collected voluntarily and under no pressure.

5/30/14   Un recuerdo que nuca boy a holbidar
            Por el resto de mi Vida

Un día melebante y se corio en toda la carcel que
el dia 17 marzo-14 seiba a ser una guelga de ambre
y nos pusimos todos de acuerdo todos los de mi Bonke
estabamos apollando a los 3 dias llego migracion y nos
dijo los que no quieran comer para la derecha y los que
quieran comer pala isquierda todos seisieron para la
isquierda y no quisieron apollar pienso que tubieron miedo O
ambre pues mesacaron y mellebaron al mentado pozo
los primeros dias en el pozo fueron muy tristes te acuerdas
de toda tu vida melapasaba resando y tomando Agua y
pensando en mí que iva a pasar conmigo si iva a salir
con Vida de ese lugar y les guro que mepuse a llorar
a los 5 dias en pese a soñar muchas cosas que no
quisiera recordar Conosi a un hombre que estaba en la
misma situacion que yo inos gritabamos de pozo a pozo
yo no lo conocia y en peso una combercasion es muy triste
estar en ese lugar el me platicaba de su vida y de su Fam.
y yo de mis hijos yo lla estaba mal y le dije a Dios que
por que seavia Olbidado de mi llorando de la tristesa
y de la desesperasion a nadie le desco lo que yo pase
estube a punto de morir y por fin sali y me pararon en
la puerta del pozo muy debil y me esposaron y les dige que
por Fabor no me esposaran pues yo estaba debil y no me esposaron
Caminando para la enfermeria estube un rato y luego me
sacaron y metope a uno que tambie estaba debil y medijo
Comote llamas y ledije ███████ y me contesto yo soy
████████ mi compañero que no conocia el era con el
que platicabamos en el pozo mediomucho Justo Verlo vivo
esto es un poco de lo que yo Vivi en este lugar ⑦ dias
                              en el pozo ←

5/30/14

One memory I will never forget for the rest of my life.

One day I got up and the whole jail talked that on the 17 of March . . . there was going to be a hunger strike. We were all in agreement in my bunk. We were supporting. The third day, immigration came and told us that whoever didn't want to eat to the right and those who did want to eat to the left. Everyone moved to the left and didn't want to support. I think they were scared or were hungry. Well they took me to the so-called hole [el "pozo"]. The first few days in the pozo were very sad, you remember your whole life and I spent my time praying and drinking water and thinking about what was going to happen to me, if I was going to get out alive. I swear I started to cry. On the fifth day, I started to dream lots of things I would not like to remember. I met a man who was there in the same situation as me and we would yell from pozo to pozo . . . He talked to me about his life and his family and I about my kids. I was already feeling bad and I asked God why he had forgotten about me . . . I do not wish what I went through to anyone, I was about to die when I finally got out. They picked me up at the door of the pozo. I was very weak and they handcuffed me. I told them not to handcuff me please because I was so weak and they didn't handcuff me when walking to the infirmary. I was there for a while and then they took me out and I met someone who was also weak. They asked me my name and I said [redacted] and they answered I am [redacted] my companion that I didn't know, he was the one I had talked to while we were in the pozo. I was very glad to see him alive . . .

A man that works in this place told me to eat and I said no. He made fun of me and asked me if I wanted a beer and kept making fun of me since I am in here for drunk driving. Well this is my story of the 4 days I spent in the pozo and 3 in my bunk without eating.

Detention Nation serves not only as an art installation but also as a platform for activism. The Sin Huellas collective, composed of artists, activists, and individuals directly affected by immigration policies, emphasizes the importance of community engagement. The project has been instrumental in raising awareness and even contributed to the release of at least one detained individual, David, who was featured in the exhibition.

The project also underscores the privatized nature of immigrant detention, revealing how corporations like GEO Group profit from the incarceration of undocumented individuals. By presenting detention centers as spaces of profit rather than justice, *Detention Nation* challenges public complacency and calls for policy changes.

Through its powerful visual language and immersive installations, *Detention Nation* forces audiences to confront the grim realities of immigrant detention in the United States. Whether experienced in a physical gallery or through a virtual platform, the project remains a vital disruption and intervention that challenges state violence and amplifies the voices of those most affected. Its continued evolution ensures that the pressing issues of immigration incarceration remain in the public consciousness, driving discourse and activism in pursuit of justice, which in 2025 has become even more necessary**.**

In Conversation with Delilah Montoya, Orlando Lara, and Demetria Martinez: *Detention Nation*

Demetria: Migrants who do survive the crossing all too often end up in hellish detention centers, which have become a big business, particularly under the Trump administration. Individuals in these places become mere numbers, faceless and rendered virtually powerless to improve their conditions. Orlando and Delilah, the two of you collaborated on a video sound and sculpture installation called *Detention Nation*. It is nothing if not an invitation to act. Artist and activist roles merge.

Delilah: *Detention Nation* was a large project with many contributors. Orlando and I coordinated the project. We wanted to think about new ways of presenting the information because it was evolving. James "Jim" Harithas, (the Houston-based artist, curator, patron, and museum director) asked us to be part of *Degrees of Separation*, an exhibition at the Station Museum in Houston. I thought that he was just going to give us a small space, but it ended up being the whole back room. We had four

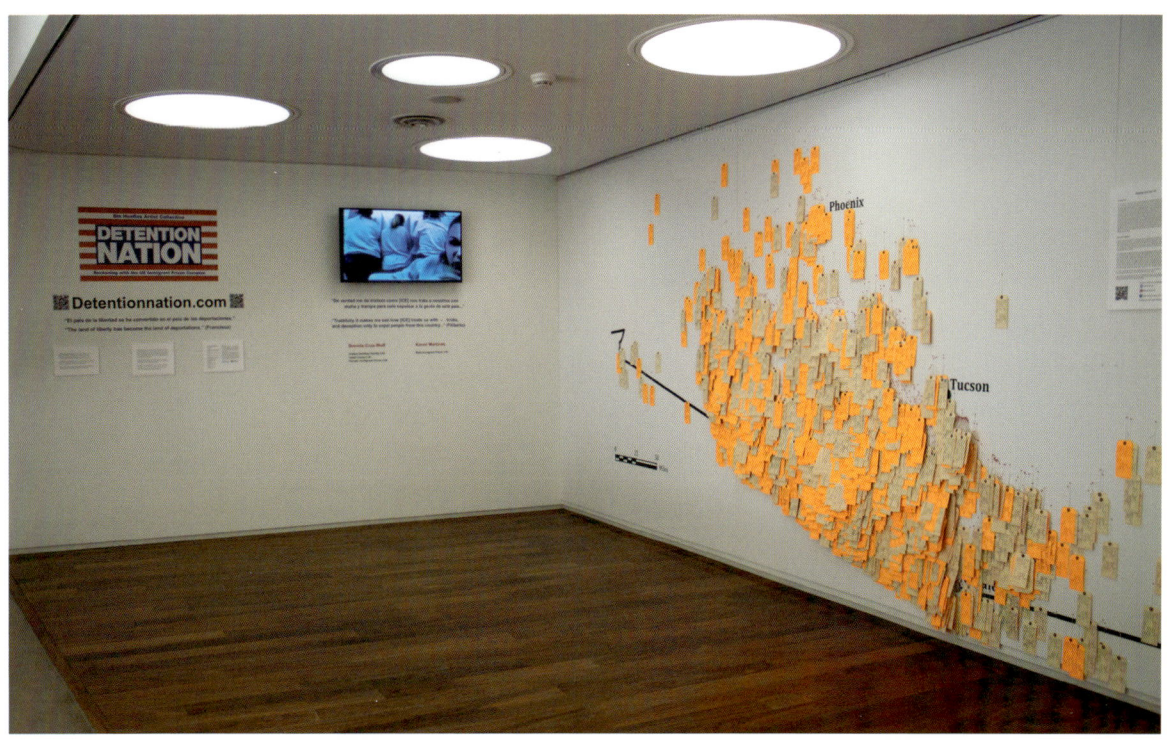

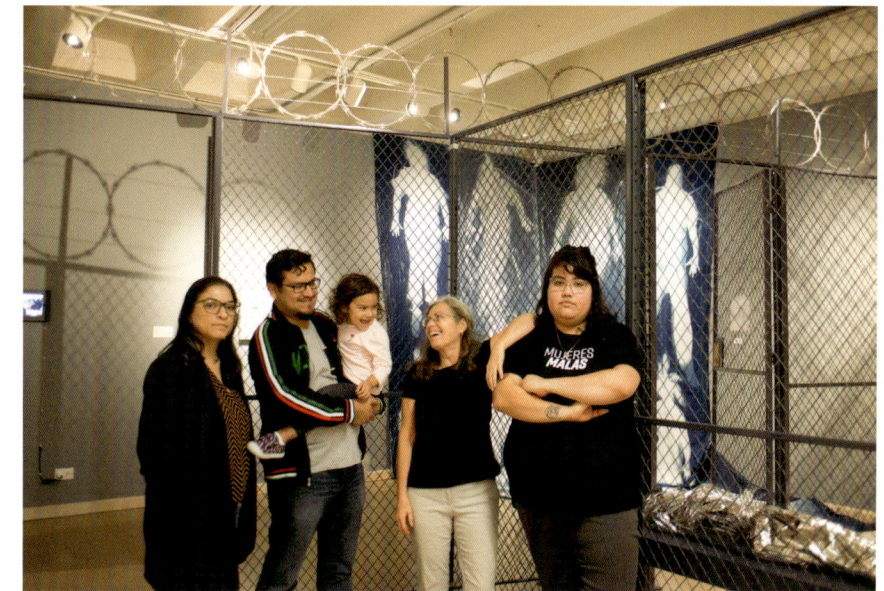

(*top*) Sin Huellas Artist Collective
Detention Nation WEB premier, with Hostile Terrain 94, University of Houston School of Art Blaffer Museum 2021
Toe tags mural, vinyl, and monitor

(*bottom*) *Detention Nation*: Sin Huellas Collective Installation Exhibition, TTU School of Art Landmark Gallery, 2018
left to right: Deyadira Arellano, Orlando Lara, Katalina Lara, Delilah Montoya, and Jessica Carolina González

months to pull the installation together. Orlando was doing activist work with immigration centers. We invited artists and activists to collaborate, and we met regularly to discuss how to present this material. For Orlando, it was important to put the letters sent by detainees up on the wall. The letters proved to be an important element.

It was 2015, and detention centers were really starting to gear up. They weren't allowing people inside. Nobody knew what it looked like inside, and the only descriptions we would get were from people that came out of them. That is when I realized that those letters were significant because of the descriptions written in those letters. The conditions were not good. We decided to recreate the inside of a detention center as an installation that included razor wire gated, mats on the floor, Mylar covered bodies, and a toilet sitting on the floor. Jim provided funding for the project, so all we had to do was put it all together. We decided to make cyanotype body prints of detainees and their families as a large tapestry entitled *Rapture*. It is a train of people who are floating from the floor to the ceiling. It dominated the installation. On one hand, it felt like surveillance; on the other hand, it felt like an abduction. It also echoed imprints of bodies or chalk lines. Brenda Cruz did a great job with the videos. She did excellent research and included video clips that expressed the narrative of how people were captured and detained. She made a soundscape that echoed throughout the room. It was impressive.

Orlando: *Detention Nation* had incredible source material and really came out of activism and organizing. It came out of working on anti-deportation campaigns. That is really how we had access to these people who were detained. Some of them who fought their deportation were able to be released. Some were still fighting their deportation. Daniel, for example, was actively fighting his deportation, and so whenever the media covered us, we would bring him on. I think it actually helped. I remember the Station Museum wrote a letter for him asking ICE not to deport him. The whole project came out of an organizing activist spirit. The most powerful thing was these letters that people wrote while they were inside. Sending a letter out was their only way to connect with the outside world other than super expensive phone calls. It is a beautiful project, and I remember in 2015, during the Obama administration, we were having a meeting, and the announcement came out that he was issuing deferred action for undocumented adults. It was a win after so much time spent trying to get Obama to help adults. It stopped and never went into effect. So much has happened since then, and the immigrant rights movement has shifted from a call for immigration reform to a call for the abolition of detention centers. We created a virtual space that brought in that voice. It's not just about raising visibility anymore. We had to be more explicit in writing about what was going on and how deep the changes needed to be.

Delilah: We showed the installation in Denver, Kansas, Lubbock, the Station Museum, and the University of Houston Campus. There were five iterations. It was on view almost every year from 2015 to 2020. There were always panel discussions connected with the exhibition. Many local people working along the same lines would show up. So it was very much activist art. More and more artists are taking up these issues. More voices were chiming in. We went virtual with Detention Nation during the pandemic. We were planning a final installation on the UH campus. I found some grant money because we had a good track record. It was quite a bit of money to put into the installation, and then everything shut down, and we lost our venue. Fortunately, we didn't lose the funding, but we had to think of something else. We all got together on Zoom and decided to take it to the web. That's the only way that we're going to be able to put out the message and give it longevity. DetentionNation.com is still up, and it's still running. We have not updated it since 2021. The weird thing is that it doesn't need updating.

Orlando: It's coming back. It's getting worse, but I think one through line of both projects is that we're never trying just to show people as victims or as powerless or as helpless. Even in detention, immigrants themselves are doing so much. Part of what the letters do is tell the story of a hunger strike that happened up in Conroe and all these acts of resistance that migrants were engaging in inside and outside of detention centers. And I hope, you know, I expect that we're going to see a lot of that in the coming years, too.

Demetria: That's a really critical point because we forget the people on the inside. We're very much in solidarity with people on the outside who are trying to change conditions and to educate people.

Delilah: It's still going on. It hasn't stopped. There have been no humanitarian improvements.

Orlando: And the profit motive I think was where. We tried to be very explicit about just the profit side of all this and how profitable it is for these companies. But even on the side of just migrant resistance, having seen the alternative, I saw recently a statistic that the majority of crossings are going through checkpoints where people are asking for political asylum and it feels to me like that's been an important shift where migrants themselves are no longer taking the risk, risking their lives to go through these dangerous crossings. More and more are presenting themselves at the border and asking for political asylum, doing it "the right way" and getting "in line." But now, you know, these white supremacists don't like "the line." Now, all of a sudden, they say, "No, that's not the line." That's not "the right way," either, but to me that's a major shift, a major act of resistance that people are saying, "I'm not going to risk my life. I'm going to go through, use your political asylum system, and put my life in your hands." Now, there are still a lot of people going through the river in South Texas. And the governor has put up those buoys. But it seems like that shift really drove people crazy in the US. They're kind of like, "Oh, shoot! We have a political asylum system. And now we have to follow it." You know, it's just created such madness, such madness when people do it "the right way."

Delilah: If we're talking about the future where Trump deports millions of people, they will pass through detention centers that are already crowded. So that means more detention centers will be built. The wall is already built. It crawls all the way from El Paso to San Diego. I think there's only one very small section in New Mexico that remains open. Hmm. Probably for political reasons, like animals need to migrate. When I was in Douglas, New Mexico, I went down there with Sherry Crider to photograph Ocotillos. I experienced the wall. It's huge, massive, and all made out of hard steel. So what's left to build? Detention centers. And so what happens when they deport millions of people? What will they do with all those detention centers when everyone has been pushed out? None of it makes sense. Will they become incarceration camps, more prisons? This country will be known for a massive prison industry funded by tax dollars. That's the part that boggles my mind. Who is next?

The solution to immigration is very simple and not expensive. It's not a difficult solution. You let Congress rewrite immigration policies. Rewrite the immigration policies so that people who want to enter into our system can in a smooth, effective way so there is not a twenty-year waiting period and the immigrant spends thousands and thousands of dollars to stay in the country legally. Instead of putting all tax money into detention centers, use it for our immigration and court system. There wasn't any problem when immigrants went through Ellis Island. They were processing thousands of immigrants at a time, giving them identification cards and a pathway to citizenship. They didn't even have computers or big data at that time; everybody's papers were stamped and ledgered in. We know that this country can do that again. We're talking about very few people in relation to the size of the United States population. It's not that many people, and this country would easily be able to bring them in. Historically, immigrants have always contributed to the greatness of our country.

Demetria: Delilah, when I think about *Sed* as well as *Detention Nation*. I see someone who's really committed to bearing witness to injustice. Where do you find hope as an artist and Chicana activist, *mujer*?

Delilah: Right now. It's a tough one. Where is the hope? The truth matters as we move forward. We've always stepped forward, even though sometimes those steps are just small baby steps. We keep moving forward. If we regress, it is more of a sidestep; then we move forward again. I believe in the younger generation. I have seen their artwork and activism. They are going to do amazing things, and I know they will. I might not see it in my lifetime, but I know it's going to happen because of their desire and hope. What will happen in terms of Latinx, as a colonized body, we'll keep going because this is our home we have always been here. This is who we are. We didn't vanish and die but joined together. We find ways to change the narrative. That's really the most crucial thing in terms of the Chicanx movement, and in terms of our activism, it is our ability to change the narrative. Once the narrative changes, then the reckoning comes.

Orlando: To me, too. It's a tough question. For me, as a Latino male, it is hard to see the role that Latino men are playing right now, allying with white supremacist ideas and fascism. All with the idea that they're somehow going to profit from it. It's very angering. The hope to me lies in a few places, one definitely in the people, in the organizing. That, I know is gonna come. And when there's that organizing, there's going to be creative production out of that organizing. It will need to be part of it. Because so much of what's happening is these false narratives that people are getting attached to and believing. So that to me tells me there's a very important role for artists and truth-tellers still as hard as the work is, but the other part, too, is just how overt the oligarchy is becoming, like they're exposing themselves. You know, with "President Musk." Now, being so right in front and center. It used to be that they kind of funded politicians from behind the scenes. Now, the donors are becoming the politicians, and I think that they have a lot of power in doing that. But they also have a huge risk that it's going to be harder for them to continue to sell this narrative to working class people that they have their interests in mind. And so we have to do a lot of work and undoing that false narrative that so many of our people are buying into, but I think it can be done, and I have a lot of hope in the resistance that is coming.

**Delilah Montoya interviewed by Demetria Martinez
on being an artist**

Demetria: What would you say are key factors that have defined your trajectory as an artist?

Delilah: I'm fortunate to have been able to concentrate on being an artist for the duration of my life. But that was something I set out to do. It is a simple thing to say, "I want to be an artist," but it is a complicated process. How do I do that? How will I get all the materials? How will I feed my daughter and myself? How will I learn new things and maintain the energy to keep going? What will I be involved with? All of these things get complicated. I think the most important thing that I did was find something to believe in. Something that I knew I could make a statement with and that I felt deeply about. Those were the ideas that came out of the Chicanx community.

Early on, when I was sixteen or so, I worked at El Charros Restaurant as a waitress. I was getting introduced more and more to the Chicanos that lived in Omaha, Nebraska. Certain families came into Omaha early, establishing residency and businesses, creating their own community. I got to know who they were. One family, the Montelongos, were involved with the Chicano movement. They were one of the founders of the Chicano Awareness Center. This center really interested me. Have you ever heard about the Sociedades Mutualistas? Well, there was a group in Omaha, and they had a building. The Chicano movement came to Omaha; they donated the building to the Chicanos. And I remember when I was in Houston. I was in the second ward, an old Latinx section of town, where the refurbished Leo Tanguma mural was located. A powerful mural that he did back in the 70s, and for all those decades, nobody tagged it because the community loved and respected the mural. And I was looking at admiring the work as I turned around there. Across the street was an old building that had Sociedades Mutualistas tiled across the front.

The Sociedades Mutualistas was something that was going on in the United States during the 20s through the 40s. It's the Latinx presence within the United States for hundreds of years, literally hundreds of years. You know, we're not immigrants. As I was involved with the Chicano Awareness Center, I was also enrolled in a photo program at Metro Technical College. Eventually, I ended up at the west side of Denver, where

Conclusion

there was a flurrying of murals and Chicanx activity with the brown beret and Corky Gonzalez. I was learning all about ideas; it was like a creative explosion in my mind. But I also knew that I wanted to learn more about photography. And I wanted to learn more about art too.

I remember just leaving Omaha and putting it in my rearview mirror. With my daughter in the back seat and a few things in the car, we just took off for Denver. My sister Paige was in Denver, so I moved in with her. My professors in Omaha told me they were hiring special effects technicians at Photosynthesis because I used a Forox duplicator while working on the Mexican Nebraskan slide show. And I remember showing up there, and they had me take a test. I aced it because I had already put together a whole slideshow with all special effects and everything so you know, they hired me on the spot.

I stayed there for almost a year, but it was really factory work, and I wanted more than that. I wanted to make art. And about that time, I photographed that whole community on the west side. The other day, I was kind of looking back at some of those images, and it was like, this was at a time when the Vietnamese refugees came to the United States. So some of my pictures have Vietnamese refugees with suitcases just kind of looking around. Some of the other pictures were of the family that moved right next door to us. The buildings are only like three feet away, so I have pictures of these little girls playing with these little pieces of paper origami.

I decided that I really wanted to go to the University of New Mexico. My family is from northern New Mexico. Also, I was told about a really great photo department at UNM. With big names, because I remember at the Technical College, they told me about people like Beaumont Newhall and Van Deren Coke were there. Again, I just threw everything in the car. Come on, Luci. Let's go. Can you imagine just . . . just blindly showing up and I had no idea, like you have to take things like SAT tests. I remember I went to enroll and was told you haven't taken an SAT test. Okay. Here, fill out these forms, and I did. I took the SAT test, never studied for it . . . I did okay. I was not a genius. I remember my scores in English and math were really low. But for some reason, I had high scores in the sciences. In the sciences, my scores were just right up there. And it's because I've been doing a lot with chemistry. You know, working with lenses and all those materials was intuitive for me. They took me because of those high science scores.

My family is here in Albuquerque; I have cousins, aunties, a daughter, grandchildren, and of course, my mother. I really began to consider the life of my grandfather who was a *penitente*, there were a lot of stories about him. My mother would tell us about her life in Las Vegas, New Mexico. I was really interested in that history and wanted to follow it with my art making. And so . . . there for a bit of time I photographed him.

Eventually I met artists in Albuquerque like Cecilio García-Camarillo as well as Francisco Lefebre who was married to Bernadette. We were all of like minds and of the same interest. I remember meeting Miguel Gandert and admired his work, it is very strong. So I guess what I'm saying is I found a real community of Chicanx artists. It was the same thing in Denver. Stevon Lucero introduced me to Chispa Productions owned by Maruca and Danny Salazar they took me in. Of course Emmanuel Martinez was producing murals and was very active and Adrianna Abarca has always been an effective patron and curator for the community.

I always relied on university labs as my studio, I don't think that I would have been able to continue making art without these connections. My inspiration came from Chicanx communities; this was where my creative juices flowed. However, getting to the equipment that I needed to make the work was also very important. So it was really the combination of the two communities. I kept going to school for the studio space and equipment.

I had a strong photo background prior to enrolling at UNM; I did a lot of drawing. I loved watercolor and mixing color. I first learned to screen print; it was a hands-on process where you could manipulate the photograph. So a lot of my early work even though it might look as though it's computer generated, it was all done by hand. I was making masks mixing my own colors and taking images to many different paper surfaces.

My day job was as a medical photographer for the UNM med school. I remember there was this work study position. My mom was going to UNM too; we were going both at the same time. She saw in the Lobo newspaper that OMI was looking for a photographer that was work study qualified. She thought it was an interesting job and encouraged me to apply. It paid way more than any other work study position listed; it was $5 an hour, and I could use that money. They hired me, that was when Joel Peter Witken was finishing his master's at UNM. I told him about being hired at OMI; he was excited for me. It was a tough job, but it was what got me into the medical world. Eventually, I was hired as a full-time medical photographer. I called that first job my still life photography and after that I just worked with living people.

Demetria: Could you say more about your art in relation to the Chicano movement? Who are some of the people and ideas that contributed to your self-understanding as a Chicana artist?

Delilah: It had a lot to do with the people I was encountering while residing in various locations. I saw other Chicanx's work, and it inspired me to continue my own work. Paul Denetclaw shipped my art to the first exhibition that included my work; I just did not know how to do that. He has always been a great ally. Wonderful people provided mentorship.

In Omaha, the Chicano Awareness Center is where I decided that I was going to be a photographer. I had a daughter, and I needed a job. I owned this little Pentex camera. I remember buying it. My palms were sweaty. I had $300 to my name, and that camera cost $150. It was half of everything I owned. I knew I had to make a living with it. I found out later that a Pentex camera was not really a high-end professional camera, but I had to make that single fixed lens camera work. I decided that I wanted to create a slideshow on the Mexican Nebraskan. The director there at the Chicano Awareness Center helped me write a grant. So that was my first photo job. I needed a script written for the project. My sister Paige started it, but then didn't complete it, and so I had a half-written script. I met Alurista at the Chicano Awareness Center, and he offered to help. It was the early Chicano movement and people were ready to help make things happen.

In Denver, I met people like Maruca Salazar, who was really helpful as a curator. She started bringing me into the Museo de las Americas. Eventually I met people like Holly Barnett Sanchez, who introduced me to the Chicano movement that was happening in Los Angeles. That is how I got into Self Help Graphics. I met artists like Laura Aguilar, Barbara Carrasco, Judy Baca, and Yolanda Lopez here in New Mexico. Cecilio García-Camarillo, and he was very helpful in many of the projects that I took on. As a poet and a writer, he introduced me to Chicano philosophies that influenced my work. He helped me write my thesis on the Sagrada Corazon, and also with Codex Delilah. We would work collaboratively. I had the idea and would formulate the stories. Everywhere I've gone or moved to, I have been able to connect with the communities that are there, and they all contributed to my way of seeing the world. Like in Massachusetts on the East Coast, Ondine Chavoya, Frank Gimpaya, Tomás Ybarra-Frausto, and Sandra Matthews helped provide visibility. In Houston, Surpik Angelini and Elia Arce were instrumental to my practice. Luis Jimenez and Adrianna Abarca helped me understand the art market, and Orlando Lara opened my eyes to what was happening in terms of immigration. For me, the borderlands in New Mexico and Texas seemed fluid with people crossing back and forth from Mexico. But in the eighties the border was becoming militarized. So these are some of the people who were helping me understand what it was to be a Chicana artist and why it was important to speak about these things and to change the narrative. Yolanda Lopez helped me understand the importance of mentorship so some of the artists whom I mentored are important to the making of the work such as artists Michael Esfera and Tina Hernandez. They all helped keep the momentum going.

Demetria: So that art becomes also a form of activism.

Delilah: Exactly.

Notes

Introduction

1. Rodolfo Acuña, *Occupied America: A History of Chicanos* (HarperCollins, 1972), 290.

2. Carlos Muñoz Jr., *Youth, Identity, Power: The Chicano Movement* (Verso, 1989, 2007), 76–84.

3. Francisco A. Rosales, *Chicano! The History of the Mexican American Civil Rights Movement* (Arte Público Press, 1996), 127–135.

4. Juan Gómez-Quiñones, *Chicano Politics: Reality and Promise, 1940–1990* (University of New Mexico Press, 1990).

5. Dolores Delgado Bernal, "Grassroots Leadership and the Chicano Movement: The East Los Angeles School Blowouts," *Frontiers: A Journal of Women Studies* 19, no. 2 (1998): 113–131.

6. Chicano Youth Liberation Conference, *Plan de Aztlán*, 1969.

7. Laura E. Gomez, *Manifest Destinies, Second Edition: The Making of the Mexican American Race* (New York University Press, 2018), xxi.

8. Delilah Montoya, "Malcriada Aesthetics/Bad Girl Realities," *Chicana/Latina Studies: The Journal of Mujeres Activas en Letras y Cambio Social* 15, no. 2 (2016): 11.

Chapter One

1. Tatiana Reinoza and Karen M. Davalos, eds., *Self Help Graphics at Fifty: A Cornerstone of Latinx Art and Collaborative Artmaking* (University of California Press, 2023), 10, 15.

2. Delilah Montoya, *Printmaking and Photography*, unpublished essay provided by the artist, 2025, 1.

3. Emily Wasserman, "Photography as Printmaking: Museum of Modern Art," *Artforum* 6, no. 10 (1968): 72.

4. "Process Work: Intersections of Photography and Print ca. 1825 to Today," RISD Museum, accessed December 2024, https://risdmuseum.org/exhibitions-events/events/process-work.

5. Jennifer L. Roberts, *Contact: Art and the Pull of Print* (Princeton University Press, 2024), 13.

6.   Roberts, *Contact*, 13.

7.   Montoya, *Printmaking and Photography*, 2.

8.   Montoya, *Printmaking and Photography*, 2.

9.   Delilah Montoya, "Artist Statement," accessed December 2024, https://www.delilahmontoya.com/Bio.html.

Chapter Two

1.   Ann Marie Leimer, "Crossing the Border with 'La Adelita': Lucha-Adelucha as 'Nepantlera' in Delilah Montoya's 'Codex Delilah.'" *Chicana/Latina Studies* 5, no. 2 (2006): 12, http://www.jstor.org/stable/23014481.

2.   Delilah Montoya, *Proposal for Codex Delilah: 6 Deer Journey from Mexicatl to Chicana* (unpublished essay, MFA proposal at the University of New Mexico), 6.

3.   Montoya, *Proposal for Codex Delilah*, 1–3.

4.   Delilah Montoya, *Bookmaking an Artist's Book: Crickets in My Mind, Codex Delilah, and Shooting the Tourist* (2025) (unpublished essay, MFA proposal at the University of New Mexico), 1–2.

5.   Montoya, *Proposal for Codex Delilah*, 18.

6.   This exhibition was organized by the Denver Art Museum.

Chapter Three

1.   Stephanie Lewthwaite, "Recovering Mestiza Genealogies in Contemporary New Mexican Art: Delilah Montoya's El Sagrado Corazón (1993)," *Frontiers* 37, no. 1 (2016): 118.

2.   Lewthwaite, "Recovering Mestiza Genealogies in Contemporary New Mexican Art," 129.

Chapter Five

1.   Delilah Montoya, *Bookmaking an Artist's Book: Crickets in My Mind, Codex Delilah, and Shooting the Tourist* (unpublished essay provided by the artist, 2025).

2.   Cecilio García-Camarillo and Delilah Montoya, *Crickets in My Mind* (Mano Isquierda flyer, 1992), 1.

3.   Cecilio García-Camarillo and Delilah Montoya, *Crickets in My Mind* (artist book in the Center for Southwest collection at the University of New Mexico, 1992).

4.   Montoya, *Bookmaking an Artist's Book*, 1.

5.   Montoya, *Bookmaking an Artist's Book*, 2.

6.   Chon Noriega, *From the West: Chicano Narrative Photography* (Mexican Museum, 1995), 9.

7.   Jennifer A. González, "Negotiated Frontiers: Contemporary Chicano Photography," in *From the West: Chicano Narrative Photography* (Mexican Museum, San Francisco, 1995) 19.

Chapter Six

1.   Delilah Montoya, *Digitizing the Photograph—Moving the Photographic Analog through Digital Space, 1999–2006* (unpublished essay provided by the artist, 2025).

Chapter Seven

1.   Delilah Montoya, *Digitizing the Photograph—Moving the Photographic Analog through Digital Space, 1999–2006* (unpublished essay provided by the artist, 2025), 1.

Chapter Eight

1.   Rudy Arispe, "The Beauty Behind the Gloves," *Conexion* (December 14, 2006).
2.   Arispe, "The Beauty Behind the Gloves."
3.   Delilah Montoya, "The New Warriors," in *Women Boxers: The New Warriors* (Arte Público Press, 2006), 19.
4.   María Teresa Márquez, "No Longer Counted Out: Fighting Isn't What It Used to Be," in *Women Boxers: The New Warriors* (Arte Público Press, 2006), 9.
5.   Montoya, "The New Warriors," 21.
6.   Márquez, "No Longer Counted Out," 9.
7.   Montoya, "The New Warriors," 19.

Chapter Nine

1.   Orlando Lara, "The Trail of Thirst," Fotofest, 2004.
2.   Elizabeth Frasco, *Crisis of Image, Crisis of Self: Delilah Montoya and the Theater of the American Borderlands* (Universidad de Alcalá, 2024), 1–3.
3.   Delilah Montoya, *Digitizing the Photograph—Moving the Photographic Analog through Digital Space, 1999–2006* (unpublished essay provided by the artist, 2025), 2.
4.   Lara, "The Trail of Thirst."
5.   Ann Marie Leimer, "Chicana Photography: The Power of Place," *National Association for Chicana and Chicano Studies Conference Proceedings* (2008) 3.
6.   Gloria Anzaldúa, "Border Arte: Nepantla, el Lugarde la Frontera: 1993," in *Chicano and Chicana Art: A Critical Anthology*, edited by Jennifer A. González, Ondine Chavoya, Chon Noriega, and Terezita Romo (Duke University Press, 2019), 341.

Chapter Ten

1.   "Detention Nation 2020 Update," Sin Huellas Artist Collective (unpublished document, 2020).
2.   "Sin Huellas," Station Museum, accessed November 2024, https://www.stationmuseum.com/past-exhibitions/degrees-of-separation/sin-huellas/.
3.   "Sin Huellas."

4.   "Updates to Detention Nation Proposal," Sin Huellas Artist Collective (unpublished document, 2021).

5.   Sin Huellas Art Collective and Department of Comparative Cultural Studies, University of Houston, "Detention Nation alongside Hostile Terrain 94 Installation with Two Online Panels: Press Release," March 3, 2021.

References

All interviews and conversations with Delilah Montoya, Demetria Martinez, and other collaborators were conducted in December 2024 and January 2025 and edited by Josie Lopez and Delilah Montoya.

Acuña, Rodolfo. 1972. *Occupied America: A History of Chicanos*. HarperCollins.

Anzaldúa, Gloria. 2019. "Border Arte: Nepantla, el Lugarde la Frontera: 1993." In *Chicano and Chicana Art: A Critical Anthology*, edited by Jennifer A. González, C. O. Chavoya, Chon Noriega, and Terezita Romo. Duke University Press.

Arispe, Rudy. 2006. "The Beauty Behind the Gloves." *Conexion* (December 14, 2006).

Carrera, Magali M. 2003. *Imagining Identity in New Spain: Race, Lineage, and the Colonial Body in Portraiture*. University of Texas Press.

Delgado Bernal, Dolores. 1998. "Grassroots Leadership and the Chicano Movement: The East Los Angeles School Blowouts." *Frontiers: A Journal of Women Studies* 19, no. 2: 113–121.

Emily, Wasserman. 1968. "Photography as Printmaking: Museum of Modern Art." *Artforum* 6, no. 10: 71–74.

García-Camarillo, Cecilio, and Delilah Montoya. 1992. *Crickets in My Mind*. Artist book in the collection of the Center for Southwest Research at the University of New Mexico.

Garcia Camarillo, Cecilio, and Delilah Montoya. n.d. *Crickets in My Mind*. Mano Isquierda flyer.

Gómez, Laura E. 2018. *Manifest Destinies, Second Edition: The Making of the Mexican American Race*. New York University Press.

Gómez-Quiñones, Juan. 1990. *Chicano Politics: Reality and Promise, 1940–1990*. University of New Mexico Press.

González, Jennifer A. 1995. "Negotiated Frontiers: Contemporary Chicano Photography." In *From the West: Chicano Narrative Photography*, edited by Chon Noriega. Mexican Museum.

Katzew, Ilona. 2004. *Casta Painting: Images of Race in Eighteenth-Century Mexico*. Yale University Press.

Lara, Orlando. 2009. "A Trail of Thirst." *Anthropology Now* 1, no. 3: 86–91.

Leimer, Ann Marie. 2008. "Chicana Photography: The Power of Place." *National Association for Chicana and Chicano Studies Conference Proceedings*, 3.

Leimer, Ann Marie. 2006. "Crossing the Border with 'La Adelita': Lucha-Adelucha as 'Nepantlera' in Delilah Montoya's 'Codex Delilah.'" *Chicana/Latina Studies* 5, no. 2: 12–59. http://www.jstor.org/stable/23014481.

Lewthwaite, Stephanie. 2016. "Recovering Mestiza Genealogies in Contemporary New Mexican Art: Delilah Montoya's El Sagrado Corazón (1993)." *Frontiers* 37, no. 1: 118–150.

Márquez, María Teresa. 2006. "No Longer Counted Out: Fighting Isn't What It Used to Be." In *Women Boxers: The New Warriors*. Arte Público Press: 9–17.

Montoya, Delilah. 2006. "The New Warriors." In *Women Boxers: The New Warriors*. Arte Público Press: 18–23.

Montoya, Delilah. 2016. "Malcriada Aesthetics/Bad Girl Realities." *Chicana/Latina Studies: The Journal of Mujeres Activas en Letras y Cambio Social* 15, no 2: 10–16.

Montoya, Delilah. 2025. *Bookmaking an Artist's Book: Crickets in My Mind, Codex Delilah, and Shooting the Tourist*. Unpublished essay provided by the artist.

Montoya, Delilah. 2025. "Collotypes—*Sagrado Corazón* and *To Be Invisible*." Unpublished essay provided by the artist.

Montoya, Delilah. 2025. *Digitizing the Photograph—Moving the Photographic Analog through Digital Space. 1999 – 2006, Women Boxers, Sed: Trail of Thirst, Guadalupe en Piel, and Doña Sebastiana*. Unpublished essay provided by the artist.

Montoya, Delilah. 2025. *Installations: Saints & Sinners, Sebastiana, and Guadalupe*. Unpublished essay provided by the artist.

Montoya, Delilah. 2025. *Printmaking and Photography*. Unpublished essay provided by the artist.

Montoya, Delilah. n.d. *Proposal for Codex Delilah: 6 Deer Journey from Mexicatl to Chicana*. Submitted for MFA thesis at the University of New Mexico.

Munoz, Carlos. 2007. *Youth, Identity, Power: The Chicano Movement*. Verso Books.

Noriega, Chon. 1995. "Many Wests." In *From the West: Chicano Narrative Photography*. The Mexican Museum, 9–15.

Reinoza, Tatiana, and Karen M. Davalos, eds. 2023. *Self Help Graphics at Fifty: A Cornerstone of Latinx Art and Collaborative Artmaking*. University of California Press.

RISD Museum. n.d. "Process Work: Intersections of Photography and Print ca. 1825 to Today." Accessed December 2024. https://risdmuseum.org/exhibitions-events/events/process-work.

Roberts, Jennifer L. 2024. *Contact: Art and the Pull of Print*. Princeton University Press.

Rosales, Francisco A. 1997. *Chicano! The History of the Mexican American Civil Rights Movement*. Arte Público Press.

Wasserman, Emily. 1968. "Photography as Printmaking: Museum of Modern Art," *Artforum* 6, no. 10: 72.

Index

Note: Page numbers in italic text indicate illustrations.

ISBN 978-0-8263-6945-1 (paper)
ISBN 978-0-8263-6946-8 (ePub)

Library of Congress Control Number: 2025945297

Founded in 1889, the University of New Mexico sits on the traditional homelands of the Pueblo of Sandia. The original peoples of New Mexico—Pueblo, Navajo, and Apache—since time immemorial have deep connections to the land and have made significant contributions to the broader community statewide. We honor the land itself and those who remain stewards of this land throughout the generations and also acknowledge our committed relationship to Indigenous peoples. We gratefully recognize our history.

This catalog includes a variety of terms to describe Latino, Chicano, and Nuevo Mexicano, identity. Usage is based on specific events, time, place, and artist and collaborator preference.

Cover illustration: *La Malinche* (from the portfolio *El Sagrado Corazón*), 1993
Designed by Felicia Cedillos
Composed in Arno Pro